How to Master CCNP ROUTE

René Molenaar

Introduction

One of the things I do in life is work as a Cisco Instructor and after teaching CCNP for a few years I've learned which topics people find difficult to understand. This is the reason I created http://gns3vault.com where I offer free Cisco labs and videos to help people learn networking. The problem with networking is that you need to know what you are doing before you can configure anything. Even if you have all the commands you still need to understand *what* and *why* you are typing these commands. I created this book to give you a compact guide which will provide you the answer to *what* and *why* to help you master the CCNP exam.

CCNP is one of the well-known certifications you can get in the world of IT. Cisco is the largest supplier of networking equipment but also famous for its CCNA, CCNP and CCIE certifications. Whether you are new to networking or already in the field for some time, getting a certification is the best way to prove your knowledge on paper! Having said that, I also love routing & switching because it's one of those fields in IT that doesn't change much...some of the protocols you are about to learn are 10 or 20 years old and still alive and kicking!

I have tried to put all the important keywords in **bold**. If you see a **term or concept** in **bold** it's something you should remember / write down and make sure you understand it since its core knowledge for your CCNP!

One last thing before we get started. When I'm teaching I always advise students to create mindmaps instead of notes. Notes are just lists with random information while mindmaps show the relationship between the different items. If you are reading this book on your computer I highly suggest you download "Xmind" which you can get for free here:

http://www.xmind.net/

If you are new to mindmapping, check out "Appendix A – How to create mindmaps" at the end of this book where I show you how I do it.

Enjoy reading my book and good luck getting your CCNP certification!

René Molenaar

P.S. If you have any questions or comments about this book, please let me know:

E-mail: info@gns3vault.com
Website: gns3vault.com
Facebook: facebook.com/gns3vault
Twitter: twitter.com/gns3vault
Youtube: youtube.com/gns3vault

Index

1. Introduction to EIGRP

The first routing protocol we will look at is called **EIGRP** (Enhanced Interior Gateway Routing Protocol). EIGRP was created by Cisco which means you can only run it on Cisco hardware. If you want routing with devices from different vendors (like Juniper) you will have to look for another routing protocol.

In this chapter I'm going to give you an introduction to EIGRP, we'll see how it works and how EIGRP is different compared to OSPF. Most of the information in this chapter is a review of EIGRP on CCNA level so if you have everything still fresh in mind you might want to skim through the chapter. Let me start by giving you an overview:

- **Advanced distance vector** or **Hybrid routing protocol**.
- Multicast or unicast is used for exchange of information.
- Multiple network layer protocols are supported.
- 100% loop-free.

Why do we call EIGRP an advanced distance vector or hybrid routing protocol? If you studied CCNA you have seen RIP. RIP is a true distance vector routing protocol and very simple:

- No neighbor discovery.
- Periodic updates.
- Vulnerable to loops.
- Simple metric (hop count).

Cisco added some of the features from link-state routing protocols to EIGRP which makes it far more advanced than a true distance vector routing protocol like RIP. This is why (probably the marketing department) calls EIGRP an advanced distance vector or hybrid routing protocol.

EIGRP does not use broadcast packets to send information to other neighbors but will use multicast or unicast. Besides IPv4 you can also use EIGRP to route IPv6 or even some older network layer protocols like IPX or AppleTalk. Last but not least...EIGRP is 100% loop-free and I'm going to show you why this is true.

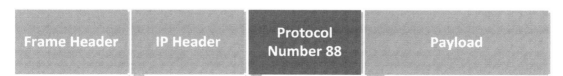

| Frame Header | IP Header | Protocol Number 88 | Payload |

EIGRP runs directly on top of the IP header. If you look at the picture above you see we have a frame header (for example an Ethernet Frame), an IP Header (we are using IPv4) and inside the IP packet you'll find EIGRP. EIGRP has its own protocol number which is 88. Other protocol numbers you are familiar with are TCP (6) and UDP (17).

EIGRP Neighbor Table	• Lists all directly connected neighbors: • Next Hop Router • Interface

EIGRP Topology Table	• Lists all learned routes from all EIGRP neighbors: • Destination • Metric

Global Routing Table	• Best routes from EIGRP topology table will be copied to the routing table.

EIGRP routers will start sending hello packets to other routers just like OSPF does, if you send hello packets and you receive them you will become neighbors. EIGRP neighbors will exchange routing information which will be saved in the topology table. The best path from the topology table will be copied in the routing table.

Selecting the best path with EIGRP works a bit different than other routing protocols so let's see it in action:

We have three routers named KingKong, Ann and Carl. We are going to calculate the best path to the destination which is behind router Carl.

EIGRP uses a rich set of metrics namely **bandwidth, delay, load and reliability** which we will cover later. These values will be put into a formula and each link will be assigned a metric. The lower these metrics the better.

In the picture above I have assigned some values on the interfaces, if you would look on a real EIGRP router you'll see the numbers are very high and a bit annoying to work with.

Router Carl will advertise to router Ann its metric towards the destination.

Basically router Carl is saying to router Ann: "It costs me 5 to get there". This is called the **advertised distance.**

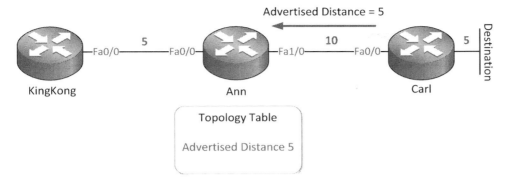

Router Ann has a topology table and in this topology table it will save this metric, the advertised distance to reach this destination is 5.

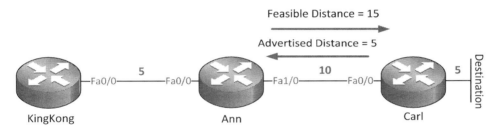

We are not done yet since there is something else that router Ann will save in its topology table. We know the advertised distance is 5 since this is what router Carl told us. We also know the metric of the link between router Ann and router Carl since this is directly connected. Router Ann now knows the metric for the total path to the destination, this total path is called the **feasible distance** and it will be saved in the topology table.

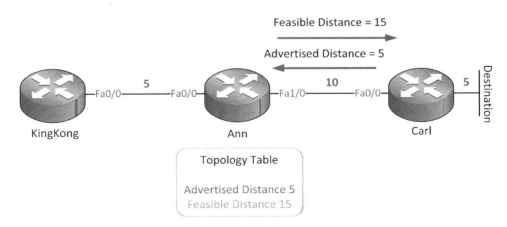

You have now learned two important concepts of EIGRP. The advertised distance, your neighbor tells you how far it is for him to reach the destination and the feasible distance which is your total distance to get to the destination.

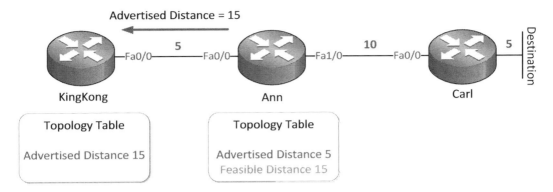

We are not done yet since router KingKong is also running EIGRP. Router Ann is sending its feasible distance towards router KingKong which is 15. Router KingKong will save this information in the topology table as the advertised distance. Router Ann is "telling" router KingKong the distance is 15.

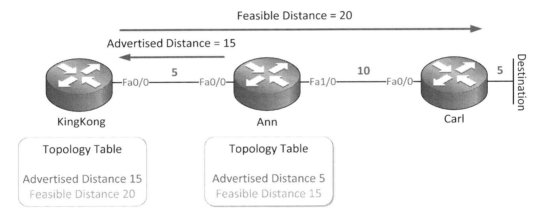

Router KingKong now knows how far the destination is away for Router Ann and since we know the metric for the link between router KingKong and Ann it can also calculate the total distance which is called the feasible distance. This information is saved in the topology table.

Are you following me so far? Let me describe these terms once again but in plain English:

- ✓ Advertised distance: How far the destination is away for your neighbor.
- ✓ Feasible distance: The total distance to the destination.

The best path to the destination is called the **successor**!

The successor will be copied from the topology table to the routing table.

With EIGRP however it's possible to have a backup path which we call the **feasible successor**. How do we find out if we have a feasible successor? Let's find out:

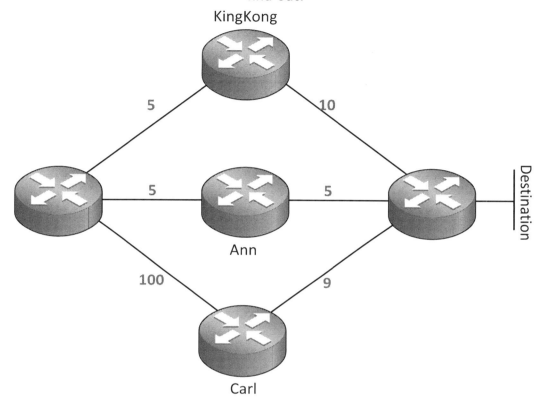

In the example above we have a couple of routers running EIGRP; we are sitting on the router without a name on the left side and would like to know two things:

✓ Which path is the successor (the best path)?
✓ Do we have any feasible successors? (backup paths)

Let's fill in the following table to find out:

	Advertised Distance	Feasible distance	
KingKong			
Ann			
Carl			

If you want to try your new-learned EIGRP skills try to fill in the advertised and feasible distance by yourself in the table above.

Router KingKong is telling us the destination is 10 away, router Ann tells us its 5 away and router Carl tells us its 9 away. We can now fill in the advertised distance part of the table:

	Advertised Distance	Feasible distance	
KingKong	10		
Ann	5		
Carl	9		

Since we know our directly connected links we can add this to the advertised distance and we'll have our feasible distance.

	Advertised Distance	Feasible distance	
KingKong	10	15	
Ann	5	10	
Carl	9	109	

The path with the lowest feasible distance will be the successor (router Ann) so now we answered the first question.

	Advertised Distance	Feasible distance	
KingKong	10	15	
Ann	5	10	SUCCESSOR
Carl	9	109	

You will find the successor in the routing table.

To answer the second question "do we have a feasible successor (backup path)?" we need to learn another formula:

Advertised distance of feasible successor < Feasible distance of successor.

This is where I get to see glazed eyes and flabbergasted students so let's do it in plain English one more time:

A router can become a backup path if he is closer to the destination than the total distance of your best path.

I think that sounds a bit better right? Let's try it and see if router KingKong or router Carl is suitable as a backup path:

The advertised distance of router KingKong is 10 which is equal to the feasible distance of router Ann which is also 10. It has to be lower...equal is not good enough so router KingKong will NOT be a feasible successor.

The advertised distance of router Carl is 9 which is lower than the feasible distance of router Ann which is 10. Router Carl will be a valid feasible successor and used as a backup path!

	Advertised Distance	Feasible distance	
KingKong	10	15	
Ann	5	10	SUCCESSOR
Carl	9	109	FEASIBLE SUCCESSOR

Excellent so router Ann is our successor and router Carl is a feasible successor. You will find both entries in the EIGRP topology but you will only find the successor in the routing table. If you lose the successor because of a link failure EIGRP will copy/paste the feasible successor in the routing table. This is what makes EIGRP a FAST routing protocol...but only if you have feasible successor in the topology table.

Now look closely to the feasible distance of router Carl and router KingKong...what do you see? The metric for router Carl is FAR worse than the one for router KingKong. Does this make any sense? Did the Cisco EIGRP engineers make a horrible mistake here by using non-optimal backup paths?

Nope this is perfectly the way it should be! Keep in mind EIGRP at heart is a distance vector protocol. It doesn't know what the complete network looks like...it's not a link-state routing protocol like OSPF which DOES have a complete map of the network. Distance vector routing protocols only know which way to go (vector) and how far away the destination is (distance). I'll show you in a bit exactly why EIGRP works like this.

EIGRP has another trick in its hat. RIP and OSPF both can do load balancing but the paths have to be equal. EIGRP can do something cool...unequal load balancing! Even better it will share traffic in a proportional way, if you have a feasible successor that has a feasible distance which is 5 times worse than the successor traffic will be shared in a 5:1 way.

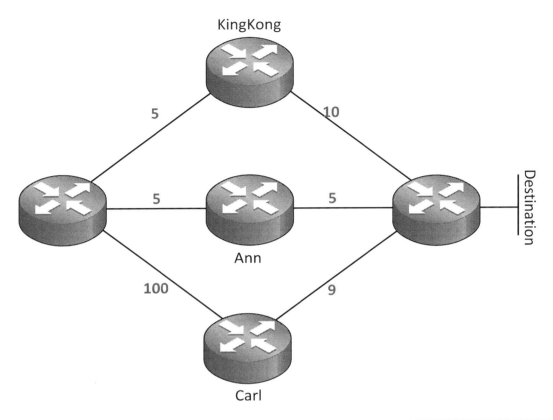

	Advertised Distance	Feasible distance	
KingKong	10	15	
Ann	5	10	SUCCESSOR
Carl	9	109	FEASIBLE SUCCESSOR

This is our first example where we found out the successor and feasible successor. If you look at the routing table you will only find the successor there. Now we are going to change things so we'll see the feasible successor in the routing table as well so it will load-balance.

You can do this by using the **variance** command. The variance command works as a multiplier:

- ✓ Our successor has a feasible distance of 10.
- ✓ Our feasible successor has a feasible distance of 109.

In order to load-balance our feasible successor needs to have a lower feasible distance than the successor X multiplier.

If we set the variance at 2, this is what we get:

Feasible distance of successor is 10 x 2 (multiplier) = 20.

109 is higher than 20 so we don't do any load balancing.

If we set the variance at 5, this is what we get:

Feasible distance of successor is 10 x 5 (multiplier) = 50.

109 is still higher than 50 so still no load balancing here.

Now I'm going to set the variance at 11 and this is what we get:

Feasible distance of successor is 10 x 11 = 110.

109 is lower than 110 so now we will put the feasible successor in the routing table and start load balancing!

Are we ever going to use the route through router KingKong? No we won't since it's not a feasible successor!

The formula you just witnessed to determine EIGRP feasible successors is how EIGRP can guarantee you that the backup path is 100% loop-free! I know this is difficult to grasp by reading text so let's do another example:

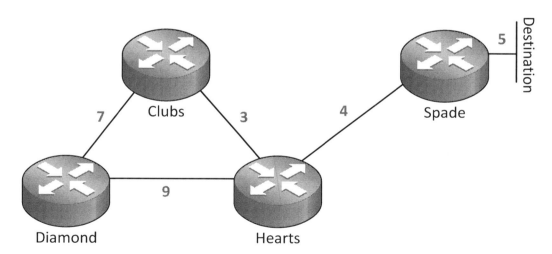

Keep in mind that EIGRP is by nature a distance vector routing protocol, we see the topology but EIGRP does not!

We are looking at the EIGRP topology table of router Hearts and we want to reach the destination behind router Spade, let's fill in the table (try it yourself if you want a good exercise):

	Advertised Distance	Feasible distance	
Spade			
Clubs			
Diamond			

1. Router Spade will advertise the destination network to router Hearts.
2. Router Hearts will advertise the network to router Clubs and Diamond.
3. Router Clubs will advertise the network to router Diamond.
4. Router Diamond will advertise the network to router Clubs.
5. Router Clubs will advertise this network back to router Hearts.
6. Router Diamond will advertise this network back to router Hearts.

	Advertised Distance	Feasible distance	
Spade	5		
Clubs	25		
Diamond	19		

Here we have the advertised distance; our neighbors are telling us how far it is for them to reach the destination network. Next step is to fill in the feasible successors.

How did I get the numbers in the advertised distance table? Let's look at all the routers:

Router Spade is easy. The destination has a distance of 5 as seen in the topology picture. This will be advertised to router Hearts and placed in its topology table.

Router Clubs will learn the destination network through router Hearts and router Diamond. Router Hearts will advertise a distance of 5+4 = 9 to router Clubs. So why didn't I place "9" in the advertised distance field in the table? Good question! Remember split-horizon? Don't advertise to your neighbor whatever you learned from them....router Clubs is not sending information about this network back to router Hearts. To be more specific: **whatever you learn on an interface you don't advertise back out of the same interface.**

How did I get to 25? Let's break it down:

Router Spade will advertise a distance of 5 towards router Hearts. Router Hearts will advertise 5+4 = 9 towards router Diamond.

Router Diamond will advertise 5+4+9 = 18 towards router Clubs. Finally router Clubs will advertise 5+4+9+7 = 25 towards router Hearts. Split-horizon doesn't apply here since router Clubs learned about the destination on another interface (router Diamond).

The same thing applies for the advertised distance of 19 for router Diamond:

1. Router Spade advertises a distance of 5 to router Hearts.
2. Router Hearts advertises a distance of 5+4 = 9 to router Clubs.
3. Router Clubs advertises a distance of 5+4+3 = 12 to router Diamond.
4. Router Diamond advertises a distance of 5+4+3+7 = 19 to router Hearts.

	Advertised Distance	Feasible distance	
Spade	5	9	
Clubs	25	28	
Diamond	19	28	

Router Hearts has learned the advertised distance from its neighbors and knows about its own directly connected interfaces so you can fill in the feasible distance. Last step is to pick our successor.

	Advertised Distance	Feasible distance	
Spade	5	9	SUCCESSOR
Clubs	25	28	
Diamond	19	28	

Router Spade has the lowest feasible distance so it will become the successor...excellent! Let's do the feasible successor check and see if there is a backup path:

Advertised distance of feasible successor < Feasible distance of successor.

The advertised distance of router Clubs (25) and Diamond (19) are higher than the feasible distance of router Spade (9) so they won't become feasible successors. This makes sense right? If these routers become backup paths we would have a loop!

If your neighbor is closer to the destination than your total path you at least know it's not getting to the destination by sending packets **through your router**. Perhaps it's not the best path but it's absolutely 100% loop-free!

This is the end of the EIGRP introduction chapter! What do you think? Was this new for you or just CCNA refreshment? Make sure you understand all the key concepts because in the next chapter we are going to dive deeper into the material.

If you want to warm up you might want to try one of my CCNA EIGRP labs that teaches you most of the EIGRP stuff on CCNA level:

http://gns3vault.com/CCNA/eigrp-for-ccna-1.html

2. EIGRP Packets and Metrics

Hello packets are sent between EIGRP neighbors for **neighbor discovery** and **recovery.** If you send hello packets and receive them then EIGRP will form a neighbor relationship with the other router. As long as you receive hello packets from the other side EIGRP will believe that the other router is still there, as soon as you don't receive them anymore you will drop the neighbor relationship called **adjacency** and EIGRP might have to look for another path for certain destinations.

EIGRP uses **RTP (Reliable Transport Protocol)** and its function is to deliver EIGRP packets between neighbors in a **reliable** and ordered way. It can use multicast or unicast and to keep things efficient not all packets are sent reliable. Reliable means that when we send a packet we want to get an **acknowledgment** from the other side to make sure that they received it.

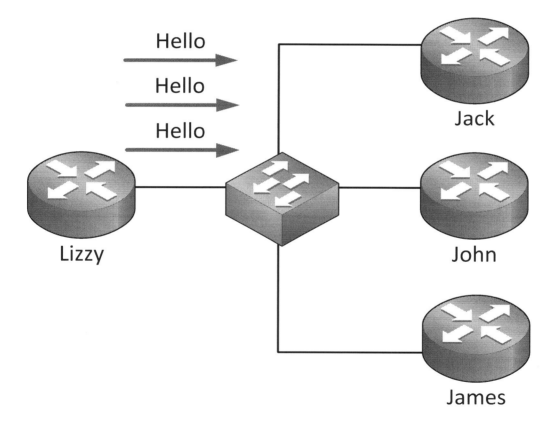

In this example we have 4 routers all running EIGRP. Hello packets are sent between routers in order to form adjacencies. As you can see router Lizzy is sending 3 hello packets meant for router Jack, John and Lizzy.

There are 2 questions that we can ask ourselves here:

- Is it really useful to send 3 different hello packets on a single link?
- Is it necessary that a hello packet gets an acknowledgement in return?

Sending 3 packets on the same link is not very useful so instead of doing this EIGRP will send hello packets by using multicast on a **multi-access** network like Ethernet.
Hello packets don't have to be acknowledged since EIGRP uses a **holddown time**. If a router doesn't receive hello packets in an X amount of time it will drop the neighbor adjacency.
So which packets should be acknowledged? Think about routing information, if there's a change in the network you want to make sure all routers receive this routing update.

Let me show you all the different EIGRP packets:

- **Hello**
- **Update**
- **Query**
- **Reply**
- **ACK** (Acknowledgement)

Hello packets are used for neighbor discovery. As soon as you send hello packets and receive them your EIGRP routers will try to form the neighbor adjacency.

Update packets have routing information and are sent reliable to whatever router that requires this information. Update packets can be sent to a single neighbor using unicast or to a group of neighbors using multicast.

Query packets are used when your EIGRP router has lost information about a certain network and doesn't have any backup paths. What happens is that your router will send query packets to its neighbors asking them if they have information about this particular network.

Reply packets are used in response to the query packets and are reliable.

ACK packets are used to acknowledge the receipt of update, query and replay packets. ACK packets are sent by using unicast.

EIGRP Neighbor Table	• *Lists all directly connected neighbors:* • Next Hop Router • Interface

EIGRP Topology Table	• *Lists all learned routes from all EIGRP neighbors:* • Destination • Metric

Global Routing Table	• *Best routes from EIGRP topology table will be copied to the routing table.*

Instead of using just a single routing table EIGRP will use multiple tables. The first one is the **neighbor table** and this is where EIGRP stores all information of directly connected neighbors. After we have become neighbors routers will exchange routing information which is stored in the **EIGRP topology table.** It's possible to have multiple entries for a network in the topology table.

The best information will be copied from the EIGRP topology table to the routing table.

Now you know about all the different packets and the EIGRP tables let's have a look at the total process of becoming EIGRP neighbors and exchanging routing information:

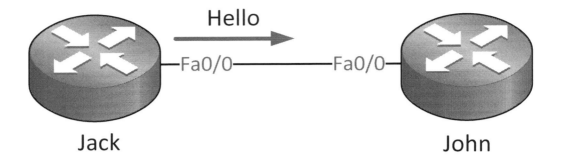

1. We have 2 routers called Jack and John and they are configured for EIGRP. As soon as we enable it for the interface they will start sending hello packets. In this example router Jack is the first router to send a hello packet.

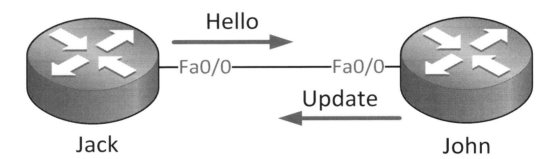

2. As soon as router John receives the hello packet from Jack it will respond by sending update packets that contain all the routing information that it has in its routing table. The only routes that are not sent on this interface are the one that John learned on this interface because of split-horizon. The update packet that router John will send has the initialization bit set so we know this is the "initialization process". At this moment there is still no neighbor adjacency until router John has sent a hello packet to Jack.

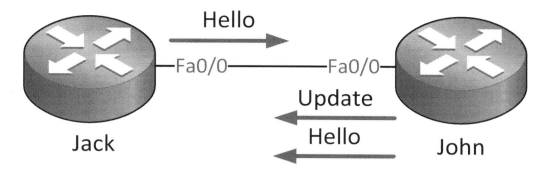

3. Router Jack is of course not the only one sending hello packets. As soon as router John sends a hello packet to Jack we can continue to setup a neighbor adjacency.

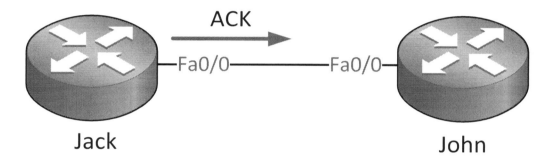

4. After both routers have exchanged hello packets we will establish the neighbor adjacency. Router Jack will send an ACK to let John know he received the update packets. The routing information in the update packets will be saved in the EIGRP topology table.

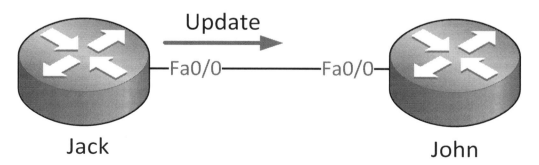

5. Router John is anxious to receive routing information as well so Jack will send update packets to John who will save this information in its EIGRP topology table.

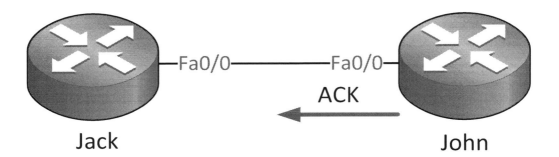

6. After receiving the update packets router John will send an ACK back to Jack to let him know everything is ok.

As soon as both routers have exchanged routing information they will select the best paths to each destination and copy those to the routing table. The best path in EIGRP is called the **successor.**

Want to see what this looks like on a real router? Let's use the following topology and see what happens:

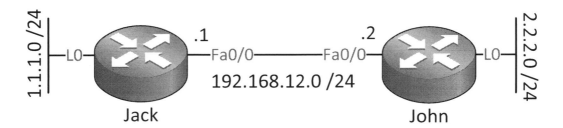

This is the topology I'm going to use to configure EIGRP. My goal is to have full connectivity and here are the configurations:

```
Jack(config)#router eigrp 1
Jack(config-router)#no auto-summary
Jack(config-router)#network 1.1.1.0 0.0.0.255
Jack(config-router)#network 192.168.12.0
Jack(config-router)#exit
```

```
John(config)#router eigrp 1
John(config-router)#no auto-summary
John(config-router)#network 2.2.2.0 0.0.0.255
John(config-router)#network 192.168.12.0
John(config-router)#exit
```

Let's break this one down. **Router eigrp 1** will start up EIGRP using AS (autonomous system) number 1. This number has to **match on both routers** or we won't become EIGRP neighbors.

No auto-summary is needed because by default EIGRP will behave like a classful routing protocol which means it won't advertise the subnet mask along the routing information. In this case that means that 1.1.1.0/24 and 2.2.2.0/24 will be advertised as 1.0.0.0/8 and 2.0.0.0/8. Disabling auto-summary will ensure EIGRP sends the subnet mask along.

Network 1.1.1.0 0.0.0.255 means that I'm advertising networks that exist on interfaces that fall within the 1.1.1.0 – 1.1.1.255 range. If I don't specify the wildcard you'll find "network 1.0.0.0" in your configuration. Does it matter? Yes and no. The same thing applies to "network 2.2.2.0 /24". It will work but also means that every interface that falls within the 1.0.0.0/8 or 2.0.0.0/8 range is going to run EIGRP. Network 192.168.12.0 without a wildcard mask is fine since I'm using a /24 on this interface which is Class C.

If you are working on a lab and are lazy (like me) you can also type in network 0.0.0.0 which will activate EIGRP on all of your interfaces...if that's what you want of course.

Let's do a debug on router John to see what is going on:

```
John#debug eigrp packets ?
  SIAquery   EIGRP SIA-Query packets
  SIAreply   EIGRP SIA-Reply packets
  ack        EIGRP ack packets
  hello      EIGRP hello packets
  ipxsap     EIGRP ipxsap packets
  probe      EIGRP probe packets
  query      EIGRP query packets
  reply      EIGRP reply packets
  request    EIGRP request packets
  retry      EIGRP retransmissions
  stub       EIGRP stub packets
  terse      Display all EIGRP packets except Hellos
  update     EIGRP update packets
  verbose    Display all EIGRP packets
  <cr>
```

As you can see we have a LOT of debug options for EIRP. I want to see the hello packets...

```
John#debug eigrp packets hello
EIGRP Packets debugging is on
     (HELLO)
```

```
John# EIGRP: Received HELLO on FastEthernet0/0 nbr 192.168.12.1
   AS 1, Flags 0x0, Seq 0/0 idbQ 0/0 iidbQ un/rely 0/0 peerQ
un/rely 0/0
```

Looking good seems we have received a hello packet from router Jack.

```
John# EIGRP: Sending HELLO on FastEthernet0/0
   AS 1, Flags 0x0, Seq 0/0 idbQ 0/0 iidbQ un/rely 0/0
```

And we are sending hello packets to router Jack as well.

```
Jack# %DUAL-5-NBRCHANGE: IP-EIGRP(0) 1: Neighbor 192.168.12.2
(FastEthernet0/0) is up: new adjacency
```

```
John# %DUAL-5-NBRCHANGE: IP-EIGRP(0) 1: Neighbor 192.168.12.1
(FastEthernet0/0) is up: new adjacency
```

You can see we have an EIGRP neighbor adjacency.

```
John# EIGRP: Sending HELLO on Loopback0
AS 1, Flags 0x0, Seq 0/0 idbQ 0/0 iidbQ un/rely 0/0

       EIGRP: Received HELLO on Loopback0 nbr 2.2.2.2
AS 1, Flags 0x0, Seq 0/0 idbQ 0/0
```

Hmm interesting it seems router John is schizophrenic and sending hello packets to its loopback0 interface and also receiving them.

This behavior is normal because the network command does two things:

- Send EIGRP packets on the interface that falls within the network command range.
- Advertise the network that is configured on the interface in EIGRP.

So what do you have to do when you want to advertise a network without sending EIGRP packets on the interface and forming EIGRP neighbors? Use the **passive interface** command.

```
John(config)#router eigrp 1
John(config-router)#passive-interface loopback 0
```

This will advertise the 2.2.2.0/24 network on router John's loopback 0 interface without sending EIGRP packets to the loopback.

```
John(config)#router eigrp 1
John(config-router)#passive-interface default
John(config-router)#no passive-interface fastEthernet 0/0
```

If you have to configure an ISP router with 50+ interfaces you probably don't want to type in this command on each of those interfaces. You can also configure **passive-interface default** and only activate the interfaces you want to run EIGRP on.

Let's look at a debug of some EIGRP update packets. I'm going to clear the EIGRP neighbor adjacency to see what it looks like:

```
John#debug eigrp packets update
EIGRP Packets debugging is on
    (UPDATE)
```

```
Jack#clear ip eigrp neighbors
```

Let's reset the EIGRP neighbor adjacency on router Jack.

```
John# %DUAL-5-NBRCHANGE: IP-EIGRP(0) 1: Neighbor 192.168.12.1
(FastEthernet0/0) is down: Interface Goodbye received
```

You can see that router Jack is being nice and at least telling router John that it's deleting the neighbor adjacency.

```
John# %DUAL-5-NBRCHANGE: IP-EIGRP(0) 1: Neighbor 192.168.12.1
(FastEthernet0/0) is up: new adjacency
```

Router Jack is back in business and our EIGRP neighbor adjacency has been reestablished.

```
John#
EIGRP: Enqueueing UPDATE on FastEthernet0/0 nbr 192.168.12.1
iidbQ un/rely 0/1 peerQ un/rely 0/0
EIGRP: Received UPDATE on FastEthernet0/0 nbr 192.168.12.1
   AS 1, Flags 0x1, Seq 13/0 idbQ 0/0 iidbQ un/rely 0/0 peerQ
un/rely 0/1
EIGRP: Sending UPDATE on FastEthernet0/0 nbr 192.168.12.1
   AS 1, Flags 0x1, Seq 13/13 idbQ 0/0 iidbQ un/rely 0/0 peerQ
un/rely 0/1
```

Here you can see router John is putting an update packet in its queue for router Jack. John is also receiving an update packet from router Jack and afterwards sending its own update packet. You'll see a couple of update packets flying back and forth.

```
John#debug eigrp packets ack
EIGRP Packets debugging is on
    (ACK)
```

We can also check out some acknowledgments by debugging ack packets.

```
Jack#clear ip eigrp neighbors
```

We'll reset the EIGRP neighbor adjacency so the update packets are resent.

```
John#
EIGRP: Received ACK on FastEthernet0/0 nbr 192.168.12.1
  AS 1, Flags 0x0, Seq 0/17 idbQ 0/0 iidbQ un/rely 0/1 peerQ
un/rely 0/1
EIGRP: Received ACK on FastEthernet0/0 nbr 192.168.12.1
  AS 1, Flags 0x0, Seq 0/18 idbQ 0/0 iidbQ un/rely 0/0 peerQ
un/rely 0/1
EIGRP: Enqueueing ACK on FastEthernet0/0 nbr 192.168.12.1
  Ack seq 18 iidbQ un/rely 0/0 peerQ un/rely 1/2
EIGRP: Sending ACK on FastEthernet0/0 nbr 192.168.12.1
  AS 1, Flags 0x0, Seq 0/18 idbQ 0/0 iidbQ un/rely 0/0 peerQ
un/rely 1/2
EIGRP: Enqueueing ACK on FastEthernet0/0 nbr 192.168.12.1
  Ack seq 19 iidbQ un/rely 0/0 peerQ un/rely 1/2
EIGRP: Sending ACK on FastEthernet0/0 nbr 192.168.12.1
  AS 1, Flags 0x0, Seq 0/19 idbQ 0/0 iidbQ un/rely 0/0 peerQ
un/rely 1/2
EIGRP: Received ACK on FastEthernet0/0 nbr 192.168.12.1
  AS 1, Flags 0x0, Seq 0/20 idbQ 0/0 iidbQ un/rely 0/0 peerQ
un/rely 0/1
```

These are the ack packets in response to some of the update packets. If you want to see the whole process we can combine some debugging.

```
John#debug eigrp packets
EIGRP Packets debugging is on
    (UPDATE, REQUEST, QUERY, REPLY, HELLO, IPXSAP, PROBE, ACK,
STUB, SIAQUERY, SIAREPLY)
```

This is how you enable debugging for all EIGRP packets.

```
Jack#clear ip eigrp neighbors
```

Reset the EIGRP neighbor adjacency again...

```
John#
EIGRP: Sending HELLO on FastEthernet0/0
  AS 1, Flags 0x0, Seq 0/0 idbQ 0/0 iidbQ un/rely 0/0
EIGRP: Received HELLO on FastEthernet0/0 nbr 192.168.12.1
  AS 1, Flags 0x0, Seq 0/0 idbQ 0/0
```

```
%DUAL-5-NBRCHANGE: IP-EIGRP(0) 1: Neighbor 192.168.12.1
(FastEthernet0/0) is up: new adjacency
John#
EIGRP: Enqueueing UPDATE on FastEthernet0/0 nbr 192.168.12.1
iidbQ un/rely 0/1 peerQ un/rely 0/0
EIGRP: Sending HELLO on FastEthernet0/0
  AS 1, Flags 0x0, Seq 0/0 idbQ 0/0 iidbQ un/rely 0/1
EIGRP: Requeued unicast on FastEthernet0/0
EIGRP: Received UPDATE on FastEthernet0/0 nbr 192.168.12.1
  AS 1, Flags 0x1, Seq 25/0 idbQ 0/0 iidbQ un/rely 0/0 peerQ
un/rely 0/1
EIGRP: Sending UPDATE on FastEthernet0/0 nbr 192.168.12.1
  AS 1, Flags 0x1, Seq 25/25 idbQ 0/0 iidbQ un/rely 0/0 peerQ
un/rely 0/1
EIGRP: Received ACK on FastEthernet0/0 nbr 192.168.12.1
  AS 1, Flags 0x0, Seq 0/25 idbQ 0/0 iidbQ un/rely 0/0 peerQ
un/rely 0/1
EIGRP: Enqueueing UPDATE on FastEthernet0/0 iidbQ un/rely 0/1
serno 1-2
EIGRP: Enqueueing UPDATE on FastEthernet0/0 nbr 192.168.12.1
iidbQ un/rely 0/0 peerQ un/rely 0/0 serno 1-2
EIGRP: Sending UPDATE on FastEthernet0/0
  AS 1, Flags 0x8, Seq 26/0 idbQ 0/0 iidbQ un/rely 0/0 serno 1-2
EIGRP: Enqueueing UPDATE on FastEthernet0/0 nbr 192.168.12.1
iidbQ un/r
John#ely 0/1 peerQ un/rely 0/1
EIGRP: Requeued unicast on FastEthernet0/0
EIGRP: Received ACK on FastEthernet0/0 nbr 192.168.12.1
  AS 1, Flags 0x0, Seq 0/26 idbQ 0/0 iidbQ un/rely 0/0 peerQ
un/rely 0/2
EIGRP: FastEthernet0/0 multicast flow blocking cleared
EIGRP: Sending UPDATE on FastEthernet0/0 nbr 192.168.12.1
  AS 1, Flags 0x8, Seq 27/25 idbQ 0/0 iidbQ un/rely 0/0 peerQ
un/rely 0/1
EIGRP: Received ACK on FastEthernet0/0 nbr 192.168.12.1
  AS 1, Flags 0x0, Seq 0/27 idbQ 0/0 iidbQ un/rely 0/0 peerQ
un/rely 0/1
EIGRP: Received UPDATE on FastEthernet0/0 nbr 192.168.12.1
  AS 1, Flags 0x8, Seq 26/0 idbQ 0/0 iidbQ un/rely 0/0 peerQ
un/rely 0/0
EIGRP: Enqueueing ACK on FastEthernet0/0 nbr 192.168.12.1
  Ack seq 26 iidbQ un/rely 0/0 peerQ un/rely 1/0
EIGRP: Sending ACK on FastEthernet0/0 nbr 192.168.12.1
  AS 1, Flags 0x0, Seq 0/26 idbQ 0/0 iidbQ un/rely 0/0 peerQ
un/rely 1/0
EIGRP: Enqueueing UPDATE on FastEthernet0/0 iidbQ un/rely 0/1
serno 9-9
EIGRP: Enqueueing UPDATE on Fa
John#stEthernet0/0 nbr 192.168.12.1 iidbQ un/rely 0/0 peerQ
un/rely 0/0 serno 9-9
EIGRP: Received UPDATE on FastEthernet0/0 nbr 192.168.12.1
```

```
    AS 1, Flags 0x8, Seq 27/27 idbQ 0/0 iidbQ un/rely 0/0 peerQ
un/rely 0/1
EIGRP: Enqueueing ACK on FastEthernet0/0 nbr 192.168.12.1
  Ack seq 27 iidbQ un/rely 0/0 peerQ un/rely 1/1
EIGRP: Sending ACK on FastEthernet0/0 nbr 192.168.12.1
    AS 1, Flags 0x0, Seq 0/27 idbQ 0/0 iidbQ un/rely 0/0 peerQ
un/rely 1/1
```

This will show you the entire process of sending hello packets to each other, becoming EIGRP neighbors, exchanging updates and sending acks.

```
John#show ip protocols
Routing Protocol is "eigrp 1"
  Outgoing update filter list for all interfaces is not set
  Incoming update filter list for all interfaces is not set
  Default networks flagged in outgoing updates
  Default networks accepted from incoming updates
  EIGRP metric weight K1=1, K2=0, K3=1, K4=0, K5=0
  EIGRP maximum hopcount 100
  EIGRP maximum metric variance 1
  Redistributing: eigrp 1
  EIGRP NSF-aware route hold timer is 240s
  Automatic network summarization is not in effect
  Maximum path: 4
  Routing for Networks:
    2.2.2.0/24
    192.168.12.0
  Passive Interface(s):
    Loopback0
    VoIP-Null0
  Routing Information Sources:
    Gateway         Distance         Last Update
    192.168.12.1          90         00:04:42
  Distance: internal 90 external 170
```

This is the last command I want to show you now. **Show ip protocols** is a very useful and powerful command in your CCNP arsenal. It will show you for which networks you are routing, passive interfaces and the administrative distance. See the external administrative distance of 170? We'll talk about that one in the redistribution chapter. This command isn't just for EIGRP it will show you all routing protocols.

Enough debugging for now let's continue by looking at the different EIGRP tables in detail:

- EIGRP Neighbor table
- EIGRP Topology table
- Routing table

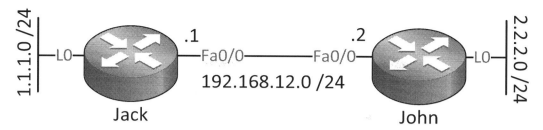

Jack   John

Router Jack and John are back and I'm going to show you what the EIGRP neighbor table looks like on a real network:

```
Jack#show ip eigrp neighbors
IP-EIGRP neighbors for process 1
H    Address                  Interface        Hold Uptime    SRTT
RTO  Q  Seq
                                               (sec)          (ms)
Cnt  Num
0    192.168.12.2             Fa0/0            10 00:06:06    19
200  0  27
```

In the output above I'm looking at the EIGRP neighbor table of router Jack. As you can see we have one neighbor (192.168.12.2) which happens to be router John on interface FastEthernet 0/0. What else do we find here?

- **H (Handle):** Here you will find the order when the neighbor adjacency was established. Your first neighbor will have a value of 0, the second neighbor a value of 1 and so on.

- **Hold Uptime** (sec): this is the **holddown timer** per EIGRP neighbor. Once this timer expires we will drop the neighbor adjacency. The default holddown timer is 15 seconds. On older IOS versions only a hello packet would reset the holddown timer but on newer IOS versions any EIGRP packet after the first hello will reset the holddown timer.

- **SRTT (Smooth round-trip time):** The number of milliseconds it takes to send an EIGRP packet to your neighbor and receive an acknowledgment packet back.

- **RTO (Retransmission timeout):** The amount of time in milliseconds that EIGRP will wait before retransmitting a packet from the retransmission queue to this neighbor.

- **Q Cnt (Q count):** The number of EIGRP packets (Update, Query or Reply) in the queue that are awaiting transmission. Ideally you want this number to be 0 otherwise it might be an indication of congestion on the network.

- **Seq Num (Sequence number):** This will show you the sequence number of the last update,query or reply packet that you received from your EIGRP neighbor.

Excellent so that's how EIGRP stores neighbor information! Our next stop is of course to take a look at the EIGRP Topology table:

```
Jack#show ip eigrp topology
IP-EIGRP Topology Table for AS(1)/ID(1.1.1.1)

Codes: P - Passive, A - Active, U - Update, Q - Query, R -
Reply,
        r - reply Status, s - sia Status

P 1.1.1.0/24, 1 successors, FD is 128256
        via Connected, Loopback0
P 2.2.2.0/24, 1 successors, FD is 156160
        via 192.168.12.2 (156160/128256), FastEthernet0/0
P 192.168.12.0/24, 1 successors, FD is 28160
        via Connected, FastEthernet0/0
```

Now that's a lot of information to look at! Let me break it down for you in chunks:

```
Jack#show ip eigrp topology
IP-EIGRP Topology Table for AS(1)/ID(1.1.1.1)

Codes: P - Passive, A - Active, U - Update, Q - Query, R -
Reply,
        r - reply Status, s - sia Status

P 1.1.1.0/24, 1 successors, FD is 128256
        via Connected, Loopback0
P 2.2.2.0/24, 1 successors, FD is 156160
        via 192.168.12.2 (156160/128256), FastEthernet0/0
P 192.168.12.0/24, 1 successors, FD is 28160
        via Connected, FastEthernet0/0
```

If you look at the red fonts you can see that we are looking at the EIGRP topology table for **AS (Autonomous System)** number 1.

Keep in mind that the AS number has to match on EIGRP routers in order to become neighbors!

```
Jack#show ip eigrp topology
IP-EIGRP Topology Table for AS(1)/ID(1.1.1.1)

Codes: P - Passive, A - Active, U - Update, Q - Query, R -
Reply,
       r - reply Status, s - sia Status

P 1.1.1.0/24, 1 successors, FD is 128256
        via Connected, Loopback0
P 2.2.2.0/24, 1 successors, FD is 156160
        via 192.168.12.2 (156160/128256), FastEthernet0/0
P 192.168.12.0/24, 1 successors, FD is 28160
        via Connected, FastEthernet0/0
```

Look at those codes...Update, Query and Reply should ring a bell since I discussed them a few pages ago. Let's focus on those codes that I didn't explain before:

- **Passive:** Passive is good...we like routing information to be passive which means that we have learned information about a network and there are no changes in the topology table.

- **Active:** Active is not good since it means we have lost information about a certain network and EIGRP doesn't know another way of reaching this network. It will go into active mode and send query packets to ALL its neighbors asking them if they know how to reach this network.

- **Reply Status:** EIGRP will track all the query packets it has sent to neighbors since you need a reply in return. By setting the reply status flag it will do this.

- **Sia Status (Stuck in Active):** This is a bad one...it means that EIGRP has not received a reply to a query packet from one of the neighbors within the allowed time (about 3 minutes). When this happens EIGRP will drop the neighbor adjacency and it will be stuck in active. More on this later!

```
Jack#show ip eigrp topology
IP-EIGRP Topology Table for AS(1)/ID(1.1.1.1)

Codes: P - Passive, A - Active, U - Update, Q - Query, R -
Reply,
        r - reply Status, s - sia Status

P 1.1.1.0/24, 1 successors, FD is 128256
        via Connected, Loopback0
P 2.2.2.0/24, 1 successors, FD is 156160
        via 192.168.12.2 (156160/128256), FastEthernet0/0
P 192.168.12.0/24, 1 successors, FD is 28160
        via Connected, FastEthernet0/0
```

One more thing to show you! Let's look at an entry of a prefix…in this case 2.2.2.0/24 and break it down in pieces:

- **P 2.2.2.0/24**: The **P** stands for **passive** and that's how we like it! As you can see EIGRP stores the network and the subnet mask.

- **1 successor**: The best path to get to a certain network is called the **successor**. It's possible to have backup paths which EIGRP calls the **feasible successor**. In this case there is only one way to get to the destination.

- **FD is 156160**: **FD** stands for **feasible distance** and in plain English we would call this the "total distance" to get to the destination.

- **Via 192.168.12.2:** That's the IP address of the neighbor where we have to send packets to in order to reach the 2.2.2.0/24 network.

- **(156160/128256):** The first value is the feasible distance. The second value is the **advertised distance.** Your EIGRP neighbor will report to you how far it is for him to reach the 2.2.2.0/24 network and this is saved as the advertised distance.

- **FastEthernet0/0**: This one is easy; it's just the interface we are using to send our packets to in order to reach this network.

Does this make sense to you? Understanding the EIGRP topology table is very important for troubleshooting or when we start playing with load balancing.

```
Jack#show ip route
Codes: C - connected, S - static, R - RIP, M - mobile, B - BGP
       D - EIGRP, EX - EIGRP external, O - OSPF, IA - OSPF inter
area
       N1 - OSPF NSSA external type 1, N2 - OSPF NSSA external
type 2
       E1 - OSPF external type 1, E2 - OSPF external type 2
       i - IS-IS, su - IS-IS summary, L1 - IS-IS level-1, L2 -
IS-IS level-2
       ia - IS-IS inter area, * - candidate default, U - per-
user static route
       o - ODR, P - periodic downloaded static route

Gateway of last resort is not set

C    192.168.12.0/24 is directly connected, FastEthernet0/0
     1.0.0.0/24 is subnetted, 1 subnets
C        1.1.1.0 is directly connected, Loopback0
     2.0.0.0/24 is subnetted, 1 subnets
D        2.2.2.0 [90/156160] via 192.168.12.2, 01:31:17,
FastEthernet0/0
```

The best information from the EIGRP topology table will be copied to the routing table. What do we find here?

- **D (DUAL or Diffusing Update Algorithm)**: DUAL is the algorithm behind EIGRP which is why we find the D here. Why are we not using the E for EIGRP? That would be nice but the letter E is already in use for EGP (Exterior Gateway Protocol) which is an old routing protocol we don't use anymore.

- **2.2.2.0 [90/156160]:** Do you recognize these values? The first one is the administrative distance which is 90 for EIGRP. 156160 is the feasible distance for this network.

- **Via 192.168.12.2 01:31:17, FastEthernet 0/0**: 192.168.12.2 is the next hop address to reach this network. 01:31:17 is the time how long this network has been in the routing table. In this case that's 1 hour, 31 minutes and 17 seconds. You can also see the interface how to reach this next hop address which is FastEthernet 0/0.

One more thing we have to talk about...the EIGRP metrics! In my introduction I showed you really low values since it's easier to explain EIGRP that way. In the examples above you could see that the feasible and advertise distance values are a bit higher which makes them annoying to work with. Let's take a good look at the EIGRP metrics and the formula.

Let's start with the formula that EIGRP uses:

$$EIGRP\ Metric = 256*((K1*Bw) + (K2*Bw)/(256-Load) + K3*Delay)*(K5/(Reliability + K4)))$$

Ewww...that looks bad! Don't worry...you don't have to remember this formula! If you look at it you can see that it incorporates bandwidth, load, delay and reliability and you can see K1, K2, K3, K4 and K5 values.

If you studied CCNA you might have seen and/or learned the following list:

- **Bandwidth (K1)**
- **Load (K2)**
- **Delay (K3)**
- **Reliability (K4)**
- **MTU (K5)**

Technically this is incorrect. K1 doesn't correspond 1:1 with bandwidth, K2 doesn't correspond 1:1 with load, delay not with K3 etc. These K values are only numbers to **scale numbers** in the metric calculation.

We can see what K values are enabled or disabled by default:

```
Jack#show ip protocols
Routing Protocol is "eigrp 1"
  Outgoing update filter list for all interfaces is not set
  Incoming update filter list for all interfaces is not set
  Default networks flagged in outgoing updates
  Default networks accepted from incoming updates
  EIGRP metric weight K1=1, K2=0, K3=1, K4=0, K5=0
  EIGRP maximum hopcount 100
  EIGRP maximum metric variance 1
  Redistributing: eigrp 1
  EIGRP NSF-aware route hold timer is 240s
  Automatic network summarization is not in effect
  Maximum path: 4
  Routing for Networks:
    1.1.1.0/24
    192.168.12.0
  Routing Information Sources:
    Gateway         Distance      Last Update
    192.168.12.2          90      00:14:30
  Distance: internal 90 external 170
```

In this example where I used the command **show ip protocols** you can see which K-values are enabled by default. Only K1 and K3 are enabled by default.

Let's walk through the different metric components to see what they are:

Bandwidth:

```
Jack#show interfaces fastEthernet 0/0
FastEthernet0/0 is up, line protocol is up
  Hardware is AmdFE, address is cc02.58a9.0000 (bia
cc02.58a9.0000)
  Internet address is 192.168.12.1/24
  MTU 1500 bytes, BW 100000 Kbit, DLY 100 usec,
```

If you use the **show interface FastEthernet 0/0** command you can see the interface information. The example above only shows part of the output. You can see the bandwidth is 100000 Kbit which is a 100Mbit interface.

```
Jack(config)#interface fa0/0
Jack(config-if)#band
Jack(config-if)#bandwidth ?
  <1-10000000>  Bandwidth in kilobits
  inherit       Specify that bandwidth is inherited
  receive       Specify receive-side bandwidth

Jack(config-if)#bandwidth 500
```

Bandwidth is a *static* value which can be changed by using the **bandwidth** command. Keep in mind this doesn't change the *actual* bandwidth of the interface! This command is ONLY used to influence routing protocols like EIGRP. It's not like you can slow down electric signals through a wire...if you want to limit the traffic on an interface you'll need QoS (Quality of Service) which is a story for another day!

```
Jack#show interfaces fastEthernet 0/0
FastEthernet0/0 is up, line protocol is up
  Hardware is AmdFE, address is cc02.58a9.0000 (bia
cc02.58a9.0000)
  Internet address is 192.168.12.1/24
  MTU 1500 bytes, BW 500 Kbit, DLY 100 usec,
```

Here you see the result of changing the bandwidth on the interface. Something to remember is that EIGRP will **use the lowest bandwidth** in the path from A to B (since this is the bottleneck).

Load:

```
Jack#show interfaces fastEthernet 0/0
FastEthernet0/0 is up, line protocol is up
  Hardware is AmdFE, address is cc02.58a9.0000 (bia
cc02.58a9.0000)
  Internet address is 192.168.12.1/24
  MTU 1500 bytes, BW 500 Kbit, DLY 100 usec,
     reliability 255/255, txload 1/255, rxload 1/255
```

Load will show you how busy the interface is based on the packet rate and the bandwidth on the interface. This is a value that can change over time so it's a *dynamic* value.

Delay:

```
Jack#show interfaces fastEthernet 0/0
FastEthernet0/0 is up, line protocol is up
  Hardware is AmdFE, address is cc02.58a9.0000 (bia
cc02.58a9.0000)
  Internet address is 192.168.12.1/24
  MTU 1500 bytes, BW 500 Kbit, DLY 100 usec,
     reliability 255/255, txload 1/255, rxload 1/255
```

Delay reflects the time it will take for packets to cross the link and is a *static* value. Cisco IOS will have default delay values for the different types of interface. A FastEthernet interface has a default delay of 100 usec.

```
Jack(config)#interface fa0/0
Jack(config-if)#delay ?
  <1-16777215>  Throughput delay (tens of microseconds)

Jack(config-if)#delay 50
```

If you use the **delay** command you can change this value to influence routing protocols like EIGRP. It doesn't actually change the delay for this interface but it is only used to influence routing protocols.

```
Jack#show interfaces fastEthernet 0/0
FastEthernet0/0 is up, line protocol is up
  Hardware is AmdFE, address is cc02.58a9.0000 (bia
cc02.58a9.0000)
  Internet address is 192.168.12.1/24
  MTU 1500 bytes, BW 500 Kbit, DLY 500 usec,
```

Above you see the delay that I changed. EIGRP will **accumulate all the delay values** in the path from A to B.

Reliability:

```
Jack#show interfaces fastEthernet 0/0
FastEthernet0/0 is up, line protocol is up
  Hardware is AmdFE, address is cc02.58a9.0000 (bia
cc02.58a9.0000)
  Internet address is 192.168.12.1/24
  MTU 1500 bytes, BW 500 Kbit, DLY 500 usec,
     reliability 255/255, txload 1/255, rxload 1/255
```

Reliability at 255/255 is 100%. This means that you don't have issues on the physical or data-link layer. If you are having issues this value will decrease. Since this is something that can change it's a *dynamic value.*

MTU:

```
Jack#show interfaces fastEthernet 0/0
FastEthernet0/0 is up, line protocol is up
  Hardware is AmdFE, address is cc02.58a9.0000 (bia
cc02.58a9.0000)
  Internet address is 192.168.12.1/24
  MTU 1500 bytes, BW 500 Kbit, DLY 500 usec,
     reliability 255/255, txload 1/255, rxload 1/255
```

MTU or Maximum Transmission Unit is being exchanged between EIGRP neighbors but not used for the metric calculation.

By default only K1 and K3 are enabled and we don't use K2 or K4. This means that only bandwidth and delay are used in the formula.

Why not? Because loading and reliability are *dynamic* values and they can change over time. You don't want your EIGRP routers calculating 24/7 and sending updates to each other just because the load or reliability of an interface has changed. We want routing protocols to be nice and quiet and only base their routing decisions on *static* values like bandwidth and delay. If you only use those two static values our EIGRP routers don't have to do any recalculation unless an interface goes down or a router died.

Since only K1 and K3 are enabled we can simplify the EIGRP formula:

Metric = bandwidth (slowest link) + delay (sum of delays)

- Bandwidth: [10^7 / minimum bandwidth in the path] * 256.
- Delay: sums of delays in the path multiplied by 256 (in tens of microseconds).

So the formula looks like:

Metric = (10⁷ / minimum bandwidth) * 256 + (sum of delays) * 256

The multiplication of 256 is done so EIGRP is compatible with IGRP (the predecessor of EIGRP).

Let me show you an example so we can break down this formula:

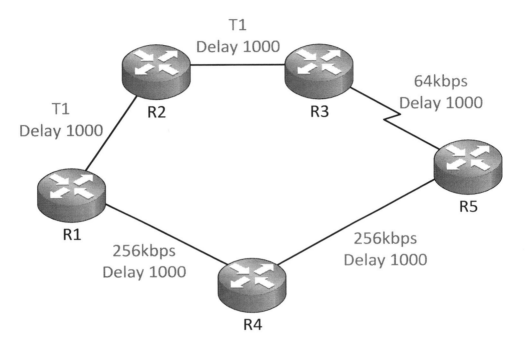

We are looking at R1 and calculating the distance to get to R5. As you can see there is an upper path with some T1 interfaces and a 64kbps link. The path below has two 256kbps links.

A T1 interface has a bandwidth of 1.554Mbit which is obviously better than 256kbps but the bottleneck in the upper path is our 64kbps link. Let's throw these numbers for the upper path in the EIGRP metric formula and see what happens:

The lowest bandwidth in the upper path is our 64kbps link so the EIGRP bandwidth calculation will look like this:

Bandwidth = (10⁷ / slowest link) * 256
Bandwidth = (10,000,000 / 64) * 256 = 156,250 * 256 = 40,000,000

Now let's look at the delay calculation for the upper path:

Delay = [sum of delays] * 256
Delay = [1000+1000+1000] * 256
Delay = 768,000

Let's add those numbers together and we'll have the total metric:

Metric = bandwidth + delay
Metric = 40,000,000 + 768,000
Metric = 40,768,000

Having fun yet? Let's do the lower path as well!

The lowest bandwidth in the lower path is 256kbps link so the EIGRP bandwidth calculation will look like this:

Bandwidth = (10^7 / slowest link) * 256
Bandwidth = (10,000,000 / 256) * 256 = 39062.5 * 256 = 10,000,000

Now let's look at the delay calculation for the lower path:

Delay = [sum of delays] * 256
Delay = [1000+1000] * 256
Delay = 512,000

Let's add those numbers together and we'll have the total metric:

Metric = bandwidth + delay
Metric = 10,000,000 + 512,000
Metric = 10,512,000

Upper path metric = 40,768,000
Lower path metric = 10,512,000

The lower metric will be installed as the successor route in the routing table so the lower path will be used in this example.

Maybe you are wondering what the formula looks like if you would enable loading (K2) and reliability (K4) as well, well here it is:

Metric = [K1*bandwidth + ((K2*bandwidth)/(256-load))+K3*delay]

If MTU (K5) is not equal to 0:

Metric = Metric*[K5/(reliability+K4)]

Phew! Does this make your head spin? I think you and I both agree we should let EIGRP do the metric calculations and not us (that's why we have routers right!). The important lesson I wanted to show you here is that EIGRP uses the **slowest bandwidth** in the path and the **sum of delays**. You don't have to know this formula by heart but **understand** it. No need to do any manual calculations on the exam!

The metrics in EIGRP are a pain to work with since the values are so LARGE! If you want to practice with EIGRP you can try to disable all the K-values except K3. This will make EIGRP only use delay as metric. The metric values will be much lower and easier to work with since you don't have to think about the lowest bandwidth in the path. I like to do this when I'm teaching people how to calculate feasible successors and configure EIGRP load balancing.

Feel like playing with the metrics and some load balancing? Try the following labs:

http://gns3vault.com/EIGRP/eigrp-maximum-path-and-variance.html

http://gns3vault.com/EIGRP/eigrp-intermediate.html

René Molenaar

3. EIGRP Summarization

If you studied and passed CCNA you probably have an idea why we use summaries:

- Decrease the size of the routing table.
- Fewer routing updates.

EIGRP has two ways of summarizing networks:

- Automatic summarization:
  - Subnets are summarized to the classful network.
  - This is the default for EIGRP.
- Manual summarization.

You should disable EIGRP automatic summarization since it can cause issues with routing.

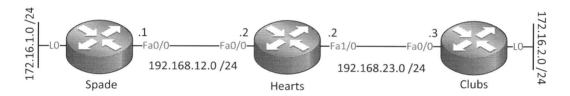

Look at the topology above. We have 3 routers and we are configuring EIGRP. Note the 172.16.1.0 and 172.16.2.0 networks. EIGRP will summarize to the classful network by default.

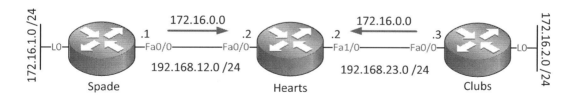

Router Spade and router Clubs don't send the subnet mask along with the routing update so it will advertise the classful network which is 172.16.0.0 in this case. So what happens with router Hearts? It thinks it can reach the 172.16.0.0 network by sending packets either left or right and if the metric is equal it will try to load-balance. Obviously this is going to cause problems.

```
Spade(config)#router eigrp 1
Spade(config-router)#no auto-summary
```

```
Clubs(config)#router eigrp 1
Clubs(config-router)#no auto-summary
```

Type in the **no auto-summary** command to make sure EIGRP behaves classless and sends the subnet mask along.

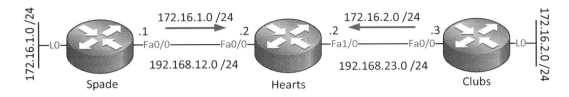

This is what we want to achieve. Router Spade and Clubs will send the subnet mask with their EIGRP update packets.

Let's take a look at manual summarization which is more fun. In the picture below we have router Jack and John, router Jack has the following networks configured:

192.168.0.0 / 24
192.168.1.0 / 24
192.168.2.0 / 24
192.168.3.0 / 24

When we configure EIGRP, all 4 networks will be advertised and seen in the routing table of Router John:

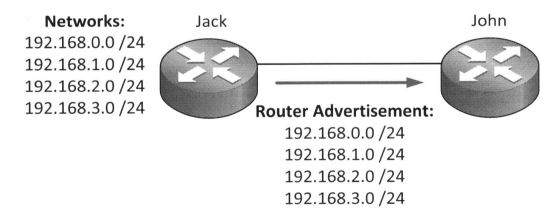

Router John's routing table:

```
John#show ip route
Codes: C - connected, S - static, R - RIP, M - mobile, B - BGP
       D - EIGRP, EX - EIGRP external, O - OSPF, IA - OSPF inter
area
       N1 - OSPF NSSA external type 1, N2 - OSPF NSSA external
type 2
       E1 - OSPF external type 1, E2 - OSPF external type 2
       i - IS-IS, su - IS-IS summary, L1 - IS-IS level-1, L2 -
IS-IS level-2
       ia - IS-IS inter area, * - candidate default, U - per-
user static route
       o - ODR, P - periodic downloaded static route

Gateway of last resort is not set

C    192.168.12.0/24 is directly connected, FastEthernet0/0
D    192.168.0.0/24 [90/156160] via 192.168.12.1, 00:00:06,
FastEthernet0/0
D    192.168.1.0/24 [90/156160] via 192.168.12.1, 00:00:06,
FastEthernet0/0
D    192.168.2.0/24 [90/156160] via 192.168.12.1, 00:00:06,
FastEthernet0/0
D    192.168.3.0/24 [90/156160] via 192.168.12.1, 00:00:06,
FastEthernet0/0
```

Let's configure a summary on router Jack to decrease the size of router John's routing table. Creating summaries for EIGRP is easy since you can do it on any interface you like.

```
Jack(config)#interface fastEthernet 0/0
Jack(config-if)#ip summary-address eigrp 1 192.168.0.0
255.255.252.0
%DUAL-5-NBRCHANGE: IP-EIGRP(0) 1: Neighbor 192.168.12.2
(FastEthernet0/0) is resync: summary configured
```

I summarized those 4 networks into 192.168.0.0 /22. You need to specify the AS number and the subnet mask to send along the network. As you can see it's resyncing with router John.

```
John#show ip route
Codes: C - connected, S - static, R - RIP, M - mobile, B - BGP
       D - EIGRP, EX - EIGRP external, O - OSPF, IA - OSPF inter
area
       N1 - OSPF NSSA external type 1, N2 - OSPF NSSA external
type 2
       E1 - OSPF external type 1, E2 - OSPF external type 2
       i - IS-IS, su - IS-IS summary, L1 - IS-IS level-1, L2 -
IS-IS level-2
```

```
         ia - IS-IS inter area, * - candidate default, U - per-
user static route
         o - ODR, P - periodic downloaded static route

Gateway of last resort is not set

C       192.168.12.0/24 is directly connected, FastEthernet0/0
D       192.168.0.0/22 [90/156160] via 192.168.12.1, 00:00:39,
FastEthernet0/0
```

This is what router John looks like now. We reduced its routing table from 4 entries to just 1 entry.

```
Jack#show ip route
Codes: C - connected, S - static, R - RIP, M - mobile, B - BGP
       D - EIGRP, EX - EIGRP external, O - OSPF, IA - OSPF inter
area
       N1 - OSPF NSSA external type 1, N2 - OSPF NSSA external
type 2
       E1 - OSPF external type 1, E2 - OSPF external type 2
       i - IS-IS, su - IS-IS summary, L1 - IS-IS level-1, L2 -
IS-IS level-2
       ia - IS-IS inter area, * - candidate default, U - per-
user static route
       o - ODR, P - periodic downloaded static route

Gateway of last resort is not set

C       192.168.12.0/24 is directly connected, FastEthernet0/0
C       192.168.0.0/24 is directly connected, Loopback0
C       192.168.1.0/24 is directly connected, Loopback1
C       192.168.2.0/24 is directly connected, Loopback2
C       192.168.3.0/24 is directly connected, Loopback3
D       192.168.0.0/22 is a summary, 00:01:09, Null0
```

Router John is not the only one who had a routing table metamorphose. Look at router Jack above and check out the last entry. 192.168.0.0/22 has been created sending packets to Null0. Our Null0 interface is like a black hole sucking up packets never to return again...ouch! Why does EIGRP do this and what is it good for? Let me show you another example.

```
Jack(config)#interface fastEthernet 0/0
Jack(config-if)#ip summary-address eigrp 1 192.168.0.0
255.255.0.0
```

The previous example was an A+ example of summarization because I summarized the following networks:

192.168.0.0 /24
192.168.1.0 /24
192.168.2.0 /24
192.168.3.0 /24

Into 192.168.0.0 /22 which is a perfect match.

If you look at the example above I made a change. I created the summary 192.168.0.0 /16 which router Jack is advertising towards router John. This is a C- example! The summary is working but I'm advertising a huge range of networks that I don't have. Let's look at router John's routing table:

```
John#show ip route
Codes: C - connected, S - static, R - RIP, M - mobile, B - BGP
       D - EIGRP, EX - EIGRP external, O - OSPF, IA - OSPF inter
area
       N1 - OSPF NSSA external type 1, N2 - OSPF NSSA external
type 2
       E1 - OSPF external type 1, E2 - OSPF external type 2
       i - IS-IS, su - IS-IS summary, L1 - IS-IS level-1, L2 -
IS-IS level-2
       ia - IS-IS inter area, * - candidate default, U - per-
user static route
       o - ODR, P - periodic downloaded static route

Gateway of last resort is not set

C    192.168.12.0/24 is directly connected, FastEthernet0/0
D    192.168.0.0/22 [90/156160] via 192.168.12.1, 00:02:29,
FastEthernet0/0
D    192.168.0.0/16 [90/156160] via 192.168.12.1, 00:00:34,
FastEthernet0/0
```

There are 2 things to mention here:

- We now have a 192.168.0.0 /16 entry in our routing table.
- You can see that my latest summary 192.168.0.0 /16 does not overwrite the old summary. You have to remove the old one yourself.

So what happens when we send a ping towards an IP address within the 192.168.0.0 /16 address space but not configured on any interface?

```
John#ping 192.168.200.20

Type escape sequence to abort.
Sending 5, 100-byte ICMP Echos to 192.168.200.20, timeout is 2
seconds:
```

```
U.U.U
Success rate is 0 percent (0/5)
```

As you can see router Jack is telling us through ICMP that this IP address is unreachable.

```
Jack(config)#access-list 100 permit ip any 192.168.200.20
0.0.0.0
Jack(config)#exit
Jack#debug ip packet 100
IP packet debugging is on for access list 100
```

Let's switch over to router Jack and do a debug. **Debug ip packet** is VERY useful but you need to use an access-list otherwise you drown in information.

```
John#ping 192.168.200.20

Type escape sequence to abort.
Sending 5, 100-byte ICMP Echos to 192.168.200.20, timeout is 2
seconds:
U.U.U
Success rate is 0 percent (0/5)
```

Let's send those pings again…

```
Jack#
IP: tableid=0, s=192.168.12.2 (FastEthernet0/0),
d=192.168.200.20 (Null0), routed via RIB
Jack#
IP: tableid=0, s=192.168.12.2 (FastEthernet0/0),
d=192.168.200.20 (Null0), routed via RIB
Jack#
IP: tableid=0, s=192.168.12.2 (FastEthernet0/0),
d=192.168.200.20 (Null0), routed via RIB
```

Those packets are boldly going where no packet has gone before…only this time there are no strange new worlds to discover….those packets are gone forever!

Why does EIGRP work like this? There's a very good reason. What if there was a 3rd router in our topology and router Jack has a default route pointing to this router?

We will end up forwarding packets for 192.168.200.20 to the default route with the chance of creating a routing loop.

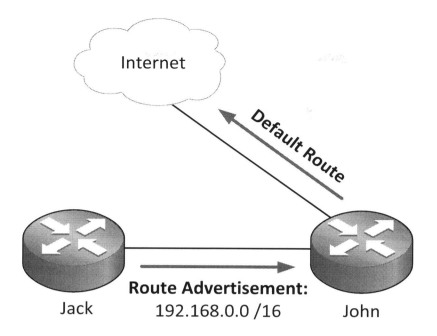

Jack   **Route Advertisement:**   John
         192.168.0.0 /16

Let's spice up our topology to see why we need this Null0 interface. Router John has another interface connected to the Internet. Router John has a default Route to the Internet.

Since we want Internet access on router Jack as well we configure a default route on router Jack towards router John.

```
Jack(config)#ip route 0.0.0.0 0.0.0.0 192.168.12.2
```

This is what the default route on router Jack pointing to John looks like.

```
Jack#show ip route | exclude C
       D - EIGRP, EX - EIGRP external, O - OSPF, IA - OSPF inter
area
       N1 - OSPF NSSA external type 1, N2 - OSPF NSSA external
type 2
       E1 - OSPF external type 1, E2 - OSPF external type 2
       i - IS-IS, su - IS-IS summary, L1 - IS-IS level-1, L2 -
IS-IS level-2
       ia - IS-IS inter area, * - candidate default, U - per-
user static route
       o - ODR, P - periodic downloaded static route

Gateway of last resort is 192.168.12.2 to network 0.0.0.0

S*    0.0.0.0/0 [1/0] via 192.168.12.2
D     192.168.0.0/22 is a summary, 00:09:40, Null0
D     192.168.0.0/16 is a summary, 00:07:45, Null0
```

This is what will happen if we don't have the Null0 interface:

1. Router John has the 192.168.0.0 /22 summary in its routing table.
2. Router John sends an IP packet to 192.168.200.20 and forwards it to router Jack.
3. Router Jack doesn't have the 192.168.200.X network in its routing table but does have a default route.
4. Router Jack will forward the IP packet to router John.
5. Uh-oh...we have a routing loop!

IP Packets have a TTL (Time to Live) field so they won't bounce around forever but it's not a good thing.

Thanks to our Null0 interface this is not going to happen, watch this:

```
John#ping 192.168.200.20

Type escape sequence to abort.
Sending 5, 100-byte ICMP Echos to 192.168.200.20, timeout is 2
seconds:
U.U.U
Success rate is 0 percent (0/5)
```

We are sending another ping from router John to router Jack.

```
Jack#show ip route | exclude C
       D - EIGRP, EX - EIGRP external, O - OSPF, IA - OSPF inter
area
       N1 - OSPF NSSA external type 1, N2 - OSPF NSSA external
type 2
       E1 - OSPF external type 1, E2 - OSPF external type 2
       i - IS-IS, su - IS-IS summary, L1 - IS-IS level-1, L2 -
IS-IS level-2
       ia - IS-IS inter area, * - candidate default, U - per-
user static route
       o - ODR, P - periodic downloaded static route

Gateway of last resort is 192.168.12.2 to network 0.0.0.0

S*    0.0.0.0/0 [1/0] via 192.168.12.2
D     192.168.0.0/22 is a summary, 00:11:19, Null0
D     192.168.0.0/16 is a summary, 00:09:25, Null0
```

Router Jack will do a lookup in its routing table to see if anything matches 192.168.200.20. Our entry with 192.168.0.0/22 is more specific than 0.0.0.0/0 so that's the one we are going to use. Packets will be forwarded to Null0 and are gone! No more routing loops...

Creating summaries has one more advantage besides reducing the size of routing tables. You will also have less routing updates on your network.

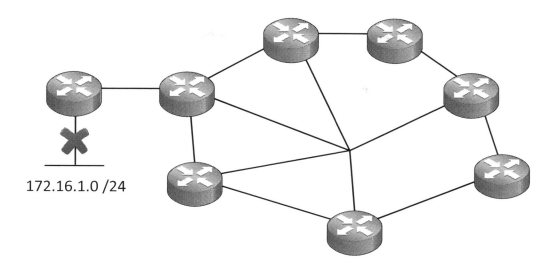

Look at the topology above. We are running EIGRP on all routers. The router on the left side has an interface that's going down.

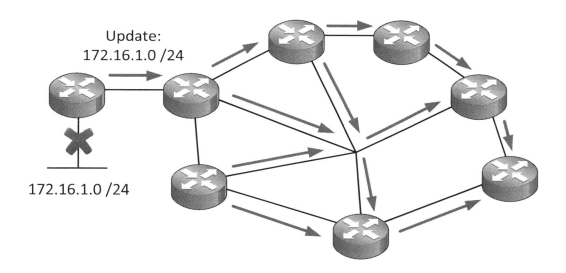

Our router will send an update to its EIGRP neighbor which will pass it along to the other routers running EIGRP. The whole network is updating itself because just a single interface went down. Summaries can help us here.

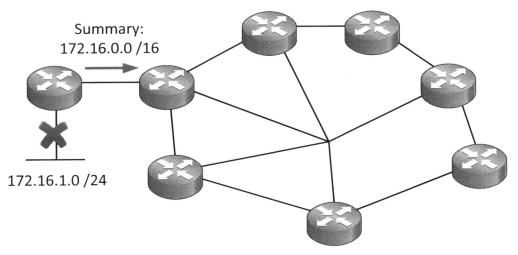

Summary:
172.16.0.0 /16

172.16.1.0 /24

If we had a summary configured on the left router to its EIGRP neighbor nothing would happen as soon as our interface goes down. All the routers on the right side have 172.16.0.0 /16 in their routing table and that's it.

What else can I tell you about EIGRP summarization?

- As soon as you delete the last specific route of the summary, your summary will be deleted from the routing table.
- The lowest metric you have for a specific route will be used for the summary route.
- If you want you can specify a different AD (administrative distance) for your summary.

That's all I have for you on EIGRP summarization! Did you enjoy this? We still have a couple of EIGRP chapters left!

If you want to see EIGRP summarization in action you should look at the following labs:

http://gns3vault.com/EIGRP/eigrp-auto-summarization.html

http://gns3vault.com/EIGRP/eigrp-summarization.html

4. EIGRP over Frame-Relay

If you studied CCNA you have seen frame-relay and the following concepts should ring a bell for you:

- NBMA (Non broadcast multi-access network)
- Inverse ARP
- Point-to-point and point-to-multipoint
- Split-horizon issues

Frame-relay is one of those topics that you might not encounter in real life very often but is still heavily tested on Cisco exams. For those of you who are new to frame-relay or a little fuzzy on the subject I'm going to start with an overview.

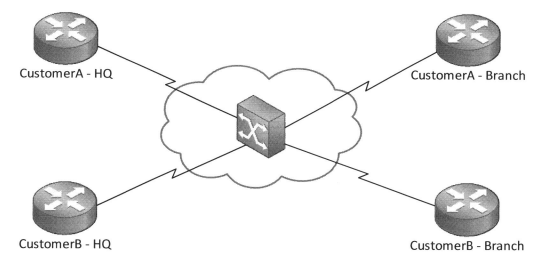

This is a picture of frame-relay. The idea behind frame-relay is that you have a single infrastructure from the service provider and multiple customers are connected to it, effectively sharing everything.

In the middle you see a cloud with an icon. This icon is the frame-relay switch. The cloud is called the **frame-relay cloud** and the reason it has this name is because for us as customer it's unknown what happens in the frame-relay cloud. This is the service provider's infrastructure and we really don't care what happens there...we are the customer and all we want is connectivity!

What else do you see? There are two customers (A and B) and each of them has a HQ (Headquarters) and a branch office.

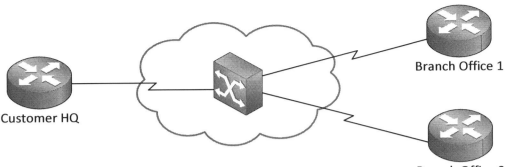

One more picture, here's a frame-relay network with three routers from one company. There's a router at the headquarters and we have two branch offices. All of them are connected to the frame-relay cloud.

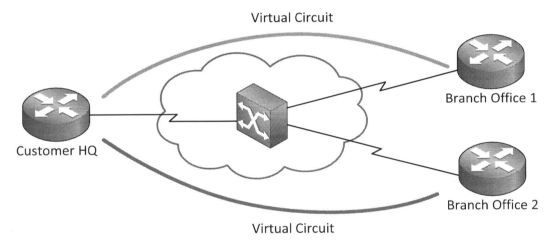

We call our service provider since we want connectivity and the first question they'll ask us is which sites should be connected? In the example above you can see two **virtual circuits**, the red and blue one. With frame-relay there's a difference between the physical and logical connections. The physical connection is just the serial cable which is connected to the provider. Our logical links are virtual circuits. As you can see there is a virtual circuit from branch Office 1 to the HQ router and another one from branch office 2 to the HQ routers.

This means that we can send traffic through our virtual circuits between:

- Branch office 1 and HQ.
- Branch office 2 and HQ.

There is no virtual circuit between branch office 1 and branch office 2. Does this mean there is no connectivity between them? No you can still have connectivity between them by sending data to the HQ router! Of course you can get another virtual circuit between branch office 1 and branch office 2 but you'll have to pay for it. Virtual circuits are also called **PVC (Permanent Virtual Circuit)**.

You also pay for a certain speed called the **CIR (Committed Information Rate).** The cool thing about frame-relay is that when no other customers are using the frame-relay network it's possible you get a higher speed than what you paid for...the CIR however is a speed that is guaranteed.

How do we know if a PVC is working or not?

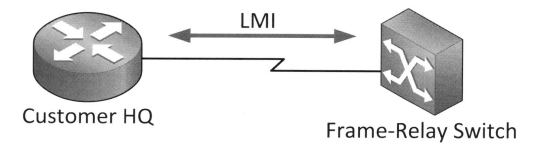

Customer HQ

Frame-Relay Switch

Frame-relay uses something called **LMI** which stands for **Local Management Interface**. LMI has two functions:

- It's a **keepalive** mechanism.
- It tells us if the PVC is active or inactive.
- It also gives us a **DLCI** (Data Link Connection Identifier). I'll get back to this in a bit

There are 3 types of LMI. They all do the same thing but there are three standards which are not compatible with each other. Whatever you choose make sure it's the same between two devices:

- ✓ Cisco
- ✓ ANSI T1.617 Annex D
- ✓ ITU-T Q.933 Annex A

So if you pick Cisco on one side, use Cisco on the other side as well.

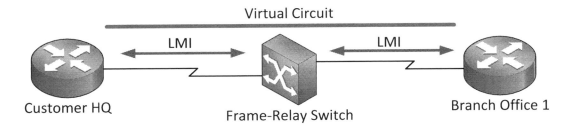

Customer HQ   Frame-Relay Switch   Branch Office 1

Here's an example of LMI in action. In the middle we have the frame-relay switch. LMI packets are sent between Router A and the frame-relay switch and router B and the frame-relay switch. The frame-relay switch tells our routers that the PVC is active.

What else do you need to know about frame-relay? Let me throw the OSI-model at you:

OSI-Model

Application
Presentation
Session
Transport
Network
Data Link
Physical

WAN protocols describe the physical (layer 1) and data link (layer 2) layer. What does frame-relay use on the data link layer? We don't use MAC addresses since that's Ethernet but we do have something else called a **DLCI (Data Link Connection Identifier).**

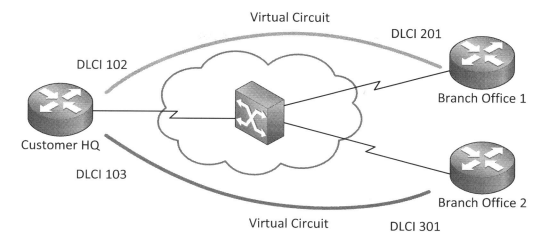

For each PVC you will get a DLCI per router. In our example above you can see that for the PVC between router HQ and branch office 1 we have DLCI 102 on the HQ router and DLCI 201 on the branch office 1 router.

Between router HQ and router branch office 2 we have DLCI 103 on HQ and DLCI 301 on branch office 2. Our DLCI is nothing more but a unique identifier for the data link layer per PVC.

Now there is an important concept to grasp and remember about DLCI. DLCI's are only **locally known** to the router! Your router does **not know** the DLCI of the router on the other side. This is different if you compare it to Ethernet. In our Ethernet world you need to know the MAC address of the computer on the other side in order to send something to it.

This is just like taking a train. If you are at the train station you walk to the correct train platform and take the train. You have no idea on which train platform you will arrive and you don't care.

Frame-relay supports multiple topologies:

- **Full-mesh**
- **Partial-mesh**
- **Hub and Spoke**

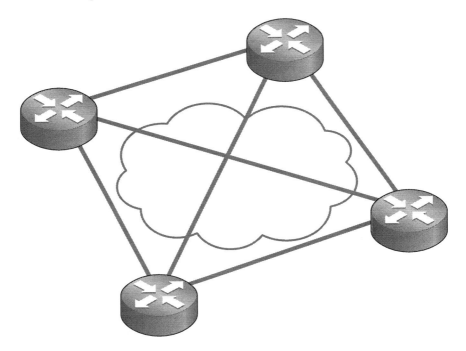

This is our full-mesh topology. As you can see there is a PVC between every router.

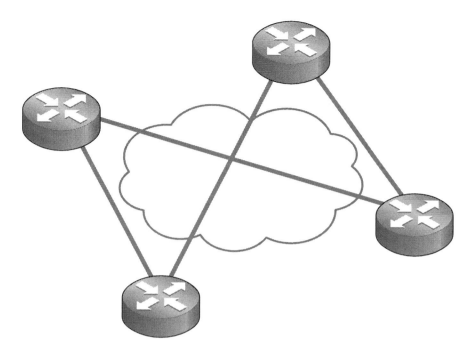

This is partial-mesh. The more important routers will have multiple connections to others.

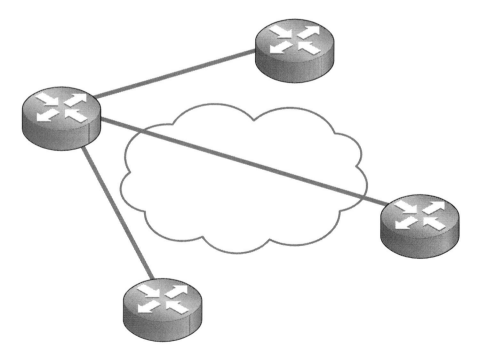

This is the hub and spoke model. The router on the left is our hub and the other routers are spokes. If the spokes want to communicate with each other they'll have to send traffic towards the hub router.

Frame-relay is **NBMA (non-broadcast multi-access)**

Keep this in mind. What it means is that frame-relay is multi-access since all routers can access the network but you are unable to send broadcasts over the frame-relay network. No broadcast also means you are unable to send multicast traffic. No multicast means you'll be in trouble with routing protocols. Rip version 2, OSPF and EIGRP all use multicast. Does this mean you can't use routing protocols with frame-relay? Well no but it's a bit tricky:

- RIP, OSPF and EIGRP can also use unicast instead of multicast.
- There is a method to "emulate" broadcasts over your frame-relay network.

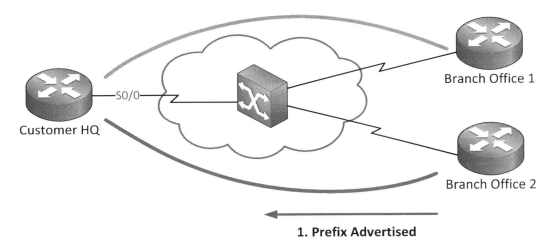

1. Prefix Advertised

What other problems might we encounter with frame-relay and routing? Do you remember the characteristics of distance vector routing protocols (RIP and EIGRP)? Split-horizon anyone?

In the picture above I have configured EIGRP on all the routers. Router branch office 1 is sending routing information towards router Customer HQ. If we look at the routing table we see this routing information on router HQ.

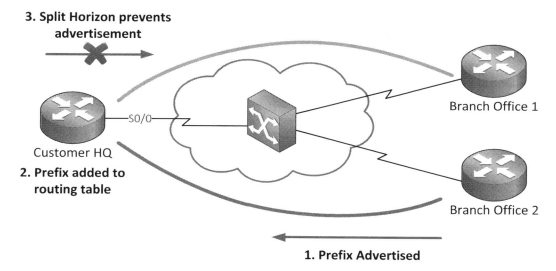

3. Split Horizon prevents advertisement

S0/0

Customer HQ

2. Prefix added to routing table

Branch Office 1

Branch Office 2

1. Prefix Advertised

Do you remember the split-horizon rule? Whatever you learn from your neighbor you don't advertise back to them. To be more specific: **whatever you learn on an interface you don't advertise it back out on the same interface.**

We are using two PVC's but on router HQ there is still only one physical interface. Split-horizon will prevent the advertisement of routing information towards router branch office 2.

How can we solve this problem?

- You can disable split-horizon (the default on physical interfaces).
- You can use sub-interfaces.

Serial 0/0

S0/0.1

S0/0.2

If you use a sub-interface you don't have the split-horizon problem since you are learning routing information on serial0/0.1 and advertising it out of serial0/0.2

Frame-relay can use **point-to-point** sub-interfaces or **point-to-multipoint** sub-interfaces. If you use point-to-point it will solve your split-horizon problem but you'll need to use a different IP subnet per PVC. Point-to-multipoint means you have the split-horizon problem but you can use a single IP subnet for all PVCs.

4

1110 René Molenaar

Remember ARP (address resolution protocol)? When we use ARP for Ethernet we need to learn the MAC address of the computer we want to send something to. ARP effectively maps the destination IP address to the destination MAC address.

Frame-relay uses **inverse ARP** and is a bit different. Remember my story about the train platform and how your router only knows it's local DLCI? You don't know the DLCI of the other side. Inverse ARP is going to map your **local DLCI to the IP address of the other side**:

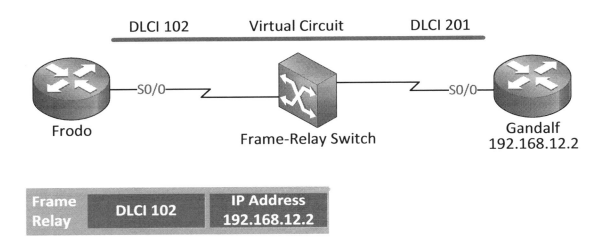

Router Frodo in my example above has mapped the IP address of router Gandalf (192.16.12.2) to its local DLCI 102. That's inverse ARP. Let's see it in more detail:

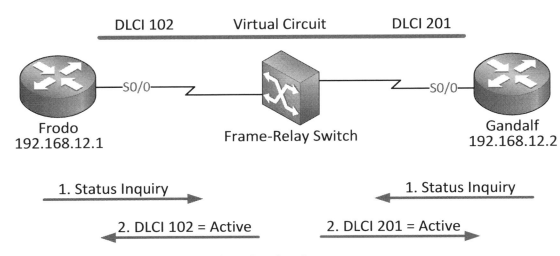

When we configure frame-relay here's what happens:

62

1. Our router will do a status enquiry using LMI.
2. The frame-relay switch will give us our DLCI number (or you can configure it yourself).

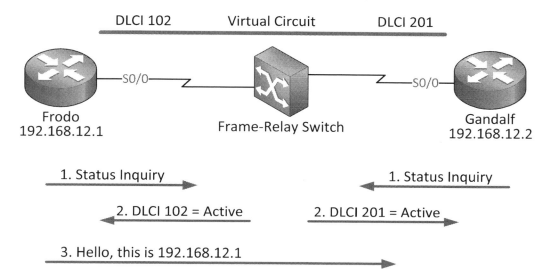

Once our routers know the PVC is active they will send a hello message with their IP address. In my example you only see router Frodo sending this but of course router Gandalf will also send its IP address.

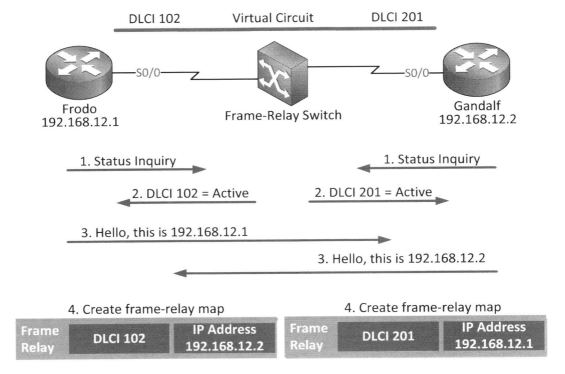

Router Frodo will now know it can reach IP address 192.168.12.2 by sending traffic through the PVC with DLCI 102. Router Gandalf will know that it can reach IP address 192.168.12.1 through the PVC with DLCI 201.

I hope this refreshes your frame-relay knowledge now I'm going to show you the different ways of configuring EIGRP over your frame-relay network.

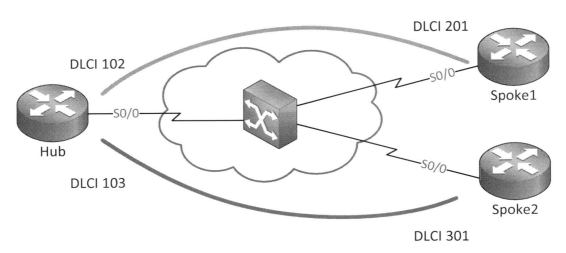

The topology above is the one I'm going to use to show you how to run EIGRP over a frame-relay network. On the left side we have a hub router and on the ight side 2 spoke routers. This is a classic example of a hub and spoke model and ideal for a lab.

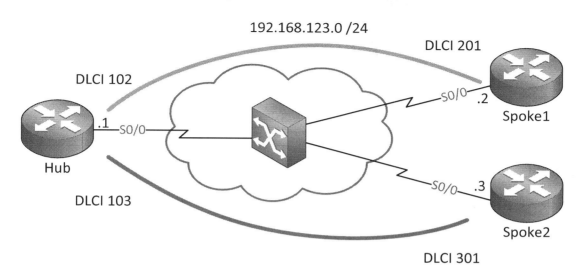

192.168.123.0 /24

DLCI 201

DLCI 102

.1 S0/0

Hub

DLCI 103

S0/0 .2

Spoke1

S0/0 .3

Spoke2

DLCI 301

Same topology but I added the 192.168.123.0 /24 subnet. As you can see our Hub router has the .1 IP address, Spoke1 has .2 and Spoke2 has .3.

Since we are using a single IP subnet we are using frame-relay point-to-multipoint. Keep in mind that with frame-relay the physical interface is point-to-multipoint by default!

```
Hub(config)#interface s0/0
Hub(config-if)#ip address 192.168.123.1 255.255.255.0
Hub(config-if)#encapsulation frame-relay
```

```
Spoke1(config)#interface serial 0/0
Spoke1(config-if)#ip address 192.168.123.2 255.255.255.0
Spoke1(config-if)#encapsulation frame-relay
```

```
Spoke2(config)#interface serial 0/0
Spoke2(config-if)#ip address 192.168.123.3 255.255.255.0
Spoke2(config-if)#encapsulation frame-relay
```

This is the configuration of the interfaces of the three routers. Just a clean simple point-to-multipoint frame-relay configuration.

```
Hub(config)#router eigrp 123
Hub(config-router)#network 192.168.123.0
```

```
Spoke1(config)#router eigrp 123
Spoke1(config-router)#network 192.168.123.0
```

```
Spoke2(config)#router eigrp 123
Spoke2(config-router)#network 192.168.123.0
```

This is the EIGRP configuration of our routers. Not so hard right? Basic EIGRP router commands and you must change the serial interface to frame-relay encapsulation.

```
Hub#
%DUAL-5-NBRCHANGE: IP-EIGRP(0) 123: Neighbor 192.168.123.2
(Serial0/0) is up: new adjacency
%DUAL-5-NBRCHANGE: IP-EIGRP(0) 123: Neighbor 192.168.123.3
(Serial0/0) is up: new adjacency
```

```
Spoke1#
%DUAL-5-NBRCHANGE: IP-EIGRP(0) 123: Neighbor 192.168.123.1
(Serial0/0) is up: new adjacency
```

```
Spoke2#
%DUAL-5-NBRCHANGE: IP-EIGRP(0) 123: Neighbor 192.168.123.1
(Serial0/0) is up: new adjacency
```

And we can see the EIGRP neighbor adjacencies are working.

```
Hub#show frame-relay map
Serial0/0 (up): ip 192.168.123.2 dlci 102(0x66,0x1860), dynamic,
          broadcast,, status defined, active
Serial0/0 (up): ip 192.168.123.3 dlci 103(0x67,0x1870), dynamic,
          broadcast,, status defined, active
```

Take a good look at the output of the **show frame-relay map** command on the hub router. Inverse ARP is enabled by default which is why you see the word **dynamic** in the frame-relay mappings. We see that it has learned about the IP addresses of the spoke routers and to which local DLCI numbers we have to map them.

There are 3 important things to learn in the output above:

- We didn't configure any frame-relay mappings which means that Inverse ARP is enabled by default.
- The word **dynamic** means we are using Inverse ARP.
- The keyword **broadcast** means its emulating broadcast traffic so we can use multicast as well. Inverse ARP enabled this for us.

Let's disable Inverse ARP on the hub router and configure some frame-relay mappings ourselves:

```
Hub(config)#interface serial 0/0
Hub(config-if)#no frame-relay inverse-arp
```

That's all there is. Type in **no frame-relay inverse-arp** under the interface and you'll disable Inverse ARP.

```
Hub#clear frame-relay inarp
```

Don't forget to remove the pre-learnt frame-relay mappings by using the **clear frame-relay inarp** command.

Next step is to configure the frame-relay mappings ourselves:

```
Hub(config)#interface serial 0/0
Hub(config-if)#frame-relay map ip 192.168.123.2 102 broadcast
Hub(config-if)#frame-relay map ip 192.168.123.3 103 broadcast
```

You configure it on the interface level by using the **frame-relay map** command.

You have to specify the **broadcast** keyword or your frame-relay network will only support unicast! Since EIGRP uses multicast you'll run into trouble if you forget to use this.

What else can we do with EIGRP and frame-relay? Let's forget about the physical interface and move our frame-relay commands to a sub-interface!

```
Hub(config)#interface s0/0
Hub(config-if)#no frame-relay map ip 192.168.123.3 103 broadcast
Hub(config-if)#no frame-relay map ip 192.168.123.2 102 broadcast
Hub(config-if)#no ip address 192.168.123.1 255.255.255.0
```

```
Hub(config)#interface s0/0.123 multipoint
Hub(config-subif)#ip address 192.168.123.1 255.255.255.0
Hub(config-subif)#frame-relay map ip 192.168.123.2 102 broadcast
Hub(config-subif)#frame-relay map ip 192.168.123.3 103 broadcast
```

I'll move the IP address and the frame-relay mappings from the physical interface to a sub-interface.

```
Hub#show running-config | begin interface Serial0/0
interface Serial0/0
 no ip address
 encapsulation frame-relay
 serial restart-delay 0
 no frame-relay inverse-arp
!
interface Serial0/0.123 multipoint
 ip address 192.168.123.1 255.255.255.0
 frame-relay map ip 192.168.123.2 102 broadcast
 frame-relay map ip 192.168.123.3 103 broadcast
```

Here's an overview of the physical and sub interface.

There are only two things I'm leaving on the physical interface:

- The encapsulation type, we want to run frame-relay right?
- Disable Inverse ARP with the no frame-relay inverse-arp command.

We don't want any frame-relay mappings on the physical interface since we need them on the sub-interface. If you create a sub-interface you need to specify whether it's a multipoint or point-to-point. I'm still using a single IP subnet for all routers so we are using multipoint in this situation.

```
Hub(config)#interface serial 0/0.123
Hub(config-subif)#no ip split-horizon eigrp 123
```

This is an important step you should not forget. On a physical interface split-horizon is **disabled** but on the sub-interface it is **enabled** by default! Don't forget to add your frame-relay mappings on the sub-interface with the broadcast keyword at the end.

```
Hub#
%DUAL-5-NBRCHANGE: IP-EIGRP(0) 123: Neighbor 192.168.123.3
(Serial0/0.123) is resync: split horizon changed
%DUAL-5-NBRCHANGE: IP-EIGRP(0) 123: Neighbor 192.168.123.2
(Serial0/0.123) is resync: split horizon changed
```

You'll see a quick message that split horizon has changed.

What happens if I forget the broadcast keyword in the frame-relay mapping? Like the following example:

```
Hub(config-subif)#no frame-relay map ip 192.168.123.2 102
broadcast
Hub(config-subif)#no frame-relay map ip 192.168.123.3 103
broadcast
Hub(config-subif)#frame-relay map ip 192.168.123.2 102
Hub(config-subif)#frame-relay map ip 192.168.123.3 103
```

Our frame-relay configuration doesn't support broadcast nor multicast anymore...only unicast.

```
Hub#
%DUAL-5-NBRCHANGE: IP-EIGRP(0) 123: Neighbor 192.168.123.3
(Serial0/0.123) is down: Interface Goodbye received
%DUAL-5-NBRCHANGE: IP-EIGRP(0) 123: Neighbor 192.168.123.2
(Serial0/0.123) is down: Interface Goodbye received
```

After a short time you'll see messages like this.
Is there still any method to get EIGRP working? Sure there is! Just use the

neighbor command. If you manually specify EIGRP neighbors we will switch over to unicast.

```
Hub(config-subif)#router eigrp 123
Hub(config-router)#neighbor 192.168.123.2 serial 0/0.123
Hub(config-router)#neighbor 192.168.123.3 serial 0/0.123
```

```
Spoke1(config)#router eigrp 123
Spoke1(config-router)#neighbor 192.168.123.1 serial 0/0
```

```
Spoke2(config)#router eigrp 123
Spoke2(config-router)#neighbor 192.168.123.1 serial 0/0
```

Here we go...specify the EIGRP neighbors and we no longer need multicast and you can forget about the broadcast keyword in your frame-relay mappings.

Those are all the options we have for running EIGRP over frame-relay using the **multipoint** physical or sub-interface.

I still need to show you the **point-to-point** sub-interface method:

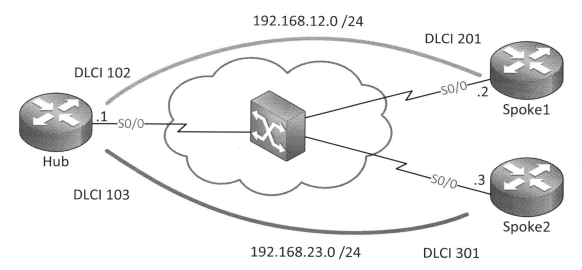

We are using the same topology to demonstrate point-to-point EIGRP over frame-relay with one difference. Point-to-point links require an **IP Subnet per PVC**:

- Hub and Spoke1: 192.168.12.0 /24
- Hub and Spoke2: 192.168.13.0 /24

```
Hub(config)#interface serial 0/0
```

```
Hub(config-if)#encapsulation frame-relay

Hub(config)#interface serial 0/0.1 point-to-point
Hub(config-subif)#ip address 192.168.12.1 255.255.255.0
Hub(config-subif)#frame-relay interface-dlci 102

Hub(config)#interface serial 0/0.2 point-to-point
Hub(config-subif)#ip address 192.168.13.1 255.255.255.0
Hub(config-subif)#frame-relay interface-dlci 103
```

```
Spoke1(config)#interface s0/0
Spoke1(config-if)#encapsulation frame-relay
Spoke1(config-if)#exit
Spoke1(config)#interface serial 0/0.1 point-to-point
Spoke1(config-subif)#ip address 192.168.12.2 255.255.255.0
Spoke1(config-subif)#frame-relay interface-dlci 201
```

```
Spoke2(config)#interface serial 0/0
Spoke2(config-if)#encapsulation frame-relay
Spoke2(config-if)#exit
Spoke2(config)#interface serial 0/0.1 point-to-point
Spoke2(config-subif)#ip address 192.168.13.3 255.255.255.0
Spoke2(config-subif)#frame-relay interface-dlci 301
```

Here is the configuration for the hub and spoke routers. You only have to specify encapsulation frame-relay on the physical interface. The rest of the commands are on the sub-interfaces. Your router can't read your mind and find out on which sub-interfaces which DLCI's should be so you have to configure it yourself. We don't use the frame-relay map command for point-to-point sub-interfaces but you have to use the **frame-relay interface-dlci** command here.

Since we are using 2 sub-interfaces on the hub router instead of a single multipoint interface we don't have to deal with pesky split-horizon issues here!

Now you have seen all the different ways of configuring EIGRP over frame-relay networks. There is one thing left you have to understand when running EIGRP over frame-relay networks and this is about bandwidth utilization.

- By default EIGRP can use up to **50% of interface bandwidth for EIGRP traffic**.
- The percentage can be changed.
- Point-to-point interfaces:
  - Bandwidth **treated as T1 interface** (1.544Mbit).
  - Configure the bandwidth yourself to reflect the true bandwidth.
- Multipoint interfaces:
  - Bandwidth on physical interface is **divided by the number of neighbors**.

What is the problem here? Let's say your frame-relay provider has given you a

PVC with a CIR of 64kbps. Your point-to-point interface is by default treated as T1 which is 1.544Mbit. EIGRP can take 50% of the bandwidth....50% of 1.544Mbit is 768kbps and voila...your PVC is flooded with EIGRP packets!

You can solve this by setting the correct bandwidth using the **bandwidth** command on the interface and/or by changing the percentage that EIGRP may use for traffic.

```
Hub(config)#interface s0/0.1 point-to-point
Hub(config-subif)#bandwidth 64
```

This is how you change the bandwidth on the sub-interface. If you change the bandwidth on the physical interface your sub-interface **will not inherit** the bandwidth! You need to specify it on each sub-interface yourself.

```
Hub#show interfaces serial 0/0.1
Serial0/0.1 is up, line protocol is up
  Hardware is M4T
  Internet address is 192.168.12.1/24
  MTU 1500 bytes, BW 64 Kbit, DLY 20000 usec,
```

You can see the new bandwidth by using the **show interface** command.

```
Hub(config)#interface s0/0.1 point-to-point
Hub(config-subif)#ip bandwidth-percent eigrp 123 25
```

By using the **ip bandwidth-percent eigrp** command you can change the percentage EIGRP may use for traffic. In my example I set it to 25% for EIGRP AS 123. Why would I want to change this percentage? Keep in mind changing the bandwidth also influences the metric so if you changed the bandwidth because of routing policy you might not want to change it. Imagine you have a FastEthernet link but set the bandwidth to 64kbps so the interface is less attractive to EIGRP. 50% of 64kbps is only 32kbps that EIGRP allows itself to use on this FastEthernet interface...that's not a lot right? That's why you can set the bandwidth percentage to above 100%.

Are you following me so far? Good! Let's crank it up a notch by looking at some funky examples with EIGRP bandwidth related issues.

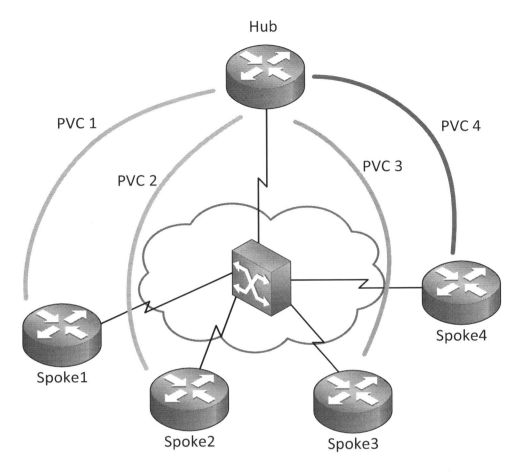

In the example above I have 5 routers in a hub and spoke model. The router on top is our hub and I have 4 spoke routers at the bottom. For each spoke there is a PVC and they each have a different CIR:

- PVC 1:   CIR 128kbps
- PVC 2:   CIR 128kbps
- PVC 3:   CIR 256kbps
- PVC 4:   CIR 64kbps

If we configure this frame-relay network as multipoint we might run into an issue. What happens when the spoke3 router sends EIGRP updates at 50% of its capacity meant for the spoke4 router?

50% of 256kbps = 128kbps

PVC4 only has a CIR of 64kbps so it will be overloaded with EIGRP traffic...not a good idea.

How can we fix this? The best method is to get rid of the multipoint setup and use point-to-point sub-interfaces since it allows you to set the bandwidth per

sub-interface and thus per neighbor. Are we going to do the easy solution? Of course not ;)
If you want to keep the multipoint setup this is what you need to do:

- Take the PVC with the lowest CIR. In our example this is PVC4 with a CIR of 64kbps.
- Multiply 64kbps with the number of PVCs and configure this as the bandwidth on the hub router.

```
Hub(config)#interface serial 0/0
Hub(config-if)#bandwidth 256
```

If you use multipoint interfaces EIGRP will divide the bandwidth over the number of neighbors. In our example this means each PVC will get 64kbps which is the bandwidth of the lowest bandwidth PVC.

This solution will not get the maximum out of the PVCs with a higher CIR but will ensure that the lower CIR PVCs are not overburdened with traffic.

Let's look at another topology:

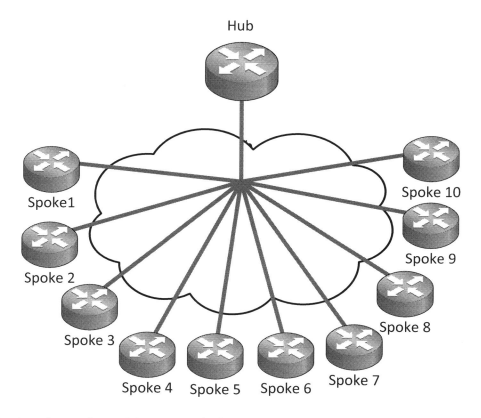

In the topology above I have one hub router and 10 spoke routers. All the PVCs are configured as point-to-point and have a CIR of 64kbps. The physical interface at the hub router only has a bandwidth of 256kbps and has been configured correctly.

```
Hub(config)#interface serial 0/0
Hub(config-if)#bandwidth 256
Hub(config-if)#exit

Hub(config)#interface serial 0/0.1 point-to-point
Hub(config-subif)#ip address 192.168.12.1 255.255.255.0
Hub(config-subif)#frame-relay interface-dlci 102

Hub(config)#interface serial 0/0.2 point-to-point
Hub(config-subif)#ip address 192.168.13.1 255.255.255.0
Hub(config-subif)#frame-relay interface-dlci 103


Hub(config)#interface serial 0/0.3 point-to-point
Hub(config-subif)#ip address 192.168.14.1 255.255.255.0
Hub(config-subif)#frame-relay interface-dlci 104
```

Here's part of the configuration of the hub router, I'm only showing the first 3 spoke routers. You can see the bandwidth has been configured correctly on the physical interface to 256kbps. Each PVC is configured as a point-to-point sub-interface.

What happens when our hub router tries to communicate with all spoke routers at the same time at full capacity? 10x 64kbps is 640kbps and our physical interface doesn't go faster than 256kbps...we'll run out of capacity! We have to make some changes to solve this problem.

```
Hub(config)#interface serial 0/0
Hub(config-if)#bandwidth 256
Hub(config-if)#exit

Hub(config)#interface serial 0/0.1 point-to-point
Hub(config-subif)#ip bandwidth-percent eigrp 123 128

Hub(config)#interface serial 0/0.2 point-to-point
Hub(config-subif)#ip bandwidth-percent eigrp 123 128

Hub(config)#interface serial 0/0.3 point-to-point
Hub(config-subif)#ip bandwidth-percent eigrp 123 128
```

We'll start with the hub router. The physical bandwidth of the interface is 256kbps and since we have 10 PVCs this bandwidth will be divided automatically between the PVCs, no need to configure the bandwidth **manually** on each point-to-point sub-interface.

256 / 10 = 25kbps for each PVC.

Each PVC has a bandwidth of 64kbps however so we need to do something to make sure EIGRP can still use 50% of the available bandwidth.

 I have changed the percentage EIGRP AS 123 can use to 128%.

128% of 25kbps = 32kbps

32kbps is exactly 50% of the available CIR rate for each PVC.

What about the spoke routers? We need to change their configuration as well so they reflect the hub router. Let me show you one of them:

```
Spoke1(config)#interface serial 0/0
Spoke1(config-if)#bandwidth 25
Spoke1(config-if)#exit

Spoke1(config)#interface serial 0/0.1 point-to-point
Spoke1(config-subif)#ip bandwidth-percent eigrp 123 128
```

We set the bandwidth at 25kbps and the percentage EIGRP can use at 128% for AS 123.

128% of 25kbps = 32kbps

32kbps is exactly 50% of the available CIR rate of our PVC.
There is one downside to this solution. Since EIGRP divides the bandwidth of multipoint interfaces automatically over the number of neighbors there shouldn't be any changes in the number of EIGRP neighbors or our calculation is incorrect.

Almost there...I promise! Now you have seen the multipoint and point-to-point solution but there's also a **hybrid** option. We are going to mix the multipoint and point-to-point interfaces for this one!

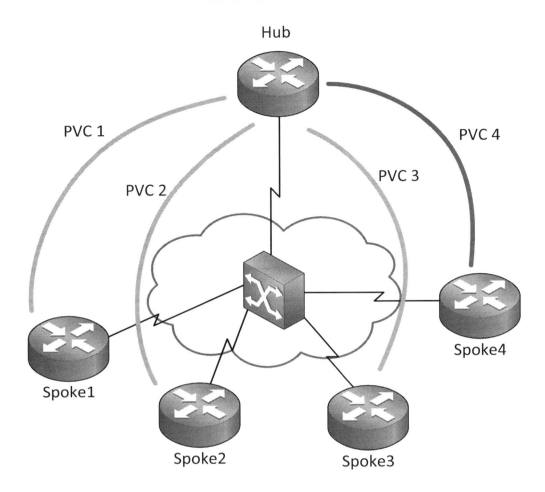

In the example above I have the same topology as our first example. The router on top is our hub and I have 4 spoke routers at the bottom. There's something different with the CIR of our PVCs:

- PVC 1,2 and 3:   CIR 256kbps
- PVC 4:   CIR 128kbps

So PVC 1, 2 and 3 have the same CIR rate of 256kbps while PVC4 is slower at 128kbps. We can combine the 3 PVCs with the 256kbps CIR on a multipoint interface while the slow PVC is configured on a separate point-to-point interface.

```
Hub(config)#interface serial 0/0.123 multipoint
Hub(config-subif)#bandwidth 768
Hub(config-subif)#exit

Hub(config)#interface serial 0/0.1 point-to-point
Hub(config-subif)#bandwidth 128
```

This is what we have to do on the hub router. PVC1, 2 and 3 we are going to configure under the multipoint sub-interface and give it a bandwidth of 768kbps. EIGRP automatically divides the bandwidth over the number of EIGRP neighbors so each of them gets 256kbps which matches the CIR rate of 256kbps.

The slower PVC number 4 will be configured as a separate point-to-point sub-interface where we set the correct bandwidth, that's it!

We made it to the end of this chapter. I believe EIGRP with frame-relay and the different bandwidth/CIR configurations is probably the most difficult part to understand about this subject. If you want some good practice check out the frame-relay labs I created for EIGRP.

If you are a little fuzzy on frame-relay you can start with this lab:

http://gns3vault.com/Frame-Relay/frame-relay-basics.html

Next stop is to configure EIGRP over frame-relay:

http://gns3vault.com/EIGRP/eigrp-over-frame-relay-with-sub-interfaces.html

http://gns3vault.com/EIGRP/eigrp-over-frame-relay-with-multipoint-interface.html

Once you feel familiar with EIGRP over frame-relay you can work on the different bandwidth pacing labs:

http://gns3vault.com/EIGRP/eigrp-multipoint-bandwidth-pacing.html

http://gns3vault.com/EIGRP/eigrp-point-to-point-bandwidth-pacing.html

http://gns3vault.com/EIGRP/eigrp-hybrid-bandwidth-pacing.html

René Molenaar

5. EIGRP Authentication

Routing protocols can be configured to prevent receiving false routing updates and EIGRP is no exception. If you don't use authentication and you are running EIGRP someone could try to form an EIGRP neighbor adjacency with one of your routers and try to mess with your network...we don't want that to happen right?

What options do we have to authenticate EIGRP?

- MD5 authentication.

EIGRP only offers MD5 authentication, there's no plaintext authentication.

What does authentication offer us?

- Your router will authenticate the source of each routing update packet that it will receive.
- Prevents false routing updates from sources that are not approved.
- Ignore malicious routing updates.

A potential hacker could be sitting on your network with a laptop running GNS3 / Dynamips, boot up a Cisco router and try the following things:

- Try to establish a neighbor adjacency with one of your routers and advertise junk routes.
- Send malicious packets and see if you can drop the neighbor adjacency of one of your authorized routers.

In order to configure EIGRP authentication we need to do the following:

- Configure a key-chain
    - Configure a key ID under the key-chain.
        - Specify a password for the key ID.
        - Optional: specify accept and expire lifetime for the key.

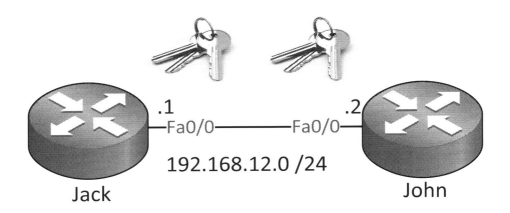

Jack   John

I'm going to use router Jack and John again and this time we will configure MD5 authentication for EIGRP.
The configuration for both routers is very basic:

```
Jack(config)#interface fastEthernet 0/0
Jack(config-if)#ip address 192.168.12.1 255.255.255.0

Jack(config)#router eigrp 12
Jack(config-router)#network 192.168.12.0
```

```
John(config)#interface fastEthernet 0/0
John(config-if)#ip address 192.168.12.2 255.255.255.0

John(config)#router eigrp 12
John(config-router)#network 192.168.12.0
```

Key ID 1
String: Banana

Keychain "KingKong"

We'll start by specifying a keychain. I called mine "KingKong" but it can be different on both routers, it doesn't matter. The Key ID is a value that has to match on both routers and the key-string is the password which has to match of course.

```
Jack(config)#key chain KingKong
Jack(config-keychain)#key 1
Jack(config-keychain-key)#key-string Banana
```

```
Jack(config)#interface fastEthernet 0/0
Jack(config-if)#ip authentication mode eigrp 12 md5
Jack(config-if)#ip authentication key-chain eigrp 12 KingKong
```

First you have to create the keychain and then you need to activate it on the interface. The "12" is the AS number of EIGRP. The configuration on router John is exactly the same.

```
John#debug eigrp packets
EIGRP Packets debugging is on
    (UPDATE, REQUEST, QUERY, REPLY, HELLO, IPXSAP, PROBE, ACK,
STUB, SIAQUERY, SIAREPLY)
```

```
John# EIGRP: FastEthernet0/0: ignored packet from 192.168.12.1,
opcode = 5 (authentication off or key-chain missing)
```

You can check if your configuration is correct by using **debug eigrp packets**. You can see that we received a packet with MD5 authentication but I didn't enable MD5 authentication yet on router John.

Let's fix it:

```
John(config)#key chain KingKong
John(config-keychain)#key 1
John(config-keychain-key)#key-string Banana

John(config)#interface fastEthernet 0/0
John(config-if)#ip authentication mode eigrp 12 md5
John(config-if)#ip authentication key-chain eigrp 12 KingKong
```

Right away I can see that the EIGRP neighbor adjacency is working:

```
John# %DUAL-5-NBRCHANGE: IP-EIGRP(0) 12: Neighbor 192.168.12.1
(FastEthernet0/0) is up: new adjacency
```

What if I entered a wrong key-string?

```
Jack(config)#key chain KingKong
Jack(config-keychain)#key 1
Jack(config-keychain-key)#key-string Apples
```

Let's see if KingKong likes apples...

```
John# EIGRP: pkt key id = 1, authentication mismatch
```

You will see the message above in the debug output on router John. At least it tells us that key 1 is the one with the error.

If you want to spice it up a bit you can set an **accept** and **expire** lifetime on keys. The idea behind this is that you can have keys that are only valid for a day, a week, a month or something else. Do you want to use this in real life? It might enhance security but it also make maintenance a bit more complex...

Before you configure keys with a limited lifetime make sure you set the correct time and date. You can do this manually on each router but it's better to use a NTP (Network Time Protocol) server so all the routers have the same time/date.

See if you can configure authentication with this lab:

http://gns3vault.com/EIGRP/eigrp-authentication-rotating-key.html

6. EIGRP Advanced Features

This is our final EIGRP chapter and we will look at some more advanced EIGRP features. We will dive a little bit more into the EIGRP query process and how stub routers can help us solve some problems.

EIGRP is designed for large enterprise networks but having one big EIGRP network (5000+ prefixes and many hops) can lead to some problems:

- Lots of EIGRP prefixes equal a large topology table and routing table.
- Calculating the successor router will take longer if you have many EIGRP neighbors and different paths.
- If there are many backup paths EIGRP will have to see if there are 1 or more feasible successors, this will take longer.
- More information means our EIGRP routers have to work harder to process everything.
- When EIGRP loses a route and there is no feasible successor the route will go from **passive** to **active** and the router starts sending queries to its neighbors.
- EIGRP sends queries on all interfaces except the interface of the successor.

We have talked about summarization before and how it helps to reduce the size of the routing table and stops the query process. Let me describe the EIGRP query process in detail for you:

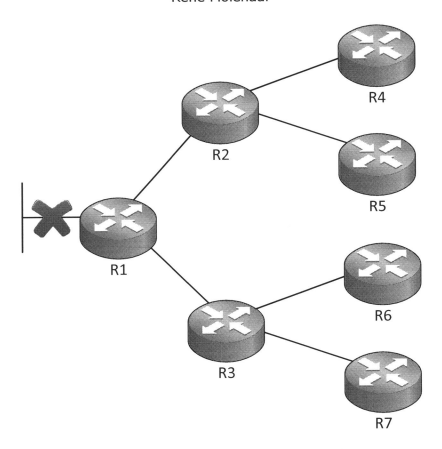

In the topology above we are running EIGRP on all of the routers. Router 1 has a link failure and as a result has lost its successor route to a particular network on the left side. There is no feasible successor so the route is going from passive to active and we will send a query to router 2 and 3.

There are 2 things that can happen at this moment:

- Router 2 or 3 has information about this particular route and will send information about it to router 1. The query process is now over.
- Router 2 or 3 don't know anything about this route and will send a query themselves to their neighbors router 4, 5 and router 6 and 7. Router 2 or 3 will not send a reply to router 1 until they heard a response from all their neighbors.

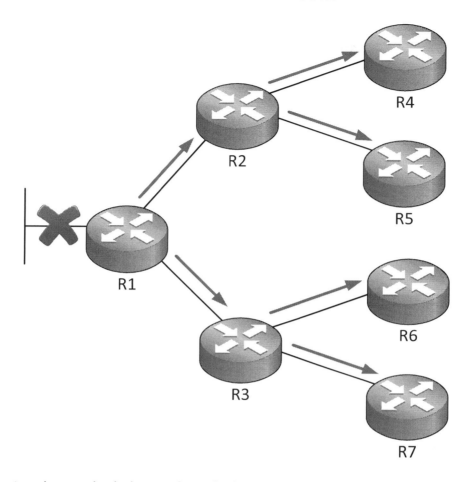

In our topology nobody has a clue which network router 1 is looking for. They will forward their queries to their own neighbors. The red arrows indicate the query packet.

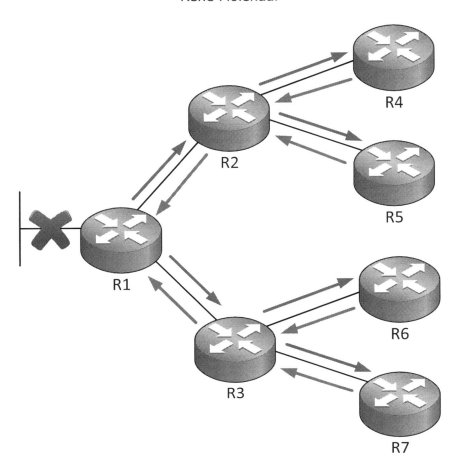

There are no other neighbors behind router 4, 5, 6 or 7. They will send a reply to router 2 and 3 to let them know they don't know the answer. Router 2 and 3 will send a reply to router 1 to tell them they are sorry but this is it. That's a lot of packets for just one route that was lost right?

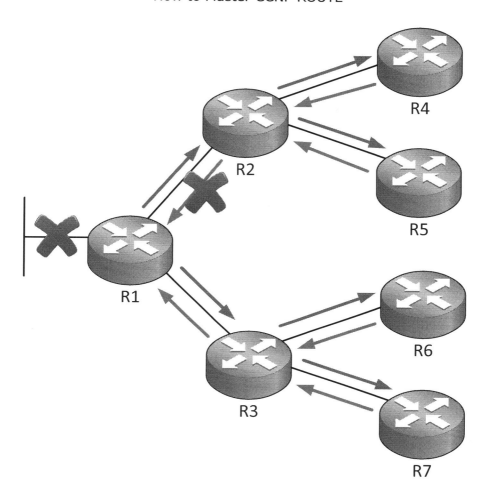

Let's make things even more interesting. Look at my picture above and you'll see that the reply from router 2 never makes it back to router 1. EIGRP is a reliable protocol and for each query a router sends to its neighbors it must **get a reply in response within 3 minutes**. If the router does not receive a reply to ALL its outstanding queries it will put the route in **SIA (Stuck in Active)** state and will kill the neighbor adjacency. By dropping the neighbor adjacency you will lose all the routes you learned from this neighbor which means the router will start sending queries for all those routes as well. Not a pretty sight right?

How is it possible that a reply never makes it back?

- The router that gets the query is too busy because of memory problems or a CPU that's too busy. It might not get the chance to process the incoming query or send a reply packet.
- There are problems with the link between the neighbors so not all packets arrive.
- You have a unidirectional link failure so packets only flow in one direction. This can happen with fiber links.

Since IOS 12.1 Cisco decided to change the stuck in active process to reduce the number of unwanted lost neighbor adjacencies. They introduced two new packets called **SIA query** and **SIA reply**.

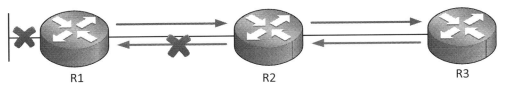

| R1 | R2 | R3 |

Before Cisco introduced SIA query and SIA reply this would happen:

1. Router 1 loses information about a network and has no feasible successor.
2. Router 1 sends a query to router 2.
3. Router 2 doesn't know the answer so sends a query as well to router 3.
4. Router 3 doesn't know the answer and sends a reply to router 2.
5. Router 2 sends a reply to router 1 to let him know he has no clue about this network.
6. Because of congestion the reply from router 2 never makes it back to router 1.
7. After 3 minutes router 1 will drop the neighbor adjacency with router 2 including all the routes it learnt from router 2.

Now we have SIA query and SIA reply and things will work a little bit different:

1. Router 1 loses information about a network and has no feasible successors.
2. Router 1 sends a query to router 2.
3. Router 2 doesn't know the answer so sends a query as well to router 3.
4. Router 3 doesn't know the answer and sends a reply to router 2.
5. Router 2 sends a reply to router 1 to let him know he has no clue about this network.
6. Because of congestion the reply from router 2 never makes it back to router 1.
7. After 1.5 minute router 1 will send a SIA query to router 2 to ask for its status.

8. Router 2 will respond with a SIA reply and the neighbor adjacency will not be dropped.

Does this make sense to you? There is something else we can do to stop queries....**EIGRP stub** to the rescue!

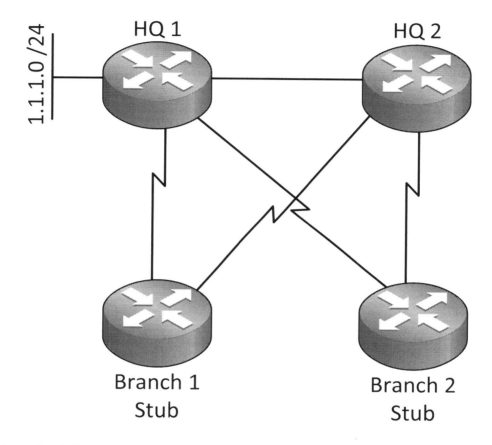

Look at the following topology. We have a company with a headquarters and 2 branch offices. The 2 HQ routers are connected on the LAN using a Gigabit link. The branch offices are connected to both HQ routers using slow 64kbps serial links. What do you think will happen once HQ 1 loses its route to the 1.1.1.0 /24 network on the left side?

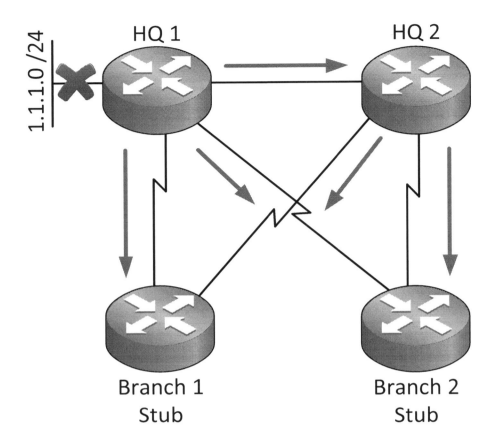

Query packets (red arrows) will fly everywhere! It doesn't sound like a good idea to use the serial links for backup so we are going to change this behavior by turning the branche routers into **EIGRP stubs.**

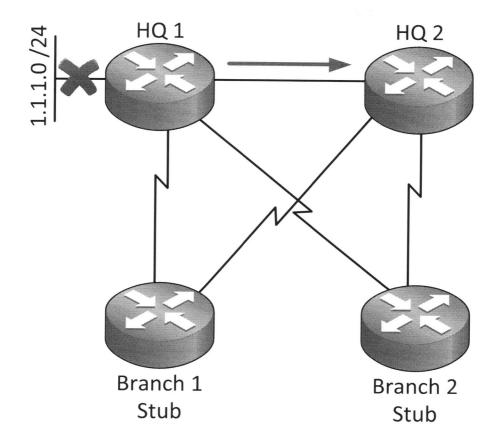

If we configure the branch routers as stub routers they will **not receive queries** from our HQ routers. This is a very good technique to stop query traffic!

Why do we call it a stub? You have probably seen one before!

A tree that is cut off is called a stub...there's nothing attached to it anymore.

If you look at our branch routers they are like the tree. There are no other routers behind the branch routers and we don't want to use them as backup paths so why bother querying them?

EIGRP stubs are not an "all or nothing" solution. We have different flavors so you can choose to which types of routes the stub router should receive queries or not.
Here are the flavors we have:

- **Receive-only**: The stub router will not advertise any network.
- **Connected**: allows the stub router to advertise directly connected networks.
- **Static**: allows the stub router to advertise static routes (you have to redistribute them).
- **Summary**: allows the stub router to advertise summary routes.
- **Redistribute**: allows the stub router to advertise redistributed routes.

The default is **connected + summary.** If you like you can mix some of the options with the exception of receive-only because it denies all advertisements. Redistribution is the importing and exporting of routing information from one routing protocol to another. This is something we will discuss later in the redistribution chapter.

Let's look at some EIGRP stub scenarios!

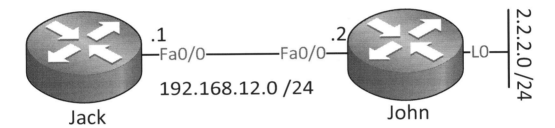

```
Jack(config)#router eigrp 123
Jack(config-router)#network 192.168.12.0
```

```
John(config-if)#router eigrp 123
John(config-router)#network 192.168.12.0
John(config-router)#network 2.2.2.0 0.0.0.255
```

I'll use the topology above and a basic EIGRP configuration. Let me first demonstrate the EIGRP query behavior to you.

```
Jack#debug eigrp packets query
EIGRP Packets debugging is on
    (QUERY)
```

```
John#debug eigrp packets query
EIGRP Packets debugging is on
    (QUERY)
```

First let me enable the debug on router Jack and John so you can see the queries.

```
John(config)#interface loopback 0
John(config-if)#shutdown
```

We'll shut the loopback0 interface on router John to see what will happen.

```
John#
EIGRP: Enqueueing QUERY on FastEthernet0/0 iidbQ un/rely 0/1
serno 33-33
EIGRP: Enqueueing QUERY on FastEthernet0/0 nbr 192.168.12.1
iidbQ un/rely 0/0 peerQ un/rely 0/0 serno 33-33
EIGRP: Sending QUERY on FastEthernet0/0
  AS 12, Flags 0x0, Seq 55/0 idbQ 0/0 iidbQ un/rely 0/0 serno
33-33
```

You can see that router John is sending a query towards router Jack.

```
Jack# EIGRP: Received QUERY on FastEthernet0/0 nbr 192.168.12.2
  AS 12, Flags 0x0, Seq 55/0 idbQ 0/0 iidbQ un/rely 0/0 peerQ
un/rely 0/0
```

And we see that router Jack has received the query. So far so good, this is normal EIGRP behavior. You lose a network...you ask your neighbors if they know where it is.

```
John(config)#interface loopback 0
John(config-if)#no shutdown
```

First I'll restore the loopback0 interface...

```
Jack(config)#router eigrp 12
Jack(config-router)#eigrp stub
```

And we'll configure router Jack as an EIGRP stub router.

```
Jack#show running-config | begin router eigrp
router eigrp 12
 network 192.168.12.0
 no auto-summary
 eigrp stub connected summary
```

Just so you know, if you configure EIGRP stub without any parameters then it will use "connected" and "summary" by default.

```
Jack#
%DUAL-5-NBRCHANGE: IP-EIGRP(0) 12: Neighbor 192.168.12.2
(FastEthernet0/0) is down: peer info changed
%DUAL-5-NBRCHANGE: IP-EIGRP(0) 12: Neighbor 192.168.12.2
(FastEthernet0/0) is up: new adjacency
John#
```

```
%DUAL-5-NBRCHANGE: IP-EIGRP(0) 12: Neighbor 192.168.12.1
(FastEthernet0/0) is down: Interface Goodbye received
%DUAL-5-NBRCHANGE: IP-EIGRP(0) 12: Neighbor 192.168.12.1
(FastEthernet0/0) is up: new adjacency
```

You can see that configuring the stub feature breaks the EIGRP neighbor adjacency. Let's see if anything is different if I shut the loopback0 interface...

```
John(config)#interface loopback 0
John(config-if)#shutdown
```

The interface goes down...let's see what will happen...

```
Jack# EIGRP: Enqueueing QUERY on FastEthernet0/0 iidbQ un/rely
0/1 serno 28-28
EIGRP: Enqueueing QUERY on FastEthernet0/0 nbr 192.168.12.2
iidbQ un/rely 0/0 peerQ un/rely 0/0 serno 28-28
EIGRP: Sending QUERY on FastEthernet0/0
  AS 12, Flags 0x0, Seq 44/0 idbQ 0/0 iidbQ un/rely 0/0 serno
28-28
```

```
John#
EIGRP: Received QUERY on FastEthernet0/0 nbr 192.168.12.1
  AS 12, Flags 0x0, Seq 44/0 idbQ 0/0 iidbQ un/rely 0/0 peerQ
un/rely 0/0
```

You can see that router Jack will send a query towards router John because it has lost the 2.2.2.0 /24 network. It's not receiving a query anymore from router John because it's a stub router!

Now you know how it deals with the queries, let's take a look at the different stub options!

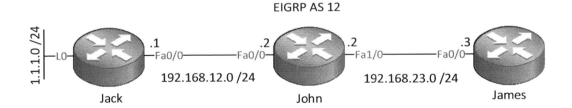

I'll use a different topology to demonstrate the different stub options. Here are the EIGRP configurations of the 3 routers:

```
Jack#show run | begin router eigrp
router eigrp 12
 network 192.168.12.0
 no auto-summary
```

```
John#show run | begin router eigrp
router eigrp 12
 network 192.168.12.0
 network 192.168.23.0
 no auto-summary
```

```
James#show run | begin router eigrp
router eigrp 12
 network 3.3.3.0 0.0.0.255
 network 192.168.23.0
 no auto-summary
```

Nothing special as you can see. Let me advertise the loopback 0 interface on router Jack in EIGRP:

```
Jack(config)#router eigrp 12
Jack(config-router)#network 1.1.1.0 0.0.0.255
```

Nothing special so far...

```
John#show ip route eigrp
      1.0.0.0/24 is subnetted, 1 subnets
D        1.1.1.0 [90/156160] via 192.168.12.1, 00:00:48,
FastEthernet0/0
```

You can see that router John has learned about network 1.1.1.0 /24. Now let's play with the stub feature.

```
Jack(config)#router eigrp 12
Jack(config-router)#eigrp stub receive-only
```

Let's make it receive-only.

```
John#show ip route eigrp
```

Easy enough...router Jack doesn't advertise anything anymore so router John doesn't know about the 1.1.1.0 /24 network anymore. That's it...let's try the next stub option:

```
Jack(config)#router eigrp 12
Jack(config-router)#no eigrp stub receive-only
```

Let's start by getting rid of the stub feature on router Jack.

```
James#show ip route eigrp
D    192.168.12.0/24 [90/30720] via 192.168.23.2, 00:12:49,
FastEthernet0/0
      1.0.0.0/24 is subnetted, 1 subnets
```

```
D          1.1.1.0 [90/158720] via 192.168.23.2, 00:11:16,
FastEthernet0/0
```

Let's take a quick look at the routing table of router James. It has learned two networks through EIGRP:

- 192.168.12.0 /24 which is the link between router Jack and John.
- 1.1.1.0 /24 which is the loopback0 interface of router Jack.

```
John(config)#router eigrp 12
John(config-router)#eigrp stub connected
```

Let's enable the eigrp stub connected option on router John.

```
John#show ip route eigrp
     1.0.0.0/24 is subnetted, 1 subnets
D        1.1.1.0 [90/156160] via 192.168.12.1, 00:10:45,
FastEthernet0/0
```

```
James#show ip route eigrp
D     192.168.12.0/24 [90/30720] via 192.168.23.2, 00:01:03,
FastEthernet0/0
```

Interesting...router James only has 192.168.12.0 /24 in its routing table now. Why? It's because this network is directly connected to router John and that's why it's advertised. 1.1.1.0/24 is not advertised from router John to James because of the stub connected option!

```
John(config)#router eigrp 12
John(config-router)#no eigrp stub connected
```

Let's clean up before we continue with the next stub option...

```
John(config)#router eigrp 12
John(config-router)#eigrp stub static
```

This time I'll turn router John into a stub static. Let's see what router James thinks of this...

```
James#show ip route eigrp
```

Router James doesn't have any EIGRP information anymore. Why? It's because router John only advertises redistributed static routes...

```
John#show ip route eigrp
     1.0.0.0/24 is subnetted, 1 subnets
D        1.1.1.0 [90/156160] via 192.168.12.1, 00:01:29,
FastEthernet0/0
```

You can see that router John still knows about network 1.1.1.0/24...

```
John(config)#ip route 1.1.1.0 255.255.255.0 192.168.12.1
```

First I'll create a static route and point it towards router Jack.

```
John(config)#router eigrp 12
John(config-router)#redistribute static
```

Secondly we'll make sure that router John redistributes this static route into EIGRP.

```
James#show ip route eigrp
     1.0.0.0/24 is subnetted, 1 subnets
D EX    1.1.1.0 [170/30720] via 192.168.23.2, 00:01:06,
FastEthernet0/0
```

There we go...since router John only advertises redistributed static routes we can now see network 1.1.1.0/24 again in the routing table of router James.

```
John(config)#router eigrp 12
John(config-router)#no eigrp stub static
John(config-router)#no redistribute static
John(config-router)#exit
John(config)#no ip route 1.1.1.0 255.255.255.0 192.168.12.1
```

Let's clean up before we continue.

```
John(config)#router eigrp 12e.
John(config-router)#eigrp stub summary
```

Let's turn router John into an EIGRP stub summary router.

```
James#show ip route eigrp
```

Of course router James is clueless again because router John will only advertise summary routes...

```
John(config)#interface fastEthernet 1/0
John(config-if)#ip summary-address eigrp 12 1.1.0.0 255.255.0.0
```

We'll configure a summary and advertise it towards router James.
```
James#show ip route eigrp
     1.0.0.0/16 is subnetted, 1 subnets
D       1.1.0.0 [90/158720] via 192.168.23.2, 00:01:10,
FastEthernet0/0
```

You can see the summary in the routing table of router James...that's it!

```
John(config)#interface fastEthernet 1/0
John(config-if)#no ip summary-address eigrp 12 1.1.0.0
255.255.0.0
John(config-if)#exit
John(config)#router eigrp 12
John(config-router)#no eigrp stub summary
```

Let's clean up and move on to the final EIGRP stub option, redistribute.

```
John(config)#router eigrp 12
John(config-router)#eigrp stub redistributed
```

Let's enable the redistributed stub option.

```
John#show run | include eigrp stub
  eigrp stub connected summary redistributed
```

First thing you might notice is that it also includes connected and summary routes.

Let's add a loopback interface on router John and redistribute it into EIGRP:

```
John(config)#interface loopback 1
John(config-if)#ip address 2.2.2.2 255.255.255.0
```

```
John(config)#router eigrp 12
John(config-router)#redistribute connected
```

Instead of the network command we'll redistribute the loopback interface into EIGRP.

```
James#show ip route | include 2.2.2.0
D EX    2.2.2.0 [170/156160] via 192.168.23.2, 00:00:42,
FastEthernet0/0
```

You can see that router James learned the 2.2.2.0/24 network.

Are you following me so far? EIGRP stubs are quite fun to play with. If you want to see all the stubs in action you should try some of my labs or watch the videos I created:

http://gns3vault.com/EIGRP/eigrp-stub.html

http://gns3vault.com/EIGRP/eigrp-stub-leak-map.html

Since IOS 15, EIGRP has a new method of configuration called **named EIGRP**. With the examples you have seen so far, we configured EIGRP globally and configured some other things like authentication on the interface(s). With named EIGRP, everything is done globally. If you try to configure EIGRP on an IOS 15.x router you'll see this:

```
R1(config)#router eigrp ?
  <1-65535>   Autonomous System
  WORD        EIGRP Virtual-Instance Name
```

Instead of an AS number we can also choose a name. Let's try this, I'll use two routers for this demonstration:

.1   .2
—Fa0/0———————Fa0/0—
192.168.12.0 /24

R1   R2

Let's start with R1:

```
R1(config)#router eigrp MY_NAME
R1(config-router)#?
Router configuration commands:
  address-family  Enter Address Family command mode
  default         Set a command to its defaults
  exit            Exit from routing protocol configuration mode
  no              Negate a command or set its defaults
  service-family  Enter Service Family command mode
  shutdown        Shutdown this instance of EIGRP
```

We'll have to select an address-family:

```
R1(config-router)#address-family ?
  ipv4  Address family IPv4
  ipv6  Address family IPv6
```

EIGRP named mode covers both IPv4 and IPv6. Let's try IPv4:

```
R1(config-router)#address-family ipv4 autonomous-system 12
```

This is where I configure everything. For example advertising a network:

```
R1(config-router-af)#network 192.168.12.0
```

Everything that used to be configured on the interface is now under the same global configuration:

```
R1(config-router-af)#af-interface FastEthernet 0/0
R1(config-router-af-interface)#?
Address Family Interfaces configuration commands:
  authentication        authentication subcommands
  bandwidth-percent     Set percentage of bandwidth percentage
limit
  bfd                   Enable Bidirectional Forwarding Detection
  dampening-change      Percent interface metric must change to
cause update
  dampening-interval    Time in seconds to check interface metrics
  default               Set a command to its defaults
  exit-af-interface     Exit from Address Family Interface
configuration mode
  hello-interval        Configures hello interval
  hold-time             Configures hold time
  next-hop-self         Configures EIGRP next-hop-self
  no                    Negate a command or set its defaults
  passive-interface     Suppress address updates on an interface
  shutdown              Disable Address-Family on interface
  split-horizon         Perform split horizon
  summary-address       Perform address summarization
```

Let's try authentication:

```
R1(config-router-af-interface)#authentication mode md5
R1(config-router-af-interface)#authentication key-chain MY_CHAIN
```

Don't forget to create that key chain:

```
R1(config)#key chain MY_CHAIN
R1(config-keychain)#key 1
R1(config-keychain-key)#key-string PASSWORD
```

Let's configure R2 with the "classic" commands:

```
R2(config)#key chain MY_CHAIN
R2(config-keychain)#key 1
R2(config-keychain-key)#key-string PASSWORD
```

```
R2(config)#router eigrp 12
R2(config-router)#network 192.168.12.0
```

```
R2(config)#interface FastEthernet 0/0
R2(config-if)#ip authentication key-chain eigrp 12 MY_CHAIN
R2(config-if)#ip authentication mode eigrp 12 md5
```

EIGRP is still the same, only the configuration commands have changed. Show commands are still the same:

```
R1#show ip eigrp neighbors
EIGRP-IPv4 VR(MY_NAME) Address-Family Neighbors for AS(12)
H    Address                 Interface       Hold Uptime    SRTT
RTO  Q  Seq

                                             (sec)          (ms)
Cnt  Num
0    192.168.12.2            Fa0/0             12 00:00:35     6
200  0  3
```

That's all there is to it.

Phew! We made it to the end of the EIGRP chapter! What do you think? There's quite some material about EIGRP you have to understand if you want to master your CCNP ROUTE exam. Cisco exams are very practical-minded so make sure you practice on labs until you fully understand EIGRP. Throughout the chapters I gave you some links to EIGRP labs that cover the different topics and now is a good time to try some of the full CCNP EIGRP labs I have for you.

These labs are a mix of all the different EIGRP items you have seen like summaries, authentication, stubs, load balancing and more. If you can beat those without too much effort you'll have mastered EIGRP!

http://gns3vault.com/CCNP/eigrp-ccnp-1.html

Here you can find all the EIGRP labs I currently have:

http://gns3vault.com/Table/EIGRP/

If you feel confident on EIGRP and are up for a challenge you should try my EIGRP troubleshooting lab:

http://gns3vault.com/Troubleshooting/eigrp-troubleshooting.html

7. Introduction to OSPF

Next to EIGRP there is one more IGP (Interior Gateway Protocol) we are going to look at which happens to be **OSPF (Open Shortest Path First).** This first chapter will be an introduction. Some of the things you might have seen from CCNA but I've added some extras.

I don't know about you but I love my navigation system. The good thing about them is you can just drive and there is no need to look for traffic signs, the bad thing is that I'm absolutely lost when it's not working.

I'm bad at reading maps (or maybe I just don't like it) and if I had to find my way to some street in any big city I'm doomed.

Link-state routing protocols are like your navigation system, they have a complete map of the network. If you have a full map of the network you can just calculate the shortest path to all the different destinations out there. This is cool because if you know about all the different paths it's impossible to get a loop since you know everything! The downside is that this is more CPU intensive than a distance vector routing protocol. It's just like your navigation system...if you calculate a route from New York to Los Angeles it's going to take a bit longer than when you calculate a route from one street to another street in the same city.

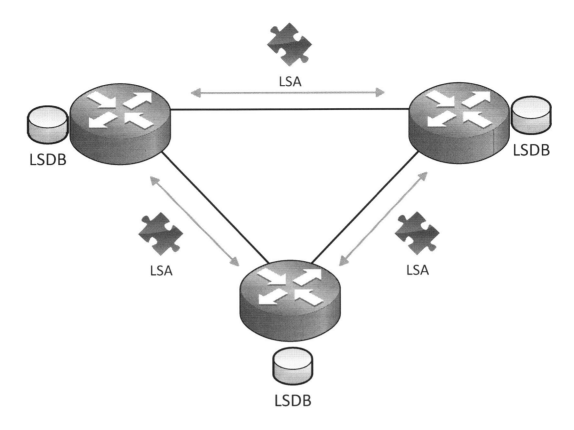

Let's take a good look at link-state and what it exactly means:

- ✓ Link: That's the interface of our router.
- ✓ State: Description of the interface and how it's connected to neighbor routers.

Link-state routing protocols operate by sending **link-state advertisements** (**LSA**) to all other link-state routers.

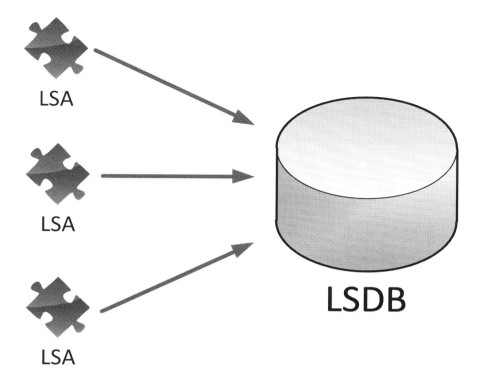

All the routers need to have these link-state advertisements so they can build their **link-state database** or **LSDB**.

Basically all the link-state advertisements are a piece of the puzzle which builds the LSDB.

This LSDB is our full picture of the network, in network terms we call this the **topology**.

You could compare the LSDB to having a full map of your country.

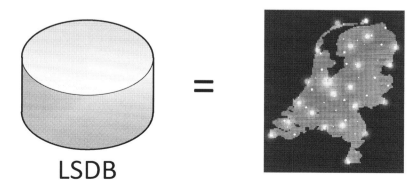

Once every router has a complete map we can start calculating the shortest path to all the different destinations by using the **shortest-path first (SPF) algorithm**. The BEST information goes into the routing table. Calculating the shortest path is like using your navigation system, it will look at the map and look at all the different ways of getting to the destination and only show you the best way of getting there.

There is only one link-state routing protocol we are going to discuss which is OSPF (Open Shortest Path First). There is another link-state routing protocol called IS-IS but it has been completely removed from CCNA, CCNP and even CCIE by Cisco.

Enough of my link-state routing protocol introduction let's take a look at OSPF and see how it operates.

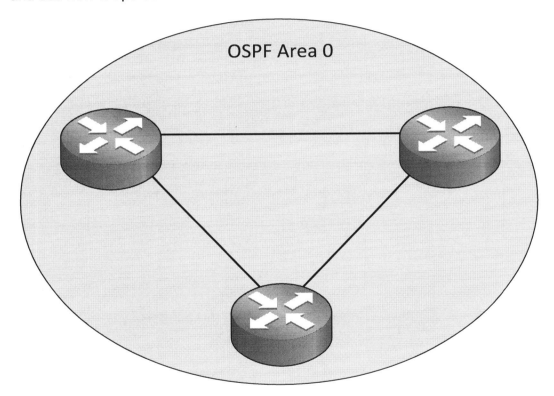

OSPF works with the concepts of **areas** and by default you will always have a single area, normally this is area 0 or also called the **backbone** area.

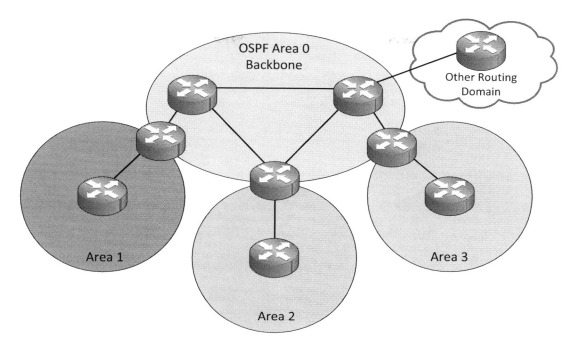

You can have multiple areas however as in the picture above, we have area 1, 2 and 3. All of these areas **must connect** to the backbone area. If you want to go from area 1 to area 2 you **must** go through the backbone area to get there. It's impossible to go from area 1 directly to area 2; you always have to pass the backbone area! Same thing if you want to go from area 3 to area 2...you must cross the backbone area.

So why do we work with areas? Remember what I just explained about your navigation system. If you tell your navigation system to calculate from New York to Los Angeles it will take much longer than calculating a route from one street to another street in the same city. This calculating is called the **shortest path first** or **SPF** algorithm and the same thing apply to OSPF. Our routers only have a full picture of the network topology within the area, the smaller your map the faster your SPF algorithm works!

Keep in mind the SPF algorithm is from the 70's and OSPF was invented somewhere in the 80's...we didn't have fancy Core 2 Duo / Quad and I7's back then.

In the picture you also see on the top right something called "other routing domain". This could be another network running another routing protocol (perhaps RIP) and it's possible to import and export routes from RIP into OSPF or the other way around, this is called **redistribution.**

- ✓ Routers in the backbone area (area 0) are called backbone routers.
- ✓ Routers between two areas (like the one between area 0 and area 1) are called **area border routers** or **ABR.**
- ✓ Routers that run OSPF and are connected to another network that runs another routing protocol (for example RIP) are called **autonomous system border routers** or **ASBR.**

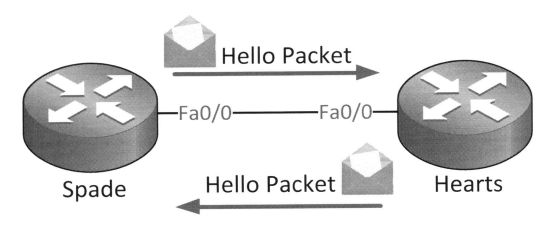

OSPF works differently than RIP or EIGRP, first of all it's a link-state compared to a distance vector but it also doesn't just send the link-state-advertisements around. Routers have to be become neighbors first; once we have become neighbors we are going to exchange link-state advertisements.

Once you configure OSPF your router will start sending hello packets. If you also receive hello packets from the other router you will become neighbors.

Router ID
Hello / Dead Interval *
Neighbors
Area ID *
Router Priority
DR IP Address
BDR IP Address
Authentication
Password *
Stub Area Flag *

There's one catch however, there are a couple of fields in the hello packet and many of them have to match (the ones with the asterisk) otherwise you won't become neighbors. Let's walk through the items in the hello packet and see what they are about:

- ✓ **Router ID:** Each OSPF router needs to have an unique ID which is the highest IP address on any active interface. More about this later.
- ✓ **Hello / Dead Interval:** Every X seconds we are going to send a hello packet, if we don't hear any hello packets from our network for X seconds we declare you "dead" and we are no longer neighbors. These values have to match on both sides in order to become neighbors.
- ✓ **Neighbors:** All other routers who are your neighbors are specified in the hello packet.
- ✓ **Area ID:** This is the area you are in. This value has to match on both sides in order to become neighbors.
- ✓ **Router Priority:** This value is used to determine who will become designated or backup designated router. More on this later.
- ✓ **DR and BDR IP address:** Designated and Backup Designated router. More on this later.
- ✓ **Authentication password:** You can use clear text and MD5 authentication for OSPF which means every packet will be authenticated. Obviously you need the same password on both routers in order to make things work.
- ✓ **Stub area flag:** Besides area numbers OSPF has different area types, we will cover this later. Both routers have to agree on the area type in order to become neighbors.

- • **Unadvertised Loopback Address**
- • Used as OSPF Router ID
- • Saves address space
- • Unable to use to connect to router

- • **Advertised Loopback Address**
- • Used as OSPF Router ID
- • Uses address space
- • Able to use to connect to router

Each OSPF router needs to have a unique router ID which is based on the **highest IP address** on any **active interface**.

If you have a loopback interface on your OSPF router then this IP address will be used as the router ID even when it's not the highest active IP address. Why does OSPF do this? Well it makes sense...your loopback interface will never go down unless your router crashes.

Using a loopback interface you can do 2 things:

- ✓ Advertise the IP address on the loopback interface in OSPF.
- ✓ Don't advertise the IP address on the loopback interface in OSPF.

What's the difference? Well if you advertise it other routers will be able to reach and ping the IP address on this loopback interface or even use it to telnet into the router. If you don't then well you can't...it's as easy as that.

Everything is well, we have configured OSPF...we have become neighbors with a bunch of routers and they have exchanged link-state advertisements. Our routers have built their LSDB and they have a full topology picture of our network. Next step is to run the SPF algorithm and see what the shortest path to our destination is.

What about the metric? OSPF uses a metric called **cost** which is based on the bandwidth of an interface, it works like this:

Cost = Reference Bandwidth / Interface Bandwidth

The reference bandwidth is a default value on Cisco routers which is a 100Mbit interface. You divide the reference bandwidth by the bandwidth of the interface and you'll get the cost.

Example: If you have a 100 Mbit interface what will the cost be?

Cost = Reference bandwidth / Interface bandwidth.

100 Mbit / 100 Mbit = COST 1

Example: If you have a 10 Mbit interface what will the cost be?

100 Mbit / 10 Mbit = COST 10

Example: If you have a 1 Mbit interface what will the cost be?

100 Mbit / 1 Mbit = COST 100

The **lower** the cost the better the path is.

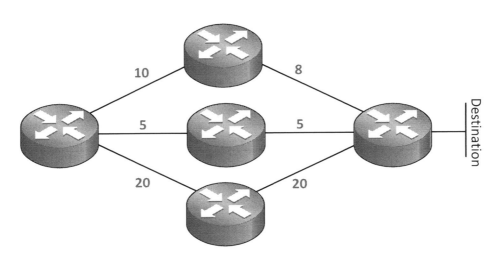

Look at the picture above, we are sitting in the router on the left and running the SPF algorithm looking for the shortest path to our destination. Which one are we going to use?

Using the router on top we would have a cost of 10+8 which is 18. The path in the middle is 5+5 = 10. The router on the bottom we would have a cost of 20+20 = 40. The path in the middle obviously has the lowest cost so this is the path we are going to use!

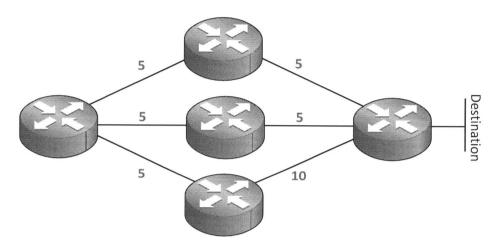

Look at this picture: As you can see the path through the router on top and the middle router have the same cost (5+5 = 10). What are we going to do here? The path is equal.

The answer is **load balancing**! We are going to use both paths and OSPF will load balance among them 50/50. Some things worth knowing about OSPF load balancing:

- ✓ Paths must have an equal cost.
- ✓ 4 equal cost paths will be placed in routing table.
- ✓ Maximum of 16 paths.
- ✓ To make paths equal cost, change the "cost" of a link

If a path is not equal we can make it so by manually changing the cost or bandwidth of an interface.

How exactly does OSPF fill the LSDB? Let's zoom in on the operation of how OSPF keeps its link-state database up-to-date.

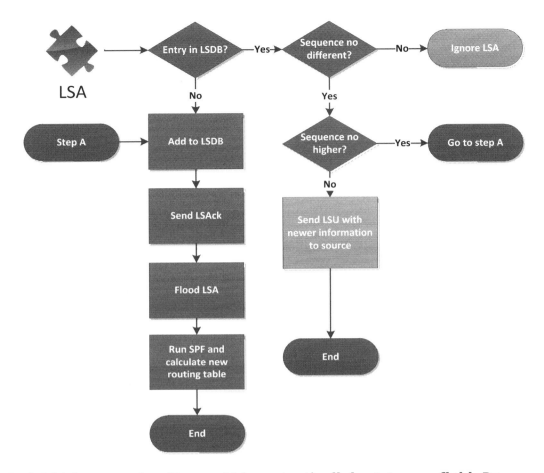

Each LSA has an **aging timer** which carries the **link-state age field.** By default each OSPF LSA is only valid for **30 minutes.** If the LSA expires then the router that created the LSA will resend the LSA and increase the **sequence number**.

Let's walk through this flowchart together. In this example a new LSA is arriving at the router and OSPF has to decide what to do with it:

1. If the LSA isn't already in the LSDB it will be added and a LSAck (acknowledgement) will be sent to the OSPF neighbor. The LSA will be flooded to all other OSPF neighbors and we have to run SPF to update our routing table.
2. If the LSA is already in the LSDB and the sequence number is the same then we will ignore the LSA.
3. If the LSA is already in the LSDB and the sequence number is different then we have to take action:
   a. If the sequence number is higher it means this information is newer and we have to add it to our LSDB.

b. If the sequence number is lower it means our OSPF neighbor has an old LSA and we should help them. We will send a **LSU (Link state update)** including the newer LSA to our OSPF neighbor. The LSU is an envelope that can carry multiple LSAs in it. More about OSPF packets in the next chapter!

It's not just the sequence number that OSPF will look at to determine if a LSA is **more recent**. It will consider the LSA to be more recent if it has:

- A higher sequence number.
- A higher checksum number.
- An age equal to the maximum age.
- If the link-state age is much younger.

What do the sequence numbers look like for OSPF LSAs?

- There are 4 bytes or 32-bits.
- Begins with 0x80000001 and ends at 0x7FFFFFFF.
- Every 30 minutes each LSA will age out and will be flooded:
  - The sequence number will increment by one.

With 32-bits we have a LOT of sequence numbers and every 30 minutes it will increase. If we make it to the last sequence number 0x7FFFFFFF it will wrap around and start again at 0x80000001. Every 30 minutes OSPF will flood a LSA to make sure the LSDB stays up to date and when it does this the sequence number will increase and OSPF will reset the max age when it receives a new LSA update.

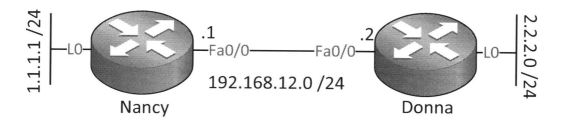

Let's use the topology above to configure OSPF and see some LSAs in action.

```
Nancy(config)#router ospf 1
Nancy(config-router)#network 0.0.0.0 255.255.255.255 area 0
Nancy(config-router)#exit
```

```
Donna(config)#router ospf 1
Donna(config-router)#network 0.0.0.0 255.255.255.255 area 0
Donna(config-router)#exit
```

I'm using the above network command to advertise any interface with an IP address, keep in mind this is not best practice. It's just my "quick and dirty" method to get OSPF going...I like to do this if I only care about "connectivity".

```
Donna#show ip ospf database

            OSPF Router with ID (2.2.2.2) (Process ID 1)

            Router Link States (Area 0)

Link ID             ADV Router          Age          Seq#          Checksum
Link count
1.1.1.1             1.1.1.1             109          0x80000002 0x004ED8
2
2.2.2.2             2.2.2.2             108          0x80000002 0x003EDB
2

            Net Link States (Area 0)

Link ID             ADV Router          Age          Seq#          Checksum
192.168.12.2        2.2.2.2             108          0x80000001 0x008F1F
```

Here is the output of the **show ip ospf database** command which shows us the LSDB. What interesting things can we see here?

- Each OSPF router has interfaces in an area. For each interface it will advertise a **router LSA**. The link ID is the OSPF router ID. Since I'm using loopback interfaces on both routers that IP address was chosen for the OSPF router ID.
- The first router LSA entry you see is from router Nancy and you can see the age, sequence number and a checksum. You can see that the LSA has been updated 2 times since the sequence number is 0x80000002 (I did a **clear ip ospf process** to demonstrate this).

So far my OSPF introduction... Throughout the OSPF chapters I'm going to tell a bit more about the OSPF database. In the upcoming chapter we'll start with looking at the different OSPF packets.

If you want to look at the OSPF LSDB yourself and play a bit you can use one of my OSPF single area labs:

http://gns3vault.com/OSPF/ospf-single-area.html

If you need more refreshment you can try one of the full OSPF CCNA labs:

http://gns3vault.com/CCNA/ospf-for-ccna-1.html

8. OSPF Packets and Neighbor discovery

In this chapter I'm going to show you the different packets OSPF uses and how neighbor discovery works.

Frame Header	IP Header	OSPF Packet	Payload

OSPF uses its own protocol like EIGRP and doesn't use a transport protocol like TCP or UDP. If you would look at the IP packet in wireshark you can see that OSPF has **protocol ID 89** for all its packets.

```
Donna#debug ip ospf packet
OSPF packet debugging is on
      OSPF: rcv. v:2 t:1 l:48 rid:1.1.1.1
      aid:0.0.0.0 chk:4D40 aut:0 auk: from FastEthernet0/0
```

If we use **debug ip ospf packet** we can look at the OSPF packet on our router. Let's look at the different fields we have:

- **V:2** stands for OSPF version 2. If you are running IPv6 you'll version 3.
- **T:1** stands for OSPF packet number 1 which is a hello packet. I'm going to show you the different packets in a bit.
- **L:48** is the packet length in bytes. This hello packet seems to be 48 bytes.
- **RID 1.1.1.1** is the Router ID.
- **AID** is the area ID in dotted decimal. You can write the area in decimal (area 0) or dotted decimal (area 0.0.0.0).
- **CHK 4D40** is the checksum of this OSPF packet so we can check if the packet is corrupt or not.
- **AUT:0** is the authentication type. You have 3 options:
  - 0 = no authentication
  - 1 = clear text
  - 2 = MD5
- **AUK:** If you enable authentication you'll see some information here.

Let's continue by looking at the different OSPF packet types:

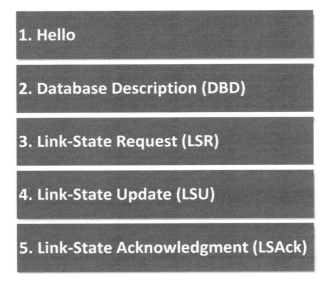

1. Hello

2. Database Description (DBD)

3. Link-State Request (LSR)

4. Link-State Update (LSU)

5. Link-State Acknowledgment (LSAck)

I'm throwing them right at you; here are all the **OSPF packet types** we have. In my **debug ip ospf packet** at the previous page you could see T:1 which stands for packet type 1. Here you see that it corresponds to an OSPF hello packet. What is the role of each OSPF packet?

- **Hello:** neighbor discovery, build neighbor adjacencies and maintain them.
- **DBD:** This packet is used to check if the LSDB between 2 routers is the same. The DBD is a **summary of the LSDB**.
- **LSR:** Requests specific link-state records from an OSPF neighbor.
- **LSU:** Sends specific link-state records that were requested. This packet is like an envelope with multiple LSAs in it.
- **LSAck:** OSPF is a reliable protocol so we have a packet to acknowledge the others.

OSPF has to get through 7 states in order to become neighbors...here they are:

1. **Down**: no OSPF neighbors detected at this moment.
2. **Init:** Hello packet received.
3. **Two-way:** own router ID found in received hello packet.
4. **Exstart:** master and slave roles determined.
5. **Exchange:** database description packets (DBD) are sent.
6. **Loading:** exchange of LSRs (Link state request) and LSUs (Link state update) packets.
7. **Full:** OSPF routers now have an adjacency.

Let's have a detailed look at this process!

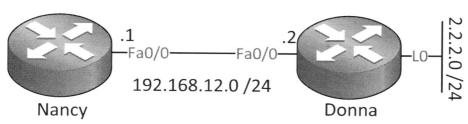

This is the topology I'm using. Router Nancy and Donna are connected using a single link and we will see how router Nancy learns about the 2.2.2.0 /24 network.

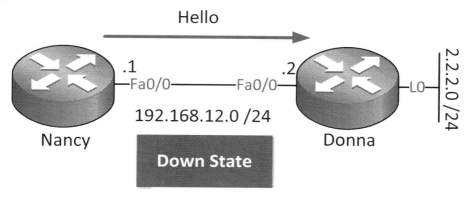

As soon as I configure OSPF on router Nancy it will start sending hello packets. Router Nancy has no clue about other OSPF routers at this moment so it's in the **down state**. The hello packet will be sent to the **multicast address 224.0.0.5.**

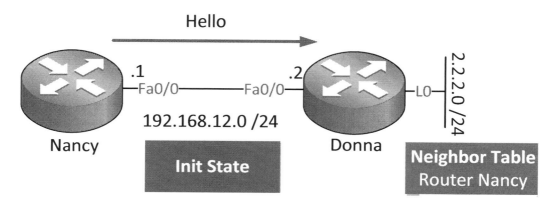

Router Donna receives the hello packet and will put an entry for router Nancy in the **OSPF neighbor table.** We are now in the **init state.**

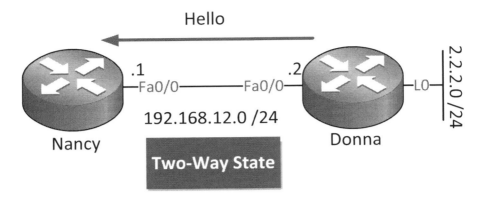

Router Donna has to respond to router Nancy with a hello packet. This packet is not sent using multicast but with **unicast** and in the neighbor field it will include **all OSPF neighbors** that router Donna has. Router Nancy will see **her own name** in the neighbor field in this hello packet.

Router Nancy will receive this hello packet and sees her own router ID. We are now in the **two-way state**.

I have to take a pause here. If the link we are using is a **multi-access network** OSPF has to elect a **DR (Designated Router)** and **BDR (Backup Designated Router)**. This has to happen before we can continue with the rest of the process. In the next chapter I'm going to teach your DR/BDR...for now just hold the thought that the DR/BDR election happens right after the two-way state ok?

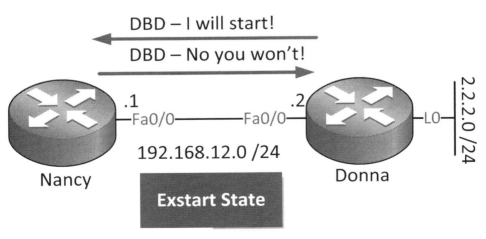

Our next stop is the **exstart state**. Our routers are ready to sync their LSDB. At this step we have to select a **master** and **slave** role. The router with the highest router ID will become the master. Router Donna has the highest router ID and will become the master.

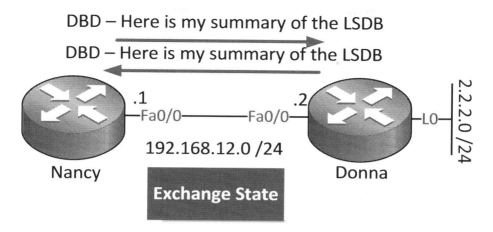

In the **exchange state** our routers are sending a DBD with a summary of the LSDB. This way the routers can find out what networks they don't know about.

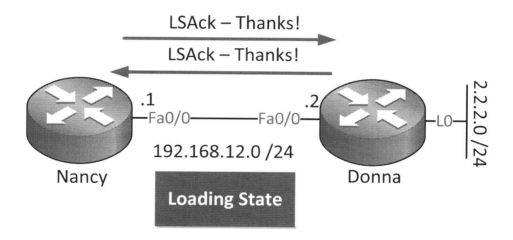

When our routers receive the DBD from the other side they will do a couple of things:

- Send an acknowledgement using the LSAck packet.
- Compare the information in the DBD with the information it already has:
  - If the neighbor has new or newer information it will send a LSR (Link State Request) packet to request for this information
- When the routers start sending a LSR (Link State Request) we are in the **loading state**.
- The other router will respond with a LSU (Link State Update) with the requested information.

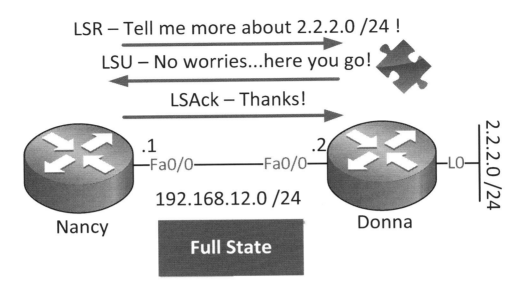

When router Nancy requested information about 2.2.2.0 /24 it used a LSR. Router Donna will send the LSU with the information. Router Nancy will send an acknowledgment using a LSAck packet to finish. We are now in the **full state.** Both routers have a synchronized LSDB and we are ready to route!

Wonder what this looks like on a real router? Doing a **debug ip ospf adj** is faster than drawing all those pictures in Microsoft Visio:

```
Donna#debug ip ospf adj
OSPF adjacency events debugging is on
```

```
Donna#clear ip ospf process
Reset ALL OSPF processes? [no]: yes
```

Let me show you the debug:

```
Donna#
OSPF: Interface Loopback0 going Down
OSPF: 2.2.2.2 address 2.2.2.2 on Loopback0 is dead, state DOWN
OSPF: Interface FastEthernet0/0 going Down
OSPF: 2.2.2.2 address 192.168.12.2 on FastEthernet0/0 is dead,
state DOWN
OSPF: Neighbor change Event on interface FastEthernet0/0
OSPF: DR/BDR election on FastEthernet0/0
OSPF: Elect BDR 0.0.0.0
OSPF: Elect DR 1.1.1.1
OSPF: Elect BDR 0.0.0.0
OSPF: Elect DR 1.1.1.1
      DR: 1.1.1.1 (Id)    BDR: none
OSPF: 1.1.1.1 address 192.168.12.1 on FastEthernet0/0 is dead,
state DOWN
```

```
%OSPF-5-ADJCHG: Process 1, Nbr 1.1.1.1 on FastEthernet0/0 from
FULL to DOWN, Neighbor Down: Interface down or detached
OSPF: Neighbor change Event on interface FastEthernet0/0
OSPF: DR/BDR election on FastEthernet0/0
OSPF: Elect BDR 0.0.0.0
OSPF: Elect DR 0.0.0.0
        DR: none      BDR: none
OSPF: Remember old DR 1.1.1.1 (id)
OSPF: Interface Loopback0 going Up
OSPF: Interface FastEthernet0/0 going Up
OSPF: 2 Way Communication to 1.1.1.1 on FastEthernet0/0, state
2WAY
OSPF: Backup seen Event before WAIT timer on FastEthernet0/0
OSPF: DR/BDR election on FastEthernet0/0
OSPF: Elect BDR 2.2.2.2
OSPF: Elect DR 1.1.1.1
OSPF: Elect BDR 2.2.2.2
OSPF: Elect DR 1.1.1.1
        DR: 1.1.1.1 (Id)    BDR: 2.2.2.2 (Id)
OSPF: Send DBD to 1.1.1.1 on FastEthernet0/0 seq 0x1E09 opt 0x52
flag 0x7 len 32
OSPF: Rcv DBD from 1.1.1.1 on FastEthernet0/0 seq 0x886 opt 0x52
flag 0x7 len 32  mtu 1500 state EXSTART
OSPF: First DBD and we are not SLAVE
OSPF: Rcv DBD from 1.1.1.1 on FastEthernet0/0 seq 0x1E09 opt
0x52 flag 0x2 len 72  mtu 1500 state EXSTART
OSPF: NBR Negotiation Done. We are the MASTER
OSPF: Send DBD to 1.1.1.1 on FastEthernet0/0 seq 0x1E0A opt 0x52
flag 0x1 len 32
OSPF: Rcv DBD from 1.1.1.1 on FastEthernet0/0 seq 0x1E0A opt
0x52 flag 0x0 len 32  mtu 1500 state EXCHANGE
OSPF: Exchange Done with 1.1.1.1 on FastEthernet0/0
OSPF: Send LS REQ to 1.1.1.1 length 24 LSA count 2
OSPF: Rcv LS UPD from 1.1.1.1 on FastEthernet0/0 length 108 LSA
count 2
OSPF: Synchronized with 1.1.1.1 on FastEthernet0/0, state FULL
%OSPF-5-ADJCHG: Process 1, Nbr 1.1.1.1 on FastEthernet0/0 from
LOADING to FULL, Loading Done
```

I highlighted some of the fields: you can see the 2 way communication, the struggle for power to determine who will be master or slave, exchange of the LSDB summary using another DBD packet and finally a LSQ and LSU.

And that's the end of this chapter. By now you have learned what OSPF is, how it forms neighbors adjacencies and the different packets it uses.

9. OSPF Network Types

In this chapter I'm going to explain you what a **DR (Designated router)** and **BDR (Backup designated router)** is and we will look at the different network types. For this chapter to understand you must have solid knowledge on frame-relay. If you are a little fuzzy you should (re)read my EIGRP over Frame-relay chapter since it covers everything you need to know about frame-relay. If you thought EIGRP over frame-relay was a pain just wait till you have seen OSPF...this is a wild rollercoaster ride!

Let me start by showing you what a **DR** and **BDR** are.

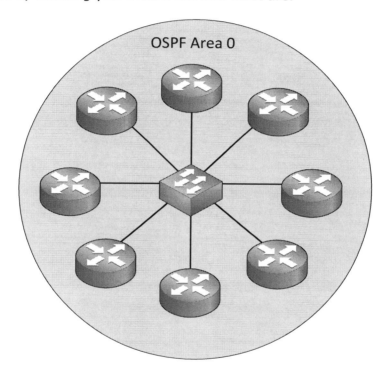

In the previous chapter I showed you how OSPF forms neighbor adjacencies and you could see this takes quite some effort. We have to send some hello's, become neighbors, send a DBD...check if our LSDB is synchronized and then send a bunch of LSRs and LSUs to get everything up-to-date.

Now look at the picture above. We have a network with 8 OSPF routers connected on a switch. Each of those routers is going to become OSPF neighbors with all of the other routers...sending hello packets, checking the LSDB, etc. etc.

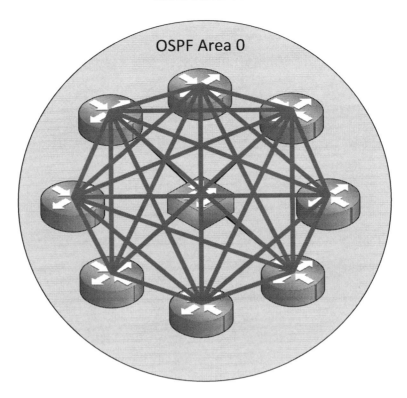

This is what we would get. A full-mesh of OSPF neighbors. Every router will become OSPF neighbors with all the others and exchange routing information. We will have a lot of OSPF packets flying around on this network just to setup and maintain OSPF neighbor adjacencies. Is there any way to make this more efficient?

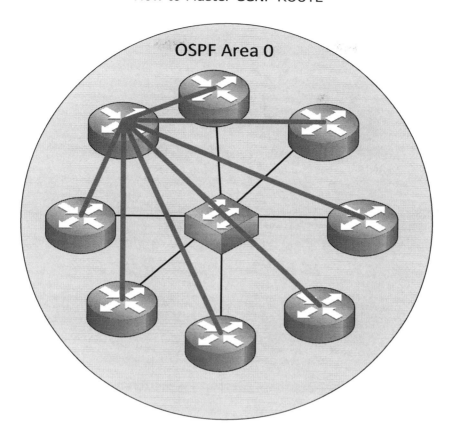

What if all our OSPF routers would just send their stuff to a single OSPF router who will then forward it to all the other OSPF routers? All our OSPF routers will know about all the routing information out there but we will have far less OSPF traffic. This is exactly what we do with a **DR (Designated router)**. Our OSPF routers will only form a full neighbor adjacency with the DR and not with all other routers!

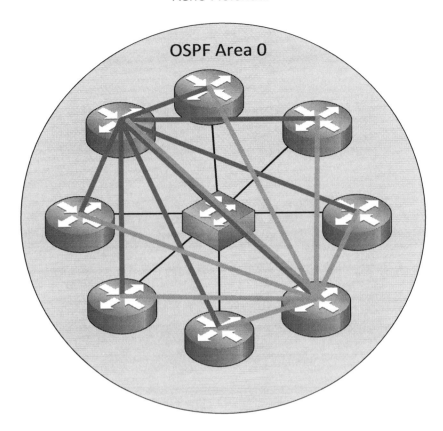

Since bad stuff can happen to our networks we want to have backup for our DR. If it crashes the **BDR (Backup Designated Router)** will take over. All our OSPF routers will only form **full neighbor adjacencies** with the DR and BDR and not with all other routers. This sounds efficient right?

We only use a DR/BDR on a **multi-access** network. There is no need to do this on a **point-to-point** link like a PPP connection. There is only one other router on the other side so why select a DR/BDR there? Makes sense right?

How do we select a DR/BDR? In the previous chapter you saw the process of becoming OSPF neighbors. Right after the two-way state that's where we elect who will become DR or BDR. Who is going to win the election?

- The router with the **highest priority** will become DR.
- The router with the **second highest priority** will become BDR.
- If the priority is the same the OSPF router ID is the tiebreaker.
- The higher router ID the better.
- DR/BDR election is non-preemptive. This means if you change the priority or router ID you have to reset OSPF in order to select a new DR/BDR.
- Routers that are not DR or BDR show up as **DROTHER**.

I always find DROTHER a funny name. Why not call it "OTHER" or something else, are we supposed to pronounce it like "BROTHER" or "DR-OTHER"? I'd say the last one but I guess someone has been creative here…nevertheless this is how it looks like on a live network:

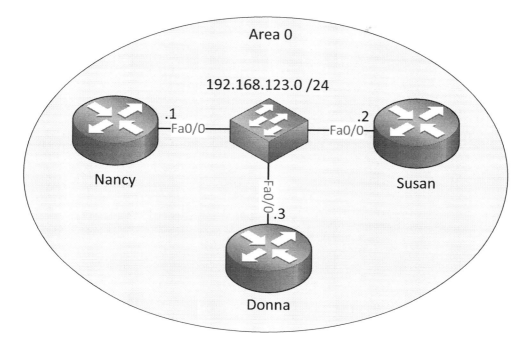

Here's an example of a network with 3 OSPF routers on a FastEthernet network. They are connected to the same switch (multi-access network) so there will be a DR/BDR election, let's take a look:

```
Nancy#show ip ospf neighbor

Neighbor ID      Pri    State         Dead Time    Address
Interface
192.168.123.2    1    FULL/BDR        00:00:32     192.168.123.2
FastEthernet0/0
192.168.123.3    1    FULL/DR         00:00:31     192.168.123.3
FastEthernet0/0
```

From router Nancy's perspective, router Susan is the BDR and Donna is the DR.

```
Donna#show ip ospf neighbor

Neighbor ID      Pri    State         Dead Time    Address
Interface
192.168.123.1    1    FULL/DROTHER    00:00:36     192.168.123.1
FastEthernet0/0
```

```
192.168.123.2    1    FULL/BDR           00:00:39      192.168.123.2
FastEthernet0/0
```

Here we can see that router Nancy is a DROTHER.

```
Susan#show ip ospf neighbor

Neighbor ID      Pri    State            Dead Time    Address
Interface
192.168.123.1    1    FULL/DROTHER       00:00:31      192.168.123.1
FastEthernet0/0
192.168.123.3    1    FULL/DR            00:00:32      192.168.123.3
FastEthernet0/0
```

And router Susan (the BDR) sees the DR and DROTHER.

Of course we can change which router becomes the DR/BDR by playing with the **priority**. Let's turn router Nancy in the DR:

```
Nancy(config)#interface fastEthernet 0/0
Nancy(config-if)#ip ospf priority 200
```

You change the priority if you like by using the **ip ospf priority** command:

- The default priority is 1.
- A priority of 0 means you will never be elected as DR or BDR.
- You need to use **clear ip ospf process** before this change takes effect.

```
Nancy#show ip ospf neighbor

Neighbor ID      Pri    State            Dead Time    Address
Interface
192.168.123.2    1    FULL/BDR           00:00:31      192.168.123.2
FastEthernet0/0
192.168.123.3    1    FULL/DR            00:00:32      192.168.123.3
FastEthernet0/0
```

As you can see router Donna is still the DR, we need to reset the OSPF neighbor adjacencies so that we'll elect the new DR and BDR.

```
Donna#clear ip ospf process
Reset ALL OSPF processes? [no]: yes
```

```
Susan#clear ip ospf process
Reset ALL OSPF processes? [no]: yes
```

I'll reset all the OPSF neighbor adjacencies.

```
Nancy#show ip ospf neighbor

Neighbor ID      Pri   State        Dead Time   Address
Interface
192.168.123.2    1     FULL/DROTHER    00:00:36    192.168.123.2
FastEthernet0/0
192.168.123.3    1     FULL/BDR        00:00:30    192.168.123.3
FastEthernet0/0
```

Now you can see router Nancy is the DR because the other routers are DROTHER and BDR.

```
Donna#show ip ospf neighbor
Neighbor ID      Pri   State        Dead Time   Address
Interface
192.168.123.1    200   FULL/DR         00:00:30    192.168.123.1
FastEthernet0/0
192.168.123.2    1     FULL/DROTHER    00:00:31    192.168.123.2
FastEthernet0/0
```

Or we can confirm it from router Donna, you'll see that router Nancy is the DR and that the priority is 200.

Something you need to be aware of is that the **DR/BDR election is per multi-access segment...not per area!** (which is what most people think). Let me give you an example:

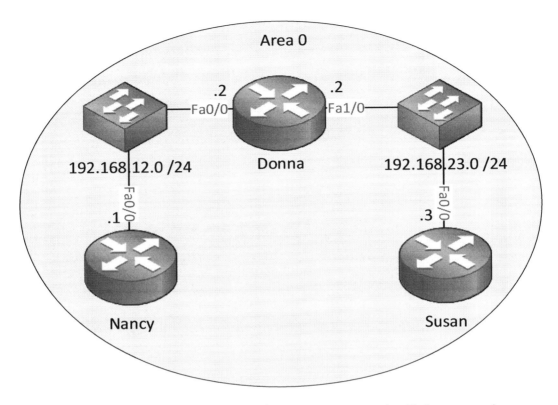

In the example above we have 2 multi-access segments. Between router Donna and Nancy, and between router Donna and Susan. For each segment there will be a DR/BDR election.

```
Donna#show ip ospf neighbor

Neighbor ID      Pri   State      Dead Time    Address
Interface
192.168.23.3     200   FULL/DR    00:00:36     192.168.23.3
FastEthernet1/0
192.168.12.1     200   FULL/DR    00:00:37     192.168.12.1
FastEthernet0/0
```

In the example above you can see that router Nancy is the DR for the 192.168.12.0/24 segment and router Susan is the DR for the 192.168.23.0/24 segment. Do we always have a DR/BDR election?

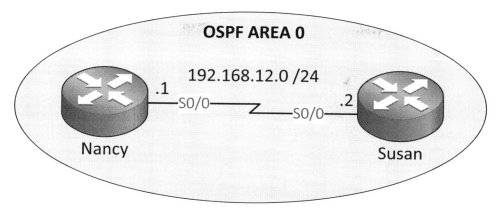

```
Nancy#show ip ospf neighbor

Neighbor ID      Pri    State            Dead Time    Address
Interface
192.168.12.2       0    FULL/   -        00:00:36     192.168.12.2
Serial0/0
```

```
Susan#show ip ospf neighbor

Neighbor ID      Pri    State            Dead Time    Address
Interface
192.168.12.1       0    FULL/   -        00:00:34     192.168.12.1
Serial0/0
```

Here's an example of a point-to-point link running HDLC. You can see that we have a neighbor but we didn't do an election for DR or BDR. Makes sense because there is always only one router on the other side.

Are you following me so far? The next part is where the fun starts! We are going to look at the different network types OSPF offers. I talked a little about multi-access and point-to-point but it's a bit more complex. Let me show you the OSPF network types:

- **Non-Broadcast (NBMA)**
- **Point-to-multipoint**
- **Point-to-multipoint non-broadcast**
- **Broadcast**
- **Point-to-Point**

Non-broadcast (NBMA) and **point-to-multipoint** are defined in RFC 2328. **Point-to-multipoint non-broadcast, broadcast** and **point-to-point** are from Cisco so you can blame them for having to learn those extra network types.

You can see what type OSPF has selected for an interface by using the **show**

ip ospf interface command.

```
Nancy#show ip ospf interface serial 0/0
Serial0/0 is up, line protocol is up
  Internet Address 192.168.12.1/24, Area 0
  Process ID 1, Router ID 192.168.12.1, Network Type
POINT_TO_POINT, Cost: 64
```

This is my serial link and you can see the network type is point-to-point.

```
Nancy#show ip ospf interface f0/0
FastEthernet1/0 is up, line protocol is up
  Internet Address 192.168.23.2/24, Area 0
  Process ID 1, Router ID 192.168.23.2, Network Type BROADCAST,
Cost: 1
```

This is an example of a FastEthernet interface. Note that I didn't do anything to set these network types...OSPF did this automatically for me. Let's walk through all the different OSPF network types:

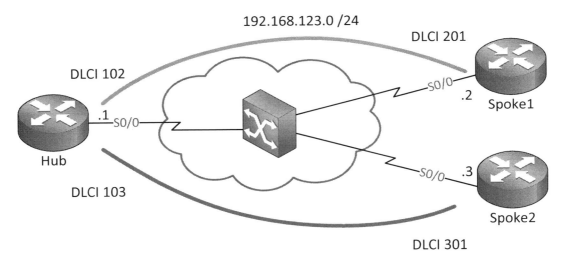

I'm going to start with the **non-broadcast** network type. If you select the non-broadcast network type then OSPF will assume you are running a **multi-access** network. Couple of key things to remember here:

- Multi-access means we have to select a DR and BDR.
- Non-broadcast means that OSPF expects us to configure neighbors ourselves.

Now take a look close look at my frame-relay network in the picture above and assume we are going to run the non-broadcast network type here. Is my network multi-access? Interesting question right?

Is there any connectivity between router Spoke1 and Spoke2? You can see I only have 2 PVCs and there is no connection between Spoke1 and Spoke2. This is where things can get funky! If we select the non-broadcast network type we are telling OSPF our network is multi-access but in reality it's not...there is only connectivity between the Hub router and the Spoke routers, not between the 2 spoke routers.

When I explained the DR/BDR to you I told you that we only have a full adjacency with the DR/BDR and not with all other routers. What do you think will happen if Spoke1 is elected as the DR?

Since Spoke2 can't reach Spoke1 it can never setup a full OSPF neighbor adjacency and we'll run into connectivity issues. How do we solve this? **We have to make sure the Hub router becomes the DR and Spoke1 or Spoke2 will never become DR or BDR**!

The Hub router can be reached by Spoke1 and Spoke2 so if it's the DR they can do the full OSPF neighbor adjacency, exchange routing information and life is all good.

```
Hub(config)#interface serial 0/0
Hub(config-if)#ip address 192.168.123.1 255.255.255.0
Hub(config-if)#encapsulation frame-relay
Hub(config-if)#ip ospf network non-broadcast
Hub(config-if)#exit
Hub(config)#router ospf 1
Hub(config-router)#network 192.168.123.0 0.0.0.255 area 0
Hub(config-router)#neighbor 192.168.123.2
Hub(config-router)#neighbor 192.168.123.3
```

Here is the configuration of the Hub router. You can see I used the **ip ospf network non-broadcast** command to change the OSPF network type. I also had to specify the neighbors so OSPF switches to unicast.

```
Spoke1(config)#interface serial 0/0
Spoke1(config-if)#ip address 192.168.123.2 255.255.255.0
Spoke1(config-if)#encapsulation frame-relay
Spoke1(config-if)#ip ospf network non-broadcast
Spoke1(config-if)#ip ospf priority 0
Spoke1(config-if)#exit
Spoke1(config)#router ospf 1
Spoke1(config-router)#network 192.168.123.0 0.0.0.255 area 0
```

```
Spoke2(config)#interface serial 0/0
Spoke2(config-if)#ip address 192.168.123.3 255.255.255.0
Spoke2(config-if)#encapsulation frame-relay
Spoke2(config-if)#ip ospf network non-broadcast
Spoke2(config-if)#ip ospf priority 0
Spoke2(config-if)#exit
Spoke2(config)#router ospf 1
```

```
Spoke2(config-router)#network 192.168.123.0 0.0.0.255 area 0
```

Here is the configuration of the spoke routers. I changed the OSPF network type as well but there's one little extra. See the **ip ospf priority 0**? That's how you make sure these routers will never become a DR or BDR. There's also a command you can use on the Hub router to make sure a spoke router never becomes a DR or BDR. Type in **neighbor <ip address> priority 0** and you are done. You have to do this under the OSPF process.

```
Hub#show ip ospf neighbor

Neighbor ID      Pri    State           Dead Time    Address
Interface
192.168.123.2     0    FULL/DROTHER     00:00:30     192.168.123.2
Serial0/0
192.168.123.3     0    FULL/DROTHER     00:00:35     192.168.123.3
Serial0/0
```

Here you can see that the hub router is the DR because the spoke routers are DROTHERS.

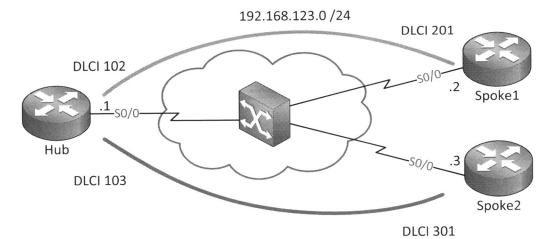

Next stop is the **broadcast** network type. If you understand non-broadcast then this one is easy. It's the EXACT same thing except we don't have to configure neighbors. OSPF will use multicast and discover OSPF neighbors automatically. The broadcast network type is the default for Ethernet interfaces as well. Let's convert the previous setup from non-broadcast to broadcast:

```
Hub(config)#router ospf 1
Hub(config-router)#no neighbor 192.168.123.2
Hub(config-router)#no neighbor 192.168.123.3
Hub(config-router)#exit
Hub(config)#interface serial 0/0
Hub(config-if)#ip ospf network broadcast
```

```
Spoke1(config)#interface serial 0/0
Spoke1(config-if)#ip ospf network broadcast
```

```
Spoke2(config)#interface serial 0/0
Spoke2(config-if)#ip ospf network broadcast
```

I'll get rid of the "neighbor" commands because we can now use multicast traffic. Second step is to change the network type to "broadcast" and that's it.

There is one thing you have to be aware of:

- Make sure you have a frame-relay map statement with the broadcast keyword or you won't be able to send multicast on your frame-relay network. By default Inverse ARP is enabled and will do this for you...if you don't have inverse ARP, make sure you add it!

Here's something for you to write down and remember...the **broadcast** and **non-broadcast** are the only 2 network types that **require** a DR or BDR. The other network types don't!

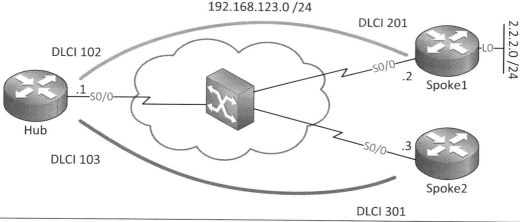

```
Spoke1(config)#interface loopback 0
Spoke1(config-if)#ip address 2.2.2.2 255.255.255.0
Spoke1(config-if)#exit
Spoke1(config)#router ospf 1
Spoke1(config-router)#network 2.2.2.0 0.0.0.255 area 0
```

Here is my frame-relay network once again but I've added a network behind Spoke1. We are using OSPF to advertise this 2.2.2.0 /24 network.

If I'm telling OSPF the network is **multi-access** by using the **broadcast** or **non-broadcast** network type then Spoke2 thinks it can reach Spoke1 directly. We will see the 2.2.2.0/24 network in its routing table like this:

```
Spoke2#show ip route ospf
      2.0.0.0/32 is subnetted, 1 subnets
O        2.2.2.2 [110/65] via 192.168.123.2, 00:00:38, Serial0/0
```

Spoke2 thinks it can reach Spoke1 directly but in reality it has to go through our Hub router to get there. By the way do you see how it shows 2.2.2.2/32 in the routing table while I configured 2.2.2.2 /24 on the interface?

```
Spoke1#show ip ospf interface loopback 0
Loopback0 is up, line protocol is up
   Internet Address 2.2.2.2/24, Area 0
   Process ID 1, Router ID 192.168.123.2, Network Type LOOPBACK,
Cost: 1
```

In fact OSPF has one more network type, it's **loopback**. OSPF will advertise a loopback as /32 no matter what you configured on the interface. If you don't want this…you can change the OSPF network type to something else.

Anyway let's continue! Is the 2.2.2.0 /24 network reachable from Spoke2?

```
Spoke2#ping 2.2.2.2

Type escape sequence to abort.
Sending 5, 100-byte ICMP Echos to 2.2.2.2, timeout is 2 seconds:
.....
Success rate is 0 percent (0/5)
```

We can't reach it…why? First check if the next hop IP address is reachable:

```
Spoke2#ping 192.168.123.2

Type escape sequence to abort.
Sending 5, 100-byte ICMP Echos to 192.168.123.2, timeout is 2
seconds:
.....
Success rate is 0 percent (0/5)
```

The next hop IP address is unreachable, let me show you why:

```
Spoke2#show frame-relay map
Serial0/0 (up): ip 192.168.123.1 dlci 301(0x12D,0x48D0),
dynamic,
                broadcast,, status defined, active
```

There's only a frame-relay map for the hub router so the spoke routers have no clue how to reach each other.

In order to fix this we'll have to create two additional frame-relay maps.

```
Spoke1(config)#interface serial 0/0
Spoke1(config-if)#frame-relay map ip 192.168.123.3 201
```

```
Spoke2(config)#interface serial 0/0
Spoke2(config-if)#frame-relay map ip 192.168.123.2 301
```

This will help the spoke routers to reach each other.

```
Spoke2#ping 2.2.2.2

Type escape sequence to abort.
Sending 5, 100-byte ICMP Echos to 2.2.2.2, timeout is 2 seconds:
!!!!!
Success rate is 100 percent (5/5), round-trip min/avg/max =
8/10/20 ms
```

There we go...problem solved!

If I tell OSPF I'm using a **point-to-point** network by using **point-to-point, point-to-multipoint** or **point-to-multipoint non-broadcast** OSPF will see the network as a collection of point-to-point links.

Let's continue with the other 3 network types so I can show you!

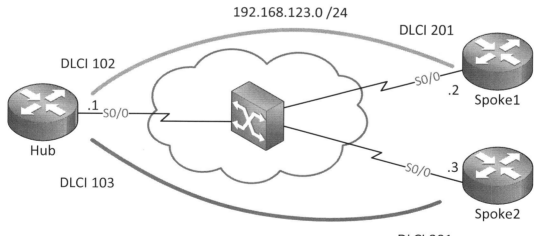

I'm going to use **point-to-multipoint** network type this time. Couple of things to be aware of:

- Automatic neighbor discovery so no need to configure OSPF neighbors yourself.
- No DR/BDR election since OSPF sees the network as a collection of point-to-point links.

- Only a single IP subnet is used.
- Make sure your frame-relay network is configured with the broadcast keyword.

Let's convert the previous configuration:

```
Hub(config)#interface serial 0/0
Hub(config-if)#ip ospf network point-to-multipoint
```

```
Spoke1(config)#interface serial 0/0
Spoke1(config-if)#ip ospf network point-to-multipoint
```

```
Spoke2(config)#interface serial 0/0
Spoke2(config-if)#ip ospf network point-to-multipoint
```

This is what you need on the interfaces. Use **ip ospf network point-to-multipoint** on your interfaces and you are ready to go.

```
Hub#show ip ospf neighbor

Neighbor ID      Pri   State          Dead Time   Address
Interface
192.168.123.3     0    FULL/   -      00:01:35    192.168.123.3
Serial0/0
192.168.123.2     0    FULL/   -      00:01:56    192.168.123.2
Serial0/0
```

Note that there's no DR/BDR election anymore.
What about the next hop IP addresses? Let me show you what I mean:

```
Spoke2#show ip route ospf | include 2.2.2.2
O       2.2.2.2 [110/129] via 192.168.123.1, 00:09:37, Serial0/0
```

Now I'm using the point-to-multipoint OSPF network type you can see that 192.168.123.1 (Hub) is the next hop IP address. This is different compared to the broadcast / non-broadcast OSPF network types, let me show that again:

```
Spoke2#show ip route ospf
     2.0.0.0/32 is subnetted, 1 subnets
O       2.2.2.2 [110/65] via 192.168.123.2, 00:00:38, Serial0/0
```

The example above is the next hop IP address for the broadcast / non-broadcast OSPF network type. You can see that in this case the next hop IP address 192.168.123.2 is the spoke1 router. The difference is that if you are using broadcast / non-broadcast you might have to add additional frame-relay maps to fix reachability problems between spoke routers.

What about the **point-to-multipoint non-broadcast** network type? It's exactly the same as point-to-multipoint but the difference is in the **non-**

broadcast. You'll have to specify neighbors yourself and you are ready to go! Let me demonstrate this:

```
Hub(config)#interface serial 0/0
Hub(config-if)#ip ospf network point-to-multipoint non-broadcast
Hub(config-if)#exit
Hub(config)#router ospf 1
Hub(config-router)#neighbor 192.168.123.2
Hub(config-router)#neighbor 192.168.123.3
```

```
Spoke1(config)#interface serial 0/0
Spoke1(config-if)#ip ospf network point-to-multipoint non-
broadcast
```

```
Spoke2(config)#interface serial 0/0
Spoke2(config-if)#ip ospf network point-to-multipoint non-
broadcast
```

We'll change the OSPF network type and on the hub router I'll configure the neighbors myself. That's all there is to it...

The last network type is **point-to-point**:

- Automatic neighbor discovery so no need to configure OSPF neighbors yourself.
- No DR/BDR election since OSPF sees the network as a collection of point-to-point links.
- Normally uses for point-to-point sub-interfaces with an IP subnet per link.
- Can also be used for single IP subnets.

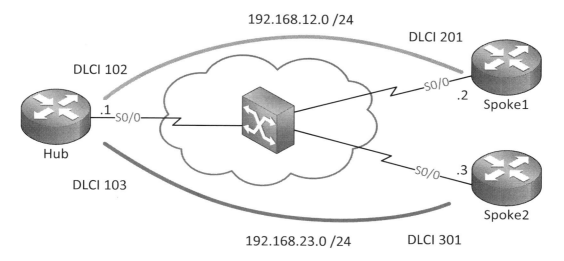

We'll use the topology above. As you can see I'm using a different subnet for the PVC between Hub/Spoke1 and Hub/Spoke2.

```
Hub(config)#default interface serial 0/0
Building configuration...

Interface Serial0/0 set to default configuration
```

```
Spoke1(config)#default interface serial 0/0
Building configuration...
```

```
Spoke2(config)#default interface serial 0/0
Building configuration...
```

If you are doing labs you might like this command...type **default interface** to reset an interface to its default configuration.

```
Hub(config)#interface serial 0/0
Hub(config-if)#encapsulation frame-relay
Hub(config-if)#exit
Hub(config)#interface serial 0/0.102 point-to-point
Hub(config-subif)#ip address 192.168.12.1 255.255.255.0
Hub(config-subif)#frame-relay interface-dlci 102
Hub(config-subif)#exit
Hub(config)#interface serial 0/0.103 point-to-point
Hub(config-subif)#ip address 192.168.13.1 255.255.255.0
Hub(config-subif)#frame-relay interface-dlci 103
```

```
Spoke1(config)#interface serial 0/0
Spoke1(config-if)#encapsulation frame-relay
Spoke1(config-if)#interface serial 0/0.201 point-to-point
Spoke1(config-subif)#ip address 192.168.12.2 255.255.255.0
Spoke1(config-if)#frame-relay interface-dlci 201
```

```
Spoke2(config)#interface serial 0/0
Spoke2(config-if)#encapsulation frame-relay
Spoke2(config-if)#interface serial 0/0.301 point-to-point
Spoke2(config-subif)#ip address 192.168.13.3 255.255.255.0
Spoke2(config-if)#frame-relay interface-dlci 301
```

Keep in mind that physical interfaces are point-to-multipoint so I'm using sub-interfaces even on the spoke routers. Also don't forget to specify the DLCI numbers on the sub-interfaces, your router can't smell which DLCI belongs to which sub-interface!

```
Hub(config)#router ospf 1
Hub(config-router)#network 192.168.12.0 0.0.0.255 area 0
Hub(config-router)#network 192.168.13.0 0.0.0.255 area 0
```

```
Spoke1(config)#router ospf 1
Spoke1(config-router)#network 192.168.12.0 0.0.0.255 area 0
```

```
Spoke2(config)#router ospf 1
Spoke2(config-router)#network 192.168.13.0 0.0.0.255 area 0
```

Configure OSPF for all subnets, nothing special here...

```
Hub#show ip ospf neighbor

Neighbor ID      Pri   State        Dead Time     Address
Interface
192.168.123.3     0   FULL/   -     00:00:34      192.168.13.3
Serial0/0.103
192.168.123.2     0   FULL/   -     00:00:36      192.168.12.2
Serial0/0.102
```

As you can see we have OSPF neighbor adjacencies, mission accomplished!

You have now seen all the OSPF network types. Let me give you an overview of all the network types:

Network Type	Hello Timer	Adjacency	RFC or Cisco
Broadcast	10	Automatic + DR/BDR	Cisco
Non-Broadcast	30	Manual + DR/BDR	RFC
Point-to-Multipoint	30	Automatic no DR/BDR	RFC
Point-to-Multipoint non-broadcast	30	Manual no DR/BDR	Cisco
Point-to-Point	10	Automatic no DR/BDR	Cisco

What else do we see here? You can see the hello timer is different for each of the network types. As you might recall the hello timer is one of the values that has to match in order to become OSPF neighbors. Here's a nice trick to remember:

- Broadcast and non-broadcast are compatible since they both require an election of DR/BDR. Set the hello timer to the same values and you are ready to go.
- Point-to-multipoint, point-to-multipoint non-broadcast and point-to-point are compatible since none of them requires a DR/BDR. Set the hello timer to the same values and off you are!

Is mixing network types a good idea? Probably not...is it something you might want to know for Cisco exams? You bet!

That's all for now about the OSPF network types. It's a good idea to try all of these network types in a lab and see for yourself how they work:

http://gns3vault.com/OSPF/ospf-over-frame-relay-point-to-point.html

http://gns3vault.com/OSPF/ospf-over-frame-relay-point-to-multipoint-non-broadcast.html

http://gns3vault.com/OSPF/ospf-over-frame-relay-point-to-multipoint.html

http://gns3vault.com/OSPF/ospf-over-frame-relay-broadcast.html

http://gns3vault.com/OSPF/ospf-over-frame-relay-non-broadcast.html

10. OSPF LSA Types

You have learned that OSPF uses a LSDB (link state database) and fills this with LSAs (link state advertisement). Instead of using 1 LSA packet OSPF has many different types of LSAs and in this chapter I'm going to show all of them to you. Let's start with an overview:

- LSA Type 1:   Router LSA
- LSA Type 2:   Network LSA
- LSA Type 3:   Summary LSA
- LSA Type 4:   Summary ASBR LSA
- LSA Type 5:   Autonomous system external LSA
- LSA Type 6:   Multicast OSPF LSA
- LSA Type 7:   Not-so-stubby area LSA
- LSA Type 8:   External attribute LSA for BGP

For many people it helps to visualize things in order to understand and remember. I like to visualize OSPF LSAs as jigsaw puzzle pieces. One jigsaw is nothing but all of them together give us the total picture...for OSPF this is the LSDB.

OSPF Area 0

Nancy   Donna

Type 1 – Router LSA

Each router within the area will flood a **type 1 router LSA** within the area. In this LSA you will find a list with all the directly connected links of this router. How do we identify a link?

- The IP prefix on an interface.
- The link type. There are 4 different link types:

Link Type	Description	Link ID
1	Point-to-point connection to another router.	Neighbor router ID
2	Connection to transit network.	IP address of DR
3	Connection to stub network.	IP Network
4	Virtual Link	Neighbor router ID

Don't worry too much about the link types; we'll see more about those later. The router LSA will always **stay within the area.**

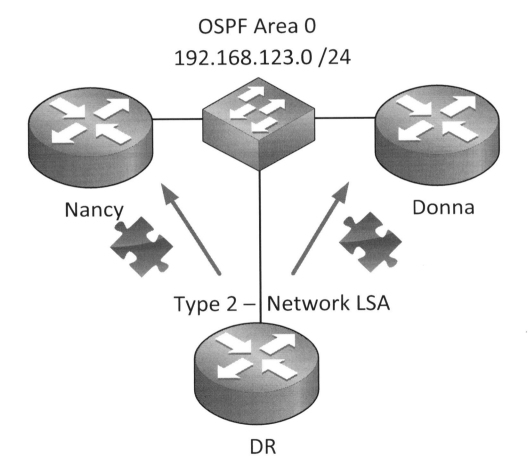

The **network LSA** or **type 2** is created for each multi-access network. Remember the OSPF network types? The broadcast and non-broadcast network types require a DR/BDR. If this is the case you will see these network LSAs being generated by the DR. In this LSA we will find all the routers that are connected to the multi-access network, the DR and of course the prefix and subnet mask.

In my example above we will find router Nancy, Donna and the DR in the network LSA. We will also see the prefix 192.168.123.0 /24 in this LSA. Last thing to mention; the network LSA always **stays within the area**.

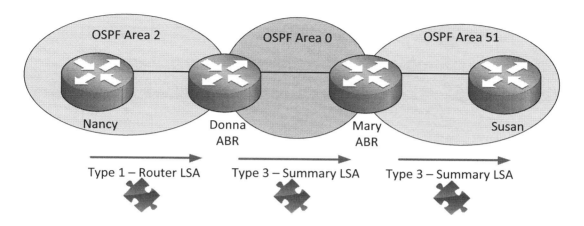

Type 1 router LSAs **always stay within the area**. OSPF however works with multiple areas and you probably want full connectivity within all of the areas. Router Nancy is flooding a router LSA within the area so router Donna will store this in her LSDB. Router Mary and Susan also need to know about the networks in Area 2.

Router Donna is going to create a **Type 3 summary LSA** and flood it into area 0. This LSA will flood into all the other areas of our OSPF network. This way all the routers in other areas will know about the prefixes from **other areas.**

The name "summary" LSA is very misleading. By default OSPF is **not going to summarize** anything for you. There is however a command that let you summarize inter-area routes. We'll talk about this in the summarization chapter. If you are looking at the routing table of an OSPF router and see some **O IA** entries you are looking at LSA type 3 summary LSAs. Those are your inter-area prefixes!

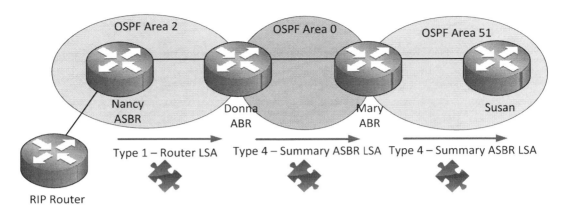

In this example we have router Nancy who is redistributing information from the RIP router into OSPF. This makes router Nancy an **ASBR (Autonomous System Border Router).** What happens is that router Nancy will flip a bit in her router LSA to identify herself as an ASBR. When router Donna who is a ABR receives this router LSA she will create a **type 4 summary ASBR LSA** and flood it into area 0. This LSA will also be flooded in all other areas and is required so all OSPF routers know where to find the ASBR.

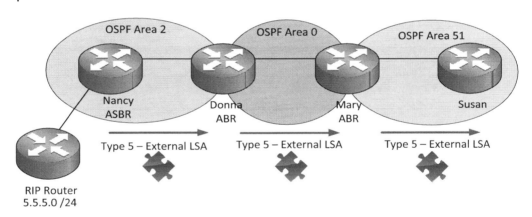

Same topology but I've added a prefix (5.5.5.0 /24) at our RIP router. This prefix will be redistributed into OSPF. Router Nancy (our ASBR) will take care of this and create a **type 5 external LSA** for this. Don't forget we still need type 4 summary ASBR LSA to locate router Nancy. If you ever tried redistribution with OSPF you might have seen **O E1 or E2** entries. Those are the external prefixes and our type 5 LSAs.

Type 6 multicast ospf LSA I can skip because it's not being used. It's not even supported by Cisco. Multicast is outside the scope of CCNP ROUTE (they removed it since BSCI which is a shame if you ask me). We use PIM (Protocol Independent Multicast) for multicast configurations.

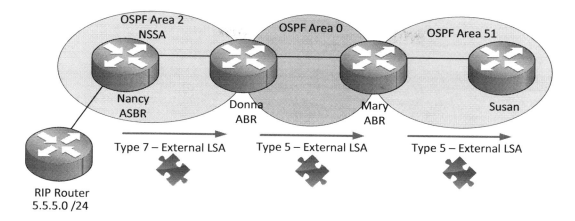

RIP Router
5.5.5.0 /24

Last LSA type...promised! You might have to read this one again after studying the OSPF Special Area Types lab since this one is about NSSA (not so stubby area). I can give you a sneak preview of special OSPF areas though. NSSA areas do not allow type 5 external LSAs. In my picture router Nancy is still our ASBR redistributing information from RIP into OSPF.

Since type 5 is not allowed we have to think of something else. That's why we have a **type 7 external LSA** that carries the exact same information but is not blocked within the NSSA area. Router Donna will translate this type 7 into a type 5 and flood it into the other areas. More about the special area types later!

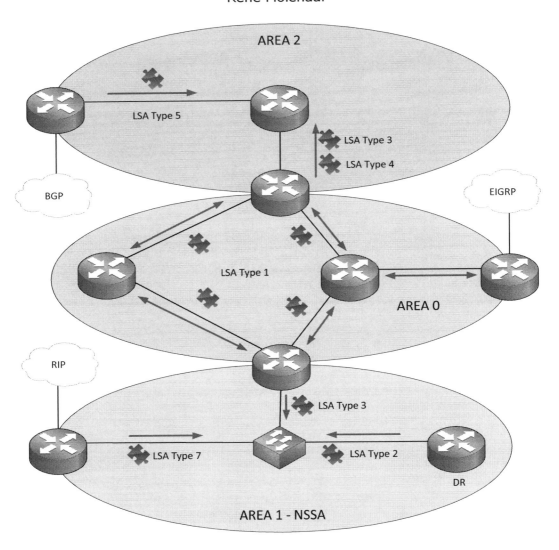

In the picture above I have a topology with 3 OSPF areas and multiple ABR and ASBRS. I'm only showing each LSA type once or twice or the picture would have become a big mess with jigsaw pieces and arrows.

Let me summarize the LSA types for you:

- Type 1 – Router LSA: The Router LSA is generated by each router for each area it is located. In the link-state ID you will find the originating router's ID. I'm showing you the router LSAs only in area 0.
- Type 2 – Network LSA: Network LSAs are generated by the DR. The link-state ID will be the router ID of the DR. In area 1 you can see a DR which is sending a network LSA.
- Type 3 – Summary LSA: The summary LSA is created by the ABR and flooded into other areas. This way area 2 will learn about the prefixes in area 0 and 1.
- Type 4 – Summary ASBR LSA: Other routers need to know where to find the ASBR. This is why the ABR will generate a summary ASBR LSA which will include the router ID of the ASBR in the link-state ID field.
- Type 5 – External LSA: also known as autonomous system external LSA: The external LSAs are generated by the ASBR. There is a ASBR in area 2 which is generating these LSAs so our OSPF domain knows about the prefixes that are redistributed from BGP.
- Type 7 – External LSA: also known as not-so-stubby-area (NSSA) LSA: As you can see area 1 is a NSSA (not-so-stubby-area) which doesn't allow external LSAs (type 5). To overcome this issue we are generating type 7 LSAs so our OSPF domain knows about the prefixes that are redistributed from RIP. More on the special OSPF area types later!

Enough LSA talk…let's see some of this stuff in action!

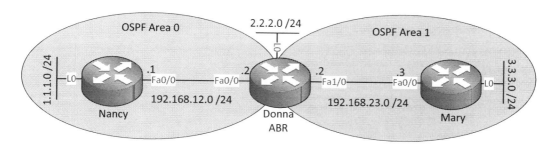

This is the topology I'm going to use. It's a simple setup with 3 routers and 2 areas. I've added a couple of loopbacks so we have prefixes to look at.

```
Nancy(config)#router ospf 1
Nancy(config-router)#network 192.168.12.0 0.0.0.255 area 0
Nancy(config-router)#network 1.1.1.0 0.0.0.255 area 0
```

```
Donna(config)#router ospf 1
Donna(config-router)#network 192.168.12.0 0.0.0.255 area 0
Donna(config-router)#network 192.168.23.0 0.0.0.255 area 1
```

```
Mary(config)#router ospf 1
Mary(config-router)#network 192.168.23.0 0.0.0.255 area 1
Mary(config-router)#network 3.3.3.0 0.0.0.255 area 1
```

Let's start by looking at the LSDB of router Nancy:

```
Nancy#show ip ospf database

            OSPF Router with ID (11.11.11.11) (Process ID 1)

          Router Link States (Area 0)

Link ID           ADV Router        Age           Seq#         Checksum
Link count
2.2.2.2           2.2.2.2           28            0x80000003 0x003CF5
1
11.11.11.11       11.11.11.11       27            0x80000003 0x003B9B
2

          Net Link States (Area 0)

Link ID           ADV Router        Age           Seq#         Checksum
192.168.12.1      11.11.11.11       27            0x80000001 0x00EF73

          Summary Net Link States (Area 0)

Link ID           ADV Router        Age           Seq#         Checksum
3.3.3.3           2.2.2.2           8             0x80000001 0x00D650
192.168.23.0      2.2.2.2           64            0x80000001 0x00A70C
```

By using the **show ip ospf** database we can look at the LSDB and we can see the type 1 router LSAs, type 2 network LSAs and the type 3 summary LSAs here. What else do we find here?

- Link ID: This is what identifies each LSA.
- ADV router: the router that is advertising this LSA.
- Age: The maximum age counter in seconds. The maximum is 3600 seconds or 1 hour.
- Seq#: Here you see the sequence number which starts at 0x80000001 and will increase by 1 for each update.
- Checksum: There is a checksum for each LSA.
- Link count: This will show the total number of directly connected links and is only used for the router LSA.

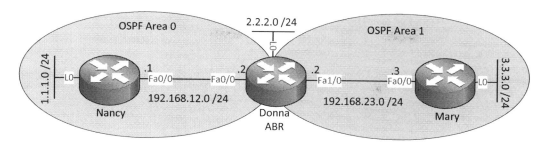

This is the same topology but I'm going to show you something else. You just saw the LSDB with LSA type 1, 2 and 3. Now I want to show you type 4 and 5 and we need an ASBR for this. To accomplish this I will redistribute something on router Nancy into OSPF.

```
Nancy(config)#interface loopback 1
Nancy(config-if)#ip address 11.11.11.11 255.255.255.0
Nancy(config-if)#exit
Nancy(config)#router ospf 1
Nancy(config-router)#redistribute connected subnets
```

I created an additional loopback interface and configured an IP address. Then I'm telling OSPF to redistribute the directly connected interfaces into OSPF. Let's look at the LSDB of router Donna and Mary.

```
Donna#show ip ospf database | begin Type-5
             Type-5 AS External Link States

Link ID          ADV Router        Age          Seq#          Checksum
Tag
11.11.11.0       11.11.11.11       36           0x80000001  0x000F44
0
```

Here you can see the type 5 external LSA in the LSDB.

Keep in mind that router Donna and Nancy are both in area 0.

```
Mary#show ip ospf database | begin Summary
           Summary Net Link States (Area 1)

Link ID          ADV Router        Age          Seq#         Checksum
1.1.1.1          2.2.2.2           149          0x80000001 0x0033FB
192.168.12.0     2.2.2.2           195          0x80000001 0x00219D

           Summary ASB Link States (Area 1)

Link ID          ADV Router        Age          Seq#         Checksum
11.11.11.11      2.2.2.2           62           0x80000001 0x004DB9

           Type-5 AS External Link States

Link ID          ADV Router        Age          Seq#         Checksum
Tag
11.11.11.0       11.11.11.11       68           0x80000001 0x000F44
0
```

Router Mary is in another area than router Nancy so it needs to know where to find the ASBR. In the LSDB you can see the type 5 external LSA but also the type 4 summary ASBR LSA which is the address of router Nancy. Because of this LSA router Mary knows how to reach the ASBR. This type 4 LSA is being generated by router Donna which is the ABR.

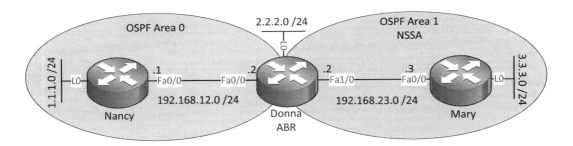

One more LSA to show you, same topology but I'm going to change area 1 into a NSSA (not-so-stubby-area). Oh by the way…in the "OSPF Special Area Types" chapter I'll cover the NSSA area type in detail.

```
Donna(config)#router ospf 1
Donna(config-router)#area 1 nssa
```

```
Mary(config)#router ospf 1
Mary(config-router)#area 1 nssa
```

Now I'm going to create an additional loopback interface on router Mary and redistribute it into OSPF.

```
Mary(config)#interface loopback 1
Mary(config-if)#ip address 33.33.33.33 255.255.255.0
Mary(config-if)#exit
Mary(config)#router ospf 1
Mary(config-router)#redistribute connected subnets
```

Let's see what happens to our LSDB:

```
Mary#show ip ospf database | begin Type-7
        Type-7 AS External Link States (Area 1)

Link ID         ADV Router      Age         Seq#        Checksum
Tag
33.33.33.0      33.33.33.33     33          0x80000001 0x005F43
0
```

You can see router Mary has generated a type 7 external LSA for the prefix on my loopback interface.

```
Donna#show ip ospf database | begin Type-7
        Type-7 AS External Link States (Area 1)

Link ID         ADV Router      Age         Seq#        Checksum
Tag
33.33.33.0      33.33.33.33     61          0x80000001 0x005F43
0


        Type-5 AS External Link States

Link ID         ADV Router      Age         Seq#        Checksum
Tag
11.11.11.0      11.11.11.11     220         0x80000001 0x000F44
0
33.33.33.0      2.2.2.2         54          0x80000001 0x00998F
0
```

Router Donna has the type 7 external LSA in its LSDB since it's in the same area as router Mary. It's also generating a type 5 external LSA to flood into area 0. This is because router Donna is an ABR.

```
Nancy#show ip ospf database | begin Type-5
        Type-5 AS External Link States

Link ID         ADV Router      Age         Seq#        Checksum
Tag
11.11.11.0      11.11.11.11     248         0x80000001 0x000F44
0
33.33.33.0      2.2.2.2         84          0x80000001 0x00998F
0
```

Router Nancy only has a type 5 external LSA in the LSDB for this prefix. This proves that our type 7 external LSA only lives within the NSSA.

That's it! Those are all the LSA types we have for OSPF and their different functions. I can recommend to look at the OSPF LSDB a couple of times when you are doing labs.

11. OSPF Summarization

If you read and understood the chapter where I talked about the different LSA types you know that we use the type 3 summary LSA for inter-area routes and the type 5 external LSAs for prefixes that are redistributed into OSPF. Type 1 and 2 you will only find within the area and they never travel across an ABR to another area.

OSPF can do summarization but it's **impossible to summarize within an area**. This means we have to configure summarization on an **ABR or ASBR.** OSPF can **only summarize our LSA type 3 and 5**.

Even though our type 3 is called a summary LSA, OSPF does **not automatically summarize anything!** This might be a little confusing. EIGRP has "auto-summary" enabled by default but OSPF doesn't do something like that. If you don't summarize yourself then all the prefixes will be advertised as they are configured on the interfaces. If you want OSPF summarization you have to **do it yourself**.

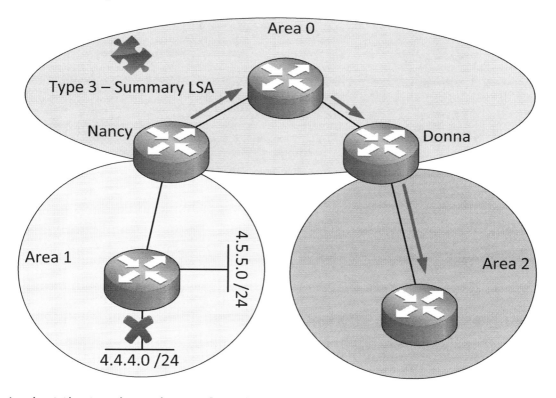

Look at the topology above. If we don't use summarization (which is the default) there will be a LSA for every specific prefix. If we have a link failure in area 1 then router Nancy (our ABR) will flood a new type 3 summary LSA and this change has to be propagated throughout all our OSPF areas. Since the LSDB will change our OSPF routers they will have to re-run the SPF algorithm which takes time and CPU power.

If we use summarization things will be different. I can create a summary on router Nancy to summarize the different type 3 summary LSAs. Instead of sending a LSA for 4.4.4.0 /24 and 4.5.5.0 /24 I could send 4.0.0.0 /8 or something alike.

If a link failure occurs in area 1 nothing will change for area 0 and area 2 since they don't have the specific 4.4.4.0 /24 prefix in their LSDB but the 4.0.0.0 /8 summary. Nothing will change in their LSDB so we don't have to re-run the SPF algorithm.

Summarization of type 3 summary LSAs means we are creating a summary of all the interarea routes. This is why we call it **interarea route summarization.** There are a couple of things to be aware of:

- A summary route will only be advertised if you have **at least one subnet** that falls within the summary range.
- A summary route will have the cost of the subnet with the lowest cost that falls within the summary range.
- Your ABR that creates the summary route will create a null0 interface to prevent loops.
- OSPF is a classless routing protocol so you can pick any subnet mask you like for prefixes.

If you look at my picture you can see that 4.4.4.0 /24 and 4.5.5.0 /24 both fall within the 4.0.0.0 /8 summary. If we have a link failure for the 4.4.4.0 /24 prefix we will still advertise the summary. If 4.5.5.0 /24 would fail as well then the summary will be withdrawn since there is no subnet left that falls within the 4.0.0.0 /8 range.

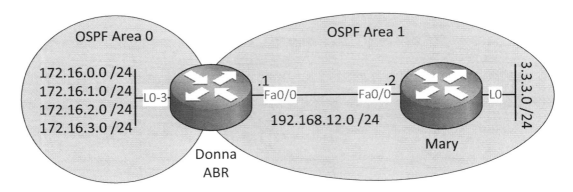

I'm going to show you an example of interarea route summarization. I'm going to use router Donna and Mary. Router Donna will have 4 loopback interfaces which are in area 0. The link between router Donna and Mary is in area 1 which turns Donna into an ABR that can do summarization.

```
Donna(config)#router ospf 1
Donna(config-router)#network 172.16.0.0 0.0.3.255 area 0
Donna(config-router)#network 192.168.12.0 0.0.0.255 area 1
```

```
Mary(config)#router ospf 1
Mary(config-router)#network 192.168.12.0 0.0.0.255 area 1
```

Here are the network commands I used to advertise all subnets.

```
Mary#show ip route ospf
      172.16.0.0/32 is subnetted, 4 subnets
O IA    172.16.1.1 [110/2] via 192.168.12.1, 00:08:04,
FastEthernet0/0
O IA    172.16.0.1 [110/2] via 192.168.12.1, 00:08:04,
FastEthernet0/0
O IA    172.16.3.1 [110/2] via 192.168.12.1, 00:08:04,
FastEthernet0/0
O IA    172.16.2.1 [110/2] via 192.168.12.1, 00:08:04,
FastEthernet0/0
```

```
Mary#show ip ospf database | begin Summary
            Summary Net Link States (Area 1)

Link ID          ADV Router        Age         Seq#          Checksum
172.16.0.1       172.16.3.1        542         0x80000003 0x005269
172.16.1.1       172.16.3.1        542         0x80000003 0x004773
172.16.2.1       172.16.3.1        542         0x80000003 0x003C7D
172.16.3.1       172.16.3.1        542         0x80000003 0x003187
```

Above you see the LSDB and routing table of router Mary. You can see there are 4 LSAs for each of the prefixes.

```
Donna(config)#router ospf 1
Donna(config-router)#area 0 range 172.16.0.0 255.255.0.0
```

By using the **area range** command we can summarize the type 3 summary LSAs. In my example I'm creating the summary 172.16.0.0 /16. To keep things interesting you need to type in a subnet mask for the summary instead of a wildcard for the network command.

```
Mary#show ip route ospf
O IA 172.16.0.0/16 [110/2] via 192.168.12.1, 00:03:26,
FastEthernet0/0
```

```
Mary#show ip ospf database | begin Summary
            Summary Net Link States (Area 1)

Link ID          ADV Router        Age         Seq#          Checksum
172.16.0.0       172.16.3.1        219         0x80000001 0x00605E
```

Once again the LSDB and routing table of router Mary. Instead of 4x type 3 summary LSA we now have just a single LSA. You can see there is only the 172.16.0.0 /16 entry in the routing table.

So far so good? Excellent! One more thing we can do with OSPF and summarization which is **external route summarization.** This is where we summarize the type 5 external LSAs.

- You can create the summary on the ABR or ASBR.
- A null0 entry will be created in the routing table for the summary route.

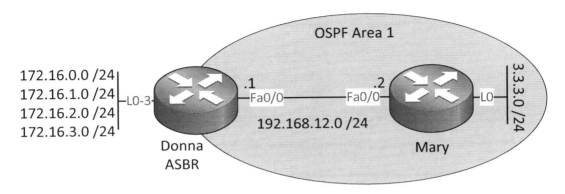

Instead of using the network command to advertise the prefixes on the loopback interfaces I'm going to redistribute them into OSPF.

```
Donna(config)#router ospf 1
Donna(config-router)#no network 172.16.0.0 0.0.3.255 area 0
Donna(config-router)#redistribute connected subnets
```

We'll remove the network command for the interfaces and redistribute the loopback interfaces into OSPF.

```
Mary#show ip route ospf
     172.16.0.0/24 is subnetted, 4 subnets
O E2    172.16.0.0 [110/20] via 192.168.12.1, 00:01:07,
FastEthernet0/0
O E2    172.16.1.0 [110/20] via 192.168.12.1, 00:01:07,
FastEthernet0/0
O E2    172.16.2.0 [110/20] via 192.168.12.1, 00:01:07,
FastEthernet0/0
O E2    172.16.3.0 [110/20] via 192.168.12.1, 00:01:07,
FastEthernet0/0
```

```
Mary#show ip ospf database | begin Type-5
         Type-5 AS External Link States

Link ID          ADV Router        Age          Seq#          Checksum
Tag
172.16.0.0       172.16.3.1        91           0x80000001 0x00B46E
0
```

172.16.1.0 0	172.16.3.1	91	0x80000001 0x00A978
172.16.2.0 0	172.16.3.1	91	0x80000001 0x009E82
172.16.3.0 0	172.16.3.1	91	0x80000001 0x00938C

Here is the LSDB and routing table of router Mary. As you can see we have type 5 external LSAs and they show up as **O E2** entries in the routing table.

```
Donna(config)#router ospf 1
Donna(config-router)#summary-address 172.16.0.0 255.255.0.0
```

This is how you summarize the type 5 external LSAs by using the **summary-address** command. This is a different command compared to summarizing the type 3 summary LSAs.

```
Mary#show ip route ospf
O E2 172.16.0.0/16 [110/20] via 192.168.12.1, 00:00:17,
FastEthernet0/0
```

```
Mary#show ip ospf database | begin Type-5
             Type-5 AS External Link States

Link ID        ADV Router     Age       Seq#        Checksum
Tag
172.16.0.0     172.16.3.1     38        0x80000002 0x00B26F
0
```

This is what the LSDB and routing table of router Mary looks like after the summarization.

Anything else we can do with OSPF? What about default routes?

```
Donna(config)#router ospf 1
Donna(config-router)#default-information originate ?
  always       Always advertise default route
  metric       OSPF default metric
  metric-type  OSPF metric type for default routes
  route-map    Route-map reference
  <cr>
```

There are a number of options, let's try something:

```
Donna(config-router)#default-information originate
```

Let's create a default route.

```
Mary#show ip route ospf
O E2 172.16.0.0/16 [110/20] via 192.168.12.1, 00:11:33,
FastEthernet0/0
```

As you can see there's no default route here...

If you use the **default-information originate** you can advertise a default route in OSPF. OSPF won't advertise a default route if you don't already have it in your routing table. If you add the **always** keyword it will advertise the default route even if you don't have it in the routing table.

```
Donna(config-router)#default-information originate always
```

Let's add the "always" keyword.

```
Mary#show ip ospf database | begin Type-5
         Type-5 AS External Link States

Link ID           ADV Router       Age          Seq#          Checksum
Tag
0.0.0.0           172.16.3.1       59           0x80000001 0x008D64
1
172.16.0.0        172.16.3.1       781          0x80000002 0x00B26F
0
```

```
Mary#show ip route ospf
O E2 172.16.0.0/16 [110/20] via 192.168.12.1, 00:12:26,
FastEthernet0/0
O*E2 0.0.0.0/0 [110/1] via 192.168.12.1, 00:00:24,
FastEthernet0/0
```

Now you can see the default route.

You can see in the LSDB of router Mary that the default route is advertised as a type 5 external LSA.

That's all I have on OSPF summarization. It's a good idea to try some OSPF summarization yourself. The following two labs will teach you exactly how to do it:

http://gns3vault.com/OSPF/ospf-lsa-type-3-summarization.html

http://gns3vault.com/OSPF/ospf-lsa-type-5-summarization.html

René Molenaar

12. OSPF Special Area Types

By now you should have a good understanding of OSPF. In the previous chapters I showed you all the different LSA types and what the LSDB looks like. You know OSPF can use multiple areas and the difference between the backbone (area 0) and regular areas.

OSPF however has multiple area types and this is what we are going to cover in this chapter. In the previous chapters I talked a little bit about NSSA (not-so-stubby area) and promised I would get back to you...in this chapter I'm going to deliver my promise. Let me start by summing up the special area types:

- **Stub area**
- **Totally stub area**
- **NSSA (not so stubby area)**
- **Totally NSSA (totally not so stubby area)**

Do you feel stubby now? Don't worry I'm going to show you everything step by step. These special area types are used to insert default routes into an area and replace type 3 summary LSAs and type 5 external LSAs. This will keep the LSA flooding to a minimum, LSDB smaller, less SPF calculations and a smaller routing table.

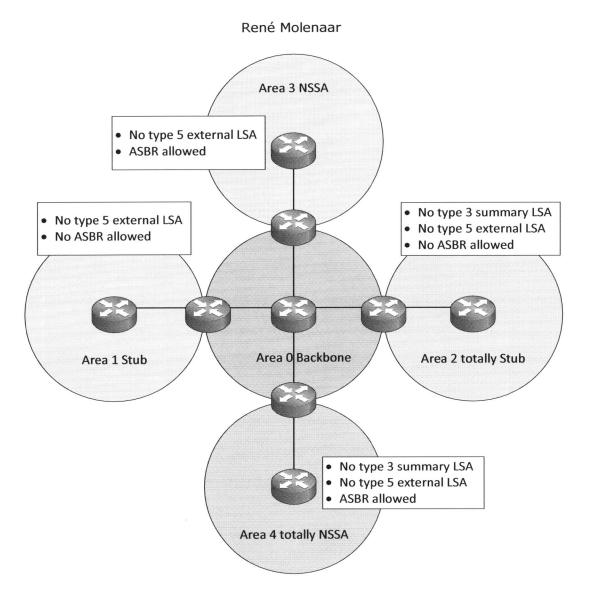

- No type 5 external LSA
- ASBR allowed

- No type 5 external LSA
- No ASBR allowed

- No type 3 summary LSA
- No type 5 external LSA
- No ASBR allowed

Area 3 NSSA

Area 1 Stub

Area 0 Backbone

Area 2 totally Stub

- No type 3 summary LSA
- No type 5 external LSA
- ASBR allowed

Area 4 totally NSSA

Let's start with a nice topology with 5 areas. In the middle you'll find the backbone area and the other areas are configured as the different stub area types.

If you configure an area as stub it will **block all type 5 external LSAs.** All the prefixes that you redistributed into OSPF from another routing protocol are not welcome in the **stub area**. Since you are not allowed to have type 5 external LSAs in the stub area it's also impossible to have an ASBR in the stub area. In order to reach networks in other areas there will be a **default route**.

Of course there's always an exception. So what if you want an area to be stub area but you also have an ASBR in this area? You can use the **NSSA (not-so-stubby-area)**. This is the same thing as the stub area with the **exception** that you are **allowed to have an ASBR within the area**. How does it work? This is where the **type 7 external LSA** kicks in. Since we are not allowed to use the type 5 external LSA we'll just use a new LSA type.

What about **totally stub?** This area type will **block type 5 external LSAs and type 3 summary LSAs.** It's impossible to have an ASBR in the totally stub area since type 5 external LSAs are blocked.

If you want to block type 3 summary LSAs and type 5 external LSAs but still need an ASBR within the totally stub area you can turn it into a **totally NSSA (totally not-so-stubby-area).** This will block both LSA types but you can still have an ASBR in this area type.

Anything else you need to know? Here are some of the rules when dealing with the **stub** and **totally stub** areas:

- There should be at least one ABR in the area.
- All routers in the stub area have to be configured as stub router.
- There is no ASBR within the stub or totally stub area.
- The backbone area cannot become stub or totally stub area.

Let's look at the area types in more detail and how to configure them!

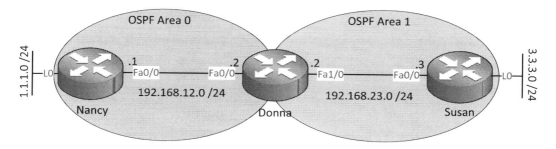

In the picture above we have 2 areas...area 0 and area 1. I'll use this topology to demonstrate all the OSPF area types to you. Let me show you the configuration:

```
Nancy(config)#router ospf 1
Nancy(config-router)#network 192.168.12.0 0.0.0.255 area 0
Nancy(config-router)#redistribute connected subnets
```

```
Donna(config)#router ospf 1
Donna(config-router)#network 192.168.12.0 0.0.0.255 area 0
Donna(config-router)#network 192.168.23.0 0.0.0.255 area 1
```

```
Susan(config)#router ospf 1
Susan(config-router)#network 192.168.23.0 0.0.0.255 area 1
```

I advertised all the interfaces in the correct OSPF areas with the exception of the loopback0 interface on router Nancy. This interface is redistributed into OSPF so it becomes a LSA Type 5.

```
Susan#show ip route ospf
O IA 192.168.12.0/24 [110/2] via 192.168.23.2, 00:08:53,
FastEthernet0/0
     1.0.0.0/24 is subnetted, 1 subnets
O E2    1.1.1.0 [110/20] via 192.168.23.2, 00:01:16,
FastEthernet0/0
```

When we look at router Susan you'll see network 192.168.12.0 /24 as inter-area (LSA Type 3) and 1.1.1.0 /24 as external type 2 (LSA Type 5). Now let's change area 1 in a stub area:

```
Donna(config)#router ospf 1
Donna(config-router)#area 1 stub
```

```
Susan(config)#router ospf 1
Susan(config-router)#area 1 stub
```

This is how you change it into a stub area. Now let's see what has changed:

```
Susan#show ip route ospf
O IA 192.168.12.0/24 [110/2] via 192.168.23.2, 00:00:42,
FastEthernet0/0
O*IA 0.0.0.0/0 [110/2] via 192.168.23.2, 00:00:42,
FastEthernet0/0
```

The stub area blocks LSA type 5 so you don't see network 1.1.1.0 /24 anymore. It does however insert a default route.

What about the totally stub area? Let me show you!

```
Donna(config)#router ospf 1
Donna(config-router)#area 1 stub no-summary
```

You only have to configure this on the ABR, we don't have to make any changes to router Susan.

```
Susan#show ip route ospf
O*IA 0.0.0.0/0 [110/2] via 192.168.23.2, 00:02:27,
FastEthernet0/0
```

Now we only have a default route. LSA Type 3 and 5 are both blocked. Now you have seen the stub and totally stub area, let me show you why you need the NSSA or totally NSSA!

```
Susan(config)#router ospf 1
Susan(config-router)#redistribute connected subnets
```

I didn't advertise the 3.3.3.0 /24 network in OSPF on router Susan so the command above will ensure that it will be redistributed into OSPF, here's what you'll see:

```
Susan# %OSPF-4-ASBR_WITHOUT_VALID_AREA: Router is currently an
ASBR while having only one area which is a stub area
```

The stub and totally stub area block LSA Type 5 so it's impossible to have an ASBR within these areas. Let me show you how the NSSA and Totally NSSA solve this problem.

```
Donna(config)#router ospf 1
Donna(config-router)#no area 1 stub
Donna(config-router)#area 1 nssa
```

```
Susan(config)#router ospf 1
Susan(config-router)#no area 1 stub
Susan(config-router)#area 1 nssa
```

We'll convert area 1 into a NSSA area. What is different this time?

```
Susan#show ip route ospf
O IA 192.168.12.0/24 [110/2] via 192.168.23.2, 00:00:44,
FastEthernet0/0
```

First of all you can see that it only allows inter-area routes. LSA Type 5 is blocked but I also don't see any default routes...you have to **do this yourself** for the NSSA area otherwise router Susan will be unable to reach network 1.1.1.0 /24.

```
Donna(config)#router ospf 1
Donna(config-router)#area 1 nssa default-information-originate
```

We'll add the default route on router Donna. Be careful: I'm using a different command this time...**area nssa default-information-originate.**

```
Susan#show ip route ospf
O IA 192.168.12.0/24 [110/2] via 192.168.23.2, 00:06:21,
FastEthernet0/0
O*N2 0.0.0.0/0 [110/1] via 192.168.23.2, 00:00:54,
FastEthernet0/0
```

Now we see a default route on router Susan, it shows up as a N2 route (OSPF NSSA External Type 2).

The reason I configured the NSSA area is so we could redistribute the loopback0 interface on router Susan into OSPF. Did this work? Let's find out:

```
Nancy#show ip route ospf
     3.0.0.0/24 is subnetted, 1 subnets
```

```
O E2    3.3.3.0 [110/20] via 192.168.12.2, 00:07:25,
FastEthernet0/0
O IA 192.168.23.0/24 [110/2] via 192.168.12.2, 00:07:41,
FastEthernet0/0
```

There you go. We can see network 3.3.3.0 /24 as an external type 2 route on router Nancy.

The last area type we need to cover is the totally NSSA, let's see what it does:

```
Donna(config-router)#no area 1 nssa default-information-
originate
Donna(config-router)#area 1 nssa no-summary
```

First I'll get rid of the default route and secondly I'll turn the area into a totally NSSA. I only have to do this on the ABR.

```
Susan#show ip route ospf
O*IA 0.0.0.0/0 [110/2] via 192.168.23.2, 00:00:39,
FastEthernet0/0
```

Now you can see router Susan only has a default route since LSA type 3 and 5 are blocked. We don't have to enable the default route for the totally NSSA area, only for the NSSA. To be honest I have no idea why they don't enable the default route by default for the NSSA but it's something to remember!

```
Nancy#show ip route ospf
     3.0.0.0/24 is subnetted, 1 subnets
O E2    3.3.3.0 [110/20] via 192.168.12.2, 00:23:17,
FastEthernet0/0
O IA 192.168.23.0/24 [110/2] via 192.168.12.2, 00:23:33,
FastEthernet0/0
```

Router Nancy still has the 3.3.3.0 /24 route in the routing table.
In case you are wondering, this is what the LSA for network 3.3.3.0 /24 looks like on each of the routers:

```
Susan#show ip ospf database | begin Type-7
          Type-7 AS External Link States (Area 1)

Link ID         ADV Router      Age       Seq#        Checksum
Tag
3.3.3.0         192.168.23.3    1791      0x80000001 0x00ADD8
0
```

On router Susan it's a type 7 because the NSSA and totally NSSA areas use type 7 for external routes (remember LSA type 5 is blocked).

```
Donna#show ip ospf database | begin Type-7
          Type-7 AS External Link States (Area 1)

Link ID          ADV Router       Age       Seq#        Checksum
Tag
3.3.3.0          192.168.23.3     29        0x80000002  0x00ABD9
0

          Type-5 AS External Link States

Link ID          ADV Router       Age       Seq#        Checksum
Tag
1.1.1.0          1.1.1.1          544       0x80000002  0x00A3F4
0
3.3.3.0          192.168.23.2     1797      0x80000001  0x004849
0
```

On router Donna it's also a type 7 LSA but it will be converted to a type 5 LSA and flooded into area 0.

```
Nancy#show ip ospf database | begin Type-5
          Type-5 AS External Link States

Link ID          ADV Router       Age       Seq#        Checksum
Tag
1.1.1.0          1.1.1.1          597       0x80000002  0x00A3F4
0
3.3.3.0          192.168.23.2     1852      0x80000001  0x004849
0
```

And router Nancy only has the LSA type 5 for network 3.3.3.0 /24.

What do you think? Are you following me so far with all the special area types? I think it's a good moment for a break and some lab action. If you like I have a couple of labs for all the different special area types so you can try to configure them.

http://gns3vault.com/OSPF/ospf-stub-area.html

http://gns3vault.com/OSPF/ospf-totally-stub.html

http://gns3vault.com/OSPF/ospf-nssa-not-so-stubby-area.html

http://gns3vault.com/OSPF/ospf-totally-nssa.html

13. OSPF Authentication

All routing protocols can be protected by using authentication and OSPF is no exception. OSPF can use plaintext or MD5 authentication and will check each OSPF packet that is received. If you have read about EIGRP authentication you might recall the keychain configuration. OSPF doesn't use a keychain and is a bit easier to configure.

There are two options for authentication:

- Plaintext authentication
- MD5 authentication

Each OSPF packet will be authenticated if you enable any form of authentication.

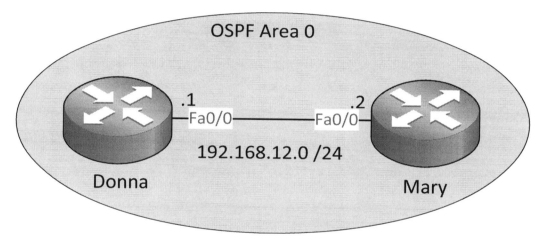

Above you see the topology I'm going to use for authentication. Just two routers but we can use it to check all different methods of authentication.

```
Donna(config)#router ospf 1
Donna(config-router)#network 192.168.12.0 0.0.0.255 area 0
```

```
Mary(config)#router ospf 1
Mary(config-router)#network 192.168.12.0 0.0.0.255 area 0
```

First I'll enable OSPF, nothing fancy here.

```
Donna(config)#interface fastEthernet 0/0
Donna(config-if)#ip ospf authentication
Donna(config-if)#ip ospf authentication-key MYPASS
```

```
Mary(config)#interface fastEthernet 0/0
Mary(config-if)#ip ospf authentication
Mary(config-if)#ip ospf authentication-key MYPASS
```

By using the **ip ospf authentication** command we enable plaintext authentication on the interface level. I configured the password MYPASS by using the **ip ospf authentication-key** command.

```
Donna(config)#router ospf 1
Donna(config-router)#area 0 authentication
```

If you have a lot of interfaces you probably don't want to enable OSPF authentication for each interface. You can also enable area-wide authentication by using the **area authentication** command. In my example above I enabled authentication for area 0.

```
Donna#show ip ospf interface fastEthernet 0/0
FastEthernet0/0 is up, line protocol is up
  Internet Address 192.168.12.1/24, Area 0
  Process ID 1, Router ID 192.168.12.1, Network Type BROADCAST,
Cost: 1
  Transmit Delay is 1 sec, State BDR, Priority 1
  Designated Router (ID) 192.168.12.2, Interface address
192.168.12.2
  Backup Designated router (ID) 192.168.12.1, Interface address
192.168.12.1
  Flush timer for old DR LSA due in 00:01:49
  Timer intervals configured, Hello 10, Dead 40, Wait 40,
Retransmit 5
    oob-resync timeout 40
    Hello due in 00:00:01
  Supports Link-local Signaling (LLS)
  Index 1/1, flood queue length 0
  Next 0x0(0)/0x0(0)
  Last flood scan length is 1, maximum is 1
  Last flood scan time is 0 msec, maximum is 0 msec
  Neighbor Count is 1, Adjacent neighbor count is 1
    Adjacent with neighbor 192.168.12.2  (Designated Router)
  Suppress hello for 0 neighbor(s)
  Simple password authentication enabled
```

If you use the **show ip ospf interface** command you can see OSPF information per interface. You can also check if authentication is enabled.

You can see the neighbor count is 1 and simple password authentication is enabled.

```
Donna#debug ip ospf packet
OSPF packet debugging is on

OSPF: rcv. v:2 t:1 l:48 rid:192.168.12.2
       aid:0.0.0.0 chk:B9F0 aut:1 auk: from FastEthernet0/0
```

I love debugs...when it comes to Cisco not Google but debug is your friend. It gives you so much information. If you use **debug ip ospf packet** you can see that authentication is enabled. In my example I receive a packet and it says **aut:1** which means that plain-text authentication is enabled.

- Aut:0 is no authentication.
- Aut:1 is plaintext authentication.
- Aut:2 is MD5 authentication.

Next step is to enable MD5 authentication!

```
Donna(config)#interface fastEthernet 0/0
Donna(config-if)#ip ospf message-digest-key 1 md5 MYPASS
Donna(config-if)#ip ospf authentication message-digest
```

```
Mary(config)#interface fastEthernet 0/0
Mary(config-if)#ip ospf message-digest-key 1 md5 MYPASS
Mary(config-if)#ip ospf authentication message-digest
```

For MD5 authentication you need different commands. First use **ip ospf message-digest-key X md5** to specify the key number and a password. It doesn't matter which key number you choose but it has to be the same on both ends. To enable OSPF authentication you need to type in **ip ospf authentication message-digest.**

```
Donna(config)#router ospf 1
Donna(config-router)#area 0 authentication message-digest
```

If you don't want to enable OSPF authentication per interface you can use the **area authentication message-digest** command.

```
Donna#show ip ospf interface fastEthernet 0/0
FastEthernet0/0 is up, line protocol is up
  Internet Address 192.168.12.1/24, Area 0
  Process ID 1, Router ID 192.168.12.1, Network Type BROADCAST,
Cost: 1
  Transmit Delay is 1 sec, State BDR, Priority 1
  Designated Router (ID) 192.168.12.2, Interface address
192.168.12.2
  Backup Designated router (ID) 192.168.12.1, Interface address
192.168.12.1
  Flush timer for old DR LSA due in 00:01:53
  Timer intervals configured, Hello 10, Dead 40, Wait 40,
Retransmit 5
    oob-resync timeout 40
    Hello due in 00:00:05
  Supports Link-local Signaling (LLS)
  Index 1/1, flood queue length 0
  Next 0x0(0)/0x0(0)
  Last flood scan length is 1, maximum is 1
  Last flood scan time is 0 msec, maximum is 0 msec
  Neighbor Count is 1, Adjacent neighbor count is 1
    Adjacent with neighbor 192.168.12.2  (Designated Router)
  Suppress hello for 0 neighbor(s)
  Message digest authentication enabled
    Youngest key id is 1
```

Using show ip ospf interface we see MD5 authentication is enabled and we are using key ID 1. We have a neighbor so it seems to be working.

```
Donna#debug ip ospf packet
OSPF packet debugging is on

OSPF: rcv. v:2 t:1 l:48 rid:192.168.12.2
      aid:0.0.0.0 chk:0 aut:2 keyid:1 seq:0x3C7EC653 from
FastEthernet0/0
```

Debug shows us that MD5 authentication is enabled (aut:2) and we are using key ID 1. Debug is also great to fix authentication errors, here's why:

```
Donna(config)#interface fastEthernet 0/0
Donna(config-if)#no ip ospf message-digest-key 1 md5 MYPASS
Donna(config-if)#ip ospf message-digest-key 1 md5 MYWRONGPASS
```

First we'll enter a wrong password...

```
Donna#debug ip ospf adj
OSPF adjacency events debugging is on
```

```
Donna#clear ip ospf process
```

```
Reset ALL OSPF processes? [no]: yes
```

I'll debug the OSPF neighbor adjacency and reset the OSPF neighbors.

```
Donna#
OSPF: Rcv pkt from 192.168.12.2, FastEthernet0/0 : Mismatch
Authentication Key - Message Digest Key 1
```

Somewhere in the debug you'll see the message above. This means that we are using MD5 key ID 1 on both sides but that the password is incorrect.

If one router is configured for MD5 authentication and the other one as plaintext authentication you get to see this as well.

Let me show you:

```
Mary(config)#interface fastEthernet 0/0
Mary(config-if)#ip ospf authentication
Mary(config-if)#ip ospf authentication-key PLAINKEY
```

Router Donna is still configured for MD5 authentication and I switched router Mary to plaintext authentication, this is what you'll see:

```
Donna#
OSPF: Rcv pkt from 192.168.12.2, FastEthernet0/0 : Mismatch
Authentication type. Input packet specified type 1, we use type
2
```

Your router will tell you that we received type 1 (plaintext) while we are configured for type 2 (MD5).

That's all I have on OSPF authentication. This isn't that bad right? Only a few commands to use but you need to keep in mind there is a difference command for enabling authentication for MD5 or plaintext. You feel like doing a lab and see if you can configure OSPF authentication?

http://gns3vault.com/OSPF/ospf-authentication.html

René Molenaar

14. OSPF Virtual Links

This is the final chapter of OSPF and the last topic I'm going to show you is **virtual-links.**

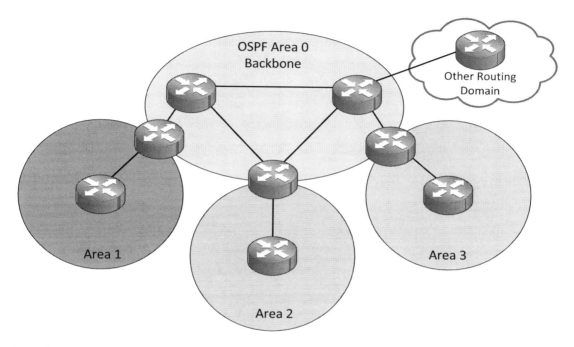

You know that all areas have to be connected to area 0 which is the backbone area. What happens when an area is not connected to the backbone area? Can it still work?

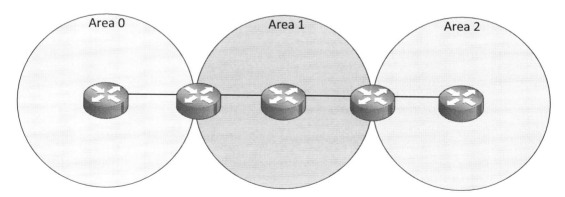

Look at my picture above. We have three areas and on the left side is area 0. Area 2 is behind area 1. Normally this is not going to work since area 2 has to be directly connected to area 0. We can make this work by using a **virtual link**. By using a virtual link we can extend area 0 through area 1 so area 2 will be "directly connected" to area 0.

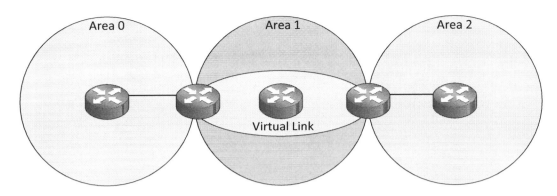

This is basically how a virtual link works. It's like a tunnel through area 1 to reach area 2. This way area 2 will be directly connected. Now let me show you how to configure a virtual link:

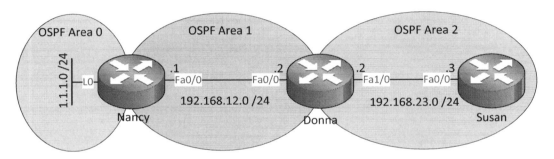

In the example above area 2 is not directly connected to area 0 so we'll have to use a virtual link between router Nancy and Donna, here's how we do it:

```
Nancy(config)#router ospf 1
Nancy(config-router)#network 1.1.1.0 0.0.0.255 area 0
Nancy(config-router)#network 192.168.12.0 0.0.0.255 area 1
```

```
Donna(config)#router ospf 1
Donna(config-router)#network 192.168.12.0 0.0.0.255 area 1
Donna(config-router)#network 192.168.23.0 0.0.0.255 area 2
```

```
Susan(config)#router ospf 1
Susan(config-router)#network 192.168.23.0 0.0.0.255 area 2
```

I'll start with a default OSPF configuration.

```
Nancy(config)#router ospf 1
Nancy(config-router)#area 1 virtual-link 192.168.23.2
```

```
Donna(config)#router ospf 1
Donna(config-router)#area 1 virtual-link 1.1.1.1
```

We configure the virtual-link **between ABRs** and we use the **area virtual-link** command. First you need to specify the area 1 where we need the virtual-link which is area 1 in my example. Second step is to configure the **OSPF router ID** of the other ABR. Keep this in mind...you need to configure the OSPF router ID and NOT the IP address of the ABR. If everything is OK area 2 will have be directly connected to area 0 through our virtual-link.

```
Nancy# %OSPF-5-ADJCHG  Process 1, Nbr 192.168.23.2 on OSPF_VL0
from LOADING to FULL, Loading Done
```

```
Donna# %OSPF-5-ADJCHG: Process 1, Nbr 1.1.1.1 on OSPF_VL0 from
LOADING to FULL, Loading Done
```

You will see the message above that tells us the virtual link is established.

```
Nancy#show ip ospf virtual-links
Virtual Link OSPF_VL0 to router 192.168.23.2 is up
  Run as demand circuit
  DoNotAge LSA allowed.
  Transit area 1, via interface FastEthernet0/0, Cost of using 1
  Transmit Delay is 1 sec, State POINT_TO_POINT,
  Timer intervals configured, Hello 10, Dead 40, Wait 40,
Retransmit 5
    Hello due in 00:00:06
    Adjacency State FULL (Hello suppressed)
    Index 1/2, retransmission queue length 0, number of
retransmission 0
    First 0x0(0)/0x0(0) Next 0x0(0)/0x0(0)
    Last retransmission scan length is 0, maximum is 0
    Last retransmission scan time is 0 msec, maximum is 0 msec
```

```
Donna#show ip ospf virtual-links
Virtual Link OSPF_VL0 to router 1.1.1.1 is up
  Run as demand circuit
  DoNotAge LSA allowed.
  Transit area 1, via interface FastEthernet0/0, Cost of using 1
  Transmit Delay is 1 sec, State POINT_TO_POINT,
  Timer intervals configured, Hello 10, Dead 40, Wait 40,
Retransmit 5
    Hello due in 00:00:05
    Adjacency State FULL (Hello suppressed)
    Index 1/3, retransmission queue length 0, number of
retransmission 0
    First 0x0(0)/0x0(0) Next 0x0(0)/0x0(0)
    Last retransmission scan length is 0, maximum is 0
    Last retransmission scan time is 0 msec, maximum is 0 msec
```

You can use the **show ip ospf virtual-links** command to check if your virtual-link is working.

```
Nancy#show ip ospf database

          OSPF Router with ID (1.1.1.1) (Process ID 1)

          Router Link States (Area 0)

Link ID          ADV Router        Age        Seq#        Checksum
Link count
1.1.1.1          1.1.1.1           189                    0x80000004 0x00E333
2
192.168.23.2     192.168.23.2      1      (DNA) 0x80000002 0x009816
1
```

```
Donna#show ip ospf database

          OSPF Router with ID (192.168.23.2) (Process ID 1)

          Router Link States (Area 0)

Link ID          ADV Router        Age        Seq#        Checksum
Link count
1.1.1.1          1.1.1.1           1    (DNA) 0x80000004 0x00E333
2
192.168.23.2     192.168.23.2      159                    0x80000002 0x009816
1
```

If you look at the LSDB you will see that the virtual-link shows up as a type 1 router LSA. You can also see **DNA** which means **do not age.**

Any other situation where we need a virtual-link? Sure is!

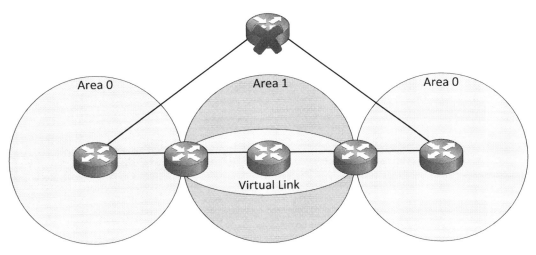

Imagine the router on top was in area 0. Unfortunately this router crashed and the result is that area 0 is now split in two pieces. We call this a **Discontiguous area 0.** We can use a virtual-link through area 1 to solve this problem. Let me show you how to fix this problem:

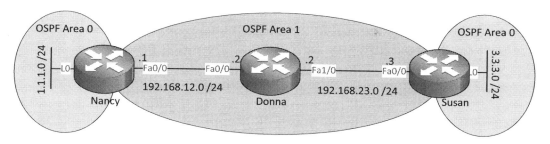

The topology above has a broken area 0. We'll configure a virtual link between router Nancy and Susan to fix it.

```
Nancy(config)#router ospf 1
Nancy(config-router)#network 1.1.1.0 0.0.0.255 area 0
Nancy(config-router)#network 192.168.12.0 0.0.0.255 area 1
```

```
Donna(config)#router ospf 1
Donna(config-router)#network 192.168.12.0 0.0.0.255 area 1
Donna(config-router)#network 192.168.23.0 0.0.0.255 area 1
```

```
Susan(config)#router ospf 1
Susan(config-router)#network 192.168.23.0 0.0.0.255 area 1
Susan(config-router)#network 3.3.3.0 0.0.0.255 area 0
```

First I'll advertise all the networks, nothing special here.

```
Nancy#show ip ospf | include ID
  Routing Process "ospf 1" with ID 1.1.1.1
```

```
Susan#show ip ospf | include ID
  Routing Process "ospf 1" with ID 192.168.23.3
```

I need to configure a virtual link between router Nancy and Susan and I'll need to use the router IDs for this.

```
Nancy(config)#router ospf 1
Nancy(config-router)#area 1 virtual-link 192.168.23.3
```

```
Susan(config)#router ospf 1
Susan(config-router)#area 1 virtual-link 1.1.1.1
```

This is how we do it.

```
Nancy# %OSPF-5-ADJCHG: Process 1, Nbr 192.168.23.3 on OSPF_VL1
from LOADING to FULL, Loading Done
```

```
Susan# %OSPF-5-ADJCHG: Process 1, Nbr 1.1.1.1 on OSPF_VL0 from
LOADING to FULL, Loading Done
```

The configuration is the same as my previous example. Just make sure to configure the area you have to get through and the OSPF router ID of the other ABR.

```
Nancy#show ip ospf virtual-links
Virtual Link OSPF_VL1 to router 192.168.23.3 is up
   Run as demand circuit
   DoNotAge LSA allowed.
   Transit area 1, via interface FastEthernet0/0, Cost of using 2
   Transmit Delay is 1 sec, State POINT_TO_POINT,
   Timer intervals configured, Hello 10, Dead 40, Wait 40,
Retransmit 5
      Hello due in 00:00:04
      Adjacency State FULL (Hello suppressed)
      Index 1/2, retransmission queue length 0, number of
retransmission 0
      First 0x0(0)/0x0(0) Next 0x0(0)/0x0(0)
      Last retransmission scan length is 0, maximum is 0
      Last retransmission scan time is 0 msec, maximum is 0 msec
```

```
Susan#show ip ospf virtual-links
Virtual Link OSPF_VL0 to router 1.1.1.1 is up
   Run as demand circuit
   DoNotAge LSA allowed.
   Transit area 1, via interface FastEthernet0/0, Cost of using 2
   Transmit Delay is 1 sec, State POINT_TO_POINT,
   Timer intervals configured, Hello 10, Dead 40, Wait 40,
Retransmit 5
      Hello due in 00:00:07
      Adjacency State FULL (Hello suppressed)
      Index 1/2, retransmission queue length 0, number of
retransmission 0
      First 0x0(0)/0x0(0) Next 0x0(0)/0x0(0)
      Last retransmission scan length is 0, maximum is 0
      Last retransmission scan time is 0 msec, maximum is 0 msec
```

This is how we can verify if the virtual link is up and running.

```
Nancy#show ip route  ospf | include 3.3.3.3
      3.0.0.0/32 is subnetted, 1 subnets
O        3.3.3.3 [110/3] via 192.168.12.2, 00:05:13,
FastEthernet0/0
```

```
Susan#show ip route ospf | include 1.1.1.1
O        1.1.1.1 [110/3] via 192.168.23.2, 00:05:52,
FastEthernet0/0
```

We can also verify that 1.1.1.1 and 3.3.3.3 show up as intra-area prefixes on router Nancy and Susan. This is because area 0 is extended through area 1.

That's all I have for you on virtual-links. How about a lab? I have a lab for you to practice the configuration of virtual-links:

http://gns3vault.com/OSPF/ospf-virtual-link.html

This is also everything I have on OSPF for you. OSPF is one of the core topics you fully need to understand to pass your CCNP so make sure spend some serious time at it.

Here you can find all the labs on OSPF that you should practice on:

http://gns3vault.com/Table/OSPF/

If you feel like doing something else you should look at my OSPF troubleshooting lab:

http://gns3vault.com/Troubleshooting/ospf-troubleshooting.html

15. Route Selection

This chapter covers a couple of things that have to do with "route selection".

Routers use routing tables to check where they should forward incoming IP packets. We'll see how CEF (Cisco Express Forwarding) is used to allow really fast forwarding.

Another topic is PBR (Policy Based Routing) that allows us to overrule routing table decisions .

We'll also take a look at IP SLA (IP Service Level Agreement). IP SLA allows us to "monitor" the network and change routing decisions.

Last but not least, we'll take a look at VRF (Virtual Routing and Forwarding) which allows us to divide the global routing table into multiple "virtual" routing tables.

Let's get started with CEF!

When we take a close look at routers, we see a "separation of duties". We have to build a table for the MAC addresses, fill a routing table, ARP requests, check if an IP packet matches an access-list etc and we need to forward our IP packets. These tasks are divided between the "**control plane**" and the "**data plane**". Let me give you an illustration:

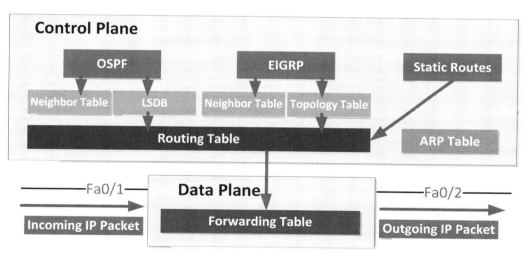

The control plane is responsible for exchanging routing information using routing protocols, building a routing table and ARP table.The data plane is responsible for the actual forwarding of IP packets. The routing table isn't very suitable for fast forwarding because we have to deal with **recursive routing**. What is recursive routing? Let me give you an example:

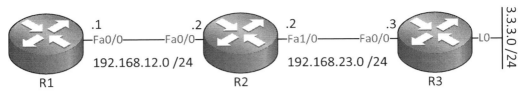

In the example above I have three routers. R3 has a loopback interface that we want to reach from R1. I will use static routes for reachability:

```
R1(config)#ip route 3.3.3.0 255.255.255.0 192.168.23.3
R1(config)#ip route 192.168.23.0 255.255.255.0 192.168.12.2
```

The first static route is to reach the loopback0 interface of R3 and points to the FastEthernet0/0 interface of R3. The second static route is required to reach network 192.168.23.0/24.

```
R1#show ip route
Codes: C - connected, S - static, R - RIP, M - mobile, B - BGP
       D - EIGRP, EX - EIGRP external, O - OSPF, IA - OSPF inter
area
       N1 - OSPF NSSA external type 1, N2 - OSPF NSSA external
type 2
       E1 - OSPF external type 1, E2 - OSPF external type 2
       i - IS-IS, su - IS-IS summary, L1 - IS-IS level-1, L2 -
IS-IS level-2
       ia - IS-IS inter area, * - candidate default, per-user
static route
       o - ODR, P - periodic downloaded static route

Gateway of last resort is not set

C     192.168.12.0/24 is directly connected, FastEthernet0/0
      3.0.0.0/24 is subnetted, 1 subnets
S        3.3.3.0 [1/0] via 192.168.23.3
S     192.168.23.0/24 [1/0] via 192.168.12.2
```

Whenever R1 wants to reach 3.3.3.0/24 we have to do 3 lookups:

- The first lookup is to check the entry for 3.3.3.0 /24. It's there and the next hop IP address is 192.168.23.3
- The second lookup is for 192.168.23.3. There's an entry and the next hop IP address is 192.168.12.2.
- The third and last lookup is for 192.168.12.2. There's an entry and it is directly connected.

R1 has to check the routing table 3 times before it knows where to send its traffic. Doesn't sound very efficient right? Doing multiple lookups to reach a certain network is called **recursive routing**.

Most of the time all incoming and outgoing IP packets will be processed and forwarded by the data plane but there are some exceptions, first let me show you this picture:

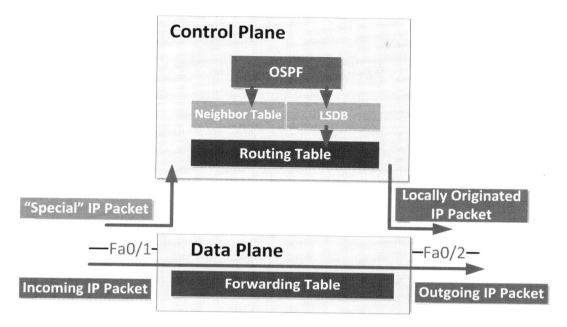

Most of the IP packets can be forwarded by the data plane. However there are some "special" IP packets that can't be forwarded by the data plane immediately and they are sent to the control plane, here are some examples:

- IP packets that are destined for one of the IP addresses of the router.
- Routing protocol traffic like OSPF, EIGRP or BGP.
- IP packets that have some of the options set in the IP header.
- IP packets with an expired TTL.

The control plane can forward outgoing IP packets to the data plane or use its own forwarding mechanism to determine the outgoing interface and the next hop IP address. An example of this is local policy based routing. If you have never heard about policy based routing, don't worry...it's covered in CCNP ROUTE.

Our router has many more steps to take than layer 2 switches so theoretically it should be slower right?

One reason that routers are able to forward frames and packets at wirespeed is because of special hardware called ASICs in the dataplane.

Information like MAC addresses, the routing table or access-lists are stored into these ASICs. The tables are stored in **content-addressable memory (CAM)** and **ternary content addressable memory (TCAM)**.

- The CAM table is used to store layer 2 information like:

o   The source MAC address.
o   The interface where we learned the MAC address on.
o   To which VLAN the MAC address belongs.

Table lookups are fast! Whenever the switch receives an Ethernet frame it will use a hashing algorithm to create a "key" for the destination MAC address + VLAN and it will compare this hash to the already hashed information in the CAM table. This way it is able to quickly lookup information in the CAM table.

- The TCAM table is used to store "higher layer" information like:
  o   Access-lists.
  o   Quality of service information.
  o   Routing table.
- The TCAM table can match on 3 different values:
  o   0 = Don't look.
  o   1 = Compare.
  o   X = Any value acceptable.
- Longest match will return a hit.
- Useful for a lookup where we don't need an exact match. (routing table or ACLs for example).

Because there are 3 values we call it *ternary*.

So why are there 2 types of tables?

When we look for a MAC address we always require an **exact match**. We require the exact MAC address if we want to forward an Ethernet frame. The MAC address table is stored in a CAM table.

Whenever we need to match an IP packet against the routing table or an access-list we **don't always need an exact match**. For example an IP packet with destination address 192.168.20.44 will match:

- 192.168.20.44 /32
- 192.168.20.0 /24
- 192.168.0.0 /16

Information like the routing table are stored in a TCAM table for this reason. We can decide whether all or some bits have to match.

Here's an example of a TCAM table:

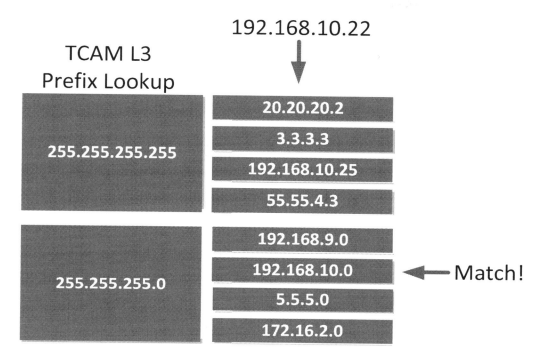

If we want to match IP address 192.168.10.22 the router will first see if there's a "most specific match". There is nothing that matches 192.168.10.22 /32 so we'll continue if there is anything else that matches. In this case there is an entry that matches 192.168.10.0 /24. The example above applies to routing table lookups, access-lists but also quality of service, VLAN access-lists and more.

Now you know all the steps a router has to take when it has to forward ip packets, the control/data plane and that we use different tables stored in special hardware called ASICs. Let's take a closer look at the actual 'forwarding' of IP packets.

There are different **switching methods** to forward IP packets. Here are the different switching options:

- **Process switching**:
  - All packets are examined by the CPU and all forwarding decisions are made in software...very slow!
- **Fast switching** (also known as **route caching**):
  - The first packet in a flow is examined by the CPU; the forwarding decision is cached in hardware for the next packets in the same flow. This is a faster method.
- **(CEF) Cisco Express Forwarding** (also known as **topology based switching**):

o Forwarding table created in hardware beforehand. All packets will be switched using hardware. This is the fastest method but there are some limitations. Multilayer switches and routers use CEF.

When using **process switching** the router will remove the header for each Ethernet frame, look for the destination IP address in the routing table for each IP packet and then forward the Ethernet frame with the rewritten MAC addresses and CRC to the outgoing interface. Everything is done in software so this is very CPU-intensive.

Fast switching is more efficient because it will lookup the first IP packet but it will store the forwarding decision in the fast switching cache. When the routers receive Ethernet frames carrying IP packets in the same flow it can use the information in the cache to forward them to the correct outgoing interface.

The default for routers is **CEF (Cisco Express Forwarding)**. Let's take a closer look at CEF:

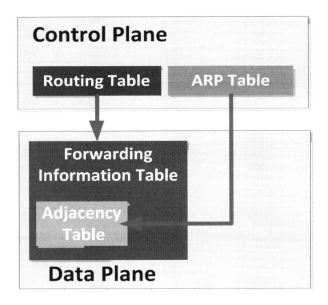

The router will use the information from tables that are built by the (control plane) **to build hardware tables**. It will use the routing table to build **the FIB (Forwarding Information Base)** and the ARP table to build the **adjacency table**. This is the fastest switching method because we now have all the layer 2 and 3 information required to forward IP packets in hardware.

Are you following me so far? Let's take a look at the forwarding information table and the adjacency table on some routers. If you want to follow me along you can take a look at a multilayer switch OR use routers in GNS3:

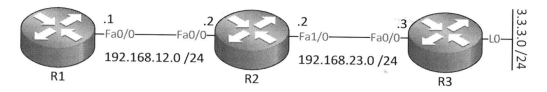

I'll use the same topology that I showed you earlier. 3 routers and R3 has a loopback0 interface.

I'll use static routes to have full connectivity:

```
R1(config)#ip route 3.3.3.0 255.255.255.0 192.168.23.3
R1(config)#ip route 192.168.23.0 255.255.255.0 192.168.12.2
```

```
R2(config)#ip route 3.3.3.0 255.255.255.0 192.168.23.3
```

```
R3(config)#ip route 192.168.12.0 255.255.255.0 192.168.23.2
```

These are the static routes that I'll use.
Now let me show you the routing and FIB table:

```
R1#show ip route
Codes: C - connected, S - static, R - RIP, M - mobile, B - BGP
       D - EIGRP, EX - EIGRP external, O - OSPF, IA - OSPF inter
area
       N1 - OSPF NSSA external type 1, N2 - OSPF NSSA external
type 2
       E1 - OSPF external type 1, E2 - OSPF external type 2
       i - IS-IS, su - IS-IS summary, L1 - IS-IS level-1, L2 -
IS-IS level-2
       ia - IS-IS inter area, * - candidate default, U - per-
user static route
       o - ODR, P - periodic downloaded static route

Gateway of last resort is not set

C    192.168.12.0/24 is directly connected, FastEthernet0/0
     3.0.0.0/24 is subnetted, 1 subnets
S       3.3.3.0 [1/0] via 192.168.23.3
S    192.168.23.0/24 [1/0] via 192.168.12.2
```

```
R1#show ip cef
Prefix                 Next Hop              Interface
```

```
0.0.0.0/0              drop                  Null0 (default route
handler entry)
0.0.0.0/32             receive
3.3.3.0/24             192.168.12.2          FastEthernet0/0
192.168.12.0/24        attached              FastEthernet0/0
192.168.12.0/32        receive
192.168.12.1/32        receive
192.168.12.2/32        192.168.12.2          FastEthernet0/0
192.168.12.255/32      receive
192.168.23.0/24        192.168.12.2          FastEthernet0/0
224.0.0.0/4            drop
224.0.0.0/24           receive
255.255.255.255/32     receive
```

Show ip cef reveals the FIB table to us.

You can see there's quite some stuff in the FIB table, let me explain some of the entries:

- 0.0.0.0/0 is for the null0 interface. When we receive IP packets that match this rule then it will be dropped.
- 0.0.0.0/32 is for all-zero broadcasts. Forget about this one since we don't use it anymore.
- 3.3.3.0/24 is the entry for the loopback0 interface of R3. Note that the next hop is 192.168.12.2 and NOT 192.168.23.3 as in the routing table!
- 192.168.12.0/24 is our directly connected network.
- 192.168.12.0/32 is reserved for the exact network address.
- 192.168.12.1/32 is the IP address on interface FastEthernet 0/0.
- 192.168.12.2/32 is the IP address on R2's FastEthernet 0/0 interface.
- 192.168.12.255/32 is the broadcast address for network 192.168.12.0/24.
- 224.0.0.0/4 matches all multicast traffic. It will be dropped if multicast support is disabled globally.
- 224.0.0.0/24 matches all multicast traffic that is reserved for local network control traffic (for example OSPF, EIGRP).
- 255.255.255.255/32 is the broadcast address for a subnet.

Let's take a detailed look at the entry for network 3.3.3.0 /24:

```
R1#show ip cef 3.3.3.0
3.3.3.0/24, version 8, epoch 0, cached adjacency 192.168.12.2
0 packets, 0 bytes
  via 192.168.23.3, 0 dependencies, recursive
    next hop 192.168.12.2, FastEthernet0/0 via 192.168.23.0/24
    valid cached adjacency
```

The version number tells us how often this CEF entry was updated since the table was generated. We can see that in order to reach 3.3.3.0/24 we need to go to 192.168.23.3 and that a recursive lookup is required. The next hop is 192.168.12.2. It also says that it's a **valid cached adjacency**. There are a number of different adjacencies:

- **Null adjacency**: used to send packets to the null0 interface.
- **Drop adjacency**: you'll see this for packets that can't be forwarded because of encapsulation errors, routes that cannot be resolved or protocols that are not supported.
- **Discard adjacency**: This is for packets that have to be discarded because of an access-list or other policy.
- **Punt adjacency**: Used for packets that are sent to the control plane for processing.

Packets that are not forwarded by CEF are handled by the CPU. If you have many of those packets then you might see performance issues.

You can see how many packets have been handled by the CPU:

```
R1#show cef not-cef-switched
CEF Packets passed on to next switching layer
Slot   No_adj No_encap Unsupp'ted Redirect   Receive   Options
Access       Frag
RP           0        0          0        0         17        0
0            0
```

You can use the **show cef not-cef-switched** command to verify this; the number of packets are listed per reason:

- **No_adj**: adjacency is incomplete.
- **No_encap**: ARP information is incomplete.
- **Unsupp'ted**: packet has features that are not supported.
- **Redirect**: ICMP redirect.
- **Receive**: These are the packets that were destined for an IP address configured on a layer 3 interface, packets that are meant for our router.
- **Options:** There are IP options in the header of the packet.
- **Access:** access-list evaluation failure.
- **Frag:** packet fragmention error.

We can also take a look at the adjacency table that stores the layer 2 information for each entry:

```
R1#show adjacency summary
Adjacency Table has 1 adjacency
  Table epoch: 0 (1 entry at this epoch)

  Interface                   Adjacency Count
  FastEthernet0/0             1
```

You can use the **show adjacency summary** command to take a quick look how many adjacencies we have. An adjacency is a mapping from layer 2 to 3 and comes from the ARP table.

```
R1#show adjacency
Protocol Interface                    Address
IP       FastEthernet0/0              192.168.12.2(9)
```

R1 only has a single interface that is connected to R2. You can see the entry for 192.168.12.2 which is the FastEthernet 0/0 interface of R2. Let's zoom in on this entry:

```
R1#show adjacency detail
Protocol Interface                    Address
IP       FastEthernet0/0              192.168.12.2(9)
                                      0 packets, 0 bytes
                                      CC011D800000CC001D8000000800
                                      ARP          03:55:00
                                      Epoch: 0
```

We can see there's an entry for 192.168.12.2 and it says:

CC011D800000CC001D8000000800

What does this number mean? It's the MAC addresses that we require and the Ethertype...let me break it down for you:

- CC011D800000 is the MAC address of R2's FastEthernet0/0 interface.

```
R2#show interfaces fastEthernet 0/0
FastEthernet0/0 is up, line protocol is up
  Hardware is AmdFE, address is cc01.1d80.0000 (bia
cc01.1d80.0000)
```

- CC001D800000 is the MAC address of R1's FastEthernet0/0 interface.

```
R1#show interfaces fastEthernet 0/0
FastEthernet0/0 is up, line protocol is up
  Hardware is AmdFE, address is cc00.1d80.0000 (bia
cc00.1d80.0000)
```

- 0800 is the Ethertype. 0x800 stands for IPv4.

Thanks to the FIB and adjacency table we have all the layer 2 and 3 information that we require to rewrite and forward packets.

Keep in mind before actually forwarding the packet we first have to rewrite the header information:

- Source MAC address.
- Destination MAC address.
- Ethernet frame checksum.
- IP Packet TTL.
- IP Packet Checksum.

Once this is done we can forward the packet. Now you have an idea what CEF is about and how packets are dealt with.

Next topic is PBR (Policy Based Routing)!

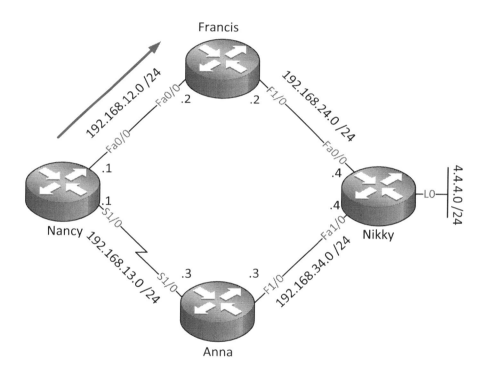

Look at the topology picture above. EIGRP has been configured on all routers and all IP packets from router Nancy towards network 4.4.4.0/24 on the right are sent towards router Francis. What if I wanted to use the link between router Nancy and Anna to get to this destination? Sure I could influence EIGRP by playing with the metrics but we can also use **policy based routing** and be a bit more creative, let me show you how!

```
Nancy#show ip route eigrp | include 4.4.4.0
D        4.4.4.0 [90/158720] via 192.168.12.2, 00:00:15,
FastEthernet0/0
```

Note that right now router Nancy is sending everything to IP address 192.168.12.2 (router Francis). Let's change this:

```
Nancy(config)#route-map PBR permit 10
Nancy(config-route-map)#match ip address NEXTHOPCHANGE
Nancy(config-route-map)#set ip next-hop 192.168.13.3
Nancy(config)#ip access-list extended NEXTHOPCHANGE
Nancy(config-ext-nacl)#permit ip any 4.4.4.0 0.0.0.255
```

I created a route-map called "PBR" and it says that whatever packets match an access-list called "NEXTHOPCHANGE" that it should **set** the next-hop IP address to 192.168.13.3. My access-list matches network 4.4.4.0/24.

I still have to activate the route-map, there are two methods how we can do this:

```
Nancy(config)#ip local policy route-map PBR
```

A router makes a difference between traffic that is **originating** from the router and traffic that is **flowing through** the router. The command above will activate policy based routing for traffic that I originate from router Nancy. If I want to activate policy based routing for traffic flowing through router Nancy I need to use another command:

```
Nancy(config)#interface fastEthernet 0/0
Nancy(config-if)#ip policy route-map PBR
```

The example above is how you enable policy based routing for traffic flowing THROUGH router Nancy.

Let's see if its working shall we?

```
Nancy#show ip route | include 4.4.4.0
D        4.4.4.0 [90/158720] via 192.168.12.2, 00:18:27,
FastEthernet0/0
```

My configuration didn't change the routing table but let me prove to you that it's working...

```
Nancy#debug ip policy
Policy routing debugging is on
```

First we'll enable policy routing debugging...

```
Nancy#ping 4.4.4.4 repeat 1

Type escape sequence to abort.
Sending 1, 100-byte ICMP Echos to 4.4.4.4, timeout is 2 seconds:
!
```

```
Success rate is 100 percent (1/1), round-trip min/avg/max =
12/12/12 ms
```

Next step is to send a ping...

```
Nancy#
IP: s=192.168.12.1 (local), d=4.4.4.4, len 100, policy match
IP: route map PBR, item 10, permit
IP: s=192.168.12.1 (local), d=4.4.4.4 (Serial1/0), len 100,
policy routed
IP: local to Serial1/0 192.168.13.3
```

Above you'll see the output of the debug and you can see that it changed the next hop IP address to 192.168.13.3 for packets heading towards 4.4.4.4. Pretty cool right?

```
Nancy#show route-map
route-map PBR, permit, sequence 10
  Match clauses:
    ip address (access-lists): NEXTHOPCHANGE
  Set clauses:
    ip next-hop 192.168.13.3
  Policy routing matches: 11 packets, 1100 bytes
```

This is another method how you can verify your configuration, just use show route-map and you'll see the matches.

In the previous example I used the set command to change the next hop IP address but we can use it for other actions as well:

```
Nancy(config)#route-map PBR permit 10
Nancy(config-route-map)#set ?
  as-path             Prepend string for a BGP AS-path attribute
  automatic-tag       Automatically compute TAG value
  clns                OSI summary address
  comm-list           set BGP community list (for deletion)
  community           BGP community attribute
  dampening           Set BGP route flap dampening parameters
  default             Set default information
  extcommunity        BGP extended community attribute
  interface           Output interface
  ip                  IP specific information
  ipv6                IPv6 specific information
  level               Where to import route
  local-preference    BGP local preference path attribute
  metric              Metric value for destination routing
protocol
  metric-type         Type of metric for destination routing
protocol
  mpls-label          Set MPLS label for prefix
```

nlri	BGP NLRI type
origin	BGP origin code
tag	Tag value for destination routing protocol
traffic-index	BGP traffic classification number for accounting
vrf	Define VRF name
weight	BGP weight for routing table

You can see there are a lot of things we can tell the route-map to do by using the **set** command. Don't worry about everything you see here...a lot of items here are used for BGP (Border Gateway Protocol) and you'll be using them when you read the BGP chapters.

If you want to try policy based routing then you can check this lab:

http://gns3vault.com/Network-Services/policy-based-routing.html

Next topic is SLA...

P SLA is a great tool on Cisco routers that allows us to generate traffic which can be used to check delay/latency, jitter but can also be combined with **object tracking**. This allows us to check the reachability of a certain IP address (by pinging) or a certain service by connecting to it (using TCP). If the IP address/service is unreachable we can apply a certain "action".

A simple example to demonstrate IP SLA is when you have a single router that is connected to two ISPs:

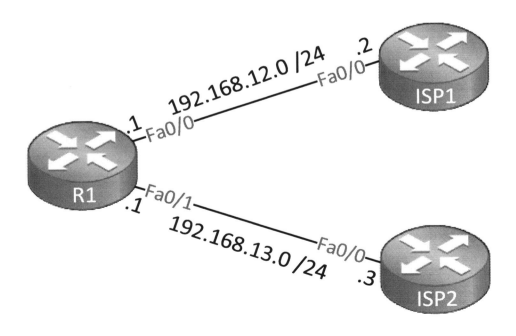

Above we have a router (R1) that is connected to two ISPs. We want to use ISP1 as the primary and ISP2 as the backup link. All traffic will be sent towards ISP1 but when it's unreachable we'll switch over to ISP2. You can achieve this by using two default routes:

```
R1(config)#ip route 0.0.0.0 0.0.0.0 192.168.12.1
R1(config)#ip route 0.0.0.0 0.0.0.0 192.168.13.3 2
```

By default a static route has an AD (Administrative Distance) of 1, that's why I configured the second static route towards ISP2 to have an AD of 2. Having a static route with a higher administrative distance is also called a floating static route. When we look at the routing table of R1 this is what you'll see:

```
R1#show ip route static
S*    0.0.0.0/0 [1/0] via 192.168.12.2
```

Above you will only see the route towards ISP1 because it has a lower AD. Now let's shut the interface towards ISP1 to see what will happen with the routing table:

```
R1(config)#interface fa0/0
R1(config-if)#shutdown
R1(config-if)#exit
```

This is what you will find:

```
R1#show ip route static
S*    0.0.0.0/0 [2/0] via 192.168.13.3
```

Now everything will be sent towards ISP2 which is great. This solution is quick and simple but it has some potential problems...a static route will always remain in the routing table unless the interface goes down. It's possible that the link towards ISP1 is up and running but that the ISP1 router itself is unreachable or that ISP1 has problems on their network that prevents us from reaching the Internet through them. This is why we'll use IP SLA to make our default route more reliable. First let's unshut the interface:

```
R1(config)#interface fa0/0
R1(config-if)#no shutdown
```

I will create an IP SLA instance that pings the IP address of the ISP1 router:

```
R1(config)#ip sla 1
R1(config-ip-sla)#icmp-echo 192.168.12.2
R1(config-ip-sla-echo)#timeout 100
R1(config-ip-sla-echo)#frequency 1
R1(config-ip-sla-echo)#exit
R1(config)#ip sla schedule 1 start-time now life forever
```

We will ping IP address 192.168.12.2 each second and when we don't get a response within 100 Ms we will believe it's unreachable. You might want to play with these values a bit on a production network. Let's see if IP SLA works:

```
R1#show ip sla statistics

Round Trip Time (RTT) for      Index 1
      Latest RTT: 4 milliseconds
Latest operation start time: *00:09:07.235 UTC Fri Mar 1 2002
Latest operation return code: OK
Number of successes: 43
Number of failures: 1
Operation time to live: Forever
```

It seems to be working, right now it only takes 4 milliseconds to get a response. As long as it stays below 100 milliseconds we'll be fine. Let's configure the default route to use IP SLA:

```
R1(config)#no ip route 0.0.0.0 0.0.0.0 192.168.12.2
R1(config)#ip route 0.0.0.0 0.0.0.0 192.168.12.2 track 1
```

First I'll remove the old default route and replace it with one that says "track 1". I can't connect IP SLA directly with the static route, I have to do this with object tracking. This is how you combine object tracking with IP SLA:

```
R1(config)#track 1 rtr 1
```

The command above combines object tracking instance 1 with the IP SLA instance that I configured. Let's see if this will work...

```
R1#show ip route static
S*    0.0.0.0/0 [1/0] via 192.168.12.2
```

Right now everything is working as it should, we use ISP1 for the default route. Curious what happens once ISP1 becomes unreachable?

```
ISP1(config)#interface fastEthernet 0/0
ISP1(config-if)#shutdown
```

We'll shut the interface on ISP1 and this is what you will find on R1:

```
R1#
%TRACKING-5-STATE: 1 rtr 1 state Up->Down
```

Object tracking will kick in because we are no longer able to ping the IP address of ISP1.

This is what you'll see in the routing table:

```
R1#show ip route static
S*    0.0.0.0/0 [2/0] via 192.168.13.3
```

We now send all traffic towards ISP2. What will happen once ISP1 is reachable again?

```
ISP1(config)#interface fastEthernet 0/0
ISP1(config-if)#no shutdown
```

Bring back the interface to the land of the living and this is what you'll discover on R1:

```
R1#
%TRACKING-5-STATE: 1 rtr 1 state Down->Up
```

Object tracking tells us that we can reach ISP1 again and the routing table will be updated:

```
R1#show ip route static
S*    0.0.0.0/0 [1/0] via 192.168.12.2
```

There we go, ISP1 is being used again as the primary ISP. You can use IP SLA for many things. Static routes work but you can also use this for PBR or routing protocols.

If you want to use this for PBR then you only need to make one change to your route-map:

```
Router(config-route-map)#set ip next-hop 192.168.13.3
```

Change this to:

```
Router(config-route-map)#set ip next-hop verify-availability
192.168.13.3 track 1
```

Add the parameter **verify-availability** and specify the object to track.

The last topic in this chapter is VRF (Virtual Routing and Forwarding). When you look at a router, it only has one **global routing table**. VRF allows us to create "virtual routers" within a single router, each virtual router has its own routing table. Let me show you an example:

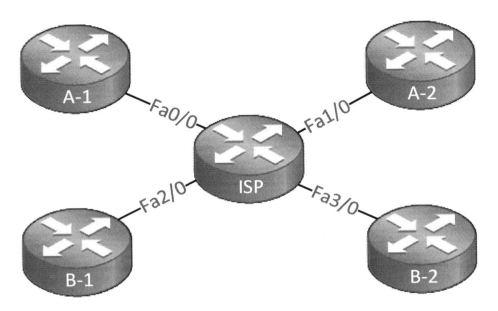

Let's say that we have an ISP with two customers...customer "A" and "B". Each customer has two sites and the ISP is connecting the different sites. The ISP router has only one global routing table so there's no way to separate routing information from customer A and B. Here's what the routing table might look like:

```
ISP#show ip route   connected
C    192.168.4.0/24 is directly connected, FastEthernet3/0
C    192.168.1.0/24 is directly connected, FastEthernet0/0
C    192.168.2.0/24 is directly connected, FastEthernet1/0
C    192.168.3.0/24 is directly connected, FastEthernet2/0
```

There's one routing table and it has all the networks on the interfaces of the ISP router, let's use VRFs to change this:

```
ISP(config)#ip vrf A
ISP(config-vrf)#exit
ISP(config)#ip vrf B
ISP(config-vrf)#exit
```

First we create two VRFs, one for each customer. Now we need to add the interfaces to the correct VRF:

```
ISP(config)#interface FastEthernet 0/0
ISP(config-if)#ip vrf forwarding A
% Interface FastEthernet0/0 IP address 192.168.1.1 removed due
to enabling VRF A
ISP(config-if)#ip address 192.168.1.1 255.255.255.0
```

Once you add the interface to the VRF, you'll have to add the IP address again.

Let's configure the remaining interfaces:

```
ISP(config)#interface FastEthernet 1/0
ISP(config-if)#ip vrf forwarding A
ISP(config-if)#ip address 192.168.2.1 255.255.255.0

ISP(config)#interface FastEthernet 2/0
ISP(config-if)#ip vrf forwarding B
ISP(config-if)#ip address 192.168.3.1 255.255.255.0

ISP(config)#interface FastEthernet 3/0
ISP(config-if)#ip vrf forwarding B
ISP(config-if)#ip address 192.168.4.1 255.255.255.0
```

All interfaces are now configured. There's a nice command that will give you an overview of all VRFs and their interfaces:

```
ISP#show ip vrf
  Name                          Default RD
Interfaces
  A                             <not set>              Fa0/0
                                                       Fa1/0
  B                             <not set>              Fa2/0
                                                       Fa3/0
```

Let's take a look at the routing table(s) now:

```
ISP#show ip route connected
```

The global routing table has no entries, this is because all interfaces were added to a VRF. Let's check the VRF routing tables:

```
ISP#show ip route vrf A connected
C    192.168.1.0/24 is directly connected, FastEthernet0/0
C    192.168.2.0/24 is directly connected, FastEthernet1/0
```

```
ISP#show ip route vrf B connected
C    192.168.4.0/24 is directly connected, FastEthernet3/0
C    192.168.3.0/24 is directly connected, FastEthernet2/0
```

There we go, separated routing tables with their interfaces.

If you want to do something on the router like sending a ping then you'll have to specify which VRF you want to use. By default it will use the global routing table.

Here's an example how to send a ping:

```
ISP#ping vrf A 192.168.1.1

Type escape sequence to abort.
Sending 5, 100-byte ICMP Echos to 192.168.1.1, timeout is 2
seconds:
!!!!!
Success rate is 100 percent (5/5), round-trip min/avg/max =
1/2/4 ms
```

The same thing applies to routing, if you want to create a static route you'll have to specify the VRF:

```
ISP(config)#ip route vrf A 1.1.1.0 255.255.255.0 192.168.1.2
```

```
ISP#show ip route vrf A static
      1.0.0.0/24 is subnetted, 1 subnets
S        1.1.1.0 [1/0] via 192.168.1.2
```

This also applies to routing protocols. For example if you want to use OSPF within VRF B:

```
ISP(config)#router ospf 1 vrf B
ISP(config-router)#network 192.168.1.0 0.0.0.0 area 0
```

This will enable OSPF only for VRF B.

The implementation of VRF that I just showed you is called **VRF lite**. It works very well but it has one downside. If you have multiple routers that use VRF then the configuration becomes quite complex. Here's an example:

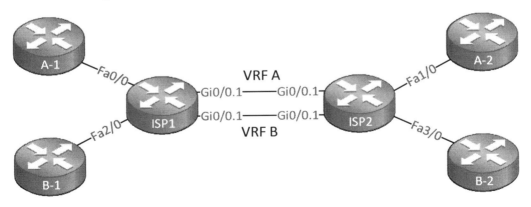

Instead of one ISP router we now have two. The problem with VRF lite is that an interface can only belong to one VRF. If we need a VRF behind ISP1 and ISP2 then we have to create sub-interfaces between the two ISP routers for each VRF that we use. With many VRFs, this becomes an administrative nightmare.

To solve this problem, we can use **EVN (Easy Virtual Networking)**. EVN uses a **Virtual Network Trunk (VNET Trunk)** that carries VRF traffic. It works similar to a L2 trunk for VLANs. All traffic that flows through the VNET trunk is tagged with a VNET tag. Here's an example:

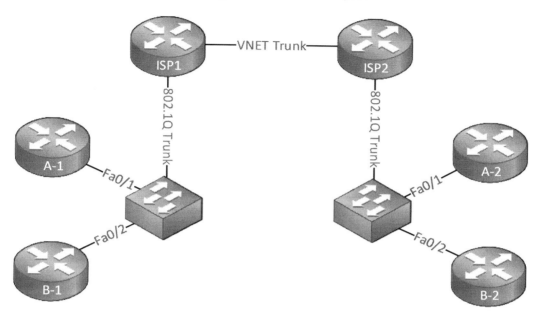

Between the two ISP routers we have a VNET trunk that carries all VRF traffic. The ISP routers are connected to switches using a 802.1Q trunk for the different VLANs for each virtual network that we have.

Each virtual network is completely isolated from other virtual networks but EVN makes it possible to share certain networks from one VRF with another. This is useful for "shared" services like DNS or DHCP servers. Sharing is done through a service called **route replication**.

That's the end of this chapter. If you want to play a bit with VRFs then you can take a look at the following lab:

http://gns3vault.com/mpls/vrf-lite/

16. Route Manipulation

Before you continue with this chapter you should have a solid understanding of OSPF and EIGRP. I'm going to teach you how to manipulate routing with the following tools:

- **Distribute lists**
- **Prefix lists**
- **Route maps**

These tools can be used for many things including **route filtering**. When we filter routes we can choose which routes we are going to allow in our routing table or what routes we don't want to send to our neighbors.

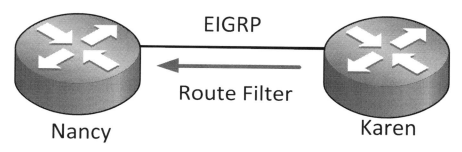

I'm going to use router Nancy and Karen to show you how route filtering works. We are using EIGRP and router Nancy has an inbound route filter so we don't accept everything that router Karen is advertising to us.

1. Router Nancy receives a routing update from router Karen on a certain interface. First we have to check if there is a route filter on the interface where we receive this routing update.
2. If there is no route filter we will just process the routing update and life is good.
3. If we do have a route filter we have to check if there is an entry for the network that is in the routing update. If there is no entry that the routing update packet will be dropped. It's just like an access-list...if you don't permit something it will be denied by default!
4. If we do find an entry in the route filter for the network address in the routing update we will process it and the network address will be permitted or denied.

Are you following me? Let's look at a real life example...

EIGRP AS 12

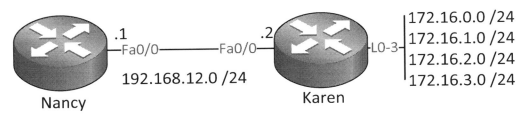

Router Nancy and Karen are back but I've added some networks. Router Karen has a couple of loopback interfaces and we are going to advertise those to router Nancy.

```
Nancy(config)#router eigrp 12
Nancy(config-router)#no auto-summary
Nancy(config-router)#network 192.168.12.0
```

```
Karen(config)#router eigrp 12
Karen(config-router)#no auto-summary
Karen(config-router)#network 192.168.12.0
Karen(config-router)#network 172.16.0.0 0.0.3.255
```

EIGRP is configured so all networks are advertised.

```
Nancy#show ip route eigrp
     172.16.0.0/24 is subnetted, 4 subnets
D       172.16.0.0 [90/156160] via 192.168.12.2, 00:01:07,
FastEthernet0/0
D       172.16.1.0 [90/156160] via 192.168.12.2, 00:01:07,
FastEthernet0/0
D       172.16.2.0 [90/156160] via 192.168.12.2, 00:01:07,
FastEthernet0/0
D       172.16.3.0 [90/156160] via 192.168.12.2, 00:01:07,
FastEthernet0/0
```

If we look at the routing table of router Nancy we can see all those networks on the loopback interfaces as it should be. Now we'll see if we can do some filtering.

```
Nancy(config)#router eigrp 12
Nancy(config-router)#distribute-list ?
  <1-199>      IP access list number
  <1300-2699>  IP expanded access list number
  WORD         Access-list name
  gateway      Filtering incoming updates based on gateway
  prefix       Filter prefixes in routing updates
  route-map    Filter prefixes based on the route-map
```

Go to the configuration of the EIGRP process and use the **distribute-list**

command to see your options. As you can see we can choose between an
access-list, a prefix-list or a route-map. Let's start with the access-list.
You are probably familiar with the concept of access-lists if you studied CCNA.

```
Nancy(config-router)#distribute-list 1 ?
   in    Filter incoming routing updates
   out   Filter outgoing routing updates
```

If you specify an access-list number you can choose if this route filter has to be
inbound or **outbound.**

```
Nancy(config-router)#distribute-list 1 in ?
   Async              Async interface
   BVI                Bridge-Group Virtual Interface
   CDMA-Ix            CDMA Ix interface
   CTunnel            CTunnel interface
   Dialer             Dialer interface
   FastEthernet       FastEthernet IEEE 802.3
   Lex                Lex interface
   Loopback           Loopback interface
   MFR                Multilink Frame Relay bundle interface
   Multilink          Multilink-group interface
   Null               Null interface
   Port-channel       Ethernet Channel of interfaces
   Tunnel             Tunnel interface
   Vif                PGM Multicast Host interface
   Virtual-PPP        Virtual PPP interface
   Virtual-Template   Virtual Template interface
   Virtual-TokenRing  Virtual TokenRing
   <cr>
```

If you want you can choose the interface where to apply the inbound route
filter to. If you don't specify an interface it will apply to **all interfaces.**

```
Nancy(config-router)#distribute-list 1 in FastEthernet 0/0
```

I'm going to apply it to the FastEthernet 0/0 interface since that's the one
where we receive information from router Karen on.

```
Nancy(config)#access-list 1 deny 172.16.1.0 0.0.0.255
Nancy(config)#access-list 1 permit any
```

Let's create an access-list that will filter 172.16.1.0 /24 and permit all the
other networks.

```
Nancy#
%DUAL-5-NBRCHANGE: IP-EIGRP(0) 12: Neighbor 192.168.12.2
(FastEthernet0/0) is resync: route configuration changed
```

You'll see a message showing you that the route filter has changed.

```
Nancy#show ip route eigrp
     172.16.0.0/24 is subnetted, 3 subnets
D        172.16.0.0 [90/156160] via 192.168.12.2, 00:06:26,
FastEthernet0/0
D        172.16.2.0 [90/156160] via 192.168.12.2, 00:06:26,
FastEthernet0/0
D        172.16.3.0 [90/156160] via 192.168.12.2, 00:06:26,
FastEthernet0/0
```

```
Nancy#show access-lists
Standard IP access list 1
    10 deny    172.16.1.0, wildcard bits 0.0.0.255 (2 matches)
    20 permit any (3 matches)
```

You can see 172.16.1.0 /24 has been filtered from the routing table. The matches in the access-list also tell us we have filtered this network.

```
Nancy(config-router)#distribute-list ?
  <1-199>        IP access list number
  <1300-2699>    IP expanded access list number
  WORD           Access-list name
  gateway        Filtering incoming updates based on gateway
  prefix         Filter prefixes in routing updates
  route-map      Filter prefixes based on the route-map
```

Using an access-list is the simplest method of filtering.

If you want a break you can try it with one my labs:

http://gns3vault.com/Network-Services/distribute-list-filtering.html

What about the other options we have? Let's look at **prefix lists**. Prefix lists are very powerful and are similar to access-lists since you need permit and/or deny statements...they are a bit different though.

Let's say I want to filter all networks within the 10.0.0.0 range that have a subnet mask between /24 and /28. Do you think you could do this with an access-list? It'll be interesting right? With prefix lists this is very easy to do! Let me walk you through some prefix lists examples:

```
Nancy#show access-lists
Standard IP access list 1
    10 deny    172.16.1.0, wildcard bits 0.0.0.255 (2 matches)
    20 permit any (3 matches)
```

This is the access-list I just created. Let's create a prefix list that does the same thing.

```
Nancy(config)#ip prefix-list FILTERTHIS seq 5 deny 172.16.1.0/24
Nancy(config)#ip prefix-list FILTERTHIS seq 10 permit 0.0.0.0/0
le 32
```

By using the **ip prefix-list** command you can create prefix lists. As you can see it looks a bit similar as my access-list but instead of typing wildcards we just specify the number of bits. The first line denies 172.16.1.0/24 and the second line permits 0.0.0.0/0 (all networks) if they have a subnet mask of /32 or smaller...in other words "everything". This line is the equivalent of "permit ip any any".

Let's enable it on router Nancy to see what the result is:

```
Nancy(config)#router eigrp 12
Nancy(config-router)#no distribute-list 1 in FastEthernet 0/0
```

First we'll get rid of the old access-list.

```
Nancy(config)#router eigrp 12
Nancy(config-router)#distribute-list prefix FILTERTHIS in
```

And we'll enable the new prefix-list.

```
Nancy#show ip route eigrp
      172.16.0.0/24 is subnetted, 3 subnets
D        172.16.0.0 [90/156160] via 192.168.12.2, 00:01:54,
FastEthernet0/0
D        172.16.2.0 [90/156160] via 192.168.12.2, 00:01:54,
FastEthernet0/0
D        172.16.3.0 [90/156160] via 192.168.12.2, 00:01:54,
FastEthernet0/0
```

As you can see we have the same result. 172.16.1.0/24 has been filtered and all the other networks are permitted.

The true power of the prefix list is in the **ge (Greater than or Equal to)** and **le (less than or equal to)** operators. Let's look at some examples:

```
Nancy(config)#ip prefix-list RENETEST permit 10.0.0.0/8 le 19
```

In this example I'm using the **le** operator. This prefix-list statement says that all networks that fall within the 10.0.0.0/8 range AND that have a subnet mask of /19 or less are permitted.

If I have a network with 10.0.0.0 /21 it will be denied by this prefix list. It falls within the 10.0.0.0 /8 range but it has a subnet mask of /21. I'm using the **le** operator which says that the subnet mask should be /19 or smaller.

Let's say I have another network with 10.0.0.0 /17 then it will be permitted by this prefix-list. It falls within the 10.0.0.0/8 range and has a subnet mask that is smaller than /19.

Are you following me here? Let me give you an example on our routers:

```
Karen(config)#interface loopback 10
Karen(config-if)#ip address 10.1.1.1 255.255.0.0
Karen(config-if)#interface loopback 11
Karen(config-if)#ip address 10.2.2.2 255.255.128.0
Karen(config-if)#interface loopback 12
Karen(config-if)#ip address 10.3.3.3 255.255.192.0
Karen(config-if)#interface loopback 13
Karen(config-if)#ip address 10.4.4.4 255.255.224.0
Karen(config-if)#interface loopback 14
Karen(config-if)#ip address 10.5.5.5 255.255.240.0
Karen(config-if)#interface loopback 15
Karen(config-if)#ip address 10.6.6.6 255.255.248.0
```

First we'll add a couple of loopback interfaces on router Karen. If you look closely you can see I'm using different subnetmasks.

```
Karen(config)#router eigrp 12
Karen(config-router)#network 10.0.0.0
```

And I'll advertise them in EIGRP.

```
Nancy(config)#router eigrp 12
Nancy(config-router)#no distribute-list prefix FILTERTHIS in
```

Let's get rid of the prefix-list on router Nancy...

```
Nancy#show ip route eigrp
     172.16.0.0/24 is subnetted, 4 subnets
D       172.16.0.0 [90/156160] via 192.168.12.2, 00:06:11,
FastEthernet0/0
D       172.16.1.0 [90/156160] via 192.168.12.2, 00:00:35,
FastEthernet0/0
D       172.16.2.0 [90/156160] via 192.168.12.2, 00:06:11,
FastEthernet0/0
D       172.16.3.0 [90/156160] via 192.168.12.2, 00:06:11,
FastEthernet0/0
     10.0.0.0/8 is variably subnetted, 6 subnets, 6 masks
D       10.2.0.0/17 [90/156160] via 192.168.12.2, 00:02:22,
FastEthernet0/0
D       10.3.0.0/18 [90/156160] via 192.168.12.2, 01:14:57,
FastEthernet0/0
D       10.1.0.0/16 [90/156160] via 192.168.12.2, 00:06:11,
FastEthernet0/0
D       10.6.0.0/21 [90/156160] via 192.168.12.2, 01:02:35,
FastEthernet0/0
```

```
D         10.4.0.0/19 [90/156160] via 192.168.12.2, 01:14:46,
FastEthernet0/0
D         10.5.0.0/20 [90/156160] via 192.168.12.2, 01:02:35,
FastEthernet0/0
```

Now we see all the networks that fall within the 172.16.0.0/16 and 10.0.0.0/8 range. Time to enable that prefix-list I just created.

```
Nancy(config)#router eigrp 12
Nancy(config-router)#distribute-list prefix RENETEST in
```

This is how we activate it and this is what we end up with:

```
Nancy#show ip route eigrp
      10.0.0.0/8 is variably subnetted, 4 subnets, 4 masks
D         10.2.0.0/17 [90/156160] via 192.168.12.2, 00:03:27,
FastEthernet0/0
D         10.3.0.0/18 [90/156160] via 192.168.12.2, 01:16:03,
FastEthernet0/0
D         10.1.0.0/16 [90/156160] via 192.168.12.2, 00:07:16,
FastEthernet0/0
D         10.4.0.0/19 [90/156160] via 192.168.12.2, 01:15:51,
FastEthernet0/0
```

Only four entries remain...why?

```
Nancy#show ip prefix-list RENETEST
ip prefix-list RENETEST: 1 entries
   seq 5 permit 10.0.0.0/8 le 19
```

Here's the prefix-list again, let me explain what happened:

- Everything in the 172.16.0.0/16 range is filtered because it's not permitted in our prefix-list.
- 10.2.0.0/17 is permitted because it's in the 10.0.0.0/8 range and has a /17 subnet mask.
- 10.3.0.0/18 is permitted because it's in the 10.0.0.0/8 range and has a /18 subnet mask.
- 10.1.0.0/16 is permitted because it's in the 10.0.0.0/8 range and has a /16 subnet mask.
- 10.4.0.0/16 is permitted because it's in the 10.0.0.0/8 range and has a /19 subnet mask.
- 10.5.0.0/20 is filtered, it's in the 10.0.0.0/8 range but has a /20 subnet mask.
- 10.6.0.0/21 is filtered, it's in the 10.0.0.0/8 range but has a /21 subnet mask.

Does this make sense? Let's walk through a couple more examples together!

```
Nancy(config)#ip prefix-list RENETEST2 permit 10.0.0.0/8 ge 20
```

This time I'm using the **ge** operator. Ge 20 means that the network needs to have a subnet mask of /20 or larger in order to be permitted. 10.0.0.0 /8 is the range we are going to check.

A network with 10.55.55.0 /25 will be permitted because it falls within the 10.0.0.0 /8 range and has a subnet mask of /25 which is larger than /20.

What about 10.60.0.0 /19? It falls within the 10.0.0.0 /8 range but it is not permitted because it has a subnet mask of /19...our ge operator says it should be /20 or larger.

Hmm interesting...what about 192.168.12.0 /25? The subnet mask of /25 matches our ge operator but it doesn't fall within the 10.0.0.0 /8 range so it's not permitted. Let's see what happens if I activate this prefix-list on router Nancy:

```
Nancy(config)#router eigrp 12
Nancy(config-router)#no distribute-list prefix RENETEST in
Nancy(config-router)#distribute-list prefix RENETEST2 in
```

First disable the old prefix-list and secondly enable the new one.

```
Nancy#show ip route eigrp
     10.0.0.0/8 is variably subnetted, 2 subnets, 2 masks
D        10.6.0.0/21 [90/156160] via 192.168.12.2, 00:01:03,
FastEthernet0/0
D        10.5.0.0/20 [90/156160] via 192.168.12.2, 00:01:03,
FastEthernet0/0
```

Only two entries remain...why?

- Everything in the 172.16.0.0/16 range is filtered because it's not permitted in our prefix-list.
- All networks in the 10.0.0.0/8 range with a subnet mask that is smaller than 20 are filtered.
- All networks in the 10.0.0.0/8 range with a subnet mask that is 20 or larger are permitted, that means only 10.6.0.0/21 and 10.5.0.0/20.

```
Nancy(config)#ip prefix-list RENETEST3 permit 10.0.0.0/8 ge 16
le 18
```

We can also combine the ge and le operators. Look at my prefix-list above. It's permitting all networks that fall within the 10.0.0.0 /8 range and that have a subnet mask of /16, /18 and everything in between.

10.22.0.0 /18 will be permitted because it falls within the 10.0.0.0 /8 range and has a subnet mask of /18.

10.55.0.0 / 26 will be denied. It falls within the 10.0.0.0 /8 range but the subnet mask is /26 which doesn't match my ge or le operators.

10.4.4.0 /14 will be denied. It falls within the 10.0.0.0 /8 range but the subnet mask is /14 which doesn't match my ge or le operators.

192.168.12.0 /18 will be denied. It matches my ge and le operators but it doesn't fall within the 10.0.0.0 /8 range.

Let's activate it on router Nancy and see what the result is:

```
Nancy(config)#router eigrp 12
Nancy(config-router)#no distribute-list prefix RENETEST2 in
Nancy(config-router)#distribute-list prefix RENETEST3 in
```

First we'll remove the old prefix-list and activate the new one...

```
Nancy#show ip route eigrp
      10.0.0.0/8 is variably subnetted, 3 subnets, 3 masks
D        10.2.0.0/17 [90/156160] via 192.168.12.2, 00:00:36,
FastEthernet0/0
D        10.3.0.0/18 [90/156160] via 192.168.12.2, 00:00:36,
FastEthernet0/0
D        10.1.0.0/16 [90/156160] via 192.168.12.2, 00:00:36,
FastEthernet0/0
```

And here's the result. What happened?

- Everything in the 172.16.0.0/16 range is filtered because it's not permitted in our prefix-list.
- Only networks in the 10.0.0.0/8 range with a subnet mask of /16, /17 or /18 are permitted, everything else is filtered.

Do you see how powerful these prefix-lists are? With a single line I can create very flexible permit or deny statements! Let me show you a couple more examples of prefix-lists:

```
Nancy(config)#ip prefix-list CLASSB permit 128.0.0.0/2 ge 17
```

This one is interesting...let's break it down in pieces. It's permitting 128.0.0.0 /2 and the ge operator says the subnet mask should be /17 or larger. 128.0.0.0 is the start of the class B range and the /2 says that we have to check the first two bits. 128.0.0.0 /2 covers the entire class B network range. This prefix-list will permit any subnet in the class B network range that has a subnet mask of /17 or larger.

```
Nancy(config)#ip prefix-list ALL permit 0.0.0.0/0 le 32
```

I showed you this one before...this one says permit 0.0.0.0 /0 which covers the entire network range. We have a le 32 operator which says that the subnet mask should be /32 or smaller. What does this mean? It means its matching ALL networks!

```
Nancy(config)#ip prefix-list DEFAULTROUTE permit 0.0.0.0/0
```

We don't have any ge or le operators and this prefix-list shows 0.0.0.0 /0. It's only permitting the default route...

```
Nancy(config)#ip prefix-list CLASSA permit 0.0.0.0/1 le 27
```

Last one...promise! The network range to check is 0.0.0.0 and we have /1 which means we are only checking the first bit. This effectively matches the whole class A range.
We have a le operator with 27 which tells us the subnet mask should be /27 or smaller. This prefix-list matches all subnets within the class A range that has a subnet mask of /27 or smaller.

If you feel you get the hang of this you should try some of my prefix-lists lab, you can find it here:

http://gns3vault.com/Network-Services/prefix-list-filtering.html

```
Nancy(config-router)#distribute-list ?
  <1-199>        IP access list number
  <1300-2699>    IP expanded access list number
  WORD           Access-list name
  gateway        Filtering incoming updates based on gateway
  prefix         Filter prefixes in routing updates
  route-map      Filter prefixes based on the route-map
```

By now you have seen access-lists and prefix-lists for route filtering. There is one option left and that's the **route-map.** You have seen a quick example in the previous chapter where I used it for policy based routing.

Route-maps are very useful. They work with **match** and **set** statements. You can use a route-map to match on a certain criteria and then configure it to take action. We can use route-maps for filtering but they are also used for BGP policies (more on this in the BGP chapter) and policy-based routing (used to overrule routing protocols).

I'm going to show you a couple of route-maps and explain to you what they do.

```
Nancy(config)#route-map TEST permit 10
Nancy(config-route-map)#match ?
  as-path            Match BGP AS path list
  clns               CLNS information
  community          Match BGP community list
  extcommunity       Match BGP/VPN extended community list
  interface          Match first hop interface of route
  ip                 IP specific information
  ipv6               IPv6 specific information
  length             Packet length
  local-preference   Local preference for route
  metric             Match metric of route
  mpls-label         Match routes which have MPLS labels
  nlri               BGP NLRI type
  policy-list        Match IP policy list
  route-type         Match route-type of route
  source-protocol    Match source-protocol of route
  tag                Match tag of route
```

You can create route-maps by using the **route-map** command. They use sequence numbers like access-lists and prefix-lists do. I'm creating a route-map called TEST and the first statement is a permit with sequence number 10. As you can see there is a big list of things you can match on...don't worry about everything you see here at this moment.

```
Nancy(config-route-map)#match ip ?
  address        Match address of route or match packet
  next-hop       Match next-hop address of route
  route-source   Match advertising source address of route
```

If we look at **match ip** you can see that we can match on address or even a next-hop or route-source address. I want to match on a certain address...

```
Nancy(config-route-map)#match ip address ?
  <1-199>      IP access-list number
  <1300-2699>  IP access-list number (expanded range)
  WORD         IP access-list name
  prefix-list  Match entries of prefix-lists
  <cr>
```

This should look familiar...you can choose to match on an access-list or prefix-list! I'm going to match on an access-list...let's pick (lucky number) 7.

```
Nancy(config-route-map)#match ip address 7
```

I just told my route-map to match everything that matches access-list 7. You can see route-maps offer far more options to match on than access-lists or prefix-lists can do.

```
Nancy(config)#access-list 7 permit 172.16.0.0 0.0.255.255

Nancy(config)#router eigrp 12
Nancy(config-router)#no distribute-list prefix RENETEST3 in
Nancy(config-router)#distribute-list route-map TEST in
```

Let's create that access-list number 7 and change EIGRP to filter using the route-map.

```
Nancy#show ip route eigrp
     172.16.0.0/24 is subnetted, 4 subnets
D       172.16.0.0 [90/156160] via 192.168.12.2, 00:01:05,
FastEthernet0/0
D       172.16.1.0 [90/156160] via 192.168.12.2, 00:01:05,
FastEthernet0/0
D       172.16.2.0 [90/156160] via 192.168.12.2, 00:01:05,
FastEthernet0/0
D       172.16.3.0 [90/156160] via 192.168.12.2, 00:01:05,
FastEthernet0/0
```

You can see that it's working, only networks that match access-list 7 are now permitted.

Route-maps work just like access-lists or prefix-lists: they work with sequence numbers. We start at the top and process the statement with sequence number 10. If nothing matches we will look for statement 20 and then 30, 40, 50 and so on. If packets match on a certain statement we will apply the set statement and we are done!

```
Nancy(config)#route-map PBR permit 40
Nancy(config-route-map)#match ip address 7 8 9
Nancy(config-route-map)#set ip next-hop 192.168.23.3
```

We can also have **multiple match** statements in a single sequence. In the example above it has to match access-list 7 **OR** 8 **OR** 9.

```
Nancy(config)#route-map PBR permit 50
Nancy(config-route-map)#match ip address 7
Nancy(config-route-map)#match interface FastEthernet 0/0
Nancy(config-route-map)#set ip next-hop 192.168.23.3
```

This route-map is different. The match statements are not OR but **AND**. In this example it has to match access-list 7 **and** the interface has to be FastEthernet0/0 before we set the next-hop IP address to 192.168.23.3.

That's all I have for you on route manipulation. If you want some good practice you should try labs that cover route-filtering using access-lists, prefix-lists and route-maps. To learn the true power of route-maps you can try policy-based-routing at this moment. See if you can filter routing information for EIGRP, OSPF and RIP.

Don't worry if you are unsure why you want to use route-maps at this moment. Once you start the BGP chapter you'll see how valuable route-maps are.

René Molenaar

17. Redistribution

Most networks you encounter will probably only run a single routing protocol like OSPF or EIGRP. Maybe you find some old small networks that are still running RIP that need migration to OSPF or EIGRP. What if you have a company that is running OSPF and you just bought another company and their network is running EIGRP?

It's possible that we have multiple routing protocols on our network and we'll need some method to exchange routing information between the different protocols. This is called **redistribution.** We'll look into some of the issues that we encounter. What are we going to do with our metrics? OSPF uses cost and EIGRP uses K-values and they are not compatible with each other....RIP uses hop count.

Redistribution also adds another problem. If you "import" routing information from one routing protocol into another it's possible to create routing loops. I'll show you how to deal with all these problems.

If you don't feel 100% confident about your knowledge on OSPF and EIGRP then I suggest you re-read some of the chapters and do some labs. One routing protocol can be bad enough but when you mix a couple of them that's where the real fun starts!

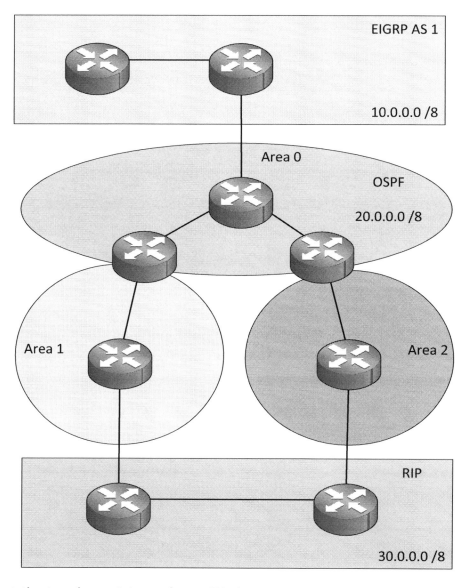

Look at the topology picture above. We have routers running EIGRP in AS 1 with the 10.0.0.0 /8 network. OSPF has multiple areas and we have 20.0.0.0 /8 there. At the bottom there are two RIP routers in the 30.0.0.0 /8 network. If we want to have full connectivity in this network we'll have to do some redistribution.

Redistribution is not just for between routing protocols, we have multiple options:

- **Between routing protocols** (RIP, OSPF, EIGRP, BGP).
- **Static routes** can be redistributed into a routing protocol.
- **Directly connected routes** can be redistributed into a routing protocol.

Normally you use the network command to advertise directly connected routes into your routing protocol. You can also use the **redistribute connected** command which will redistribute it into the routing protocol. I'll show you the difference in a bit.

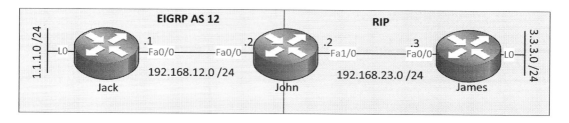

In the topology picture above I have three routers. Router Jack is running EIGRP and router James is running RIP. Router John is in the middle and is running EIGRP and RIP. If we want to do redistribution we'll have to do it on router John. Let's take a look shall we?

```
Jack(config)#router eigrp 12
Jack(config-router)#no auto-summary
Jack(config-router)#network 192.168.12.0
Jack(config-router)#network 1.1.1.0 0.0.0.255
```

```
John(config)#router eigrp 12
John(config-router)#no auto-summary
John(config-router)#network 192.168.12.0
John(config-router)#exit
John(config)#router rip
John(config-router)#version 2
John(config-router)#no auto-summary
John(config-router)#network 192.168.23.0
```

```
James(config)#router rip
James(config-router)#version 2
James(config-router)#no auto-summary
James(config-router)#network 192.168.23.0
James(config-router)#network 3.3.3.0
```

Here are the router configurations, nothing special...I only advertised the links to get EIGRP and RIP up and running.

```
Jack#show ip route

Gateway of last resort is not set

C    192.168.12.0/24 is directly connected, FastEthernet0/0
     1.0.0.0/24 is subnetted, 1 subnets
C       1.1.1.0 is directly connected, Loopback0
```

```
John#show ip route

Gateway of last resort is not set

C    192.168.12.0/24 is directly connected, FastEthernet0/0
     1.0.0.0/24 is subnetted, 1 subnets
D       1.1.1.0 [90/156160] via 192.168.12.1, 00:05:01,
FastEthernet0/0
R    3.0.0.0/8 [120/1] via 192.168.23.3, 00:00:12,
FastEthernet1/0
C    192.168.23.0/24 is directly connected, FastEthernet1/0
```

```
James#show ip route

Gateway of last resort is not set

     3.0.0.0/24 is subnetted, 1 subnets
C       3.3.3.0 is directly connected, Loopback0
C    192.168.23.0/24 is directly connected, FastEthernet0/0
```

Here are the routing table of all three routers after configuring RIP and EIGRP.
You can see router John has learned the loopback interfaces of router James
and Jack. Router Jack and James don't have anything in their routing table
because router John is not advertising anything. As you can see
redistribution is not done automatically.

Before I show you the redistribution configurations there are two things you
should be aware of:

- Redistribution happens **outbound**. If I configure redistribution on
  router John then **nothing will change** in the routing table of router
  John.
  - Router John will redistribute EIGRP routing information into RIP
    and advertise it to router James.
  - Router John will redistribute RIP routing information into EIGRP
    and advertise it to router Jack.
- You need the networks in your local routing table before you can do
  redistribution. You can't advertise (or redistribute) what you don't
  have…

When we redistribute from one routing protocol into another we have to use a **seed metric**. Each routing protocols uses a different metric:

- OSPF: Cost
- EIGRP: Bandwidth, delay, load, reliability and MTU.
- RIP: Hop count

Somehow we have to convert the metric from one routing protocol to another. This is something that doesn't happen automatically...we have to **tell the router what metric to use** and it's different for each routing protocol.

Protocol	Default Seed Metric
RIP	Infinity
EIGRP	Infinity
OSPF	20 except BGP is 1.
BGP	BGP metric is set to IGP metric

This table is important to remember. If you redistribute something into RIP then the **default seed metric** is infinity. What does RIP do with routes that have an infinite metric? That's right...they don't show up in your routing table! This means you have to configure a default hop count for everything you redistribute into RIP or it's not going to work.

The same thing applies to redistributing into EIGRP. You have to configure the bandwidth, delay, load, reliability and MTU yourself otherwise redistribution is not going to work.

OSPF is friendlier...if you redistribute into OSPF then the redistributed routes will have a default cost of 20 unless the routing information comes from BGP...which has a cost of 1.

You can forget about BGP for now but it's the only routing protocol that copies the original metric value.

```
John(config)#router rip
John(config-router)#default-metric 5
```

```
John(config)#router eigrp 12
John(config-router)#default-metric 1500 100 255 1 1500
```

Here's an example how you can configure the default seed metric by using the **default-metric** command. Default-metric 5 sets the hop count to 5 for everything we redistribute into RIP.

For EIGRP you have to specify the bandwidth, delay, load, reliability and MTU yourself. In my example I'm using a bandwidth of 1500, a delay of 100, reliability 255 (which means 100%), load of 1 (1%) and a MTU of 1500. In case you are wondering these are just values that I made up. Everything we redistribute into EIGRP will have this metric.

Let's look at some redistribution scenarios and the problems we might encounter!

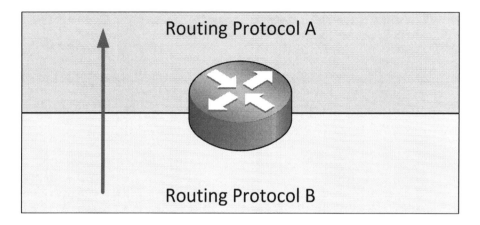

The picture above shows you **one-way redistribution.** We will redistribute Routing protocol B into routing protocol A but not vice-versa. If you want full reachability you will need static routes or a default route in the domain of routing protocol A to reach networks in routing protocol B.

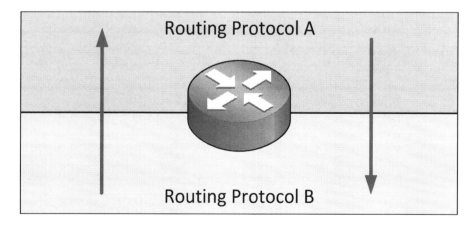

Two-way redistribution occurs when we redistribute between both routing protocols. Both forms of redistribution are called **one-point redistribution** because there is only one router doing the redistribution. One-point redistributions are always safe because there is only one exit and entrance from one routing protocol to another. Because of this we cannot have any routing loops.

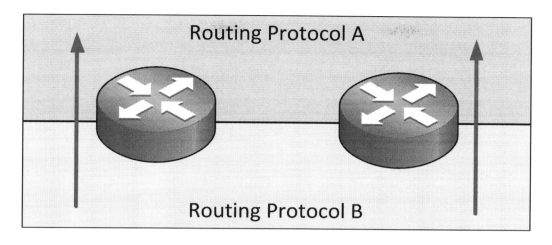

In this scenario we have two routers and both are performing redistribution. We call this **multipoint redistribution** and it might sounds like a good idea since we don't want to have a single point of failure in our network. This example only redistributes routing protocol B into routing protocol A and is thus called **one-way multipoint redistribution.**

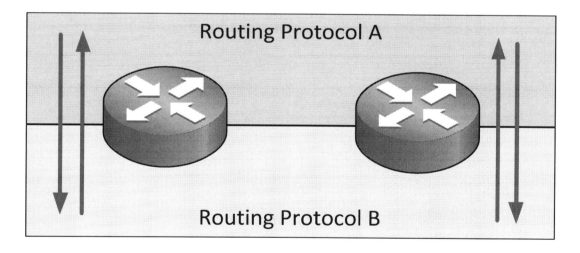

This time we are redistributing routing protocol A into routing protocol B and vice versa. This is called **two-way multipoint redistribution.**

Multipoint redistribution is **VERY likely to introduce problems** like routing loops and/or sub-optimal routing. Let's walk through a couple of scenarios to see what is wrong.

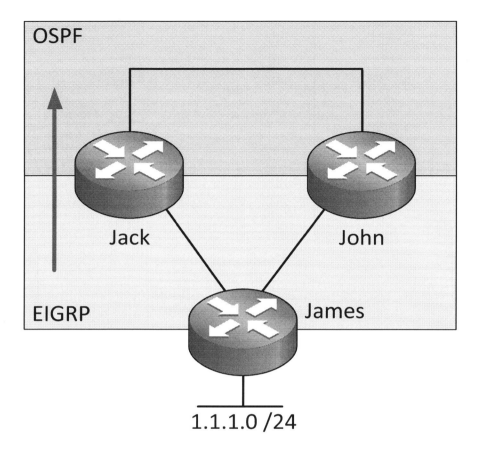

In the picture above I have three routers. Router Jack, John and James are running EIGRP. Router Jack and John are running OSPF. Router Jack is configured for one-way redistribution.

Router James has the 1.1.1.0 /24 network in its routing table but it's an external network. EIGRP uses two different administrative distance values:

- Internal: AD 90
- External: AD 170

Everything you redistribute into EIGRP will show up with an administrative distance of 170. EIGRP sees external routing information as not-so-reliable which is why it will assign it this high administrative distance.

The following will happen:

1. Router James has the 1.1.1.0 /24 network in its routing table as an EIGRP external network with an administrative distance of 170.
2. Router James will advertise the 1.1.1.0 /24 network to router Jack and John who happily store it in their routing table as EIGRP with an administrative distance of 170.
3. Router Jack has been configured to redistribute EIGRP into OSPF and will do so.
4. Since network 1.1.1.0 /24 is in the routing table of router Jack as an EIGRP route it will be redistributed into OSPF and advertised to router John.
5. Router John receives OSPF information about 1.1.1.0 /24 and now has two choices:
   a. Use the EIGRP information about 1.1.1.0 /24 with AD 170 (EIGRP).
   b. Use the OSPF information about 1.1.1.0 /24 with AD 110 (OSPF).
6. Since the administrative distance of OSPF is lower it will remove the EIGRP information on 1.1.1.0 /24 from the routing table and insert the OSPF information.
7. Router John will forward IP packets to 1.1.1.0 /24 towards router Jack who will forward it to router James. We now have **sub-optimal routing.**

The problem in this scenario is because of the difference in administrative distance. OSPF has a lower administrative distance which is why the EIGRP information is removed from the routing table.

Would you like to see this network in action and try to configure it?

http://gns3vault.com/Redistribution/multipoint-one-way-redistribution.html

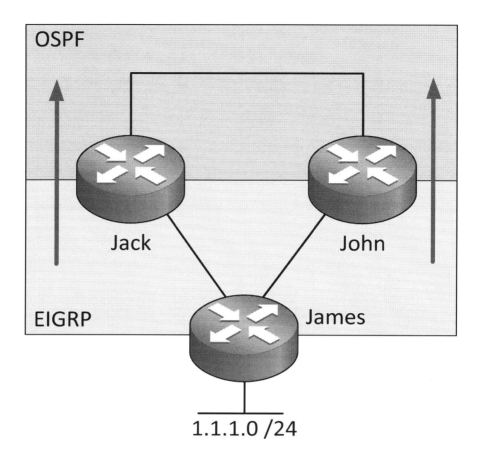

1.1.1.0 /24

This is the same scenario but now router Jack and John are both redistributing EIGRP into OSPF (one-way multipoint redistribution). Network 1.1.1.0 /24 at router James is an external EIGRP network and has an administrative distance of 170.

This is what might happen:

1. Router James has network 1.1.1.0 /24 in its routing table with an AD of 170.
2. Router James advertises network 1.1.1.0 /24 to router Jack and John and they both store it in their routing table.
3. Router Jack and router John are configured to redistribute EIGRP into OSPF and so they both will redistribute the 1.1.1.0 /24 network into OSPF.
4. There are a couple of things that can go wrong here:
   a. Router Jack receives OSPF information about network 1.1.1.0 /24 and will store it in its routing table, removing the EIGRP route because the AD of OSPF is 110 compared to EIGRP external 170.

b. Router John receives OSPF information about network 1.1.1.0 /24 and will store it in its routing table, removing the EIGRP route because the AD of OSPF is 110 compared to EIGRP external 170.

c. Router Jack and John now believe they can reach network 1.1.1.0 /24 through each other and we have a **routing loop.** Packets will bounce between each other until the TTL field has decreased to 0.

5. Another problem might be **route flapping**. Router Jack and John have replaced the EIGRP information for 1.1.1.0 /24 by the OSPF information. You cannot redistribute what you don't have in your routing table...it's like the chicken and egg problem.

Does this make your head spin? Redistribution is one of the hardest topics in routing and switching! Give yourself some time to think about this and let it sink in.

Want to see this scenario in action? One lab coming up:

http://gns3vault.com/Redistribution/multipoint-one-way-redistribution.html

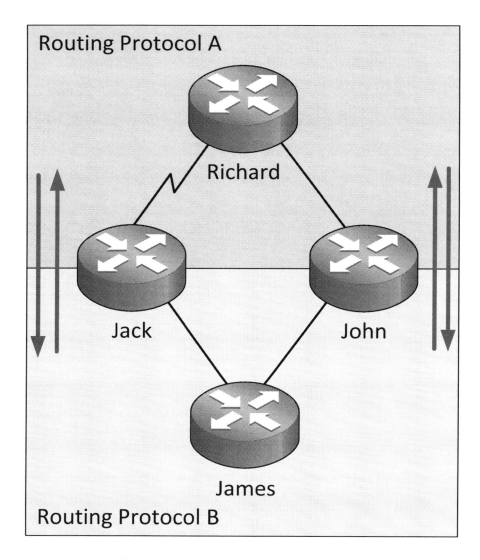

Multipoint two-way redistribution causes many problems. In the picture above I have 4 routers. On the top we have routing protocol A and on the bottom routing protocol B. Router Jack and John are both configured to redistribute between both routing protocols.

- If router James wants to reach router Richard it should send packets through router John...if you look closely you can see that between router Jack and Richard there is a (slow) serial link. The problem however is that each routing protocol uses different metrics so metric information is lost.
- Imagine router James advertises a network to router Jack (for example 1.1.1.0 /24):
  - Router Jack will redistribute network 1.1.1.0 /24 from routing protocol B into routing protocol A.

- o Router Richard will receive network 1.1.1.0 /24 and advertise it to router John.
- o Router John will redistribute network 1.1.1.0 /24 back into routing protocol B.
- o We now have a routing loop...
- The problems in the previous example with suboptimal routing can occur here as well.

There are a couple of guidelines we can use to prevent problems with redistribution:

- Redistribute **only internal** routes from routing protocol A to routing protocol B.
- Tag routes on routers doing redistribution.
- Increase the metric for redistributes routes so internal routes are used instead of the redistributed ones.
- Change the administrative distance.

Don't worry if this sounds a bit fuzzy at the moment; let's look at some of configurations on our routers.

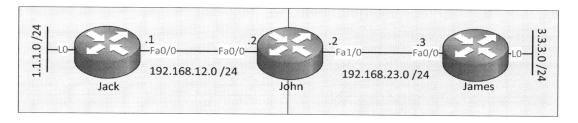

This is the topology I showed you before, I'll use it again. Just three routers...on the left site routing protocol A and on the right side routing protocol B. Router Jack and James each have a loopback interface with a network.

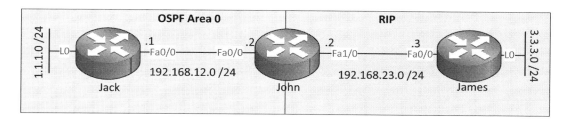

Let's start with the redistribution between OSPF and RIP.

First let me show you the router configurations:

```
Jack(config)#router ospf 1
Jack(config-router)#network 1.1.1.0 0.0.0.255 area 0
Jack(config-router)#network 192.168.12.0 0.0.0.255 area 0
```

```
John(config)#router ospf 1
John(config-router)#network 192.168.12.0 0.0.0.255 area 0

John(config)#router rip
John(config-router)#version 2
John(config-router)#no auto-summary
John(config-router)#network 192.168.23.0
```

```
James(config)#router rip
James(config-router)#version 2
James(config-router)#network 3.3.3.0
James(config-router)#network 192.168.23.0
```

Nothing special here, just OSPF and RIP advertising their networks.

```
Jack#show ip route

Gateway of last resort is not set

C    192.168.12.0/24 is directly connected, FastEthernet0/0
     1.0.0.0/24 is subnetted, 1 subnets
C        1.1.1.0 is directly connected, Loopback0
```

```
John#show ip route

Gateway of last resort is not set

C    192.168.12.0/24 is directly connected, FastEthernet0/0
     1.0.0.0/32 is subnetted, 1 subnets
O        1.1.1.1 [110/2] via 192.168.12.1, 00:11:05,
FastEthernet0/0
     3.0.0.0/24 is subnetted, 1 subnets
R        3.3.3.0 [120/1] via 192.168.23.3, 00:00:20,
FastEthernet1/0
C    192.168.23.0/24 is directly connected, FastEthernet1/0
```

```
James#show ip route

Gateway of last resort is not set

     3.0.0.0/24 is subnetted, 1 subnets
C        3.3.3.0 is directly connected, Loopback0
C    192.168.23.0/24 is directly connected, FastEthernet0/0
```

You can see router John has learned RIP and OSPF information. Time for some redistribution action!

```
John(config)#router rip
John(config-router)#redistribute ?
  bgp          Border Gateway Protocol (BGP)
  connected    Connected
  eigrp        Enhanced Interior Gateway Routing Protocol (EIGRP)
  isis         ISO IS-IS
  iso-igrp     IGRP for OSI networks
  metric       Metric for redistributed routes
  mobile       Mobile routes
  odr          On Demand stub Routes
  ospf         Open Shortest Path First (OSPF)
  rip          Routing Information Protocol (RIP)
  route-map    Route map reference
  static       Static routes
  <cr>
```

First I'm going to redistribute OSPF into RIP. You can see I can choose a lot of different protocols when you use the **redistribute** command.

```
John(config)#router rip
John(config-router)#redistribute ospf 1 metric 5
```

This is how I redistribute OSPF (process 1) into RIP. I'm setting the hop count to 5. Keep in mind the default seed metric for RIP is **infinity.** If I don't specify a metric your redistribution will fail!

```
John(config)#router rip
John(config-router)#default-metric 5
```

I also could have used the **default-metric** command to set a default hop count for everything I'm redistributing.

```
James#show ip route rip
R     192.168.12.0/24 [120/5] via 192.168.23.2, 00:00:00,
FastEthernet0/0
      1.0.0.0/32 is subnetted, 1 subnets
R         1.1.1.1 [120/5] via 192.168.23.2, 00:00:00,
FastEthernet0/0
```

This is what the routing table of router James looks like. You can see the OSPF networks that are redistributed into RIP. You can also see the seed metric (hop count) of 5….excellent!

```
John(config)#router ospf 1
John(config-router)#redistribute rip subnets
```

Let's redistribute RIP into OSPF now. I can use the **redistribute rip subnets** command here. The keyword **subnets** is needed because otherwise OSPF will redistribute classful! I want it to redistribute classless so that's why I've added the keyword subnets.

```
Jack#show ip route ospf
     3.0.0.0/24 is subnetted, 1 subnets
O E2    3.3.3.0 [110/20] via 192.168.12.2, 00:00:21,
FastEthernet0/0
O E2 192.168.23.0/24 [110/20] via 192.168.12.2, 00:00:21,
FastEthernet0/0
```

Let's look at router Jack. You can see OSPF information in the routing table. They show up as **external type 2** routes. The cost is 20 (which is the default). OSPF is a bit more sophisticated than RIP and makes a difference between internal and external routes.

If routes are redistributed into OSPF as type 2 then every router in the OSPF domain will see the same cost to reach the external networks. If routes are redistributed into OSPF as type 1, then the cost to reach the external networks could vary from router to router.

Want to see it in action?

http://gns3vault.com/Redistribution/rip-to-ospf-redistribution.html

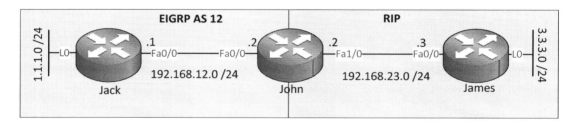

Let's do another example because I want to show you redistribution for EIGRP. Same network but I have replaced OSPF on the left side with EIGRP.

```
Jack(config)#router eigrp 12
Jack(config-router)#no auto-summary
Jack(config-router)#network 1.1.1.0 0.0.0.255
Jack(config-router)#network 192.168.12.0
```

```
John(config)#router eigrp 12
John(config-router)#no auto-summary
John(config-router)#network 192.168.12.0

John(config)#router rip
John(config-router)#no auto-summary
John(config-router)#version 2
John(config-router)#network 192.168.23.0
```

```
James(config)#router rip
James(config-router)#version 2
James(config-router)#no auto-summary
James(config-router)#network 192.168.23.0
James(config-router)#network 3.3.3.0
```

Above are the router configurations I've used, nothing special...let's move on to the redistribution:

```
John(config)#router eigrp 12
John(config-router)#redistribute rip metric 1500 100 255 1 1500
```

I'm redistributing RIP into EIGRP and I have to specify the metrics. Pick whatever values you like. In you don't specify the seed metric than the default one will be **infinity** and your redistributed routes don't show up!

```
John(config)#router eigrp 12
John(config-router)#default-metric 1500 100 255 1 1500
```

You can also configure the seed metric globally for EIGRP using the **default-metric** command.

```
Jack#show ip route eigrp
     3.0.0.0/24 is subnetted, 1 subnets
D EX    3.3.3.0 [170/1734656] via 192.168.12.2, 00:01:39,
FastEthernet0/0
D EX 192.168.23.0/24 [170/1734656] via 192.168.12.2, 00:03:49,
FastEthernet0/0
```

This is what router Jack's routing table now looks like. You can see these networks show up as EIGRP external and the administrative distance is 170.

```
John(config)#router rip
John(config-router)#redistribute eigrp 12 metric 10
```

To redistribute EIGRP into RIP we'll have to specify the AS number for EIGRP (12) and the metric (hop count).

```
James#show ip route rip
R    192.168.12.0/24 [120/10] via 192.168.23.2, 00:00:06,
FastEthernet0/0
     1.0.0.0/24 is subnetted, 1 subnets
R        1.1.1.0 [120/10] via 192.168.23.2, 00:00:06,
FastEthernet0/0
```

And here you see the RIP routes, that's all there is to it.
You can try this redistribution yourself if you like, check out my lab:

http://gns3vault.com/Redistribution/rip-to-eigrp-redistribution.html

When you are dealing with multiple routing protocols you'll have to deal with
the administrative distance. Knowing the administrative distance values is
CCNA stuff but just in case you forgot them I'll add them here:

Source	Administrative Distance
Directly connected	0
Static route	1
EIGRP summary	5
External BGP	20
EIGRP	90
IGRP	100
OSPF	110
IS-IS	115
RIP	120
ODR	160
External EIGRP	170
Internal BGP	200
Unknown	255

Keep in mind:

- The administrative distance is only **local** and can be different for each router.
- The administrative distance can be modified.

Don't worry about internal and external BGP; we'll cover that in the BGP
chapters. IGRP is the predecessor to EIGRP and you won't find it on any Cisco
exam anymore. IS-IS is another link-state routing protocol like OSPF (fun to
play with) but not on Cisco exams anymore...ODR stands for on-demand-
routing and not a CCNP-topic.

Unknown has an administrative distance of 255. If you set a network to an AD
of 255 it won't show up in the routing table.

How do we change the administrative distance? It's different for each routing protocol but you need to use the **distance** command:

```
Jack(config)#router eigrp 12
Jack(config-router)#distance eigrp 90 160
```

For example you can change the distance for EIGRP. Internal routes remain their AD of 90 while my external prefixes now have an AD of 160.

```
Jack#show ip route eigrp
      3.0.0.0/24 is subnetted, 1 subnets
D EX    3.3.3.0 [160/1734656] via 192.168.12.2, 00:00:30,
FastEthernet0/0
D EX 192.168.23.0/24 [160/1734656] via 192.168.12.2,
00:00:30,FastEthernet0/0
```

You can verify it by looking at the routing table, the external networks on router Jack now have an AD of 160.

We can change the AD of the other routing protocols as well, here are some examples:

```
Router(config)#router ospf 1
Router(config-router)#distance ospf external 150 inter-area 80
intra-area 80
```

For OSPF you can change the external, inter-area and intra-area administrative distance. In my example I've set the external distance (type 5 and 7 external LSAs) to 150. Inter-area distance is 80 and intra-area is 80. This means that your router will now prefer OSPF information above EIGRP (AD 90).

It's also possible to change the administrative distance only for certain prefixes, let me show you how:

```
James(config)#router rip
James(config-router)#distance 70 0.0.0.0 255.255.255.255
MY_PREFIXES

James(config)#ip access-list standard MY_PREFIXES
James(config-std-nacl)#permit 1.1.1.0 0.0.0.255
```

I use the distance command and combine it with a standard access-list called "MY_PREFIXES".

All networks that match this access-list will have their AD changed to 70.

```
James#show ip route rip
R    192.168.12.0/24 [120/10] via 192.168.23.2, 00:00:15,
FastEthernet0/0
     1.0.0.0/24 is subnetted, 1 subnets
R        1.1.1.0 [70/10] via 192.168.23.2, 00:00:15,
FastEthernet0/0
```

Above you see the new administrative distance for network 1.1.1.0 /24.

Changing the administrative distance might sound like fun and all that but maybe you are wondering why we would do this? Changing the administrative distance can help us to solve redistribution problems. In the following example I'm going to show you why:

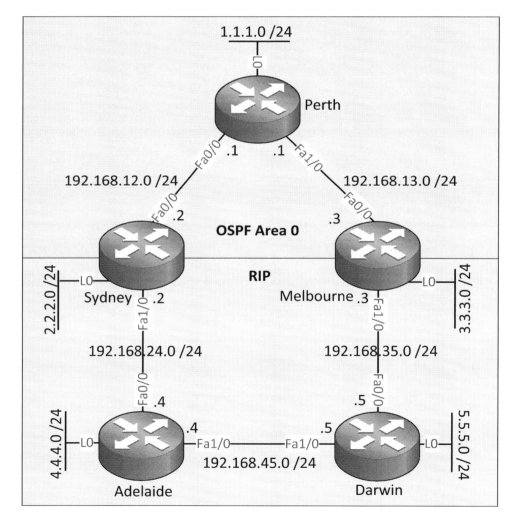

Look at my network above. Router Perth, Sydney and Melbourne are running OSPF. We also have RIP running on router Sydney, Adelaide, Melbourne and Darwin. I have configured two-way multipoint redistribution. Router Sydney and Melbourne are both redistributing between OSPF and RIP.

Do we have any problems with this network? Let's find out.

```
Sydney#traceroute 4.4.4.4

Type escape sequence to abort.
Tracing the route to 4.4.4.4

  1 192.168.12.1 4 msec 4 msec 4 msec
  2 192.168.13.3 8 msec 12 msec 8 msec
  3 192.168.35.5 12 msec 12 msec 12 msec
  4 192.168.45.4 12 msec *   8 msec
```

I'm doing a traceroute from router Sydney to 4.4.4.4 which is the loopback interface of router Adelaide. My IP packets are sent from router Sydney to Perth, Melbourne, Darwin and then arriving at Adelaide.

Doesn't look very efficient right? That's **sub-optimal routing**...

```
Sydney#show ip route | include 4.4.4.0
O E1    4.4.4.0 [110/10002] via 192.168.12.1, 00:26:57,
FastEthernet0/0
```

You can see router Sydney is using OSPF information to reach network 4.4.4.0 /24.

Why does this problem occur?

1. Router Melbourne has learned 4.4.4.0 /24 from RIP.
2. Router Melbourne is redistributing RIP information into OSPF including the 4.4.4.0 /24 network.
3. Router Sydney learns about 4.4.4.0 /24 through router Perth with OSPF.
4. OSPF has a lower administrative distance (110) compared to RIP (120).
5. Router Sydney will remove its RIP routing information for network 4.4.4.0 /24 and insert the OSPF information.
6. We now have sub-optimal routing.

The problem we are facing is that OSPF has a lower (better) administrative distance than RIP. In order to solve this problem we need to make sure that router Sydney is using RIP information for network 4.4.4.0 /24 instead of OSPF information.

How can we do this? By changing the administrative distance! I need to make sure that all the "native" RIP networks have a better administrative distance than OSPF. If I do this then RIP information will show up in the routing table instead of OSPF.

```
Sydney(config)#access-list 1 permit 192.168.24.0 0.0.0.255
Sydney(config)#access-list 1 permit 192.168.45.0 0.0.0.255
Sydney(config)#access-list 1 permit 192.168.35.0 0.0.0.255
Sydney(config)#access-list 1 permit 4.4.4.0 0.0.0.255
Sydney(config)#access-list 1 permit 5.5.5.0 0.0.0.255
Sydney(config)#access-list 1 permit 2.2.2.0 0.0.0.255
Sydney(config)#access-list 1 permit 3.3.3.0 0.0.0.255
```

First I need to create an access-list which matches all the native RIP networks. I'm using access-list 1.

```
Sydney(config)#router ospf 1
Sydney(config-router)#distance 125 0.0.0.0 255.255.255.255 1
```

Next step is to change the administrative distance. I'm changing it to 125 for all networks (0.0.0.0 255.255.255.255) but it has to match access-list 1. This effectively sets the administrative distance to 125 for all the native RIP networks.

```
Sydney#show ip route | include 4.4.4.0
R        4.4.4.0 [120/1] via 192.168.24.4, 00:00:17,
FastEthernet1/0
```

If we look at the routing table of router Sydney you can see that we are using RIP information to reach network 4.4.4.0 /24. This is because the administrative distance of RIP is 120 which is better than 125 that I've configured for the redistributed networks.

```
Sydney#traceroute 4.4.4.4

Type escape sequence to abort.
Tracing the route to 4.4.4.4

  1 192.168.24.4 4 msec *  4 msec
```

Awesome! No more sub-optimal routing. I just solved this problem by manipulating the administrative distance.

Of course you need to do the exact same thing on router Melbourne since it has the same problem as router Sydney:

```
Melbourne#traceroute 5.5.5.5

Type escape sequence to abort.
Tracing the route to 5.5.5.5

  1 192.168.13.1 4 msec 4 msec 4 msec
  2 192.168.12.2 8 msec 4 msec 12 msec
  3 192.168.24.4 16 msec 12 msec 12 msec
  4 192.168.45.5 8 msec *  8 msec
```

If I try to reach the loopback0 interface of router Darwin from Melbourne it'll go up to Perth first.

```
Melbourne#show ip route | include 5.5.5.0
O E1    5.5.5.0 [110/10002] via 192.168.13.1, 00:02:49,
FastEthernet0/0
```

You can see it's using the OSPF information. Let's use the same configuration that we used on router Sydney.

```
Melbourne(config)#access-list 1 permit 192.168.24.0 0.0.0.255
Melbourne(config)#access-list 1 permit 192.168.45.0 0.0.0.255
Melbourne(config)#access-list 1 permit 192.168.35.0 0.0.0.255
Melbourne(config)#access-list 1 permit 4.4.4.0 0.0.0.255
Melbourne(config)#access-list 1 permit 5.5.5.0 0.0.0.255
Melbourne(config)#access-list 1 permit 2.2.2.0 0.0.0.255
Melbourne(config)#access-list 1 permit 3.3.3.0 0.0.0.255

Melbourne(config)#router ospf 1
Melbourne(config-router)#distance 125 0.0.0.0 255.255.255.255 1
```

Use an access-list to "select" all the native RIP routes and then change the AD to 125.

```
Melbourne#traceroute 5.5.5.5

Type escape sequence to abort.
Tracing the route to 5.5.5.5

  1 192.168.35.5 4 msec *  0 msec
```

Now it's using the direct path to router Darwin.

```
Melbourne#show ip route | include 5.5.5.0
R       5.5.5.0 [120/1] via 192.168.35.5, 00:00:07,
FastEthernet1/0
```

As you can see above in the routing table...are we done now? I'm afraid not, let me show you:

```
Perth#show ip route ospf
     2.0.0.0/24 is subnetted, 1 subnets
O E1    2.2.2.0 [110/10001] via 192.168.13.3, 00:22:36,
FastEthernet1/0
                [110/10001] via 192.168.12.2, 00:22:36,
FastEthernet0/0
     3.0.0.0/24 is subnetted, 1 subnets
O E1    3.3.3.0 [110/10001] via 192.168.13.3, 00:28:21,
FastEthernet1/0
                [110/10001] via 192.168.12.2, 00:28:21,
FastEthernet0/0
O E1 192.168.45.0/24 [110/10001] via 192.168.13.3,
00:22:36,FastEthernet1/0
                [110/10001] via 192.168.12.2,
00:22:36,FastEthernet0/0
     4.0.0.0/24 is subnetted, 1 subnets
O E1    4.4.4.0 [110/10001] via 192.168.13.3, 00:22:36,
FastEthernet1/0
                [110/10001] via 192.168.12.2, 00:22:36,
FastEthernet0/0
O E1 192.168.24.0/24 [110/10001] via 192.168.13.3,
00:22:36,FastEthernet1/0
                [110/10001] via 192.168.12.2,
00:22:36,FastEthernet0/0
     5.0.0.0/24 is subnetted, 1 subnets
O E1    5.5.5.0 [110/10001] via 192.168.13.3, 00:22:36,
FastEthernet1/0
                [110/10001] via 192.168.12.2, 00:22:36,
FastEthernet0/0
O E1 192.168.35.0/24 [110/10001] via 192.168.13.3,
00:28:21,FastEthernet1/0
                [110/10001] via 192.168.12.2,
00:28:21,FastEthernet0/0
```

Take a look at the networks that I highlighted. The metric is the same so OSPF will load balance if it wants to reach those networks...that's not good:

- 2.2.2.0/24 is the loopback0 interface of router Sydney so going through Melbourne to get there is sub-optimal routing.
- 3.3.3.0/24 is the loopback0 interface of router Melbourne so going through Sydney to get there is sub-optimal routing.
- 4.4.4.0/24 is the loopback0 interface of router Adelaide so going through Melbourne is sub-optimal routing.
- 192.168.24.0/24 is the link between Sydney and Adelaide so going through Melbourne is sub-optimal routing.
- 5.5.5.0/24 is the loopback0 interface of router Darwin so going through Sydney is sub-optimal routing.

- 192.168.35.0/24 is the link between Melbourne and Darwin so going through Sydney is sub-optimal routing.

This is happening because router Sydney and Melbourne are using the **same metric** to redistribute information from RIP into OSPF. As a result router Perth will load balance. All networks have a cost of 10001. If we want to fix this, we'll have to play with the metrics! Let me show you how:

```
Sydney#show run | section ospf
router ospf 1
 log-adjacency-changes
 redistribute rip metric 10000 metric-type 1 subnets
 network 192.168.12.0 0.0.0.255 area 0
 distance 125 0.0.0.0 255.255.255.255 1
 redistribute ospf 1 metric 5
```

Instead of "just redistributing RIP into OSPF" I'm going to create an exception by using a route-map called "CHANGE_METRIC". Everything that matches my route-map will have a cost of 500.

```
Sydney(config)#route-map METRIC permit 10
Sydney(config-route-map)#match ip address prefix-list OPTIMAL
Sydney(config-route-map)#set metric 500
Sydney(config-route-map)#exit
Sydney(config)#route-map METRIC permit 20
```

The route-map has sequence number 10 and tells that everything that matches prefix-list "OPTIMAL" will have a cost of 500. Sequence number 20 is empty and matches on everything else. If you don't add sequence number 20 then only the networks that **match the prefix-list will be redistributed and nothing else**.

```
Sydney(config)#ip prefix-list OPTIMAL permit 2.2.2.0/24
Sydney(config)#ip prefix-list OPTIMAL permit 4.4.4.0/24
Sydney(config)#ip prefix-list OPTIMAL permit 192.168.24.0/24
```

In the prefix-list I'll match the following networks:

- 2.2.2.0/24 which is the loopback0 interface of router Sydney.
- 4.4.4.0/24 which is the loopback0 interface of router Adelaide.
- 192.168.24.0/24 which is the link between router Sydney and Adelaide.

```
Sydney(config)#router ospf 1
Sydney(config-router)#redistribute rip metric 10000 metric-type
1 subnets route-map METRIC
```

Don't forget to activate the route-map for the redistribution.

```
Perth#show ip route ospf
     2.0.0.0/24 is subnetted, 1 subnets
O E1    2.2.2.0 [110/501] via 192.168.12.2, 00:00:03,
FastEthernet0/0
     3.0.0.0/24 is subnetted, 1 subnets
O E1    3.3.3.0 [110/10001] via 192.168.13.3, 00:00:03,
FastEthernet1/0
               [110/10001] via 192.168.12.2, 00:00:03,
FastEthernet0/0
O E1 192.168.45.0/24 [110/10001] via 192.168.13.3,
00:00:03,FastEthernet1/0
               [110/10001] via 192.168.12.2,
00:00:03,FastEthernet0/0
     4.0.0.0/24 is subnetted, 1 subnets
O E1    4.4.4.0 [110/501] via 192.168.12.2, 00:00:03,
FastEthernet0/0
O E1 192.168.24.0/24 [110/501] via 192.168.12.2, 00:00:03,
FastEthernet0/0
     5.0.0.0/24 is subnetted, 1 subnets
O E1    5.5.5.0 [110/10001] via 192.168.13.3, 00:00:03,
FastEthernet1/0
               [110/10001] via 192.168.12.2, 00:00:03,
FastEthernet0/0
O E1 192.168.35.0/24 [110/10001] via 192.168.13.3,
00:00:03,FastEthernet1/0
               [110/10001] via 192.168.12.2,
00:00:03,FastEthernet0/0
```

Take a look at the highlighted networks above. You can see the cost has been changed to 500 for those networks, router Perth will send all traffic for these networks to router Sydney. Now let's implement the same route-map on router Melbourne:

```
Melbourne(config)#route-map METRIC permit 10
Melbourne(config-route-map)#match ip address prefix-list OPTIMAL
Melbourne(config-route-map)#set metric 500
Melbourne(config-route-map)#exit
Melbourne(config)#route-map METRIC permit 20
```

First I'll create the route-map.

```
Melbourne(config)#ip prefix-list OPTIMAL permit 3.3.3.0/24
Melbourne(config)#ip prefix-list OPTIMAL permit 5.5.5.0/24
Melbourne(config)#ip prefix-list OPTIMAL permit 192.168.35.0/24
```

In the prefix-list I'll match the following networks:

- 3.3.3.0/24 which is the loopback0 interface of router Melbourne.
- 5.5.5.0/24 which is the loopback0 interface of router Darwin.
- 192.168.35.0/24 which is the link between router Melbourne and Darwin.

```
Melbourne(config)#router ospf 1
Melbourne(config-router)#redistribute rip metric 10000 metric-
type 1 subnets route-map METRIC
```

And we'll activate the route-map!

```
Perth#show ip route ospf
      2.0.0.0/24 is subnetted, 1 subnets
O E1    2.2.2.0 [110/501] via 192.168.12.2, 00:06:30,
FastEthernet0/0
      3.0.0.0/24 is subnetted, 1 subnets
O E1    3.3.3.0 [110/501] via 192.168.13.3, 00:00:22,
FastEthernet1/0
O E1 192.168.45.0/24 [110/10001] via 192.168.13.3, 00:06:30,
FastEthernet1/0
                  [110/10001] via 192.168.12.2, 00:06:30,
FastEthernet0/0
      4.0.0.0/24 is subnetted, 1 subnets
O E1    4.4.4.0 [110/501] via 192.168.12.2, 00:06:30,
FastEthernet0/0
O E1 192.168.24.0/24 [110/501] via 192.168.12.2, 00:06:30,
FastEthernet0/0
      5.0.0.0/24 is subnetted, 1 subnets
O E1    5.5.5.0 [110/501] via 192.168.13.3, 00:00:22,
FastEthernet1/0
O E1 192.168.35.0/24 [110/501] via 192.168.13.3, 00:00:22,
FastEthernet1/0
```

As you can see it's now working. The only network that router Perth will still reach by load-balancing is 192.168.45.0/24 which is the link between router Adelaide and Darwin.

Are you following me here? I understand if this makes your head *spin*...redistribution is really one of the toughest topics to master. You have learned quite some things now however:

- Redistribution
- Solving sub-optimal routing by changing the administrative distance.
- Solving sub-optimal routing by changing the metric.

If you want to see this example on real routers you can try my redistribution lab. It's the exact same topology I just explained to you...you can also watch the video where I walk you through the solution:

http://gns3vault.com/Troubleshooting/ospf-rip-redistribution-ad-troubleshooting.html

Anything else we have to think about when configuring redistribution? There's something else I'd like to show you:

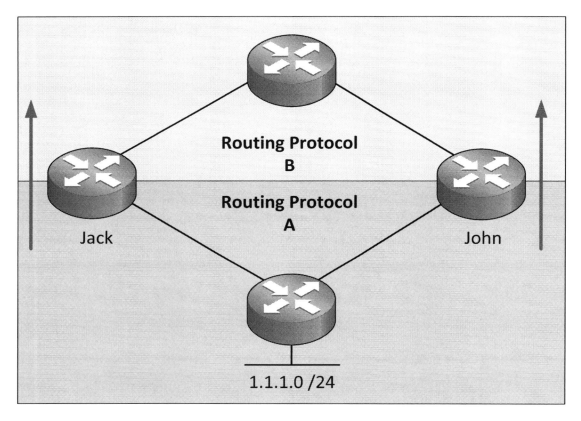

I have a bunch of routers and I am running two routing protocols. Router Jack and John are configured for redistribution so we have two-way multipoint redistribution. At the bottom there is a 1.1.1.0 /24 network. This is what will happen:

1. Network 1.1.1.0 /24 will be redistributed by router Jack from routing protocol A into B.
2. Router John will learn about network 1.1.1.0 /24 from routing Protocol B and redistribute it back into routing protocol A.

Of course it works the other way around as well. Router John is redistributing network 1.1.1.0 /24 into routing protocol B and router Jack is redistributing it back into routing protocol A.

Or to keep things simple: A → B → A

Redistributing networks back into the routing protocol where they originate from is asking for trouble and can cause routing loops.

Never redistribute routing information back into the routing protocol where it originates from.

I put it in bold so you won't forget it.
A very effective method to make sure this doesn't happen is using **route tagging**.

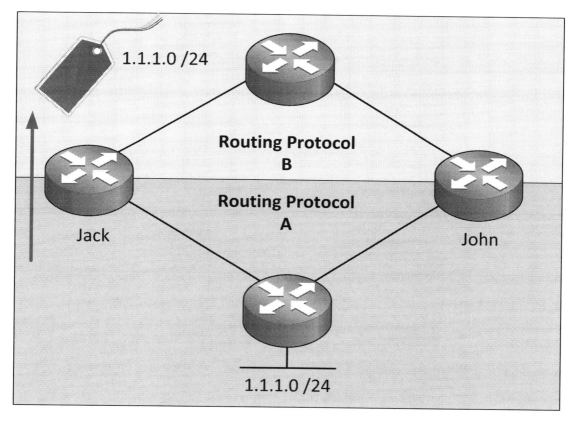

When router Jack redistributes network 1.1.1.0 /24 into routing protocol B it should **tag** it. When router John is going to redistribute routing information from routing protocol B into routing protocol A it will **notice the tag and skip** network 1.1.1.0 /24.

Of course the same thing applies to router John.

I'm only showing you the example for router Jack.

```
Jack#show ip route 1.1.1.0
Routing entry for 1.1.1.0/24
  Known via "ospf 1", distance 110, metric 20, type extern 2,
forward metric 2
  Last update from 192.168.12.2 on FastEthernet0/0, 00:00:04 ago
  Routing Descriptor Blocks:
  * 192.168.12.2, from 192.168.45.4, 00:00:04 ago, via
FastEthernet0/0
        Route metric is 20, traffic share count is 1
```

You can use **show ip route** <network> to check if a route has been tagged or not. Nothing has been tagged so far.

```
Jack(config)#route-map TAG deny 10
Jack(config-route-map)#match tag 1
Jack(config-route-map)#exit
Jack(config)#route-map TAG permit 20
Jack(config-route-map)#set tag 1
```

You can tag routes using a route-map. I created a simple route-map called TAG with two sequence numbers:
- Sequence number 10 says that when it matches tag number 1 that it should be denied.
- Sequence number 20 says that we need to set tag number 1. There's no "match" statement so EVERYTHING will match.

```
Jack(config)#router rip
Jack(config-router)#redistribute ospf 1 metric 5 route-map TAG
```

```
Jack(config)#router ospf 1
Jack(config-router)#redistribute rip subnets route-map TAG
```

Now I need to make sure we use the route-map when redistributing. The example above is for redistributing into RIP and OSPF. At the end of your redistribution command you need to specify the route-map. Everything that is redistributed INTO RIP or OSPF will have a tag of 1.

Once again I'm only showing router Jack but you need to do this on router John as well.

```
John#show ip route 1.1.1.0
Routing entry for 1.1.1.0/24
  Known via "ospf 1", distance 110, metric 20
  Tag 1, type extern 2, forward metric 3
  Redistributing via rip
  Last update from 192.168.13.1 on FastEthernet0/0, 00:00:25 ago
  Routing Descriptor Blocks:
  * 192.168.13.1, from 192.168.45.4, 00:00:25 ago, via
FastEthernet0/0
      Route metric is 20, traffic share count is 1
      Route tag 1
```

If you look at this network you can now see that it has been tagged.
This is because of the second part of our route-map:

```
route-map TAG permit 20
  set tag 1
```

Above you see the part of the route-map that did this tagging for us.

```
route-map TAG deny 10
  match tag 1
```

And this is the part of the route-map that prevents it from redistributing it again.

In other words…if your router sees something that has been tagged it will not be redistributed, otherwise it will be redistributed and a tag will be set.

This is a very simple solution to make sure you don't inject routing information back into the routing protocol where it originated from.

You have to do this on **each router** when you use multipoint redistribution!

So now you know how you can use administrative distance, playing with metrics and using route tags to solve redistribution problems.

You just made it to the end of the redistribution chapter. If you understand everything after reading this for the first time…congratulations! If you want some more practice for redistribution you can try the following labs:

http://gns3vault.com/Table/Redistribution/

I have one lab which is *way above* CCNP level for redistribution (it's for CCIE actually) but if you want an example of how complex redistribution can get this might be fun to try:

http://gns3vault.com/Redistribution/expert-redistribution.html

18. Introduction to BGP (Border Gateway Protocol)

This chapter will be interesting! **BGP (Border Gateway Protocol)** is the routing protocol that glues the Internet together. I'm going to explain in which situations we need BGP and how it works. Before you continue reading I should tell you to forget everything you know about routing protocols so far...you have learned about OSPF and EIGRP in this book and RIP was on the CCNA. Those routing protocols have one thing in common since they are all **IGPs (Interior Gateway Protocols)**. We only use them within our autonomous system but they are not scalable to use for something as large as the Internet.

RIP, OSPF and EIGRP are all different but they have one thing in common...they want to find the shortest path to the destination. When we look at the Internet we don't care as much as to find the shortest path, being able to manipulate traffic paths is far more important. There is only one routing protocol we currently use on the Internet which is BGP.

Let's start by looking at some scenarios and see why we need BGP.

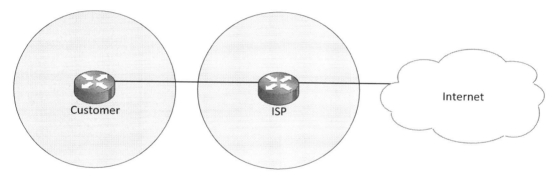

Nowadays about everyone is connected to the Internet. In the picture above we have a customer network connected to an ISP (Internet Service Provider). Our ISP is making sure we have Internet access. Our ISP has given us a single public IP address we can use to access the Internet. To make sure everyone on our LAN at the customer side can access the Internet we are using NAT/PAT (Network / Port address translation) to translate our internal private IP addresses to this single public IP address. This scenario is excellent when you only have clients that need Internet access. On our customer LAN we only need a default route pointing to the ISP router and we are done.

259

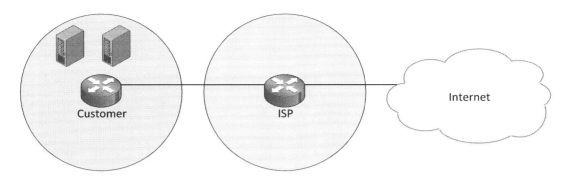

Maybe the customer has a couple of servers that need to be reachable from the Internet...perhaps a mail- or webserver. We could use port forwarding and forward the correct ports to these servers so we still only need a single IP address. Another option would be to get more public IP addresses from our ISP and use these to configure the different servers.

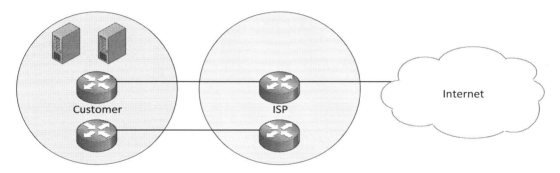

What if I want a bit more redundancy? Having a single point of failure isn't a good idea. We could add another router at the customer side and connect it to the ISP. You can use the primary link for all traffic and have another link as the backup. We still don't need BGP in this situation:

- Advertise a default route in your IGP on the primary customer router with a low metric.
- Advertise a default route in your IGP on the secondary customer router with a high metric.

This will make sure that your IGP sends all traffic to the primary link. Once the link fails your IGP will make sure all traffic is sent down the backup link. Let me ask you something to think about...can we do any load balancing across those two links? It'll be difficult right?

Your IGP will send all traffic down the primary link and nothing down the backup link unless there is a failure. You could advertise a default route with the same metric but you'd still have something like a 50/50% load share. What if I wanted to send 80% of the outgoing traffic on the primary link and 20% down the backup link? Hold the 'load share' thought for a moment...

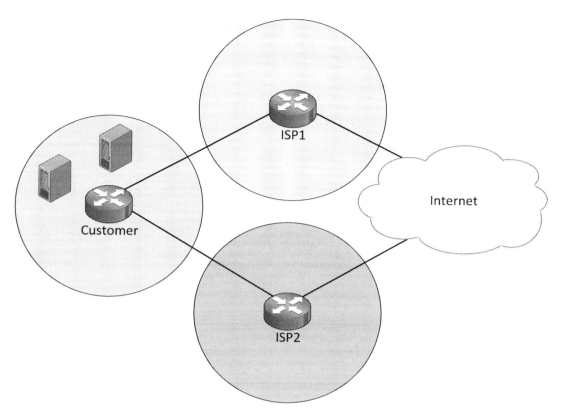

This scenario is a bit more interesting. Instead of being connected to a single ISP we now have 2 different ISPs. There's a small chance that both ISPs have connectivity issues so this setup is nice to have. What about our Customer network? We still have those 2 servers that need to be reachable from the Internet. In my previous examples we got public IP addresses from our ISP. Now I'm connected to two different ISPs so what public IP addresses should I use? From ISP1 or ISP2?

We are not going to use public IP addresses from any ISP but we'll get some public IP address space of our own from IANA (Internet Assigned Numbers Authority - http://www.iana.org/). IANA is assigning IP address space to a number of large Regional Internet Registries like RIPE (http://www.ripe.net/) or ARIN (https://www.arin.net/).

This public IP address space we are going to advertise to both our ISPs using a routing protocol...and yes, that's BGP.

If you are interested here's an overview of the IPv4 space that has been allocated by IANA:

http://www.iana.org/assignments/ipv4-address-space/ipv4-address-space.xml

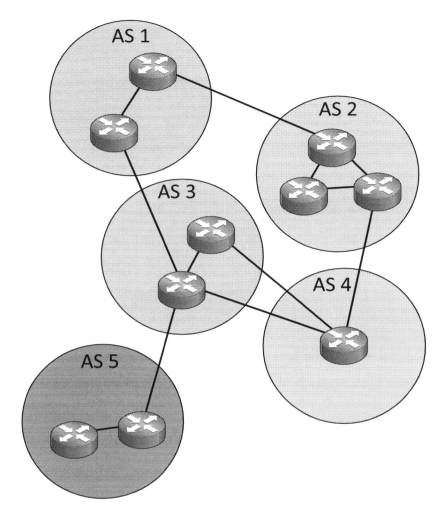

If you studied CCNA you should be familiar with the concept of an **AS (Autonomous System).** An AS is a collection of networks under a single administrative domain. The Internet is nothing more but a bunch of autonomous systems that are connected to each other. Within an autonomous system we use an IGP like OSPF or EIGRP...nobody uses RIP nowadays. For routing between the different autonomous systems we use an **EGP (external gateway protocol).** The only EGP we use nowadays is BGP.

How do we get an autonomous system number? Just like public IP address space you'll need to register one.

Autonomous system numbers are 16-bit which means we have AS 1 up to 65535. There's also a private range (64512 – 65535) you can use for non-internet usage. Since January 2009 we can also use 32-bit numbers for autonomous systems.

BGP has two flavors:

- External BGP: between autonomous systems
- Internal BGP: within the autonomous system.

External BGP is to exchange routing information between the different autonomous systems. I'll explain later why we need Internal BGP!

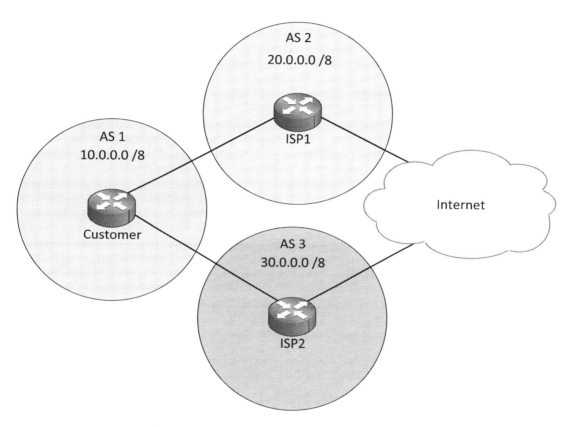

Our customer network has an autonomous system number (AS 1) and some public IP address space (10.0.0.0 /8). We are connected to two different ISPs and you can see their AS number and IP address space as well. We can reach the internet through both ISPs. What are the ISPS going to advertise to our customer network through BGP? There are a number of options:

- They advertise only a default route.
- They advertise a default route and a partial routing table.
- They advertise a full Internet routing table.

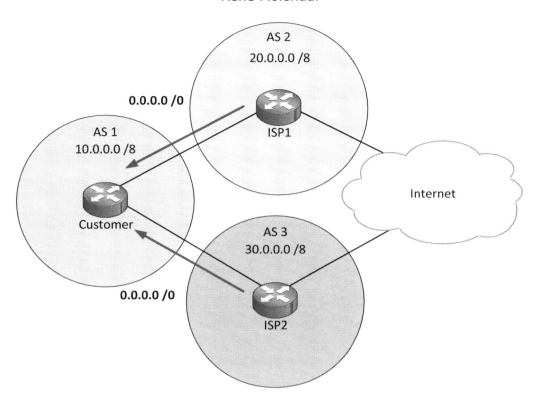

Receiving a default route requires the fewest resources on your routers since you only have a single entry to reach any external network. The customer router will advertise its 10.0.0.0 /8 network to both ISPs which will advertise it to any other AS they are connected to. The downside of this configuration is that our customer network doesn't know what is behind ISP1 and ISP2. We have connectivity because of the default routes but this can lead to sub-optimal routing. If we only have the default routes then we will send all traffic to one of the ISPs.

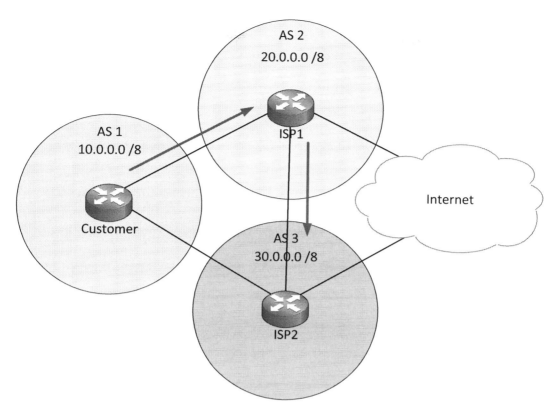

Here's what could happen if you only receive a default route from both ISPs. Our customer network only received a default route from both ISPs and we have chosen to use the default route of ISP1 to send all our outgoing traffic to. This means that whenever we send traffic meant for 30.0.0.0 /8 (ISP2) it's going to be sent to ISP1 and then to ISP2. It's not a problem but it's not optimal.

We can also receive a partial routing table along a default route. This partial update might include all the IP address space that the ISPs have assigned to their customers. Just like in real life...the more you know the better off you are. In the world of routing having more routing information means you can make better routing decisions. We'll have less sub-optimal routing problems than when we only have the default route.

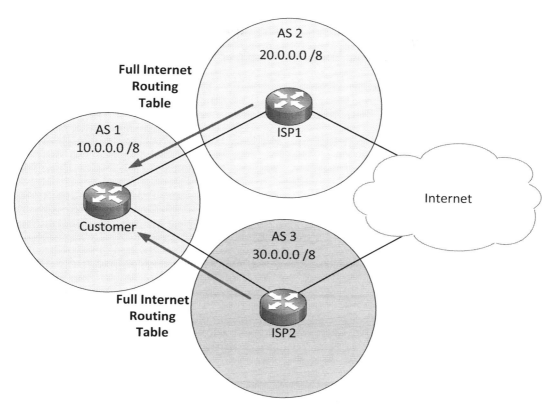

The last option that we have is that we receive the full internet routing table from both ISPs. This requires more resources but we'll be able to make the best routing decisions. In case you are wondering how large a full Internet routing table would be...you can find it online:

http://www.cidr-report.org/as2.0/

There are more than 350.000 prefixes in a full Internet routing table. This of course requires more memory and CPU power to maintain!

On the internet there are a number of looking glass servers. These are routers that have public view access and you can use them to look at the Internet routing table. If you want to see what it looks like check out:

http://www.bgp4.as/looking-glasses

Scroll down all the way to "Category 2 - IPv4 and IPv6 BGP Route Servers by region (TELNET access)". You can telnet to these devices and use **show ip route** and **show ip bgp** to check the BGP or routing table.

BGP is the routing protocol we use to route between autonomous systems:

- BGP guarantees loop-free routing information.
- BGP is completely different than IGPs.
- BGP is a **path-vector** routing protocol.
- BGP doesn't use metrics but a rich set of **BGP attributes**.

All our IGPS have in common that they want to find the fastest path to the destination. When routing between autonomous systems we don't care about the fastest path but it's more important that we are able to influence the path. BGP is also called a **policy-based** routing protocol. Influencing traffic with BGP is very easy to do.

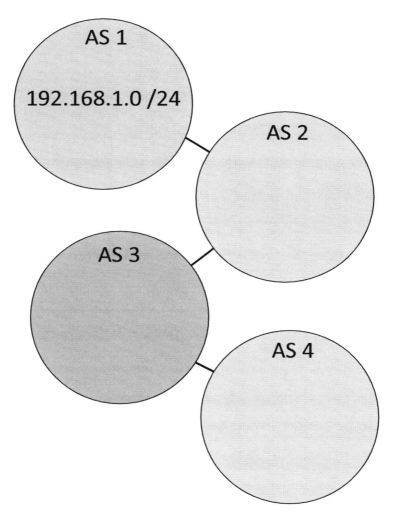

Why do we call BGP a **path-vector** routing protocol?

Look at the image above. We have 4 autonomous systems and we are running

BGP to exchange routing information.

In AS 1 we have network 192.168.1.0 /24 and this is advertised to AS 2, AS 3 and AS 4.

If we look at a BGP router in AS4 we will see network 192.168.1.0 /24 but it also stores the **path** we have to get through in order to get there. You will see that we have to get through AS 3, AS2 to get to AS 1.
This is of course different than any IGP...RIP, OSPF or EIGRP only show the next-hop IP address.

Let's look at a real BGP router so I can show you what I mean:

```
route-views.optus.net.au>show ip bgp
BGP table version is 128380331, local router ID is 203.202.125.6
Status codes: s suppressed, d damped, h history, * valid, >
best, i - internal,
           r RIB-failure, S Stale, m multipath, b backup-
path, x best-external
Origin codes: i - IGP, e - EGP, ? - incomplete

   Network          Next Hop            Metric LocPrf Weight
Path
*  1.0.0.0/24       202.160.242.71                          0
7473 15169 i
```

I used telnet to login at route-views.optus.net.au which I found at bgp4.as. This is one of the looking glass servers.

By using the **show ip bgp** command I can look at the BGP table and we see this router knows about network 1.0.0.0 /24. The next-hop IP address is 202.160.242.71. At the end of the line you see **path** with the numbers 7473 15169. These are the autonomous systems we have to get through in order to get to this network.

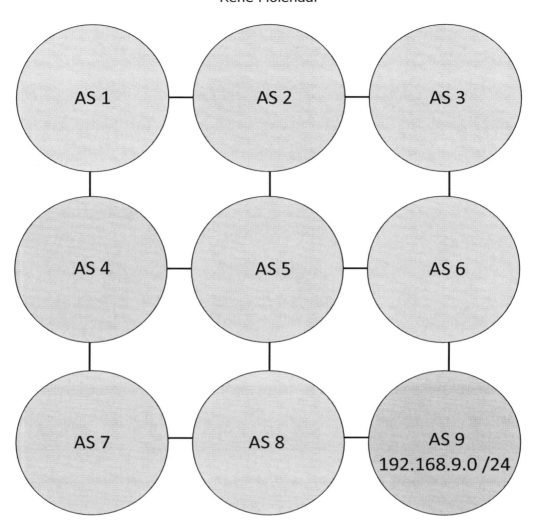

BGP allows us to use routing policies at the autonomous system level. In the picture above I have 9 autonomous systems and in AS 9 we have network 192.168.9.0 /24. If we look at AS 1 then we have a lot of different paths we can take to reach network 192.168.9.0 /24 in AS 9.

Does this mean the network administrator at AS 1 can choose the path we are going to use? Not really because of the following reasons:

- You can choose the **exit path**...so you can send your traffic to AS 2 or AS4 but you don't make routing decisions for other autonomous systems.
- Each autonomous system will only advertise the **best path** to your autonomous system. AS 1 will only learn about the **best path** from AS 2 and AS 4 unless their best path fails...only then you will learn about the second best path.

So far so good? The next part of this chapter will be fun. I'm going to explain you BGP while showing you how to configure everything!

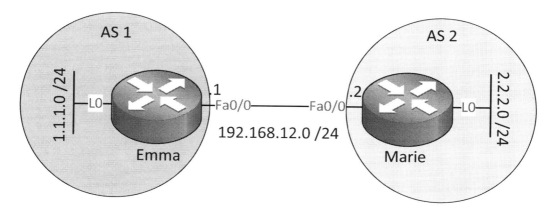

Let's start with a simple topology. Just two routers and two autonomous systems. Each router has a network on a loopback interface which we are going to advertise in BGP.

```
Emma(config)#router bgp 1
Emma(config-router)#neighbor 192.168.12.2 remote-as 2
```

```
Marie(config)#router bgp 2
Marie(config-router)#neighbor 192.168.12.1 remote-as 1
```

Use the **router bgp** command with the AS number to start BGP. Neighbors are not configured automatically this is something you'll have to do yourself with the **neighbor x.x.x.x remote-as** command. This is how we configure **external BGP.**

BGP uses **TCP port 179** to establish a neighbor adjacency.

```
Emma# %BGP-5-ADJCHANGE: neighbor 192.168.12.2 Up
```

```
Marie# %BGP-5-ADJCHANGE: neighbor 192.168.12.1 Up
```

If everything goes ok you should see a message that we have a new BGP neighbor adjacency. Behind the scenes BGP goes through a series of states when it tries to connect with another neighbor. Here's what happens:

1. Once you configure the neighbor IP address, BGP tries to reach that neighbor on destination TCP port 179.
2. When the TCP three-way handshake completes, BGP will send an **open message**. This message is similar to the hello packet that EIGRP and OSPF use.

3. When the open message has been sent and received and all other parameters match (like authentication) then the neighbors will reach the **established state**.

Here are all the BGP states that we have:

- Idle: BGP process has been shutdown or it is waiting for the next retry.
- Connect: BGP is waiting for the TCP connection to complete.
- Active: TCP connection is ready but no BGP messages have been sent yet.
- Opensent: Open message has been sent but we didn't receive one yet from the neighbor.
- Openconfirm: Open message has been sent and received from the other side.
- Established: All parameters match, we have a working BGP peering and we can exchange update messages with routing information.

```
Emma(config)#router bgp 1
Emma(config-router)#neighbor 192.168.12.2 password MYPASS
```

```
Marie(config)#router bgp 2
Marie(config-router)#neighbor 192.168.12.1 password MYPASS
```

If you like you can enable MD5 authentication by using the **neighbor password** command. Your router will calculate a MD5 digest of every TCP segment that is being sent.

```
Emma#show ip bgp summary
BGP router identifier 1.1.1.1, local AS number 1
BGP table version is 1, main routing table version 1

Neighbor        V     AS MsgRcvd MsgSent    TblVer   InQ OutQ Up/Down
State/PfxRcd
192.168.12.2 4     2       10        10         1     0    0 00:07:12
0
```

```
Marie#show ip bgp summary
BGP router identifier 2.2.2.2, local AS number 2
BGP table version is 1, main routing table version 1

Neighbor        V     AS MsgRcvd MsgSent    TblVer   InQ OutQ Up/Down
State/PfxRcd
192.168.12.1 4     1       11        11         1     0    0 00:08:33
0
```

Show ip bgp summary is an excellent command to check if you have BGP neighbors. You also see how many prefixes you received from each neighbor.

```
Emma(config)#router bgp 1
Emma(config-router)#network 1.1.1.0 mask 255.255.255.0
```

```
Marie(config)#router bgp 2
Marie(config-router)#network 2.2.2.0 mask 255.255.255.0
```

Let's advertise the loopback interface by using the **network** command. If you want to advertise something with BGP you need to make sure you type the **exact subnet mask** for the network you want to advertise. If I would type network 1.0.0.0 mask 255.0.0.0 on router Emma it will not work since this entry is not in the routing table.

```
Emma#show ip bgp
BGP table version is 3, local router ID is 1.1.1.1
Status codes: s suppressed, d damped, h history, * valid, >
best, i - internal,
            r RIB-failure, S Stale
Origin codes: i - IGP, e - EGP, ? - incomplete

   Network          Next Hop            Metric LocPrf Weight
Path
*> 1.1.1.0/24       0.0.0.0                  0           32768 i
*> 2.2.2.0/24       192.168.12.2             0               0 2 i
```

Use **show ip bgp** to look at the **BGP database**. You can see that router Emma has learned about network 2.2.2.0 /24 and the next hop IP address is 192.168.12.2. It also shows the **path** information. You can see that network 2.2.2.0 /24 is from AS 2.

```
Marie#show ip bgp
BGP table version is 3, local router ID is 2.2.2.2
Status codes: s suppressed, d damped, h history, * valid, >
best, i - internal,
            r RIB-failure, S Stale
Origin codes: i - IGP, e - EGP, ? - incomplete

   Network          Next Hop            Metric LocPrf Weight
Path
*> 1.1.1.0/24       192.168.12.1             0               0 1 i
*> 2.2.2.0/24       0.0.0.0                  0           32768 i
```

Router Marie learned about network 1.1.1.0/24 with a next hop IP address of 192.168.12.1.

```
Emma#show ip route bgp
     2.0.0.0/24 is subnetted, 1 subnets
B        2.2.2.0 [20/0] via 192.168.12.2, 00:16:13
```

```
Marie#show ip route bgp
     1.0.0.0/24 is subnetted, 1 subnets
B        1.1.1.0 [20/0] via 192.168.12.1, 00:16:59
```

In the routing table we can find an entry for BGP with an administrative distance of 20 for **external BGP**. So far so good?

In the example I just showed you router Emma and Marie used the IP addresses on their directly connected interface to establish the external BGP neighbor adjacency. It's also possible to use another interface to source the BGP updates from, let me show you how:

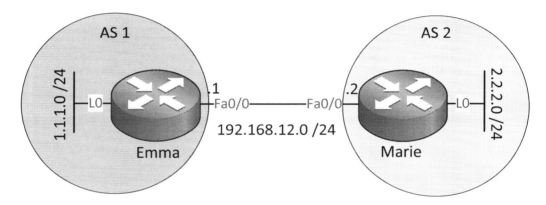

We will use the same two routers, but this time I want to establish the external BGP neighbor adjacency between the loopback0 interfaces:

```
Emma(config)#ip route 2.2.2.2 255.255.255.255 192.168.12.2
```

```
Marie(config)#ip route 1.1.1.1 255.255.255.255 192.168.12.1
```

I will use two static routes so that route Emma and Marie can reach each others loopback interface, now we can configure external BGP:

```
Emma(config)#router bgp 1
Emma(config-router)#neighbor 2.2.2.2 remote-as 2
Emma(config-router)#neighbor 2.2.2.2 update-source loopback 0
```

```
Marie(config)#router bgp 2
Marie(config-router)#neighbor 1.1.1.1 remote-as 1
Marie(config-router)#neighbor 1.1.1.1 update-source loopback 0
```

We will specify the IP addresses on the loopback interfaces as the BGP neighbor. We also have to use the **update-source** command to tell BGP to source its updates from the loopback0 interface. Let's see if this works:

```
Emma#show ip bgp summary
BGP router identifier 1.1.1.1, local AS number 1
BGP table version is 1, main routing table version 1

Neighbor        V     AS MsgRcvd MsgSent    TblVer  InQ OutQ
Up/Down    State/PfxRcd
2.2.2.2         4      2        0        0        0    0      0 never
Idle
Marie#show ip bgp summary
BGP router identifier 2.2.2.2, local AS number 2
BGP table version is 1, main routing table version 1

Neighbor        V     AS MsgRcvd MsgSent    TblVer  InQ OutQ
Up/Down    State/PfxRcd
1.1.1.1         4      1        0        0        0    0      0 never
Idle
```

As you can see it's not working, both routers show their BGP neighbor as idle. The problem is that external BGP uses a **TTL of 1** for its updates. When we source our updates from the loopback interfaces we will exceed a TTL of 1, this is something you have to change:

```
Emma(config)#router bgp 1
Emma(config-router)#neighbor 2.2.2.2 ebgp-multihop 2
```

```
Marie(config)#router bgp 2
Marie(config-router)#neighbor 1.1.1.1 ebgp-multihop 2
```

Use the **ebgp-multihop** command to change the TTL. I have set the TTL at 2 hops. Let's see if it made a difference:

```
Emma#show ip bgp summary
BGP router identifier 1.1.1.1, local AS number 1
BGP table version is 1, main routing table version 1

Neighbor        V    AS MsgRcvd MsgSent    TblVer  InQ OutQ Up/Down
State/PfxRcd
2.2.2.2         4     2        4        4        1    0      0
00:00:50        0
```

```
Marie#show ip bgp summary
BGP router identifier 2.2.2.2, local AS number 2
BGP table version is 1, main routing table version 1

Neighbor    V    AS MsgRcvd MsgSent   TblVer  InQ OutQ Up/Down
State/PfxRcd
1.1.1.1          4    1       4      4        1   0    0
00:00:55         0
```

That's better! Now it's working.

Configuring the TTL is **only required for external BGP**, you will see that we don't have to do this for internal BGP.

Let's continue by looking at **internal BGP!**

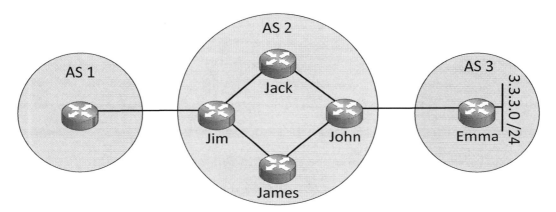

We'll start with looking at the reason why we need internal BGP. Look at the topology above. There are three autonomous systems and we have configured external BGP between AS1-AS2 and AS2-AS3. The routers within AS 2 are using OSPF as their IGP. Our goal is to make sure AS 1 can reach network 3.3.3.0 /24 in AS 3.

AS 3 has been configured to advertise network 3.3.3.0 /24 to AS 2. Router John is running BGP and now has network 3.3.3.0 /24 in its BGP and routing table.

Our next step is to make sure router Jim will advertise network 3.3.3.0 /24 to AS 1. If you want to advertise something with BGP it has to be in your routing table and we have two options to do this:

- We can redistribute network 3.3.3.0 /24 from BGP into OSPF.
- We can configure BGP between router John and Jim to exchange BGP routing information.

Does redistributing BGP into OSPF sound like a good idea? Yes and no...if we want reachability for just this single prefix then it's no problem at all. How about a full Internet routing table? 350.000+ prefixes? There is no way you can redistribute that into OSPF or any other IGP.

Internal BGP to the rescue! We can configure BGP between router John and Jim so they exchange BGP routing information. Router Jim can learn about network 3.3.3.0 /24 by using BGP and advertise it towards AS 1....problem solved!

Are we done now? Not quite yet...

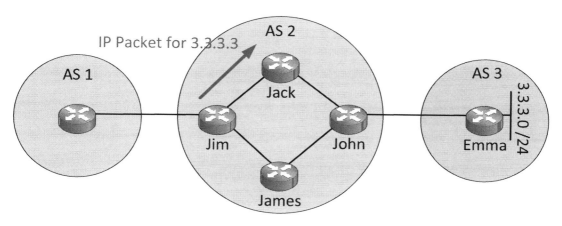

At this moment AS 1 has learned about network 3.3.3.0 /24 and knows it has to send its packets to AS 2. Router Jim receives this packet, looks at its routing table and sees it has to forward it towards router John. Router Jack or James receives this IP packet and looks at its routing table to find the destination 3.3.3.0 /24.

Uh-oh...router Jack nor router James has no idea where to find network 3.3.3.0 /24 since it's not in their routing table, they are only running OSPF. The packet will be dropped and an ICMP unreachable will be sent.

How do we solve this problem? **Configure internal BGP on all routers within the autonomous system.**

AS 2 is what we call a **transit AS.** This means that we can use AS 2 to "transit" from one autonomous system to another, in this case between AS 1 and AS 3.

If your autonomous system is a transit AS you should always run IBGP (internal BGP) on all routers within the autonomous system. Otherwise you might have reachability issues.

Let's configure the network above so I can show you how internal BGP works. I switched the network diagram from horizontal to vertical so you can see everything including the interfaces, IP addresses etc.

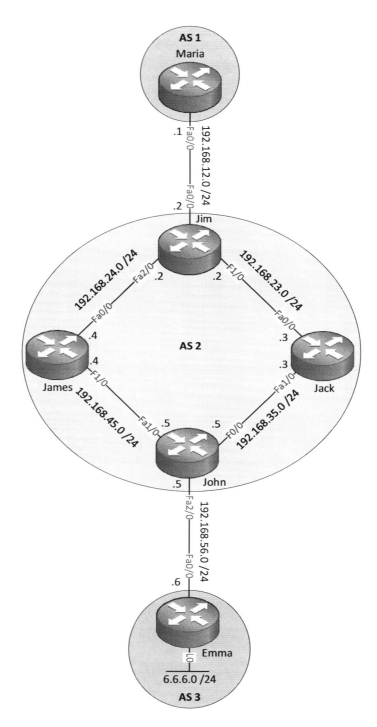

My goal is to configure this network so that AS 1 (router Maria) can reach network 6.6.6.0 /24 in AS 3 by learning it through BGP. AS 2 is a transit AS and needs internal BGP.

Let's start with the BGP configuration between AS 1 and AS 2:

```
Maria(config)#router bgp 1
Maria(config-router)#neighbor 192.168.12.2 remote-as 2
```

```
Jim(config)#router bgp 2
Jim(config-router)#neighbor 192.168.12.1 remote-as 1
```

This is how we configure EBGP between AS 1 and AS 2. Let's do the same thing for AS 2 and AS 3...

```
John(config)#router bgp 2
John(config-router)#neighbor 192.168.56.6 remote-as 3

Emma(config)#router bgp 3
Emma(config-router)#neighbor 192.168.56.5 remote-as 2
```

That's how we do it, now let's advertise that loopback0 interface on router Emma in BGP:

```
Emma(config)#router bgp 3
Emma(config-router)#network 6.6.6.0 mask 255.255.255.0
```

Keep in mind you have to specify the correct subnet mask as it is in the routing table or it won't be advertised. Let's see if it's working:

```
John#show ip bgp summary
BGP router identifier 192.168.56.5, local AS number 2
BGP table version is 2, main routing table version 2
1 network entries using 117 bytes of memory
1 path entries using 52 bytes of memory
2/1 BGP path/bestpath attribute entries using 248 bytes of
memory
1 BGP AS-PATH entries using 24 bytes of memory
0 BGP route-map cache entries using 0 bytes of memory
0 BGP filter-list cache entries using 0 bytes of memory
BGP using 441 total bytes of memory
BGP activity 1/0 prefixes, 1/0 paths, scan interval 60 secs

Neighbor       V    AS MsgRcvd MsgSent   TblVer  InQ OutQ Up/Down
State/PfxRcd
192.168.56.6   4     3      4      3       2     0    0
00:00:40            1
```

I can see that router John has a neighbor and that he has received 1 prefix.

```
John#show ip bgp
BGP table version is 2, local router ID is 192.168.56.5
Status codes: s suppressed, d damped, h history, * valid, >
best, i - internal,
             r RIB-failure, S Stale
Origin codes: i - IGP, e - EGP, ? - incomplete

   Network          Next Hop           Metric LocPrf Weight
Path
*> 6.6.6.0/24       192.168.56.6            0            0 3 i
```

It's in the BGP table of router John so it seems external BGP is working fine.

Our next step is to make sure that router Jim learns about network 6.6.6.0/24 so it can be advertised to router Maria. How are we going to do this?

- I could configure an IGP like OSPF or EIGRP within AS2 and redistribute network 6.6.6.0/24 from BGP into OSPF on router John. Router Jim can redistribute it from OSPF back into BGP and advertise it to AS 1.
- Configure internal BGP between router John and Jim so that network 6.6.6.0 /24 can be advertised.

Redistributing into OSPF will work perfectly fine for this example but it's not a scalable solution. Right now I only have one network which is no problem but redistributing a full internet routing table into OSPF is not going to happen.

Let's configure internal BGP between router John and Jim. Now we run into an issue...what IP addresses am I going to use to configure the BGP neighbors? Router John and Jim have no idea how to reach each other...

There are two options:

- I can use static routes within AS 2 so router John and Jim know how to reach each other.
- I can run an IGP like OSPF or EIGRP so router John and Jim know how to reach each other.

Of course an IGP is a far more scalable solution than static routes so that's what we'll do, I'll choose OSPF:

```
Jim(config)#router ospf 1
Jim(config-router)#network 192.168.24.0 0.0.0.255 area 0
Jim(config-router)#network 192.168.23.0 0.0.0.255 area 0
```

```
James(config)#router ospf 1
James(config-router)#network 192.168.24.0 0.0.0.255 area 0
James(config-router)#network 192.168.45.0 0.0.0.255 area 0
```

```
Jack(config)#router ospf 1
Jack(config-router)#network 192.168.23.0 0.0.0.255 area 0
Jack(config-router)#network 192.168.35.0 0.0.0.255 area 0
```

```
John(config)#router ospf 1
John(config-router)#network 192.168.45.0 0.0.0.255 area 0
John(config-router)#network 192.168.35.0 0.0.0.255 area 0
```

These are all the OSPF commands we need to achieve connectivity within AS 2. Can router John now reach router Jim?

```
John#ping 192.168.24.2

Type escape sequence to abort.
Sending 5, 100-byte ICMP Echos to 192.168.24.2, timeout is 2
seconds:
!!!!!
Success rate is 100 percent (5/5), round-trip min/avg/max =
8/11/24 ms
```

```
John#ping 192.168.23.2

Type escape sequence to abort.
Sending 5, 100-byte ICMP Echos to 192.168.23.2, timeout is 2
seconds:
!!!!!
Success rate is 100 percent (5/5), round-trip min/avg/max =
8/8/8 ms
```

Router John can ping router Jim on both IP addresses that were advertised in OSPF so now we can configure internal BGP between these routers, since I have multiple IP addresses...which one(s) am I going to use for the BGP neighbors?

Once again we can take the blue or the red pill...here are your choices:

- Pick any of the physical IP addresses on router John or Jim. Those interfaces are advertised in OSPF so they are reachable.
- Create a loopback interface and create a BGP neighbor between loopback interfaces.

Physical interfaces can go down and if that happens our BGP neighbor adjacency will drop. That's something we don't want to happen so it's a better idea to create loopback interfaces and setup the BGP neighbor adjacency between the loopback interfaces. If any of the physical interfaces goes down our IGP (OSPF) will take care of selecting a new path to the loopback interfaces, sounds good right?

```
John(config)#interface loopback 0
John(config-if)#ip address 5.5.5.5 255.255.255.0

John(config)#router ospf 1
John(config-router)#network 5.5.5.0 0.0.0.255 area 0
Jim(config)#interface loopback 0
Jim(config-if)#ip address 2.2.2.2 255.255.255.0

Jim(config)#router ospf 1
Jim(config-router)#network 2.2.2.0 0.0.0.255 area 0
```

That should take care of the loopbacks, now let's configure internal BGP:

```
Jim(config)#router bgp 2
Jim(config-router)#neighbor 5.5.5.5 remote-as 2
```

```
John(config)#router bgp 2
John(config-router)#neighbor 2.2.2.2 remote-as 2
```

By configuring the same AS number BGP knows that you are running **internal BGP.** Are we done now?

```
Jim#show ip bgp summary
BGP router identifier 192.168.24.2, local AS number 2
BGP table version is 1, main routing table version 1

Neighbor       V    AS MsgRcvd MsgSent    TblVer   InQ OutQ Up/Down
State/PfxRcd
5.5.5.5        4     2       0       0         0     0    0 never
Active
192.168.12     4     1      36      36         1     0    0 00:33:08
0
```

```
John#show ip bgp summary
BGP router identifier 192.168.56.5, local AS number 2
BGP table version is 2, main routing table version 2
1 network entries using 117 bytes of memory
1 path entries using 52 bytes of memory
2/1 BGP path/bestpath attribute entries using 248 bytes of
memory
1 BGP AS-PATH entries using 24 bytes of memory
0 BGP route-map cache entries using 0 bytes of memory
0 BGP filter-list cache entries using 0 bytes of memory
BGP using 441 total bytes of memory
BGP activity 1/0 prefixes, 1/0 paths, scan interval 60 secs

Neighbor       V    AS MsgRcvd MsgSent   TblVer  InQ OutQ Up/Down
State/PfxRcd
2.2.2.2        4     2       0       0        0   0    0 never
Active
192.168.56     4     3      30      29        2   0    0 00:26:59
1
```

Even though I configured the correct BGP neighbor IP addresses the adjacency
is not working. There's one thing missing...

```
Jim(config)#router bgp 2
Jim(config-router)#neighbor 5.5.5.5 update-source loopback 0
```

```
John(config)#router bgp 2
John(config-router)#neighbor 2.2.2.2 update-source loopback 0
```

By default BGP will use one of the physical IP addresses to setup the TCP
connection to the other BGP neighbor. If this doesn't match your neighbor
command it will not work. We need to use the **update-source** command to
tell BGP to source the update from the loopback interface.

```
Jim#show ip bgp summary
BGP router identifier 192.168.24.2, local AS number 2
BGP table version is 1, main routing table version 1
1 network entries using 117 bytes of memory
1 path entries using 52 bytes of memory
2/0 BGP path/bestpath attribute entries using 248 bytes of
memory
1 BGP AS-PATH entries using 24 bytes of memory
0 BGP route-map cache entries using 0 bytes of memory
0 BGP filter-list cache entries using 0 bytes of memory
BGP using 441 total bytes of memory
BGP activity 1/0 prefixes, 1/0 paths, scan interval 60 secs

Neighbor        V     AS MsgRcvd MsgSent   TblVer  InQ OutQ Up/Down
State/PfxRcd
5.5.5.5         4      2       5       4        1    0    0 00:00:53
1
192.168.12.0 4         1      38      38        1    0    0 00:35:09
0
```

That's better. Router Jim and John are now BGP neighbors and you can see
that router Jim has received 1 prefix from router John.

```
Jim#show ip bgp
BGP table version is 1, local router ID is 192.168.24.2
Status codes: s suppressed, d damped, h history, * valid, >
best, i - internal,
              r RIB-failure, S Stale
Origin codes: i - IGP, e - EGP, ? - incomplete

   Network          Next Hop            Metric LocPrf Weight
Path
* i6.6.6.0/24       192.168.56.6             0    100      0 3 i
```

Router Jim has even learned about network 6.6.6.0 /24 through internal
BGP...awesome! Now there's something important in the BGP table above that
you need to understand. Let me show you the difference between router Jim
and John:

```
Jim#show ip bgp | include 6.6.6.0
* i6.6.6.0/24       192.168.56.6             0    100      0 3 i
```

```
John#show ip bgp | include 6.6.6.0
*> 6.6.6.0/24       192.168.56.6             0           0 3 i
```

If you look at the comparison above you can see there's one difference. Router
John shows the > symbol and router Jim doesn't. The > symbol means that
this entry is the best one and has been **installed in the routing table**. Router
Jim didn't install this entry in its routing table, here take a look:

```
Jim#show ip route bgp
```

```
John#show ip route bgp
      6.0.0.0/24 is subnetted, 1 subnets
B        6.6.6.0 [20/0] via 192.168.56.6, 00:35:21
```

Router Jim doesn't have anything BGP-related in the routing table while router John does have network 6.6.6.0/24. Why is this route not installed from the BGP table into the routing table? Let me show you!

```
Jim#show ip bgp
BGP table version is 1, local router ID is 192.168.24.2
Status codes: s suppressed, d damped, h history, * valid, >
best, i - internal,
              r RIB-failure, S Stale
Origin codes: i - IGP, e - EGP, ? - incomplete

   Network            Next Hop          Metric LocPrf Weight
Path
*  i6.6.6.0/24        192.168.56.6           0    100      0 3 i
```

Take a look above, see that next hop IP address? That's the IP address of router Emma. Does router Jim have any idea how to reach network 192.168.56.0 /24? Let's see...

```
Jim#show ip route | include 192.168.56.
```

No it doesn't...this is something we'll have to fix.

There are two options:

- Advertise network 192.168.56.0/24 in OSPF.
- Advertise network 192.168.56.0/24 in BGP.

Both will work. If you use OSPF just make sure that you configure passive-interface otherwise you will send hello packets outside of your autonomous system. If you use BGP you need to keep in mind that these networks will be advertised to other autonomous systems. Since this chapter is about BGP that'll what I'll use:

```
John(config)#router bgp 2
John(config-router)#network 192.168.56.0 mask 255.255.255.0
```

```
Jim(config)#router bgp 2
Jim(config-router)#network 192.168.12.0 mask 255.255.255.0
```

Just add the correct network commands. I'm also advertising the link between

AS1 and AS2 otherwise we'll run into a similar problem later. So what has changed now?

```
Jim#show ip bgp
BGP table version is 4, local router ID is 192.168.24.2
Status codes: s suppressed, d damped, h history, * valid, >
best, i - internal,
             r RIB-failure, S Stale
Origin codes: i - IGP, e - EGP, ? - incomplete

   Network          Next Hop          Metric LocPrf Weight
Path
*>i6.6.6.0/24       192.168.56.6           0    100      0 3 i
*> 192.168.12.0     0.0.0.0                0         32768 i
*>i192.168.56.0     5.5.5.5                0    100      0 i
```

See the > symbol next to the 6.6.6.0/24 entry? The next hop IP address is now reachable so it can be installed in the routing table.

```
Jim#show ip route bgp
      6.0.0.0/24 is subnetted, 1 subnets
B        6.6.6.0 [200/0] via 192.168.56.6, 00:04:17
B     192.168.56.0/24 [200/0] via 5.5.5.5, 00:04:23
```

Now we see network 6.6.6.0/24 in the routing table, excellent!

Let's continue by looking at AS 1…

```
Maria#show ip bgp
BGP table version is 5, local router ID is 192.168.12.1
Status codes: s suppressed, d damped, h history, * valid, >
best, i - internal,
              r RIB-failure, S Stale
Origin codes: i - IGP, e - EGP, ? - incomplete

   Network            Next Hop          Metric LocPrf Weight
Path
*> 6.6.6.0/24        192.168.12.2                       0 2 3
i
r> 192.168.12.0      192.168.12.2          0            0 2 i
*> 192.168.56.0      192.168.12.2                       0 2 i
```

Network 6.6.6.0/24 is in the BGP table of router Maria and the > symbol indicates that it has been installed in the routing table.

```
Maria#show ip route bgp
      6.0.0.0/24 is subnetted, 1 subnets
B        6.6.6.0 [20/0] via 192.168.12.2, 00:05:58
B     192.168.56.0/24 [20/0] via 192.168.12.2, 00:06:29
```

And yes we can see it….so it is working?

```
Maria#ping 6.6.6.6

Type escape sequence to abort.
Sending 5, 100-byte ICMP Echos to 3.3.3.3, timeout is 2 seconds:
.....
Success rate is 0 percent (0/5)
```

To test this I'm sending a couple of pings but unfortunately they are failing…not good! What is going on here?

```
Maria#traceroute 6.6.6.6

Type escape sequence to abort.
Tracing the route to 6.6.6.6

  1 192.168.12.2 4 msec 4 msec 4 msec
  2  *   *   *
  3  *   *   *
```

It seems my IP packets make it to router Jim but that's it. What is going on here? Let's shift out attention to router Jim to find out!

```
Jim#show ip route | include 6.6.6.0
B       6.6.6.0 [200/0] via 192.168.56.6, 00:10:08
```

Router Jim will send traffic to 6.6.6.0/24 towards 192.168.56.6, how does it reach this IP address?

```
Jim#show ip route | include 192.168.56.0
B    192.168.56.0/24 [200/0] via 5.5.5.5, 00:13:27
```

It can reach 192.168.56.0/24 by sending traffic to IP address 5.5.5.5. This is starting to look like a rabbit hole...

```
Jim#show ip route 5.5.5.5
Routing entry for 5.5.5.5/32
  Known via "ospf 1", distance 110, metric 3, type intra area
  Last update from 192.168.23.3 on FastEthernet1/0, 00:35:08 ago
  Routing Descriptor Blocks:
  * 192.168.24.4, from 192.168.56.5, 00:35:08 ago, via
FastEthernet2/0
      Route metric is 3, traffic share count is 1
    192.168.23.3, from 192.168.56.5, 00:35:08 ago, via
FastEthernet1/0
      Route metric is 3, traffic share count is 1
```

Now we know that traffic that goes to network 6.6.6.0/24 will be forwarded towards router James and Jack. Now what do you think happens if they receive an IP packet with destination 6.6.6.0/24 ?

```
James#show ip route 6.6.6.0
% Network not in table
```

```
Jack#show ip route 6.6.6.0
% Network not in table
```

Here's the answer, it will be **dropped**! They have no idea where that network is located. So how do we fix it?

This is one of the parts that confuses most people who are new to BGP. If you have learned OSPF and EIGRP you probably got used to the idea that once something is in the routing table it is reachable (unless you have access-lists blocking stuff or are playing with frame-relay). With BGP this is definitely not the case as you can witness here.

Router Jack and James are only running OSPF. I explained you before that redistributing everything from BGP into OSPF is not a good idea so what we'll do is configure IBGP on router James and Jack.

How are we going to do this? There's something about BGP and **loop prevention** I have to tell you first.

BGP (just like any other routing protocol) has a mechanism to make sure that we don't have any routing loops. For BGP this is very simple:

If you see your own AS number in the AS path you don't accept it since you have a loop.

That sounds logical right? What about internal BGP? The AS number is the same!

To solve this problem we have something called **BGP split-horizon.** Since the AS number within the autonomous system is always the same there is no way for internal BGP routers to use the loop prevention mechanism.

When a BGP router receives an update from another internal BGP router it will not forward this information to another internal BGP router. This is called BGP split-horizon.

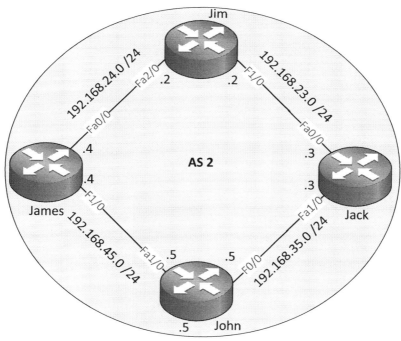

Let's zoom in on AS 2 so I can explain this better:

- Router John has learned about network 6.6.6.0/24 from AS 3 and this is stored in its BGP table.
- Router John advertises network 6.6.6.0/24 to router Jim through IBGP.
- If I configure IBGP between router James and Jim then router James won't learn about network 6.6.6.0/24 because of IBGP split horizon.

- If I configure IBGP between router Jim and Jack then router Jack won't learn about network 6.6.6.0/24 because of IBGP split horizon.

Let me demonstrate this to you!

```
James(config)#interface loopback 0
James(config-if)#ip address 4.4.4.4 255.255.255.0

James(config)#router ospf 1
James(config-router)#network 4.4.4.0 0.0.0.255

James(config-router)#network 4.4.4.0 0.0.0.255 area 0

James(config)#router bgp 2
James(config-router)#neighbor 2.2.2.2 remote-as 2
James(config-router)#neighbor 2.2.2.2 update-source loopback 0
```

```
Jim(config)#router bgp 2
Jim(config-router)#neighbor 4.4.4.4 remote-as 2
Jim(config-router)#neighbor 4.4.4.4 update-source loopback 0
```

I'll create a loopback interface, advertise in OSPF and use it for the BGP neighbor adjacency.

```
Jack(config)#interface loopback 0
Jack(config-if)#ip address 3.3.3.3 255.255.255.0

Jack(config)#router ospf 1
Jack(config-router)#network 3.3.3.0 0.0.0.255 area 0

Jack(config)#router bgp 2
Jack(config-router)#neighbor 2.2.2.2 remote-as 2
Jack(config-router)#neighbor 2.2.2.2 update-source loopback 0
```

```
Jim(config)#router bgp 2
Jim(config-router)#neighbor 3.3.3.3 remote-as 2
Jim(config-router)#neighbor 3.3.3.3 update-source loopback 0
```

And we'll do the same thing for router Jack and James.

```
James#show ip bgp
BGP table version is 2, local router ID is 4.4.4.4
Status codes: s suppressed, d damped, h history, * valid, >
best, i - internal,
              r RIB-failure, S Stale
Origin codes: i - IGP, e - EGP, ? - incomplete

   Network          Next Hop            Metric LocPrf Weight
Path
*>i192.168.12.0     2.2.2.2                  0    100      0 i
```

```
Jack#show ip bgp
BGP table version is 2, local router ID is 3.3.3.3
Status codes: s suppressed, d damped, h history, * valid, >
best, i - internal,
              r RIB-failure, S Stale
Origin codes: i - IGP, e - EGP, ? - incomplete

   Network          Next Hop           Metric LocPrf Weight
Path
*>i192.168.12.0      2.2.2.2                0    100     0 i
```

Now when we look at the BGP table of router James and Jack we can see that they only learned about the network 192.168.12.0/24 network.

Router Jack and James haven't learned about network 6.6.6.0/24. Why?

1. Router Emma advertises network 6.6.6.0 /24 to router John.
2. Router John advertises network 6.6.6.0 /24 to router Jim through internal BGP.
3. Router Jim **does not** advertise network 3.3.3.0 /24 to router James or Jack through internal BGP because of **BGP split-horizon.**

We have to do this since the loop prevention mechanism isn't working. This is the only way for BGP to be absolutely sure there are no BGP loops within the autonomous system.

I do want router James and Jack to learn about network 6.6.6.0 /24 though...how are we going to tackle this problem?

Internal BGP routers have to be configured as full-mesh.

Each internal BGP router needs a BGP neighbor adjacency with any other internal BGP router. In my example router James and Jack need to learn about network 6.6.6.0 /24 from router John. If we create a full mesh of internal BGP routers we know for sure that each internal BGP router can learn about any network out there.

Let's configure AS 2 to have a full mesh of internal BGP routers and we'll see what happens:

```
John(config)#router bgp 2
John(config-router)#neighbor 4.4.4.4 remote-as 2
John(config-router)#neighbor 4.4.4.4 update-source loopback 0
John(config-router)#neighbor 3.3.3.3 remote-as 2
John(config-router)#neighbor 3.3.3.3 update-source loopback 0
```

```
James(config)#router bgp 2
James(config-router)#neighbor 5.5.5.5 remote-as 2
James(config-router)#neighbor 5.5.5.5 update-source loopback 0
James(config-router)#neighbor 3.3.3.3 remote-as 2
James(config-router)#neighbor 3.3.3.3 update-source loopback 0
```

```
Jack(config)#router bgp 2
Jack(config-router)#neighbor 5.5.5.5 remote-as 2
Jack(config-router)#neighbor 5.5.5.5 update-source loopback 0
Jack(config-router)#neighbor 4.4.4.4 remote-as 2
Jack(config-router)#neighbor 4.4.4.4 update-source loopback 0
```

Each router within AS 2 is now internal BGP with any other router so it's a full mesh.

```
James#show ip bgp
BGP table version is 4, local router ID is 4.4.4.4
Status codes: s suppressed, d damped, h history, * valid, >
best, i - internal,
            r RIB-failure, S Stale
Origin codes: i - IGP, e - EGP, ? - incomplete

   Network          Next Hop            Metric LocPrf Weight
Path
*>i6.6.6.0/24       192.168.56.6             0     100      0 3 i
```

```
Jack#show ip bgp
BGP table version is 4, local router ID is 3.3.3.3
Status codes: s suppressed, d damped, h history, * valid, >
best, i - internal,
            r RIB-failure, S Stale
Origin codes: i - IGP, e - EGP, ? - incomplete

   Network          Next Hop            Metric LocPrf Weight
Path
*>i6.6.6.0/24       192.168.56.6             0     100      0 3 i
```

When I look at router James and Jack I can see they have learned network 6.6.6.0/24 from router John.

Are we done now? Let's find out:

```
Maria#ping 6.6.6.6

Type escape sequence to abort.
Sending 5, 100-byte ICMP Echos to 6.6.6.6, timeout is 2 seconds:
!!!!!
Success rate is 100 percent (5/5), round-trip min/avg/max =
16/16/16 ms
```

Finally it is working! So are we done now? Well yes but there is one more thing I want to show to you:

```
James#show ip route bgp
B    192.168.12.0/24 [200/0] via 2.2.2.2, 00:19:59
     6.0.0.0/24 is subnetted, 1 subnets
B       6.6.6.0 [200/0] via 192.168.56.6, 00:12:14
```

```
Jack#show ip route bgp
B    192.168.12.0/24 [200/0] via 2.2.2.2, 00:19:05
     6.0.0.0/24 is subnetted, 1 subnets
B       6.6.6.0 [200/0] via 192.168.56.6, 00:12:38
```

Let's look at router James one more time. Network 6.6.6.0 /24 is in its routing table because of internal BGP. Look closely at the next hop IP address. It's 192.168.56.6 which belongs to router Emma. The default next hop behavior of BGP is different than any IGP. **Internal BGP does not change the next hop IP address**.

The next-hop IP address is reachable for router James because network 192.168.56.0 /24 has been advertised in BGP. What if I don't advertise this network in BGP? Can I still make it work?

```
John(config)#router bgp 2
John(config-router)#no network 192.168.56.0
```

Because of this changer router James and Jack no longer can reach the next hop IP address for network 6.6.6.0/24.

Besides advertising the link between autonomous systems in BGP or an IGP like OSPF we can also change the next hop IP address using **the BGP next-hop-self** command. Here's how:

```
John(config)#router bgp 2
John(config-router)#neighbor 4.4.4.4 next-hop-self
John(config-router)#neighbor 3.3.3.3 next-hop-self
```

I'm configuring router John so that it advertises itself as the next hop IP address to router James and Jack.

```
James#show ip route bgp | include 6.6.6.0
B       6.6.6.0 [200/0] via 5.5.5.5, 00:00:37
```

```
Jack#show ip route bgp | include 6.6.6.0
B       6.6.6.0 [200/0] via 5.5.5.5, 00:00:49
```

You can see that network 6.6.6.0 /24 now shows up in the routing table with a next hop IP address of 5.5.5.5 (router John).

This is the end of the BGP introduction chapter. What do you think so far? If you never saw BGP before then this is probably completely different than any other routing protocol you have seen before. It's probably a good idea to do some labs before you continue with the next chapter to become familiar with the things you just read and implement the things just just learned.

You can try some of my BGP labs to see if you understand everything:

http://gns3vault.com/BGP/ebgp-external-bgp.html

http://gns3vault.com/BGP/ibgp-internal-bgp.html

http://gns3vault.com/BGP/bgp-md5-authentication.html

The example I just showed you with the transit AS is something you can try as well. If you can get it working you'll truly understand EBGP and IBGP:

http://gns3vault.com/BGP/bgp-transit-as.html

In the next chapter we'll look at BGP attributes and how the path selection works!

19. BGP Attributes and Path selection

In this chapter we'll look at how BGP selects the best path to each destination. In our BGP table it's possible to see multiple paths for a certain destination. BGP is not designed to do load balancing and there's a big different compared to IGPs like OSPF or EIGRP:

- IGPs choose a path on things like bandwidth, delay, hop count etc.
- BGP chooses a path based on **policy**.

You will see that BGP will choose **one best path** for each destination. BGP doesn't use a metric like hop count / cost or K-values but **BGP attributes.**

```
route-views.optus.net.au>show ip bgp
BGP table version is 129019488, local router ID is 203.202.125.6
Status codes: s suppressed, d damped, h history, * valid, >
best, i - internal,
           r RIB-failure, S Stale, m multipath, b backup-
path, x best-external
Origin codes: i - IGP, e - EGP, ? - incomplete
```

Network	Next Hop	Metric	LocPrf	Weight
Path				
* 1.0.0.0/24	202.160.242.71			0
7473 15169 i				
*	203.13.132.49			0
7474 15169 i				
*	202.139.124.130	1		0
7474 15169 i				
*	202.139.124.145	1		0
7474 15169 i				
*	202.139.124.146	1		0
7474 15169 i				
*	202.139.124.175	1		0
7474 15169 i				
*	192.65.89.98	1		0
7474 15169 i				
*	202.139.124.177	1		0
7474 15169 i				
*	192.65.89.161	1		0
7474 15169 i				
*	202.139.124.160	1		0
7474 15169 i				
*	202.139.124.140	1		0
7474 15169 i				
*	202.139.124.185			0
7474 15169 i				
*	202.139.124.159			0
7474 15169 i				
*	202.139.124.190			0
7474 15169 i				

*	203.13.132.51	0
7474 15169 i		
*	203.13.132.41	0
7474 15169 i		
*	203.13.132.47	0
7474 15169 i		
*	203.13.132.37	0
7474 15169 i		
*	203.13.132.29	0
7474 15169 i		
*	203.13.132.53	0
7474 15169 i		
*>	**203.13.132.35**	0
7474 15169 i		

I just telnetted to one of my favorite looking glass servers to look at its BGP table. This BGP router has 21 entries for network 1.0.0.0/24. Look at the **>** **symbol** at the bottom left. If you see the > symbol it means that BGP has selected this path as the **best path** and you will find it in the routing table. Why did BGP select this path as the best one?

Priority	Attribute
1.	Weight (highest)
2.	Local Preference (highest)
3.	Originate (local originate)
4.	AS Path (shortest)
5.	Origin Code (IGP < EGP < Incomplete)
6.	MED (lowest)
7.	Paths (external preferred over internal)
8.	Router ID (lowest)

<u>W</u>e <u>L</u>ove <u>O</u>ranges <u>A</u>s <u>O</u>ranges <u>M</u>eans <u>P</u>ure <u>R</u>efreshment

Whenever BGP has multiple paths to a destination they will be stored in the BGP table. Both will be in the BGP table but there will be **only one in the routing table**. Which path are we going to use? We have to start at the top of a list with BGP attributes and work our way to the bottom:

1. We start with weight because it's at the top of the BGP attributes list. If there is a difference in weight then we can make a decision and choose the BGP path with the best weight.
2. If weight is equal we move down to local preference. If one of the paths has a better local preference we will choose that path but if both paths

have the same local preference we move down the list of BGP attributes.

3. If all the BGP attributes are the same then we end up at the router ID. The router ID of course always different for each router so only one path will end up in the routing table. BGP by default does **no load balancing!** *There can be only one ~Highlander*

This list of BGP attributes is definitely something you have to remember and to make your life a bit easier you can use the memory aid "we love oranges as oranges means pure refreshment". The first letter of each word is one of the BGP attributes in the right order!

Let's find out what each BGP attribute does and how it works!

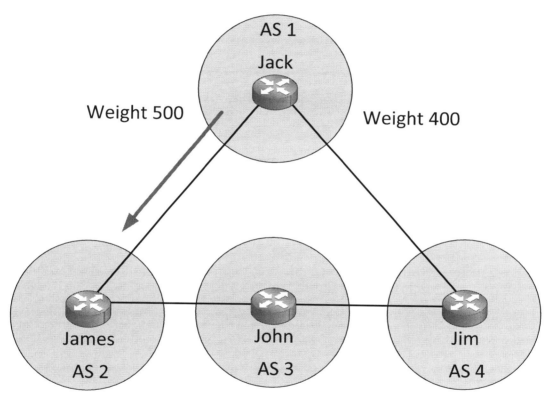

- **Weight** is the first BGP attribute in the list.
- **Cisco proprietary** so you won't find it on other vendor routers.
- Weight is not exchanged between BGP routers.
- Weight is only **local** on the router.
- The path with the **highest** weight is preferred.

Router Jack in AS 1 can reach AS 3 through AS 2 or AS 4. If we want to ensure AS 2 is always used as the best path you can change the weight. In my example the weight for the path to AS 2 is set to 500 and higher than the weight of 400 for AS 4.

Let me give you a demonstration of weight:

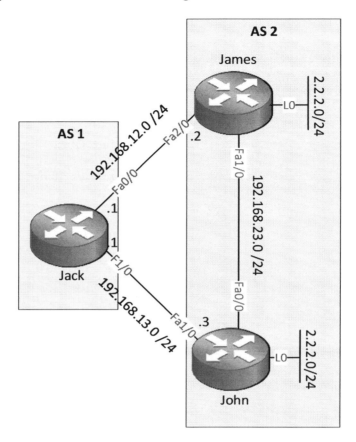

Above we have a simple scenario with two autonomous systems. Router James and John both have network 2.2.2.0/24 configured on their loopback0 interface and I'll advertise that in BGP.

```
Jack(config)#router bgp 1
Jack(config-router)#neighbor 192.168.12.2 remote-as 2
Jack(config-router)#neighbor 192.168.13.3 remote-as 2
```

```
James(config)#router bgp 2
James(config-router)#neighbor 192.168.12.1 remote-as 1
James(config-router)#neighbor 192.168.23.3 remote-as 2
James(config-router)#network 2.2.2.0 mask 255.255.255.0
```

```
John(config)#router bgp 2
John(config-router)#neighbor 192.168.13.1 remote-as 1
John(config-router)#neighbor 192.168.23.2 remote-as 2
John(config-router)#network 2.2.2.0 mask 255.255.255.0
```

Above you'll find the configuration for BGP, now let's take a detailed look at router Jack:

```
Jack#show ip bgp
BGP table version is 2, local router ID is 192.168.13.1
Status codes: s suppressed, d damped, h history, * valid, >
best, i - internal,
             r RIB-failure, S Stale
Origin codes: i - IGP, e - EGP, ? - incomplete

   Network          Next Hop          Metric LocPrf Weight
Path
*> 2.2.2.0/24       192.168.12.2           0             0 2 i
*                   192.168.13.3           0             0 2 i
```

Router Jack decided to use 192.168.12.2 as the next hop. All the BGP attributes are the same so it came down to the router ID to select a winner. Now let's change this behavior using the weight attribute...

```
Jack(config)#router bgp 1
Jack(config-router)#neighbor 192.168.13.3 weight 500
```

You can configure weight **per neighbor** using the **weight** command. All prefixes from this neighbor will have a weight of 500.

```
Jack#clear ip bgp *
```

Sometimes BGP behaves like an oil tanker so to speed things up in your lab, reset it.

```
Jack#show ip bgp
BGP table version is 2, local router ID is 192.168.13.1
Status codes: s suppressed, d damped, h history, * valid, >
best, i - internal,
             r RIB-failure, S Stale
Origin codes: i - IGP, e - EGP, ? - incomplete

   Network          Next Hop          Metric LocPrf Weight
Path
*  2.2.2.0/24       192.168.12.2           0             0 2 i
*>                  192.168.13.3           0           500 2 i
```

Now you can see that 192.168.13.3 has been selected as the next hop because the weight is now 500.

What if I want to set the weight to 500 for just a couple of prefixes from AS 2?

```
James(config)#interface loopback 1
James(config-if)#ip address 22.22.22.22 255.255.255.0

James(config)#router bgp 2
James(config-router)#network 22.22.22.0 mask 255.255.255.0
```

```
John(config)#interface loopback 1
John(config-if)#ip address 22.22.22.22 255.255.255.0

John(config)#router bgp 2
John(config-router)#network 22.22.22.0 mask 255.255.255.0
```

I'll create a new loopback interface on router James and John and I'll advertise network 22.22.22.0/24 in BGP. Here's what router Jack now looks like:

```
Jack#show ip bgp
BGP table version is 5, local router ID is 192.168.13.1
Status codes: s suppressed, d damped, h history, * valid, >
best, i - internal,
               r RIB-failure, S Stale
Origin codes: i - IGP, e - EGP, ? - incomplete

    Network          Next Hop          Metric LocPrf Weight
Path
*   2.2.2.0/24       192.168.12.2           0           0 2 i
*>                   192.168.13.3           0         500 2 i
*> 22.22.22.0/24     192.168.13.3           0         500 2 i
*                    192.168.12.2           0           0 2 i
```

As you can see above router Jack will use 192.168.13.3 as the next hop for both prefixes. What if I want to change the weight for just 1 prefix? Route-maps to the rescue!

```
Jack(config)#router bgp 1
Jack(config-router)#no neighbor 192.168.13.3 weight 500
```

First we'll get rid of the command above.

```
Jack(config)#route-map SETWEIGHT permit 10
Jack(config-route-map)#match ip address 1
Jack(config-route-map)#set weight 400
Jack(config-route-map)#exit
Jack(config)#route-map SETWEIGHT permit 20
Jack(config-route-map)#set weight 0
Jack(config-route-map)#exit
Jack(config)#access-list 1 permit 22.22.22.0 0.0.0.255
```

Here's the route-map that I will use. If the prefixes match access-list 1 we will set the weight to 400.

```
Jack(config-router)#neighbor 192.168.13.3 route-map SETWEIGHT in
```

To complete the configuration we have to apply it to our neighbor in AS 2.
Using a route-map gives you a lot of control!

```
Jack#clear ip bgp *
```

This will speed things up...

```
Jack#show ip bgp
BGP table version is 3, local router ID is 192.168.13.1
Status codes: s suppressed, d damped, h history, * valid, >
best, i - internal,
              r RIB-failure, S Stale
Origin codes: i - IGP, e - EGP, ? - incomplete

    Network          Next Hop          Metric LocPrf Weight
Path
*   2.2.2.0/24       192.168.13.3           0            0 2 i
*>                   192.168.12.2           0            0 2 i
*> 22.22.22.0/24     192.168.13.3           0          400 2 i
*                    192.168.12.2           0            0 2 i
```

See how the weight changed for network 22.22.22.0/24 ? Use route-maps to
influence the BGP attributes per neighbor/prefix.

Let's continue with the next BGP attribute; local preference.

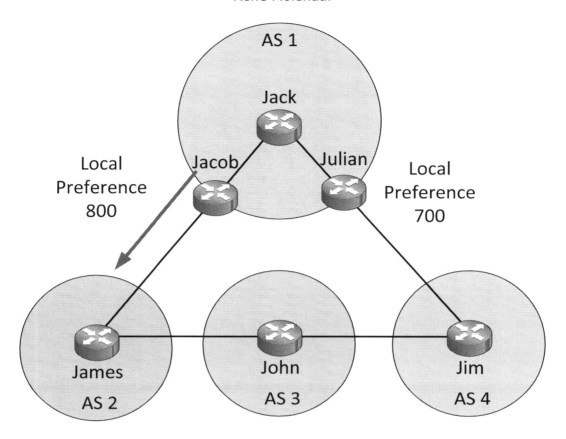

- **Local preference** is the second BGP attribute.
- You can use local preference to **choose the outbound external BGP path**.
- Local preference is sent to **all internal BGP** routers in your autonomous system.
- Not exchanged between external BGP routers.
- Local preference is a **well-known** and **discretionary** BGP attribute.
- Default value is 100.
- The path with the **highest** local preference is preferred.

You can use local preference to configure your autonomous system to select a certain exit point. Instead of configuring weight on each router you can use local preference because it is exchanged on all internal BGP routers. By increasing the local preference to 800 we can make AS 1 send all traffic towards AS 2.

A **well-known discretionary** BGP attribute must be recognized by all BGP routers per RFC but its presence in a BGP update is optional.

Let's take a look at a configuration example:

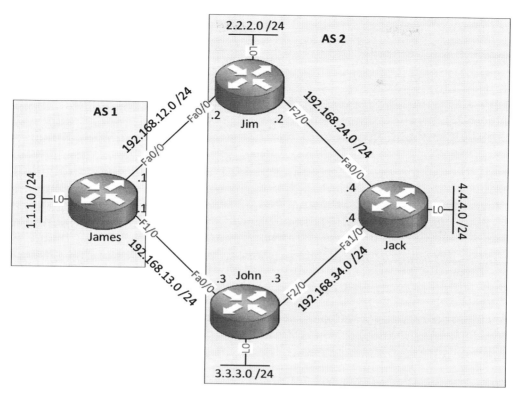

In the picture above we have two autonomous systems. Router James will advertise network 1.1.1.0/24 towards AS 2 and router Jack will have to make a choice when it wants to reach this network. It can go through router Jim or Jack, we'll see how local preference influence this.

```
James(config)#router bgp 1
James(config-router)#neighbor 192.168.12.2 remote-as 2
James(config-router)#neighbor 192.168.13.3 remote-as 2
James(config-router)#network 1.1.1.0 mask 255.255.255.0
```

This is the configuration of router James, nothing spectacular here.

```
Jim(config)#router ospf 1
Jim(config-router)#network 192.168.24.0 0.0.0.255 area 0
Jim(config-router)#network 2.2.2.0 0.0.0.255 area 0
```

```
John(config)#router ospf 1
John(config-router)#network 192.168.34.0 0.0.0.255 area 0
John(config-router)#network 3.3.3.0 0.0.0.255 area 0
```

```
Jack(config)#router ospf 1
Jack(config-router)#network 192.168.24.0 0.0.0.255 area 0
Jack(config-router)#network 192.168.34.0 0.0.0.255 area 0
Jack(config-router)#network 4.4.4.0 0.0.0.255 area 0
```

I'll configure OSPF within AS2 to prepare it for IBGP.

```
John(config)#router bgp 2
John(config-router)#neighbor 192.168.13.1 remote-as 1
John(config-router)#neighbor 2.2.2.2 remote-as 2
John(config-router)#neighbor 2.2.2.2 update-source loopback0
John(config-router)#neighbor 4.4.4.4 remote-as 2
John(config-router)#neighbor 4.4.4.4 update-source loopback0
John(config-router)#neighbor 4.4.4.4 next-hop-self
```

```
Jim(config)#router bgp 2
Jim(config-router)#neighbor 192.168.12.1 remote-as 1
Jim(config-router)#neighbor 3.3.3.3 remote-as 2
Jim(config-router)#neighbor 3.3.3.3 update-source loopback0
Jim(config-router)#neighbor 4.4.4.4 remote-as 2
Jim(config-router)#neighbor 4.4.4.4 update-source loopback0
Jim(config-router)#neighbor 4.4.4.4 next-hop-self
```

```
Jack(config)#router bgp 2
Jack(config-router)#neighbor 2.2.2.2 remote-as 2
Jack(config-router)#neighbor 2.2.2.2 update-source loopback 0
Jack(config-router)#neighbor 3.3.3.3 remote-as 2
Jack(config-router)#neighbor 3.3.3.3 update-source loopback 0
```

And above you can see the BGP configurations.

Now let's find out what path router Jack will use to reach network 1.1.1.0/24:

```
Jack#show ip bgp
BGP table version is 2, local router ID is 4.4.4.4
Status codes: s suppressed, d damped, h history, * valid, >
best, i - internal,
            r RIB-failure, S Stale
Origin codes: i - IGP, e - EGP, ? - incomplete

   Network          Next Hop           Metric LocPrf Weight
Path
*  i1.1.1.0/24      3.3.3.3                 0    100      0 1 i
*>i                 2.2.2.2                 0    100      0 1 i
```

All attributes are the same so it's the router ID that makes the decision. All traffic is sent to router Jim right now. Let's play with the local preference...

```
John(config)#router bgp 2
John(config-router)#bgp default local-preference 600
```

The default local preference is **100** and you can change it if you like with the **bgp default local-preference** command.

```
Jack#show ip bgp
BGP table version is 3, local router ID is 4.4.4.4
Status codes: s suppressed, d damped, h history, * valid, >
best, i - internal,
              r RIB-failure, S Stale
Origin codes: i - IGP, e - EGP, ? - incomplete

   Network          Next Hop           Metric LocPrf Weight
Path
*>i1.1.1.0/24       3.3.3.3                 0    600     0 1 i
* i                 2.2.2.2                 0    100     0 1 i
```

Now we see that router Jack prefers to send traffic to network 1.1.1.0/24 towards router John because the local preference is 600 > 100.

Of course we can accomplish the same thing with a route-map, here's how:

```
John(config)#router bgp 2
John(config-router)#no bgp default local-preference 600
```

Let's clean up first...

```
John(config)#route-map LOCALPREF permit 10
John(config-route-map)#set local-preference 700

John(config)#router bgp 2
John(config-router)#neighbor 192.168.13.1 route-map LOCALPREF in
```

Route-maps are a more flexible solution. If you don't use a match statement in a route-map then everything is matched by default. You can use it to set the local preference to another value. Don't forget to activate the route-map by binding it to a BGP neighbor.

```
Jack#show ip bgp
BGP table version is 5, local router ID is 4.4.4.4
Status codes: s suppressed, d damped, h history, * valid, >
best, i - internal,
              r RIB-failure, S Stale
Origin codes: i - IGP, e - EGP, ? - incomplete

   Network          Next Hop           Metric LocPrf Weight
Path
*>i1.1.1.0/24       3.3.3.3                 0    700     0 1 i
* i                 2.2.2.2                 0    100     0 1 i
```

And as you can see above the local preference has changed. Time for the next

BGP attribute!

If the weight and local preference for a path is the same then the third BGP attribute **originate** will kick in. Your BGP router will prefer a route if it's locally originated (means that its next hop IP address is 0.0.0.0 in the BGP table). Let's move on the AS Path BGP attribute.

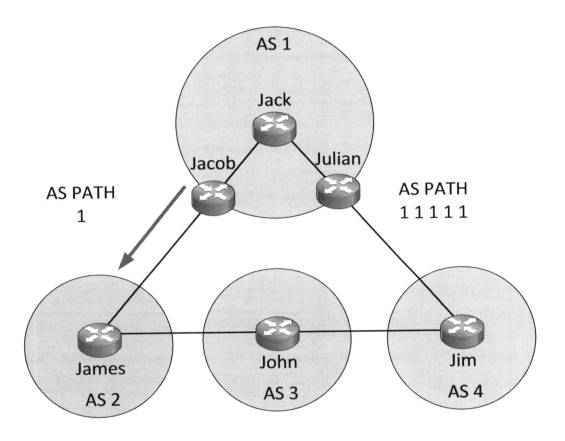

The fourth BGP attribute is called **AS path:**

- BGP prefers the **shortest AS path** to get to a destination. Less is better!
- We can manipulate this by using **AS path prepending.**

In my example AS 1 wants to make sure traffic enters the autonomous system through router Jacob. We can add our own autonomous system number multiple times so the as path becomes longer. Since BGP prefers a shorter AS path we can influence our routing. This is called **AS path prepending.** Let me demonstrate this to you:

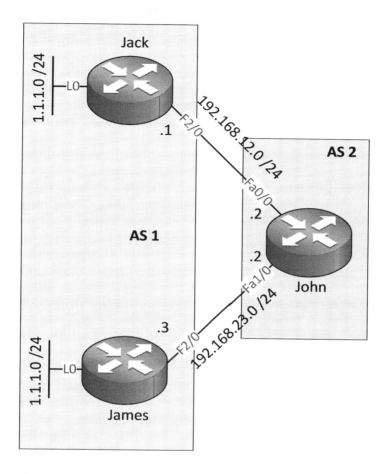

Here we have 3 routers. Router Jack and James are both in AS 1 advertising the same network (1.1.1.0/24) to router John. We can use AS Path prepending to make router Jack prefer a certain path.

```
Jack(config)#router bgp 1
Jack(config-router)#neighbor 192.168.12.2 remote-as 2
```

```
James(config)#router bgp 1
James(config-router)#neighbor 192.168.23.2 remote-as 2
```

```
John(config)#router bgp 2
John(config-router)#neighbor 192.168.12.1 remote-as 1
John(config-router)#neighbor 192.168.23.3 remote-as 1
```

First we'll configure BGP between the three routers.

```
Jack(config)#router bgp 1
Jack(config-router)#network 1.1.1.0 mask 255.255.255.0
```

```
James(config)#router bgp 1
James(config-router)#network 1.1.1.0 mask 255.255.255.0
```

And we'll advertise both networks in BGP.

```
John#show ip bgp
BGP table version is 2, local router ID is 192.168.23.2
Status codes: s suppressed, d damped, h history, * valid, >
best, i - internal,
              r RIB-failure, S Stale
Origin codes: i - IGP, e - EGP, ? - incomplete

   Network          Next Hop            Metric LocPrf Weight
Path
*  1.1.1.0/24       192.168.23.3              0             0 1 i
*>                  192.168.12.1             0             0 1 i
```

In the table above you can see that it prefers 192.168.12.1 as its path. Because everything is the same it boils down to the router ID. Let's change the AS path so that we'll use 192.168.23.3 as the preferred path.

```
Jack(config)#route-map PREPEND permit 10
Jack(config-route-map)#set as-path prepend 1 1 1 1 1
Jack(config-route-map)#exit
Jack(config)#router bgp 1
Jack(config-router)#neighbor 192.168.12.2 route-map PREPEND out
```

Here's an example for you. First create a route-map and use **set as-path prepend** to add your own A number multiple times.
Don't forget to add the route-map to your BGP neighbor configuration and since you are sending this to your remote neighbor it should be **outbound!**

```
John#show ip bgp
BGP table version is 2, local router ID is 192.168.23.2
Status codes: s suppressed, d damped, h history, * valid, >
best, i - internal,
              r RIB-failure, S Stale
Origin codes: i - IGP, e - EGP, ? - incomplete

   Network          Next Hop            Metric LocPrf Weight
Path
*> 1.1.1.0/24       192.168.23.3              0             0 1 i
*                   192.168.12.1             0             0 1 1
1 1 1 i
```

Now we see that 192.168.23.3 is the next hop IP address that we use. You can also see that the AS Path has become longer for the second entry. Let's move on to the next BGP attribute!

The fifth BGP attribute is origin code. There are three origin codes you could see in the BGP table:

- IGP (shows up as **i**)
- EGP (shows up as **e**)
- Incomplete (shows up as **?**)

You will see IGP when you use the **network** command for BGP. It means you advertised the network yourself in BGP. EGP is historical and you won't see it in the BGP table anymore. EGP is an old routing protocol we don't use it anymore. Incomplete means you have redistributed something **into** BGP. Here's a demonstration:

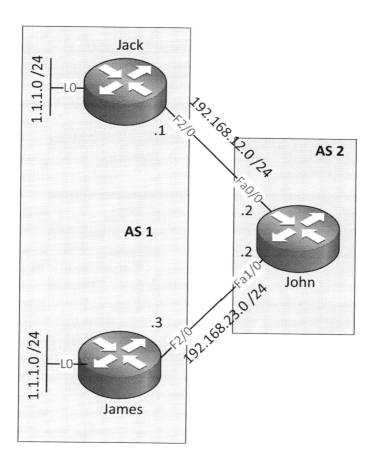

Above you can see the topology that I will use. Router Jack and James are in AS1 and connected to router John in AS2. Both routers have a loopback0 interface with network 1.1.1.0/24 configured on it.

```
Jack(config)#router bgp 1
Jack(config-router)#neighbor 192.168.12.2 remote-as 2
```

```
James(config)#router bgp 1
James(config-router)#neighbor 192.168.23.2 remote-as 2
```

```
John(config)#router bgp 2
John(config-router)#neighbor 192.168.12.1 remote-as 1
John(config-router)#neighbor 192.168.23.3 remote-as 1
```

First we'll configure BGP. Next step is to get network 1.1.1.0/24 in the BGP table:

```
Jack(config)#router bgp 1
Jack(config-router)#network 1.1.1.0 mask 255.255.255.0
```

```
James(config)#router bgp 1
James(config-router)#redistribute connected
```

On router Jack I'll advertise network 1.1.1.0/24 in BGP with the network command, on router James we'll redistribute it. Let's see what router John thinks of this...

```
John#show ip bgp
BGP table version is 4, local router ID is 192.168.23.2
Status codes: s suppressed, d damped, h history, * valid, > best,
i - internal,
              r RIB-failure, S Stale
Origin codes: i - IGP, e - EGP, ? - incomplete

   Network          Next Hop            Metric LocPrf Weight Path
*  1.1.1.0/24       192.168.23.3             0             0 1 ?
*>                  192.168.12.1             0             0 1 i
```

In the output above you can see that router John learned both networks through BGP. There's one small difference however. The first entry shows a ? symbol and the second entry shows an 'i'. As you can see router John prefers the entry with the 'i'. Next stop is MED!

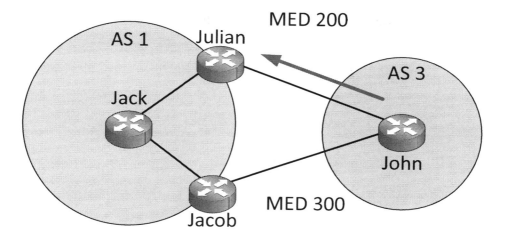

MED (or **metric)** is the sixth BGP attribute:

- MED can be used to advertise to your neighbors how they should **enter your AS**.
- MED is exchanged **between** autonomous systems.
- The **lowest MED** is the preferred path.
- MED is propagated to all routers within the neighbor AS but not passed along any other autonomous systems.

MED (also called metric) is exchanged between autonomous systems and you can use it to let the other AS know which path they should use to enter your AS. Router Julian is sending a MED of 200 towards AS 3. Router Jacob is sending a MED of 300 to AS 3. AS 3 will prefer the lower metric and send all traffic for AS 1 through AS 1.

Local preference is used for **outbound** traffic and MED is for **inbound** traffic. Let's look at an example:

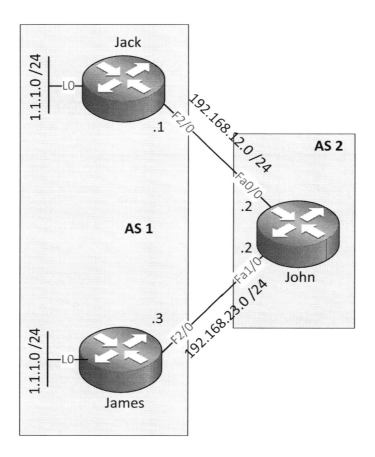

I'm using the same example as I used previously. Let me show you the configuration:

```
Jack(config)#router bgp 1
Jack(config-router)#neighbor 192.168.12.2 remote-as 2
Jack(config-router)#network 1.1.1.0 mask 255.255.255.0
```

```
James(config)#router bgp 1
James(config-router)#neighbor 192.168.23.2 remote-as 2
James(config-router)#network 1.1.1.0 mask 255.255.255.0
```

```
John(config)#router bgp 2
John(config-router)#neighbor 192.168.12.1 remote-as 1
John(config-router)#neighbor 192.168.23.3 remote-as 1
```

This is the BGP configuration, nothing special so far.

```
John#show ip bgp
BGP table version is 2, local router ID is 192.168.23.2
Status codes: s suppressed, d damped, h history, * valid, >
best, i - internal,
              r RIB-failure, S Stale
Origin codes: i - IGP, e - EGP, ? - incomplete

   Network            Next Hop           Metric LocPrf Weight
Path
*   1.1.1.0/24        192.168.23.3            0            0 1 i
*>                    192.168.12.1            0            0 1 i
```

You have seen the example above before. Router John prefers the path through 192.168.12.1. Note that the metric (MED) is 0. Let's play with the MED now:

```
Jack(config)#route-map MED permit 10
Jack(config-route-map)#set metric 700
Jack(config-route-map)#exit

Jack(config)#router bgp 1
Jack(config-router)#neighbor 192.168.12.2 route-map MED out
```

```
James(config)#route-map MED permit 10
James(config-route-map)#set metric 500
James(config-route-map)#exit

James(config)#router bgp 1
James(config-router)#neighbor 192.168.23.2 route-map MED out
```

I'll use route-maps so that router Jack advertises everything with a med of 700 and James will advertise everything with a med of 500.

```
John#show ip bgp
BGP table version is 2, local router ID is 192.168.23.2
Status codes: s suppressed, d damped, h history, * valid, >
best, i - internal,
              r RIB-failure, S Stale
Origin codes: i - IGP, e - EGP, ? - incomplete

   Network            Next Hop           Metric LocPrf Weight
Path
*   1.1.1.0/24        192.168.12.1          700            0 1 i
*>                    192.168.23.3          500            0 1 i
```

You can see router John prefers the path through 192.168.23.3 because the med is lower. That's it!

The seventh BGP attribute is **paths**. BGP will prefer external paths (external BGP) over internal paths (internal BGP). You hardly ever make it this far because normally we already made a decision because of weight, local preference, AS paths or the MED.

The last BGP attribute is **router ID.** If everything is the same then the router ID will be the decision maker...the router with the lowest router ID will be used for the path. We have seen this behavior a couple of times now when I demonstrated you the other BGP attributes.

Was this helpful for you? Path selection is one of the most important things to understand in BGP so make sure you get familiar with them.
If you want some practice you should try the following labs:

http://gns3vault.com/BGP/bgp-attribute-weight.html

http://gns3vault.com/BGP/bgp-attribute-local-preference.html

http://gns3vault.com/BGP/bgp-attribute-as-path.html

http://gns3vault.com/BGP/bgp-attribute-med.html

There is one more small thing I'd like to show you about BGP which is **route filtering**. Filtering for BGP is important because you might receive a lot of prefixes and when you are using BGP for internet connectivity you have to be careful what networks you advertise / receive.

If you are a little fuzzy on prefix-lists you should re-read the route filtering chapter before you continue.

```
James(config)#ip prefix-list 8TO24 permit 0.0.0.0/0 ge 8 le 24

James(config)#router bgp 1
James(config-router)#neighbor 192.168.23.2 prefix-list 8TO24 in
```

It might be a good idea to use a prefix-list like this. It matches the range 0.0.0.0/0 which is any network but the subnet mask has to be between /8 and /24. This will ensure you don't receive small subnets like /25, /26, /27, /28, /29 and /30 or anything larger than /8. This is something that you might see at Internet Service Providers. Basically they tell their customers to do their homework and create summaries for their networks.

Preventing the smaller subnets from entering your BGP table will save you memory and CPU cycles.

```
James(config)#route-map FILTER permit 10
James(config-route-map)#match ip address prefix-list 8TO24
James(config-route-map)#exit

James(config)#router bgp 1
James(config-router)#neighbor 192.168.23.2 route-map FILTER in
```

You can also use a route-map to achieve the same result. In the route-map you can refer to an access-list or a prefix-list to match. Don't forget to activate it for each neighbor you want to filter.

Here we are…you made it all the way through the end of the BGP chapter! Was BGP new for you? If so it might be a bit confusing after learning OSPF and EIGRP. If you have trouble with some of the concepts you should try some of the labs (or watch my videos) and re-read these chapters at a later moment.

Here are some other labs you can try:

http://gns3vault.com/BGP/bgp-basic.html

http://gns3vault.com/BGP/bgp-advanced.html

And for even more BGP action here's an overview of all labs:

http://gns3vault.com/Table/BGP/

20. Introduction to IPv6

In this chapter we'll take a look at IPv6, the reason why we need it and some of the differences with IPv4. As long as the Internet exists, IPv4 has been the protocol that is used for addressing and rouing. The problem with IPv4 however is that we are running out of addresses.

So what happened to IPv4? What went wrong? We have 32-bits which gives us 4,294,467,295 IP addresses. Remember our Class A,B and C story at the beginning of this book? When the Internet was born you would get a Class A,B or C network. Class C gives you a block of 256 IP addresses, a class B is 65.535 IP addresses and a class A even 16,777,216 IP addresses. Large companies like Apple, Microsoft, IBM etc. got one or more Class A networks...but do they really need 16 million IP addresses? Many IP addresses were just wasted.

So we started using VLSM (Variable Length Subnet Mask) so we could use any subnet mask we like and create smaller subnets, no longer just the class A,B or C networks. We also have NAT and PAT so we can have many private IP addresses behind a single public IP addresses.

Nevertheless the Internet has grown in a way nobody expected 20 years ago. Despite all our cool tricks like VLSM and NAT/PAT we needed more IP addresses and so IPv6 was born.

What happened to IPv5? Good question...IP version 5 was used for an experimental project called "Internet Stream Protocol". It's defined in a RFC if you are interested for historical reasons: http://www.faqs.org/rfcs/rfc1819.html
IPv6 has 128-bit addresses compared to our 32-bit IPv4 addresses. Keep in mind every additional bit doubles the number of IP addresses...so we go from 4 billion to 8 billion, 16,32,64, etc. Keep doubling until you reach 128-bit. Just for fun I looked up how many IPv6 addresses this will give us:

- 340,282,366,920,938,463,463,374,607,431,768,211,456

Can we even pronounce this? Let's try this:

- 340- undecillion
- 282- decillion
- 366- nonillion
- 920- octillion
- 938- septillion
- 463- sextillion
- 463- quintillion
- 374- quadrillion
- 607- trillion
- 431- billion
- 768- million

- 211- thousand
- 456

That's mind boggling... This gives us enough IP addresses for networks on earth, the moon, mars and the rest of the universe. IPv6 addresses are written down in hexadecimal.

IPv4 and IPv6 are **not compatible with each other** so many protocols have been updated or replaced to work with IPv6, here are some examples:

- OSPF has been upgraded from version 2 (IPv4) to version 3 (IPv6).
- ICMP has been upgraded to ICMP version 6.
- ARP has been replaced with **NDP (Neighbor Discovery Protocol)**.

The header of an IPv6 packet contains the source and destination addresses but compared to IPv4 it has become much simpler:

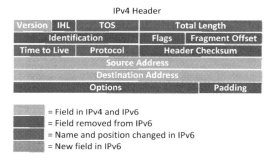
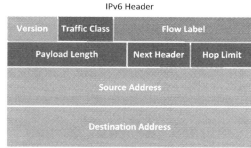

Instead of adding all the fields to the header already, the IPv6 header uses a "next header" that refers to optional headers. Since the header is much simpler routers will have less work to do.

What about routing? Is there a difference between IPv4 and IPv6? Let's look at the routing options:

- Static Routing
- RIPng
- OSPFv3
- MP-BGP4
- EIGRP

You can still use static routes just like in IPv4, nothing new here. RIP has been upgraded and is now called **RIPng** or **RIP Next Generation** (from the Star Trek TV series).

OSPF for IPv4 is actually version 2 and for IPv6 we have version 3. This is a separate protocol, it only runs IPv6. There are only minor changes made to OSPFv3.

BGP (Border Gateway Protocol) is the routing protocol that glues the Internet together. It's not a CCNA topic but it's good to know that it supports IPv6. MP-BGP stands for Multi-Protocol BGP and it can route IPv6.

EIGRP supports IPv6 as well.

Just keep in mind that OSPF and EIGRP support IPv6 but those are separate protocols. If you have a network with IPv4 and IPv6 you will run a routing protocol for IPv4 and another one for IPv6. Running IPv4 and IPv6 at the same time is called **dual stack**.

Since the two protocols are not compatible the future will be a migration from IPv4 to IPv6. This means you will run both protocols on your network and perhaps one day you can pull the plug on IPv4 since the whole Internet has been configured for IPv6.

Let's take a look at the format of an IPv6 address:

2041:0000:140F:0000:0000:0000:875B:131B

First of all it's hexadecimal and it's a much longer than an IPv4 address. There are eight pieces that consist of 4 hex digits each, so a 128-bit address can be represented with 32-bit hex characters. If you are unsure how hexadecimal works, take a look at the table below:

Hexadecimal	Binary	Hexadecimal	Binary
0	0000	8	1000
1	0001	9	1001
2	0010	A	1010
3	0011	B	1011
4	0100	C	1100
5	0101	D	1101
6	0110	E	1110
7	0111	F	1111

In hexadecimal we count from 0 to F just like we would count from 0 to 15 in decimal:

- A = 10
- B = 11
- C = 12
- D = 13
- E = 14
- F = 15

Using hexadecimal helps to make our addresses shorter but typing in an IPv6 address is still a lot of work. Imagine calling a friend and asking him if he can ping IPv6 address 2041:0000:140F:0000:0000:0000:875B:131B to see if he can reach his default gateway.

To help us out, it's possible to make IPv6 addresses **shorter**. Here's an example:

- Original: 2041:0000:140F:0000:0000:0000:875B:131B
- Short: 2041:0000:140F::875B:131B

If there is a string of zeroes you can remove them by replacing them with a double colon (::). In the IPv6 address above I removed the zeroes making the address a bit shorter. You can only do this **once**.

We can make this IPv6 address even shorter using another trick:

- Short: 2041:0000:140F::875B:131B
- Shorter: 2041:0:140F::875B:131B

If you have a block with 4 zeroes you can remove them and leave only a single zero there.

We can also remove any leading zeroes:

- Original: 2001:0001:0002:0003:0004:0005:0006:0007
- Short: 2001:1:2:3:4:5:6:7

Let me summarize the rules:

- A string of zeroes can be removed leaving only a colon (::). You can only do this once.
- 4 zeroes can be removed leaving only a single zero.
- Leading zeroes can be removed within a block.

You can't remove all zeroes otherwise your IPv6 device has no idea where to fill in the zeroes to make it 128-bit again.

IPv4 addresses have a subnet mask but instead of typing something like 255.255.255.0 we use a **prefix length** for IPv6. Here is an example of an IPv6 prefix:

2001:1111:2222:3333::/64

This is pretty much the same as using 192.168.1.1 /24. The number behind the / are the number of bits that we use for the prefix. In the example above it means that 2001:1111:2222:3333 is the prefix (64 bits) and everything behind it can be used for hosts.

When calculating subnets for IPv4 we can use the subnet mask to determine the network address and for IPv6 we can do something alike. For any given IPv6 address we can calculate what the prefix is but it works a bit different.

Let me show you what I'm talking about, here's an IPv6 address that could be assigned to a host:

2001:1234:5678:1234:5678:ABCD:EF12:1234/64

What part from this IPv6 address is the prefix and what part identifies the host?

Prefix   Host

2001:1234:5678:1234 | **2001:1234:5678:1234**

Since we use a /64 it means that the first 64 bits are the prefix. Each hexadecimal character represents 4 binary bits so that means that this part is the prefix:

2001:1234:5678:1234

This part has 16 hexadecimal characters. 16 x 4 means 64 bits. So that's the prefix right there. The rest of the IPv6 address identifies the host:

5678:ABCD:EF12:1234

So we figured out that "2001:1234:5678:1234" is the prefix part but writing it down like this is not correct. To write down the prefix correctly we need to add 0s at the end of this prefix so that it is a 128 bit address again and add the prefix length:

2001:1234:5678:1234:0000:0000:0000:0000/64 is a valid prefix but we can make it shorter. This string of 0s can be removed and replace by a single ::

2001:1234:5678:1234::/64

That's the shortest way to write down the prefix. Let's look at another example:

3211::1234:ABCD:5678:1010:CAFE/64

Before we can see what the prefix is, we should write down the complete address as this one has been shortened (see the :: ?). Just add the 0s until we have a full 128 bit address again:

3211:0000:0000:1234:ABCD:5678:1010:CAFE/64

We still have a prefix length of 64 bits. A single hexadecimal character represents 4 binary bits, so the first 16 hexadecimal characters are the prefix:

3211:0000:0000:1234

Now we can add 0s at the end to make it a 128 bit address again and add the prefix length:

3211:0000:0000:1234::/64

That's a good looking prefix but we can make it a little shorter:

3211:0:0:1234::/64

4 zeroes in a row can be replaced by a single one, so "3211:0:0:1234::/64" is the shortest we can make this prefix.

Depending on the prefix length it makes the calculations very easy or (very) difficult. In the examples I just showed you both prefixes had a length of 64. What if I had a prefix length of /53 or something?

Each hexadecimal character represents 4 binary bits. When your prefix length is a multiple of 16 then it's easy to calculate because 16 binary bits represent 4 hexadecimal characters. Here's an illustration:

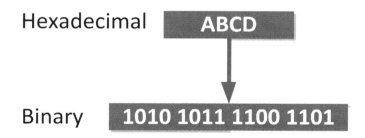

So with a prefix length of 64 we have 4 "blocks" with 4 hexadecimal characters each which makes it easy to calculate. When the prefix length is a multiple of 4 then it's still not too bad because the boundary will be a single hexadecimal character.

When the prefix length is not a multiple of 16 or 4 it means we have to do some binary calculations. Let me give you an example!

2001:1234:abcd:5678:9877:3322:5541:aabb/53

This is our IPv6 address and I would like to know the prefix for this address. Where do I start?

First I have to determine in what "block" my 53th bit is located:

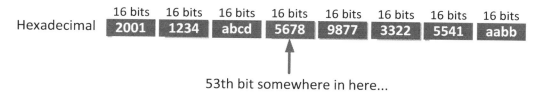

53th bit somewhere in here...

Somewhere in the blue block we will find the 53th bit. To know what the prefix is we will have to calculate those hexadecimal characters to binary:

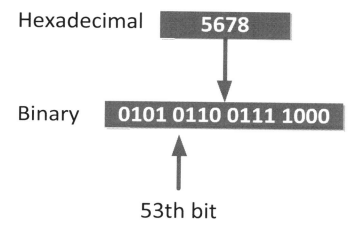

53th bit

We now have the block that contains the 53th, this is where the boundary is between "prefix" and "host":

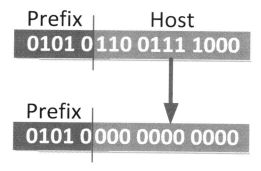

Now we will set the host bits to 0 so that only the prefix remains. Finally we calculate from binary back to hexadecimal:

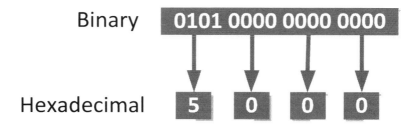

Put this block back into place and set all the other host bits to 0 as well:

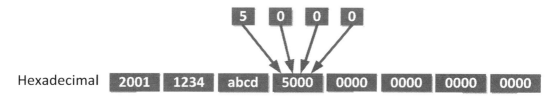

We have now found our prefix! 2001:1234:abcd:5000::/53 is the answer. It's not that bad to calculate but you do have to get your hands dirty with binary...

It will take some time to get used to IPv6 addressing and finding the prefixes, but the more you do it the easier it will become.

In the remainder of this chapter we'll talk some more about the different IPv6 addressing types.

IPv4 addresses are organized with a "class system" where Class A,B & C are for unicast IP addresses and class D are for multicast. Most of the IP addresses in these classes are public IP addresses and some are private IP addresses meant for our internal networks.

There is no such thing as classes for IPv6 but IANA did reserve certain IPv6 ranges for specific purposes. We also have private and public IPv6 addresses.

Originally the idea behind IPv4 was that each and every host that is connected to the Internet would have a public IP address. Each company would get a class A,B or C network and the network engineers at the company would further subnet it so that each host and network device would have a public IP address.
The problem however is that the IPv4 address space was too small and giving out complete A,B or C networks wasn't very wise. Even if you only required a small number of IP addresses you would still receive a class C network which gives you 254 usable IP addresses. A company that required 2.000 IP address would get a class B that gives you over 65.000 IP addresses.

Since we were running out of IP addresses we started using things like VLSM (getting rid of the class A, B, C idea) and configured private IP addresses on our LANs and used NAT/PAT instead.

IPv6 offers two options for unicast addresses:

- **Global Unicast**
- **Unique Local**

 There used to be a third range of addresses called "site local" that start with FEC0::/10. This range was originally intended to be used on internal networks but has been removed from the IPv6 standard.

The global unicast IPv6 are similar to IPv4 public addresses. Each company that wants connectivity to the Internet with IPv6 will receive a block of IPv6 addresses that they can further subnet into smaller prefixes so that all their devices have a unique IPv6 address. The reserved block is called a **global routing prefix**.

Since the IPv6 address space is so huge, everyone can get a global routing prefix. Let's take a look at how the IPv6 addresses prefixes are assigned. Let's say a company receives prefix 2001:828:105:45::/64. How did they get it?

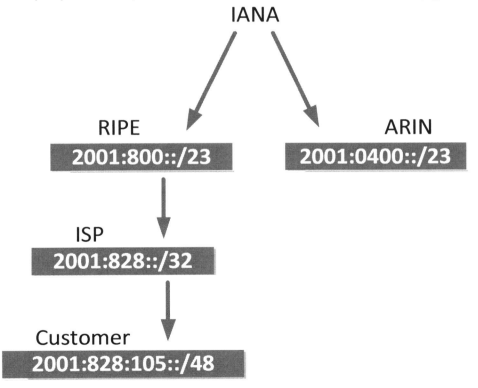

We'll walk through this picture from top to bottom:

- IANA is responsible for the allocation of all IPv6 prefixes. They will assign different blocks to the registries. ARIN is for North America, RIPE is for Europe, Middle East and central Asia. In total there are 5 of these registries. IANA assigns 2001:800::/23 to RIPE and 2001:0400::/23 to ARIN (and many other prefixes).
- An ISP that falls under the registry of RIPE requests a block of IPv6 space. They receive 2001:0828::/32 from them that they can use for customers.
- The ISP will further subnet their 2001:0828::/32 address space for their customers. In this example the customer receives the 2001:828:105::/48 prefix.

IANA has reserved certain IPv6 address ranges for different purposes, just like they did for IPv4. Originally they reserved IPv6 addresses thart with with hexadecimal 2 or 3 as global unicast addresses. This can be written as **2000::/3**. Nowadays they use everything for global unicast that is not reserved for other purposes.

Some of the prefixes that are reserved are:

- **FD: Unique Local**
- **FF: Multicast**
- **FE80: Link-Local**

We will discuss the unique local and link-local prefixes later in this chapter.
In my example the customer received 2001:828:105::/48 from the ISP but before I can do anything with this prefix I will have to subnet it for the different VLANs and point-to-point links that I might have. Subnetting for IPv6 is kinda the same as for IPv4 but the math is easier most of the times. Since the address space is so huge almost everyone **uses the /64 prefix for subnets**. It doesn't make sense to use smaller subnets like a /88 or /90 because we have plenty of room when we use IPv6.

Using IPv4 we had a "network" and "host" part and class A, B or C determines how many bits we use for the network part:

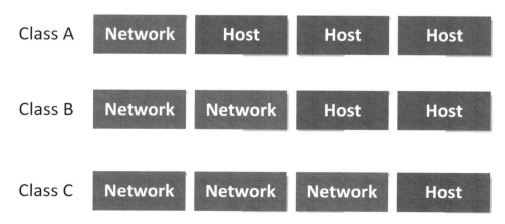

Class A | Network | Host | Host | Host

Class B | Network | Network | Host | Host

Class C | Network | Network | Network | Host

When we subnet in IPv4 we take some extra bits from the host part so that we can create more subnets:

And of course as a result we will have fewer hosts per subnet. Subnetting for IPv6 uses a similar structure that looks like this:

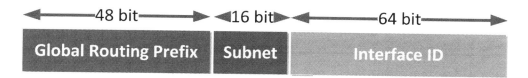

The global routing prefix was assigned to you by the ISP and in my example the customer received 2001:828:105::/48. The last 64 bits are called the **interface ID** and this is the equivalent of the host part in IPv4.

This leaves us with 16 bits in the middle that I can use to create subnets. If I want I can steal some more bits from the Interface ID to create even more subnets but there's no need for this.

Using 16 bits we can create 65.536 subnets ...more than enough for most of us. And with 64 bits for the interface ID per subnet, we can have eighteen quintillion, four hundred fourty-six quadrillion, seven hundred fourty-four trillion, seventy-four billion, seven hundred nine million, five hundred fifty-one thousand, six hundred and something hosts per subnet. That should be more than enough!

Using a 64 bit Interface ID is also very convenient because it cuts your IPv6 address exactly in half!

Let's say our customer with prefix 2001:828:105::/48 wants to create some subnets for his internal network. What addresses can we use?

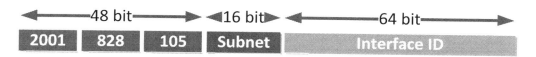

16 bit gives us 4 hexadecimal characters. So all the possible combinations we can make with those 4 characters are our possible subnets. Everything between 0000 and FFFF are valid subnets:

- 2001:828:105:**0000**::/64
- 2001:828:105:**0001**::/64

- 2001:828:105:**0002**::/64
- 2001:828:105:**0003**::/64
- 2001:828:105:**0004**::/64
- 2001:828:105:**0005**::/64
- 2001:828:105:**0006**::/64
- 2001:828:105:**0007**::/64
- 2001:828:105:**0008**::/64
- 2001:828:105:**0009**::/64
- 2001:828:105:**000A**::/64
- 2001:828:105:**000B**::/64
- 2001:828:105:**000C**::/64
- 2001:828:105:**000D**::/64
- 2001:828:105:**000E**::/64
- 2001:828:105:**000F**::/64
- 2001:828:105:**0010**::/64
- 2001:828:105:**0011**::/64
- 2001:828:105:**0012**::/64
- 2001:828:105:**0013**::/64
- 2001:828:105:**0014**::/64
- And so on...

In total there are 65,535 possible subnets so unfortunately I can't add all of them in the book...we can now assign these prefixes to different point-to-point links, VLANs, etc.

Here's an example of what it could look like:

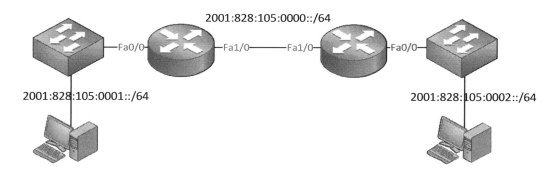

Now you know how the global prefixes work and how to subnet, what about the interface ID? We haven't talked about assigning IPv6 addresses to our hosts yet. Assigning addresses to hosts is almost the same as for IPv4:

- Addresses have to be unique for each host.
- You can't use the prefix address as a host address.

You can configure the IPv6 address **manually** along with a default gateway, DNS server and so on or your hosts can learn an IPv6 addres automatically either through DHCP or something new called **SLAAC (Stateless Address**

Autoconfiguration).

Here's an example of IPv6 addresses you could pick for the topology I just showed you:

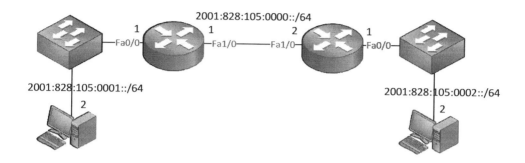

For the router interfaces I would suggest to use low numbers since they are easy to remember. This example shows a unique global unicast IPv6 address for each device.

This is all I have for you about global unicast addresses, we still have to cover the unique local unicast addresses.

Unique local addresses work like the IPv4 private addresses. You can use these addresses on your own network if you don't intend to connect to the Internet or if you plan to use IPv6 NAT. The advantage of unique local addresses is that you don't need to register at an authority to get some addresses.

You can recognize these addresses because they all start with **FD** in hexadecimal. There are still some rules you have to follow if you want to use unique local addresses:

- Make sure FD are **the first two hexadecimal** characters.
- You need to make up a **40 bit global ID**, you can pick whatever you like.
- Add the 40 bit global ID after the "FD" to **create a 48-bit prefix**.
- The next 16 bits have to be used for subnets.

This leaves you the last 64 bits to use for the interface ID. Here's what the unique local address looks like:

This gives us a unique local address that we can use on our own networks. Subnetting global unicast or unique local addresses is exactly the same with the exception that this time we make up the prefix ourselves instead of the ISP assigning us a global prefix.

The global ID can be anything you like, with 40 bits you will have 10 hexadecimal characters to play with. You could pick something like 00 0000 0001, so when you put "FD" in front of it you will have FD00:0000:0001::/48 as your prefix. You can remove some zeroes and make this prefix shorter, it will look like this: FD00:0:1::/48

Now you can add different values behind the prefix to make unique subnets:

- FD00:0:1:**0000**::/64
- FD00:0:1:**0001**::/64
- FD00:0:1:**0002**::/64
- FD00:0:1:**0003**::/64
- FD00:0:1:**0004**::/64
- FD00:0:1:**0005**::/64
- FD00:0:1:**0006**::/64
- FD00:0:1:**0007**::/64
- FD00:0:1:**0008**::/64
- FD00:0:1:**0009**::/64
- FD00:0:1:**000A**::/64
- FD00:0:1:**000B**::/64
- FD00:0:1:**000C**::/64
- FD00:0:1:**000D**::/64
- FD00:0:1:**000E**::/64
- FD00:0:1:**000F**::/64
- FD00:0:1:**0010**::/64
- FD00:0:1:**0011**::/64
- FD00:0:1:**0012**::/64
- FD00:0:1:**0013**::/64
- FD00:0:1:**0014**::/64
- And so on…

When you are doing labs it's a good idea to pick a simple global ID so that you end up with a short and simple to remember prefix. For production networks, it's better to use a global ID that it truly unique. Perhaps one day you want to connect your network to another network, or perhaps your company buys another company so you have to merge networks. When both networks have the same global ID you will have to renumber IPv6 address for one network, while if the global IDs are different you can just connect them to each other without any issues.

In the remaining of this chapter we'll take a look at how we can configure IPv6 on our routers. When you want to configure an IPv6 address on a router you have two options:

- Manually configure the full 128 bit IPv6 address.
- Use EUI-64.

I'll show you how to manually configure the IPv6 address first and then I'll explain what EUI-64 is all about. This is how you do it:

```
Router(config)#interface fastEthernet 0/0
Router(config-if)#ipv6 address 2001:1234:5678:abcd::1/64
```

You need to use the **ipv6 address** command and then you can type in the IPv6 address. The prefix that I am using is 2001:1234:5678:abcd and this router will have "1" as its "host" address. You can also type the full IPv6 address if you want:

```
Router(config)#interface fastEthernet 0/0
Router(config-if)#ipv6 address
2001:1234:5678:abcd:0000:0000:0000:0001/64
```

This command will have the exact same result. We can verify the subnet and IPv6 address like this:

```
Router#show ipv6 interface fa0/0
FastEthernet0/0 is up, line protocol is up
  IPv6 is enabled, link-local address is FE80::C000:18FF:FE5C:0
  No Virtual link-local address(es):
  Global unicast address(es):
    2001:1234:5678:ABCD::1, subnet is 2001:1234:5678:ABCD::/64
```

This shows us the global unicast address and our subnet. There is one more important thing when we configure IPv6 on a router. By default, the router will not forward any IPv6 packets and it will not build a routing table. To enable the "processing" of IPv6 packets we need to enable it:

```
Router(config)#ipv6 unicast-routing
```

Most of the "ip" commands will work, just try "ipv6" instead and see what it does:

```
Router#show ipv6 interface brief
FastEthernet0/0                 [up/up]
    FE80::C000:18FF:FE5C:0
    2001:1234:5678:ABCD::1
```

```
Router#show ipv6 route connected
IPv6 Routing Table - 3 entries
Codes: C - Connected, L - Local, S - Static, R - RIP, B - BGP
       U - Per-user Static route, M - MIPv6
       I1 - ISIS L1, I2 - ISIS L2, IA - ISIS interarea, IS -
ISIS summary
       O - OSPF intra, OI - OSPF inter, OE1 - OSPF ext 1, OE2 -
OSPF ext 2
       ON1 - OSPF NSSA ext 1, ON2 - OSPF NSSA ext 2
       D - EIGRP, EX - EIGRP external
C   2001:1234:5678:ABCD::/64 [0/0]
       via ::, FastEthernet0/0
```

Now you know how to configure an IPv6 address yourself and how to verify it. The second method we can use to configure an address is called **EUI-64 (Extended Unique Identifier)**. This can be used to make the router **generate its own interface ID** instead of typing it in ourselves.

The router will take the MAC address of its interface and use it as the interface ID. However, a MAC address is 48 bit and the interface ID is 64 bit. What are we going to do with the missing bits?

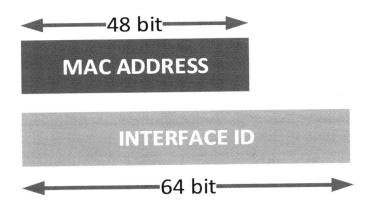

Here's what we will do to fill the missing bits:

1. We take the MAC address and split it into two pieces.
2. We insert "FFFE" in between the two pieces so that we have a 64 bit value.
3. We invert the 7th bit of the interface ID.

So if my MAC address would be 1234.5678.ABCD then this is what the interface ID will become:

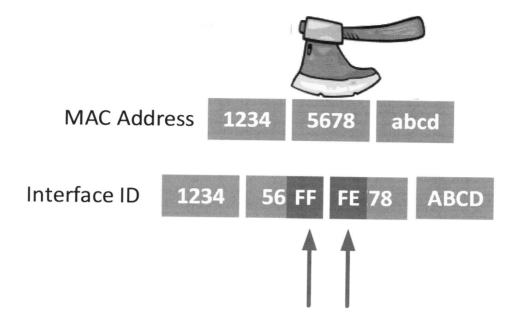

MAC Address | 1234 | 5678 | abcd

Interface ID | 1234 | 56 FF | FE 78 | ABCD

Above you see how we split the MAC address and put FFFE in the middle. It doesn't include the final stip which is "inverting the 7th" bit. To do this you have to convert the first two hexadecimal characters of the first byte to binary, lookup the 7th bit and invert it. This means that if it's a 0 you need to make it a 1, and if it's a 1 it has to become a 0.

The 7th bit represents the "universal unique" bit. A burned in MAC address will always have this bit set to 0. When you change the MAC address this bit has to be set to 1. Normally people don't change the MAC address of this router which means that EUI-64 will change the 7th bit from 0 to 1 most of the time. Here's what it looks like:

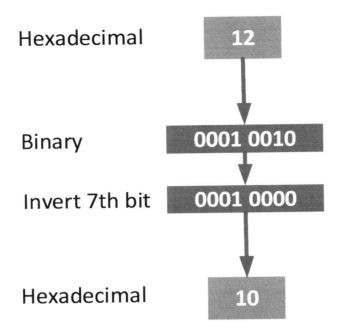

We take the first two hexadecimal characters of the first byte which are "12" and convert those back to binary. Then we invert the 7th bit from 1 to 0 and make it hexadecimal again. So in fact my EUI-64 interface ID will look like this:

Now let's take a look at the configuration of EUI-64 on a router! I'll use 2001:1234:5678:abcd::/64 as the prefix:

```
Router(config)#interface fastEthernet 0/0
Router(config-if)#ipv6 address 2001:1234:5678:abcd::/64 eui-64
```

In this I configured the router with the IPv6 prefix and I used **EUI-64** at the end. This is how we can automatically generate the interface ID using the mac address. Now take a look at the IPv6 address that it created:

```
Router#show interfaces fastEthernet 0/0 | include Hardware
   Hardware is Gt96k FE, address is c200.185c.0000 (bia
c200.185c.0000)
```

```
Router#show ipv6 interface fa0/0
FastEthernet0/0 is up, line protocol is up
  IPv6 is enabled, link-local address is FE80::C000:18FF:FE5C:0
  No Virtual link-local address(es):
  Global unicast address(es):
    2001:1234:5678:ABCD:C000:18FF:FE5C:0, subnet is
2001:1234:5678:ABCD::/64 [EUI]
```

See the C000:18FF:FE5C:0 part? That's the MAC address that is split in 2, FFFE in the middle and the "2" in "C200" of the MAC address has been inverted which is why it now shows up as "C000".
When you use EUI-64 on an interface that doesn't have a MAC address then it will select the MAC address of the lowest numbered interface on the router.

When you use EUI-64 you should type a 64-bit prefix, not a full IPv6 128-bit address. When you do this, you won't get an error but Cisco IOS will only keep the 64-bit prefix of whatever you typed in and generates the interface ID anyway.

Normally you probably won't use EUI-64 on a router to configure an interface but this is a very useful technique for normal hosts like windows, linux or mac computers. You will probably configure an IPv6 address manually on your router's interface or use an autoconfiguration technique like DHCP or SLAAC.

When you take a close look at the output of the show ipv6 interface you might noticed that there is one more IPv6 address in there:

```
Router#show ipv6 interface fa0/0
FastEthernet0/0 is up, line protocol is up
  IPv6 is enabled, link-local address is FE80::C000:18FF:FE5C:0
```

This address is called a **link-local address** and it has some special purposes for IPv6.

Each device that has IPv6 enabled will **automatically** generate a link-local address. These addresses are unicast, **can't be routed** and are only used within the subnet, which is why they are called "link-local".

A number of protocols use the link-local addresses instead of the global unicast addresses, a good example is NDP (Neighbor Discovery Protocol) which is used to discover the MAC addresses of other IPv6 devices in the subnet (NDP replaces ARP for IPv4).

Routing protocols also use these link-local addresses to establish neighbor adjacencies and also as the next hop for routes. We'll see this when we talk about IPv6 routing.

The FE80::/10 address space has been reserved for link-local addresses which covers FE8, FE9, FEA and FEB. However the RFC that describes link-local addresses states that the next 54 bits have to be zeroes so the link-local addresses will always look like this:

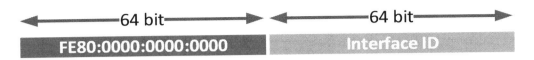

The link-local address will always start with FE80:0000:0000:0000 and the interface ID can be configured using different methods. Cisco routers will use EUI-64 to create a interface ID while other operating systems like Microsoft use a random method to create the interface ID. In the example below you can see that EUI-64 was used to create the link-local address:

```
Router#show interfaces fastEthernet 0/0 | include Hardware
   Hardware is Gt96k FE, address is c200.185c.0000 (bia
c200.185c.0000)
```

```
Router#show ipv6 interface fa0/0
FastEthernet0/0 is up, line protocol is up
   IPv6 is enabled, link-local address is FE80::C000:18FF:FE5C:0
```

The first part is FE80:: and the second part is the EUI-64 created interface ID:

C000:18FF:FE5C:0.

Cisco routers will create a link-local address when you configure an IPv6 address on the interface (global unicast or unique local) or when you enable IPv6 on the interface, you can do it like this:

```
Router(config)#interface fa0/0
Router(config-if)#ipv6 enable
```

Use the **ipv6 enable** command to make the router generate a link-local address.

```
Router#show ipv6 int fa0/0
FastEthernet0/0 is up, line protocol is up
   IPv6 is enabled, link-local address is FE80::C000:15FF:FE94:0
```

By default Cisco IOS will use EUI-64 to create the link-local address but you can also configure one yourself. Just make sure the address starts with FE80::/10 (FE8,FE9,FEA or FEB). Here's how you can configure the link-local address:

```
Router(config-if)#ipv6 address FE90:1234:5678:ABCD::1 link-local
```

Just use the **link-local keyword** to tell the router this should be a link-local address. Let's verify it:

```
Router#show ipv6 int fa0/0
FastEthernet0/0 is up, line protocol is up
  IPv6 is enabled, link-local address is FE90:1234:5678:ABCD::1
```

I can't think of any good reason why you might want to change the link-local address but it's something you might encounter on the exam.

Besides the link-local addresses there is one more addressing type we have to discuss and that's multicast.

Somewhere in the beginning of this book you learned about unicast and broadcast domains. When a host sends a broadcast, all other devices within the subnet will receive it whether they want it or not. Sending broadcasts is very inefficient and they have been **removed from IPv6**.

Multicast is also used to send something from one host to multiple receivers but the difference is that multicast traffic only ends up at hosts that want to receive it. Everyone that listens to a certain multicast address will receive the packets. It's just like a radiostation, if you want to listen...you have to *tune in* at the right frequency.

IPv6 uses multicast for many reasons. IPv6 hosts that want to send something to all hosts running IPv6 can use the **FF02::1** multicast address. Everyone that has IPv6 enabled listens to this address.

When an IPv6 router wants to send something to all other IPv6 routers (but not hosts!) it can send it to **FF02::2**.

Routing protocols also use multicast addresses. For example, EIGRP uses **FF02::A** and OSPF uses **FF02::5** and **FF02::6**.

Multicast traffic is routable but some traffic should stay within the subnet. When this is the case then these addresses will have a **link-local scope** and they won't be forwarded by routers from one subnet to another.

The **FF00::/8** range has been reserved for IPv6 multicast while the **FF02::/16** range is reserved for link-local scope multicast addresses. On a Cisco router you can see per interface to which multicast addresses the router is listening:

```
Router#show ipv6 int fa0/0
FastEthernet0/0 is up, line protocol is up
  IPv6 is enabled, link-local address is FE90:1234:5678:ABCD::1
  No Virtual link-local address(es):
  No global unicast address is configured
  Joined group address(es):
    FF02::1
    FF02::2
    FF02::1:FF00:1
```

This particular router is listening to the "all IPv6 hosts" and "all IPv6 routers" multicast addresses. Once you configure OSPF or EIGRP for IPv6 you will notice that the interface will join the corresponding multicast addresses.

The third address that we have (FF02::1:FF00:1) is called the **solicited-node multicast address**. It is used for *neighbor discovery* which we will discuss in the next chapter.

The solicited-node multicast address is based on the unicast IPv6 address of the host, and to be more precise...the **last six hecadecimal characters of the unicast address**. All hosts that have the same 6 hexadecimal characters in their unicast IPv6 address will end up with the same solicited-node address.

When you send something to this solicited-node address, all hosts with the same address will receive the packets. It's kinda like the "all IPv6 hosts" multicast address but this time we have a private room where the only members are VIPs that share the same last 6 hexadecimal characters.

All solicited-node addresses start with FF02::1:FF so they look like this:

My router has a solicited node address of FF02::1:FF00:1 while the link-local address is FE90:1234:5678:ABCD::1.

When we write down the link-local address completely it looks like this:

FE90:1234:5678:ABCD:0000:0000:0000:0001

Take the last 6 hexadecimal characters from this address:

00:0001

And put those behind the solicited node address prefix to get the full solicited node address:

FF02:0000:0000:0000:0000:0001:FF00:0001

We can remove some of the zeroes to make it shorter and it will look like this:

FF02::1:FF00:1

That's how to calculate the solicited-node address.

Something new to IPv6 is **autoconfiguration** which is almost a "mini-DHCP" server and some protocols have been removed or changed. Just like IPv4, hosts configured for IPv6 need to learn the MAC address of other devices but we don't use ARP anymore, it has been replaced by a protocol called **NDP (Neighbor Discovery Protocol)**.

Besides learning MAC addresses, NDP is used for a number of tasks:

- **Router Discovery**: NDP is used to learn about all available IPv6 routers in the subnet.
- **MAC Address Discovery**: Once a host has done the DAD check and is using an IPv6 address it will have to discover the MAC addresses of hosts it wants to communicate with.
- **DAD (Duplicate Address Detection)**: Each IPv6 host will wait to use its address unless it knows that no other device is using the same address. This process is called DAD and NDP does this for us.
- **SLAAC (Stateless Address Autoconfiguration)**: We'll cover SLAAC in a bit in more detail, but NDP is used to learn what address and prefix length the host should use.

We'll walk through the different tasks to see how they work. We'll start with the router discovery. When a host is configured for IPv6 it will automatically discover the routers on the subnet.

An IPv6 host can use NDP to detect all routers on the subnet that could be used as a default gateway. Basically the host will send a message asking if there are any routers out there, and the routers will respond. The two messages used are:

- **RS (Router Solicitation)** which is send to the "all ipv6 routers" FF02::2 multicast address.
- **RA (Router Advertisement)** is sent by the router and includes its link-local IPv6 address.

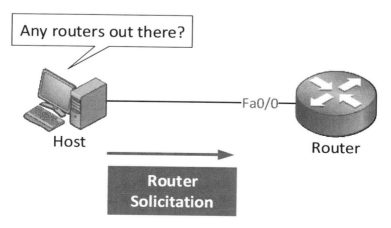

341

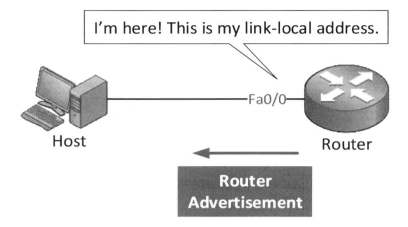

When a host sends the router solicitation a router will respond to the unicast address of the host. Routers will also periodically send router advertisements for everyone that's interested, they will use the FF02::1 "all nodes" address for this.

Most routers will also have a global unicast address configured on the interface, when this is the case the hosts will not only learn about the link-local address but also the **prefix** that is used on the subnet.

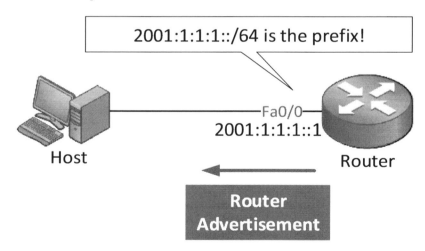

This prefix can be used for SLAAC (Stateless Address Autoconfiguration) that we'll look at later.

NPD is also used as a replacement for ARP. It uses two kind of messages for this:

- **NS (Neighbor Solicitation)**
- **NA (Neighbor Advertisement)**

The neighbor solicitation works similar to the ARP request, it will ask a certain host for its MAC address and the neighbor advertisement is like the ARP reply as it is used to send the MAC address. Basically it looks like this:

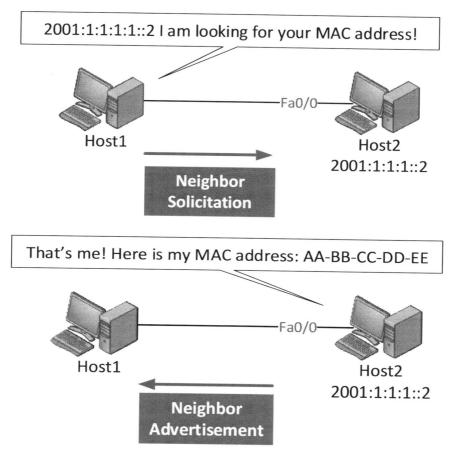

Whenever a host sends a neighbor solicitation it will first check its cache to see if it already knows the MAC address of the device it is looking for. If it's not there, it will send the neighbor solicitation. These neighbor solicitation messages use the **solicited-node multicast address**.

Besides discovering MAC addresses, the NS and NA messages are also used to **detect duplicate IPv6 addresses**. Before an IPv6 device uses a unicast address it will perform **DAD (Duplicate Address Detection)** to see if someone else is already using the same IPv6 address. If the address is in use, the host will not use it. Here's what it looks like:

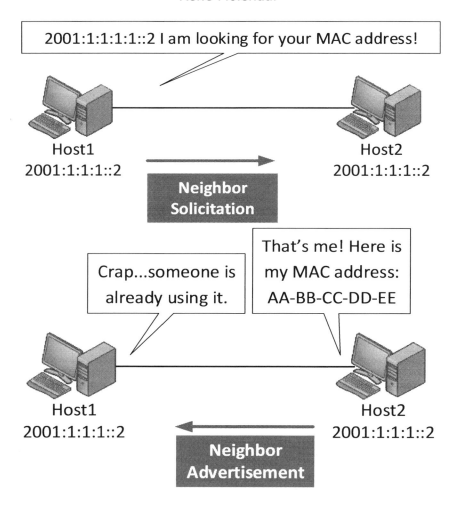

Host1 has configured 2001:1:1:1::2 as its IPv6 address which is already in use by host2. It will send a neighbor solicitation but because host2 has the same IPv6 address it will reply with a neighbor advertisement. Host1 now knows that this is a duplicate IPv6 address. This check is performed for all of the unicast addresses including the link-local addresses. It occurs when you configure them and each time the interface is 'up'.

The last NPD that we will look at is SLAAC (Stateless Address Autoconfiguration), which lets hosts automatically configure their IPv6 address. For IPv4 we have always used DHCP to automatically assign an IP address, default gateway and DNS server to our hosts and this option is still available for IPv6 (we'll look at it in a minute).

DHCP works really well but the downside is that you need to install a DHCP server, configure the pool with address ranges, default gateways and DNS servers.

When we use SLAAC our hosts will not receive an IPv6 address from a central server but it will **learn the prefix** that is used on the subnet and then creates its own interface ID to generate a unique IPv6 address. This is how SLAAC works:

1. The host first learns about the prefix by using NDS RS & RA messages.
2. The host takes the prefix and creates an interface ID to make a unique IPv6 address.
3. The host performs a DAD to make sure the IPv6 address is not used by anyone else.

Cisco routers will use EUI-64 to create the interface ID but some operating systems will use a random value. Thanks to SLAAC the host will have an IPv6 address and a default router but one ingredient is still missing...**the DNS server**. SLAAC can't help us with finding a DNS server so for this step we still require DHCP.

DHCP for IPv6 is called DHCPv6 and comes in two forms:

- Stateful
- Stateless

We'll cover DHCPv6 in a minute but for SLAAC we need to understand what **stateless DHCPv6** is about. Normally a DHCP server will keep track of the IP addresses that is has leased to clients, in other words it has to keep the "state" of what IP addresses have been leased and when they expire.
A stateless DHCPv6 server **doesn't keep track of anything** for clients. It has a simple configuration with the IPv6 addresses of a few DNS servers. When an IPv6 host asks the DHCPv6 server for the IPv6 address of the DNS server it will give this address and that's it.

So when you use SLAAC, you still need stateless DHCPv6 to learn about the DNS servers.

You have now seen all the tasks that NPD does for us:

- Router Discovery
- MAC Address Discovery
- Duplicate Address Detection
- Stateless Address Autoconfiguration

Let's take a look at NPD on some real routers so you can see how it works in action. I'll use the following topology to demonstrate this:

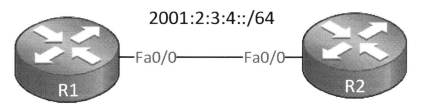

2001:2:3:4::/64

Fa0/0————————Fa0/0

R1   R2

I will use R1 as a host that will autoconfigure itself using SLAAC and R2 as the router. 2001:2:3:4//64 is the prefix that we will use. Let's configure R2 first:

```
R2(config)#ipv6 unicast-routing
```

Before R2 will act as a router we need to make sure IPv6 unicast routing is enabled. Now let's configure an IPv6 address on the interface:

```
R2(config)#interface fa0/0
R2(config-if)#no shutdown
R2(config-if)#ipv6 address 2001:2:3:4::1/64
```

Before we configure R1 we will enable NPD debugging on both routers so you can see the different messages:

```
R1#debug ipv6 nd
ICMP Neighbor Discovery events debugging is on
```

```
R2#debug ipv6 nd
ICMP Neighbor Discovery events debugging is on
```

The **debug ipv6 nd** command is very useful as it will show all the different messages that NPD uses.

Let's configure R1 now:

```
R1(config)#interface fa0/0
R1(config-if)#no shutdown
R1(config-if)#ipv6 address autoconfig
```

R1 will be configured to use SLAAC with the **ipv6 address autoconfig** command. With the debug enabled you will see the following items on your console:

```
R1#
ICMPv6-ND: Sending NS for FE80::C000:6FF:FE7C:0 on
FastEthernet0/0
ICMPv6-ND: DAD: FE80::C000:6FF:FE7C:0 is unique.
```

It sends a NS for its own IPv6 address and when nobody responds, it understands that it is the only host using this address.

You can also see that R1 sends a neighbor advertisement towards R2:

```
R1#
ICMPv6-ND: Sending NA for FE80::C000:6FF:FE7C:0 on
FastEthernet0/0
```

```
R2#
ICMPv6-ND: Received NA for FE80::C000:6FF:FE7C:0 on
FastEthernet0/0 from FE80::C000:6FF:FE7C:0
```

We can view the database with the L2 and L3 information like this:

```
R2#show ipv6 neighbors
IPv6 Address                                Age Link-layer Addr
State Interface
FE80::C000:6FF:FE7C:0                         21 c200.067c.0000
STALE Fa0/0
```

Show ipv6 neighbors will show you the IPv6 addresses and MAC addresses.

R1 will also send a router solicitation and R2 will send a router advertisement in return:

```
R1#
ICMPv6-ND: Sending RS on FastEthernet0/0
```

```
R2#
ICMPv6-ND: Received RS on FastEthernet0/0 from
FE80::C000:6FF:FE7C:0
ICMPv6-ND: Sending solicited RA on FastEthernet0/0
ICMPv6-ND: Sending RA from FE80::C001:6FF:FE7C:0 to FF02::1 on
FastEthernet0/0
ICMPv6-ND:     MTU = 1500
ICMPv6-ND:     prefix = 2001:2:3:4::/64 onlink autoconfig
ICMPv6-ND:         2592000/604800 (valid/preferred)
```

```
R1#
ICMPv6-ND: Received RA from FE80::C001:6FF:FE7C:0 on
FastEthernet0/0
ICMPv6-ND: Selected new default router FE80::C001:6FF:FE7C:0 on
FastEthernet0/0
```

If you want to see all the routers that your host knows about you can use the following command:

```
R1#show ipv6 routers
Router FE80::C001:6FF:FE7C:0 on FastEthernet0/0, last update 0
min
  Hops 64, Lifetime 1800 sec, AddrFlag=0, OtherFlag=0, MTU=1500
  HomeAgentFlag=0, Preference=Medium
  Reachable time 0 msec, Retransmit time 0 msec
  Prefix 2001:2:3:4::/64 onlink autoconfig
    Valid lifetime 2592000, preferred lifetime 604800
```

Since R1 is configured for SLAAC it will use the prefix in the router advertisement to configure itself:

```
R1#
ICMPv6-ND: Prefix Information change for 2001:2:3:4::/64, 0x0 ->
0xE0
ICMPv6-ND: Adding prefix 2001:2:3:4::/64 to FastEthernet0/0
ICMPv6-ND: Sending NS for 2001:2:3:4:C000:6FF:FE7C:0 on
FastEthernet0/0
ICMPv6-ND: Autoconfiguring 2001:2:3:4:C000:6FF:FE7C:0 on
FastEthernet0/0
ICMPv6-ND: DAD: 2001:2:3:4:C000:6FF:FE7C:0 is unique.
```

It will use the prefix and configure an IPv6 address automatically. Before it uses the address it will use DAD to make sure the address is unique. Let's take a look what the IPv6 address is:

```
R1#show ipv6 int brief
FastEthernet0/0                [up/up]
    FE80::C000:6FF:FE7C:0
    2001:2:3:4:C000:6FF:FE7C:0
```

You can see that R1 used the 2001:2:3:4::/64 prefix to configure itself. If you want to configure this yourself and look at the debug, you might want to try this lab that I created for you:

http://gns3vault.com/IPv6/ipv6-autoconfiguration.html

That's all I have about NPD for you now, let's continue by taking a closer look at DHCPv6! **Stateful DHCPv6** works similar to DHCP for IPv4. We still use it to give addresses, default gateways, DNS servers and some other options to clients but one of the key differences are the messages that we now use.

DHCP for IPv4 uses the Discover, Offer, Request and ACK messages. DHCPv6 uses a **Solicit, Advertise, Request and Reply message**.

The solicit message is similar to the discover message. A host will use this message when it's looking for the IPv6 address of the DHCPv6 server. The advertise message is used to give an IPv6 address, default gateway and DNS server to the host. The request message is used by the host to ask if it's ok to use this information and the ACK is sent by the server to confirm this.

Just like DHCP for IPv4, when your DHCP server is not on the same subnet you will require **DHCP relay** to forward the DHCP messages to a central DHCP server.

You don't have to configure a DHCPv6 server for CCNP ROUTE but you do have to understand how the different addresses are used. Let's look at an example:

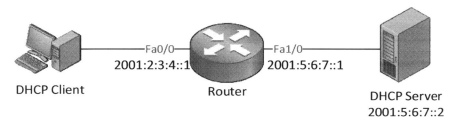

In this example we have a DHCP client, a router and a DHCP server. Since the DHCP client and DHCP server are not on the same subnet we will have to configure the router to relay the DHCP messages.

When the client is looking for an IPv6 address it will start with the solicit message:

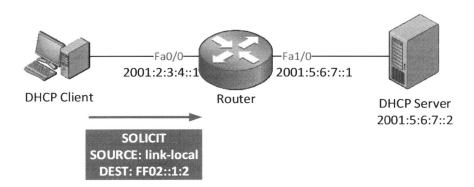

The client will use its link-local address as the source and the destination will be multicast address **FF02::1:2 (all-DHCP-agents)**. This is a link-local multicast address so it won't leave the subnet. As a result the DHCP server will never receive this solicit message.

On the router we will configure DHCP relay so that the solicit message will be forwarded to the DHCP server:

```
Router(config)#interface fa0/0
Router(config-if)#ipv6 dhcp relay destination 2001:5:6:7::2
```

This will ensure that the router forwards DHCP messages between the client and DHCP server. This is what it looks like:

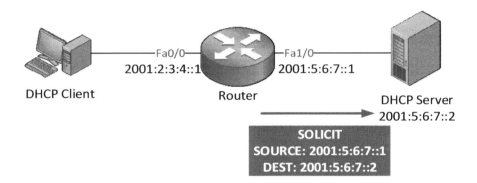

The router will forward the solicit message and the addresses will change. The source will be the IPv6 address on the Fa1/0 interface of our router and the destination will be the IPv6 address of the DHCP server. This is a big difference compared to DHCP relay for IPv4 where the IP address on the Fa0/0 would have been used.

The other DHCP messages will use the same addresses. Between the router and DHCP server we will use the 2001:5:6:7::1 and 2001:5:6:7::2 addresses. The router will forward traffic to the DHCP client by using its link-local address as the destination.

That's all we have for this chapter, the most important part is understanding NPD and how it replaced some of the things from the IPv4 world. In the next chapter we'll take a look at IPv6 routing!

21. IPv6 Routing Protocols

Routing protocols have been updated so they can support IPv6. The IGPs you have to know for CCNP ROUTE are RIP, EIGRP and OSPF. BGP also supports IPv6. You will see that the configuration of IPv6 routing protocols isn't very hard.

The first protocol we will look at is RIP or I should say **RIPNG (Next Generation).** If you are a Star Trek fan this probably sounds familiar. Besides the awesome name the protocol is exactly the same with some minor differences:

	RIP version 2 (IPv4)	RIPNG (IPv6)
UDP Port	520	521
Auto-Summary	Possible	Unavailable
Multicast address	224.0.0.9	FF02::9
Authentication	MD5 / plaintext	IPv6 AH/ESP

All the major details are the same. We still have a hop count limit of 15 (16 is unreachable). We have split-horizon, route poisoning, poison reverse etc. RIPNG doesn't form neighbor adjacencies and just sends period updates. The big difference is of course that we use an IPv6 header instead of an IPv4 header. RIPNG uses a different UDP port number and as you can see the multicast address for IPv6 looks a bit like the IPv4 equivalent. Instead of using MD5 or plaintext authentication we can use IPSEC for IPv6.

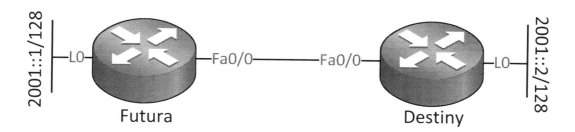

Let's use this topology to configure RIPNG. I'm going to create a loopback interface on each router to advertise in RIPNG. Note that I don't have any global unicast IPv6 addresses on the FastEthernet interface because the RIPNG updates will be sent using the link-local addresses.

```
Futura(config)#ipv6 unicast-routing
Futura(config)#interface loopback 0
Futura(config-if)#ipv6 address 2001::1/128
```

```
Destiny(config)#ipv6 unicast-routing
Destiny(config)#interface loopback 0
Destiny(config-if)#ipv6 address 2001::2/128
```

Don't forget to enable **IPv6 unicast routing** otherwise no routing protocol will work for IPv6.

```
Futura#show ipv6 interface brief
FastEthernet0/0              [up/up]
Loopback0                    [up/up]
    FE80::CE09:18FF:FE0E:0
    2001::1
```

```
Destiny#show ipv6 interface brief
FastEthernet0/0              [up/up]
Loopback0                    [up/up]
    FE80::CE0A:18FF:FE0E:0
    2001::2
```

After configuring the IPv6 addresses on the loopback interface you can see the global unicast and the link-local IPv6 addresses. There is no link-local address on the FastEthernet interfaces however.

```
Futura(config)#interface fastEthernet 0/0
Futura(config-if)#ipv6 enable
```

```
Destiny(config)#interface fastEthernet 0/0
Destiny(config-if)#ipv6 enable
```

```
Futura#show ipv6 interface brief
FastEthernet0/0              [up/up]
    FE80::CE09:18FF:FE0E:0
Loopback0                    [up/up]
    FE80::CE09:18FF:FE0E:0
    2001::1
```

```
Destiny#show ipv6 interface brief
FastEthernet0/0              [up/up]
    FE80::CE0A:18FF:FE0E:0
Loopback0                    [up/up]
    FE80::CE0A:18FF:FE0E:0
    2001::2
```

Use the **IPv6 enable** command to generate a link-local address for the FastEthernet interfaces.

```
Futura(config)#ipv6 router rip RIPNGTEST
Futura(config-rtr)#exit
Futura(config)#interface fastEthernet 0/0
Futura(config-if)#ipv6 rip RIPNGTEST enable
Futura(config-if)#exit
Futura(config)#interface loopback 0
Futura(config-if)#ipv6 rip RIPNGTEST enable
```

```
Destiny(config)#ipv6 router rip RIPNGTEST
Destiny(config-rtr)#exit
Destiny(config)#interface fastEthernet 0/0
Destiny(config-if)#ipv6 rip RIPNGTEST enable
Destiny(config-if)#exit
Destiny(config)#interface loopback 0
Destiny(config-if)#ipv6 rip RIPNGTEST enable
```

To enable RIPNG you first have to start the process with the **IPV6 router rip** command. You have to give it a tag name and I called mine "RIPNGTEST". It doesn't matter what tag name you choose and it doesn't have to be the same on both routers. Second step is to activate RIPNG on the interfaces you want by using the **IPv6 rip enable** command. That's not too bad right? No stinky network commands! Just enable it on the interface and you are ready to go. The ipv6 rip enable command does two things:

- Activate the prefix on the interface in RIPNG.
- Send RIPNG updates out of this interface.

```
Futura#debug ipv6 rip
RIP Routing Protocol debugging is on

RIPng: Sending multicast update on FastEthernet0/0 for RIPNGTEST
       src=FE80::CE09:18FF:FE0E:0
       dst=FF02::9 (FastEthernet0/0)
       sport=521, dport=521, length=32
       command=2, version=1, mbz=0, #rte=1
       tag=0, metric=1, prefix=2001::1/128
RIPng: Process RIPNGTEST received own response on Loopback0
RIPng: response received from FE80::CE0A:18FF:FE0E:0 on
FastEthernet0/0 for RIPNGTEST
       src=FE80::CE0A:18FF:FE0E:0 (FastEthernet0/0)
       dst=FF02::9
       sport=521, dport=521, length=32
       command=2, version=1, mbz=0, #rte=1
       tag=0, metric=1, prefix=2001::2/128
```

Here's part of the output of the **debug IPv6 rip** command. You can see that the link-local IPv6 addresses are used as source of the updates.

The destination address is multicast FF02::9.

```
Futura#show ipv6 route rip
IPv6 Routing Table - 4 entries
Codes: C - Connected, L - Local, S - Static, R - RIP, B - BGP
       U - Per-user Static route
       I1 - ISIS L1, I2 - ISIS L2, IA - ISIS interarea, IS -
ISIS summary
       O - OSPF intra, OI - OSPF inter, OE1 - OSPF ext 1, OE2 -
OSPF ext 2
       ON1 - OSPF NSSA ext 1, ON2 - OSPF NSSA ext 2
R   2001::2/128 [120/2]
     via FE80::CE0A:18FF:FE0E:0, FastEthernet0/0
```

```
Destiny#show ipv6 route rip
IPv6 Routing Table - 4 entries
Codes: C - Connected, L - Local, S - Static, R - RIP, B - BGP
       U - Per-user Static route
       I1 - ISIS L1, I2 - ISIS L2, IA - ISIS interarea, IS -
ISIS summary
       O - OSPF intra, OI - OSPF inter, OE1 - OSPF ext 1, OE2 -
OSPF ext 2
       ON1 - OSPF NSSA ext 1, ON2 - OSPF NSSA ext 2
R   2001::1/128 [120/2]
     via FE80::CE09:18FF:FE0E:0, FastEthernet0/0
```

A quick look at the routing table with the **show IPv6 route** command shows us that RIP has learned about the networks.

Want to give it a try and see if you can configure RIPNG? I have a nice lab for you:

http://gns3vault.com/IPv6/ipv6-ripng.html

Next stop is EIGRP for IPv6. Cisco originally created EIGRP so it could advertise routes for IPX, AppleTalk and IPv4. Because of this it was easy to add another protocol like IPv6.

	EIGRP (IPv4)	**EIGRP (IPv6)**
Protocol header	88	88
Auto-Summary	Possible	Unavailable
Multicast address	224.0.0.10	FF02::10
Authentication	MD5	IPv6 AH/ESP

EIGRP is similar to RIPNG. New multicast address and authentication has changed, the rest is pretty much the same. Let's look at the configuration which is similar to RIPNG. We'll use the same two routers.

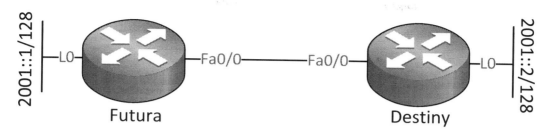

This is how you enable EIGRP for IPv6:

```
Futura(config)#ipv6 router eigrp 1
Futura(config-rtr)#router-id 1.1.1.1
Futura(config-rtr)#no shutdown
Futura(config-rtr)#exit
Futura(config)#interface fastEthernet 0/0
Futura(config-if)#ipv6 eigrp 1
Futura(config-if)#exit
Futura(config)#interface loopback 0
Futura(config-if)#ipv6 eigrp 1
```

```
Destiny(config)#ipv6 router eigrp 1
Destiny(config-rtr)#router-id 2.2.2.2
Destiny(config-rtr)#no shutdown
Destiny(config-rtr)#exit
Destiny(config)#interface fastEthernet 0/0
Destiny(config-if)#ipv6 eigrp 1
Destiny(config-if)#exit
Destiny(config)#interface loopback 0
Destiny(config-if)#ipv6 eigrp 1
```

First you need to start EIGRP with the **ipv6 router eigrp** command. The number you see is the autonomous system number and it has to match on both routers. Each EIGRP router needs a **router ID** which is the highest IPv4 address on the router. If you don't have any IPv4 addresses you need to specify it yourself with the **router-id** command. By default the EIGRP process is in shutdown mode and you need to type **no shutdown** to activate it.

Last step is to enable it on the interfaces with the **ipv6 eigrp** command.

```
Futura#show ipv6 eigrp neighbors
IPv6-EIGRP neighbors for process 1
H    Address                    Interface        Hold Uptime    SRTT
RTO  Q  Seq
                                                 (sec)          (ms)
Cnt Num
0    Link-local address:        Fa0/0            13 00:01:25    3
300  0  3
     FE80::C00F:1AFF:FEA7:0
Destiny#show ipv6 eigrp neighbors
IPv6-EIGRP neighbors for process 1
H    Address                    Interface        Hold Uptime    SRTT
RTO  Q  Seq
                                                 (sec)          (ms)
Cnt Num
0    Link-local address:        Fa0/0            13 00:01:46 1589
5000 0  3
     FE80::C00E:1AFF:FEA7:0
```

Use **show ipv6 eigrp neighbors** to verify you have an adjacency.

```
Futura#show ipv6 route eigrp
IPv6 Routing Table - 3 entries
Codes: C - Connected, L - Local, S - Static, R - RIP, B - BGP
       U - Per-user Static route, M - MIPv6
       I1 - ISIS L1, I2 - ISIS L2, IA - ISIS interarea, IS -
ISIS summary
       O - OSPF intra, OI - OSPF inter, OE1 - OSPF ext 1, OE2 -
OSPF ext 2
       ON1 - OSPF NSSA ext 1, ON2 - OSPF NSSA ext 2
       D - EIGRP, EX - EIGRP external
D    2001::2/128 [90/409600]
     via FE80::C00F:1AFF:FEA7:0, FastEthernet0/0
```

```
Destiny#show ipv6 route eigrp
IPv6 Routing Table - 3 entries
Codes: C - Connected, L - Local, S - Static, R - RIP, B - BGP
       U - Per-user Static route, M - MIPv6
       I1 - ISIS L1, I2 - ISIS L2, IA - ISIS interarea, IS -
ISIS summary
       O - OSPF intra, OI - OSPF inter, OE1 - OSPF ext 1, OE2 -
OSPF ext 2
       ON1 - OSPF NSSA ext 1, ON2 - OSPF NSSA ext 2
       D - EIGRP, EX - EIGRP external
D    2001::1/128 [90/409600]
     via FE80::C00E:1AFF:FEA7:0, FastEthernet0/0
```

Here we go...we have an EIGRP prefix in the routing table. The last IGP routing protocol we will look at is OSPF. Before we continue you might want to try to configure EIGRP for IPv6 yourself:

http://gns3vault.com/IPv6/ipv6-eigrp.html

The OSPF version you are used to work with is technically OSPFv2 and built for IPv4. To support IPv6 some changes were necessary to the protocol and the result is OSPFv3 which supports IPv6.

OSPFv2 and OSPFv3 are pretty much the same but there are some differences. The metrics, network types and packet types are the same. There are some changes to the LSAs however:

- LSA type 3 has been renamed from summary LSA to **Inter-Area Prefix LSA**. The function of this LSA remains the same, it's used to advertise internal prefixes to another area.
- LSA type 4 has been renamed from ASBR summary LSA to **Inter-Area Router LSA**.
- LSA type 8 is new and called the **Link LSA**. They only exist on the local link and are used by routers to advertise their link-local IPv6 address to other routers.
- LSA type 9 is new and called **Intra-Area Prefix LSA**. It is used to send information about IPv6 prefixes (we use LSA type 1 for this in OSPFv2) and intra-area network information (LSA type 2 in OSPFv2). The advantage of using this new LSA type is that the prefixes that are advertised are separated from the calculation of the SPF tree. In OSPFv2, advertising a new prefix or removing one triggered a SPF calculation, in OSPFv3 it doesn't.

Here are some of the other differences between OSPFv2 and OSPFv3:

	OSPF (IPv4)	OSPF (IPv6)
Multicast all OSPF routers	224.0.0.5	FF02::5
Multicast DR/BDR	224.0.0.6	FF02::6
Authentication	MD5 / plaintext	IPv6 AH/ESP
Multiple instances per interface	Not possible	Possible

The multicast addresses have changed but they still end with 5 and 6. Authentication is also different, OSPFv2 uses its own authentication but OSPFv3 relies on the native IPv6 authentication. Something new with OSPFv3 is that you can run multiple instances of OSPFv3 on a single interface.

Also, the router ID for OSPFv3 still uses an "IPv4 style" ID. Let's take a look at the configuration of OSPFv3!

Also, the router ID for OSPFv3 still uses an "IPv4 style" ID. Let's take a look at the configuration of OSPFv3! Here's the topology:

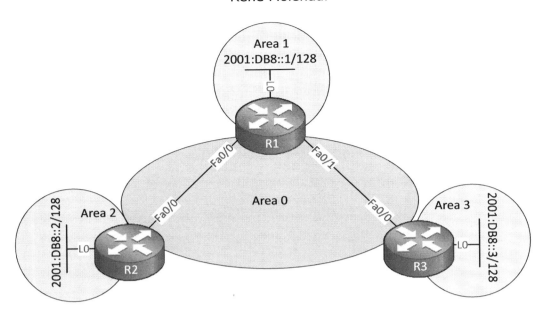

Make sure IPv6 routing is enabled:

```
R1,R2 & R3
(config)#ipv6 unicast-routing
```

Let's enable IPv6 on the FastEthernet interfaces. We only need link-local addresses for the routers to communicate with each other:

```
R1(config)#interface FastEthernet 0/0
R1(config-if)#ipv6 enable

R1(config)#interface FastEthernet 0/1
R1(config-if)#ipv6 enable
```

```
R2(config)#interface FastEthernet 0/0
R2(config-if)#ipv6 enable
```

```
R3(config)#interface FastEthernet 0/0
R3(config-if)#ipv6 enable
```

Let's configure some prefixes on the loopback interfaces:

```
R1(config)#interface Loopback 0
R1(config-if)#ipv6 address 2001:DB8::1/128
```

```
R2(config)#interface Loopback 0
R2(config-if)#ipv6 address 2001:DB8::2/128
```

```
R3(config)#interface Loopback 0
```

```
R3(config-if)#ipv6 address 2001:DB8::3/128
```

Now we configure OSPFv3:

```
R1(config)#ipv6 router ospf 1
R1(config-rtr)#router-id 1.1.1.1
```

You start the process with **ipv6 router ospf** and then you need to specify a router ID. I'll pick 1.1.1.1 for R1. Now we'll enable it on the interfaces:

```
R1(config)#interface FastEthernet 0/0
R1(config-if)#ipv6 ospf 1 area 0

R1(config)#interface FastEthernet 0/1
R1(config-if)#ipv6 ospf 1 area 0

R1(config)#interface Loopback 0
R1(config-if)#ipv6 ospf 1 area 1
```

This is much easier than the network commands for OSPFv2, just specify the process ID and area number and that's it. Let's configure R2 and R3 as well:

```
R2(config)#ipv6 router ospf 1
R2(config-rtr)#router-id 2.2.2.2

R2(config)#interface FastEthernet 0/0
R2(config-if)#ipv6 ospf 1 area 0

R2(config)#interface Loopback 0
R2(config-if)#ipv6 ospf 1 area 2
```

```
R3(config)#ipv6 router ospf 1
R3(config-rtr)#router-id 3.3.3.3

R3(config)#interface FastEthernet 0/0
R3(config-if)#ipv6 ospf 1 area 0

R3(config)#interface Loopback 0
R3(config-if)#ipv6 ospf 1 area 3
```

Let's verify our work:

```
R1#show ipv6 ospf neighbor

Neighbor ID     Pri   State              Dead Time   Interface ID
Interface
3.3.3.3          1    FULL/DR            00:00:36    4
FastEthernet0/1
2.2.2.2          1    FULL/BDR           00:00:33    4
FastEthernet0/0
```

This command looks exactly the same as the OSPFv2 output. The neighbors are shown with their router ID. Here's what the routing table looks like:

```
R1#show ipv6 route ospf
IPv6 Routing Table - 4 entries
Codes: C - Connected, L - Local, S - Static, R - RIP, B - BGP
       U - Per-user Static route, M - MIPv6
       I1 - ISIS L1, I2 - ISIS L2, IA - ISIS interarea, IS -
ISIS summary
       O - OSPF intra, OI - OSPF inter, OE1 - OSPF ext 1, OE2 -
OSPF ext 2
       ON1 - OSPF NSSA ext 1, ON2 - OSPF NSSA ext 2
       D - EIGRP, EX - EIGRP external
OI  2001:DB8::2/128 [110/10]
     via FE80::C002:19FF:FE64:0, FastEthernet0/0
OI  2001:DB8::3/128 [110/10]
     via FE80::C003:BFF:FE34:0, FastEthernet0/1
```

We can see R1 has learned about the prefixes from R2 and R3. Let's see what R2 and R3 have in their routing tables:

```
R2#show ipv6 route ospf
IPv6 Routing Table - 4 entries
Codes: C - Connected, L - Local, S - Static, R - RIP, B - BGP
       U - Per-user Static route, M - MIPv6
       I1 - ISIS L1, I2 - ISIS L2, IA - ISIS interarea, IS -
ISIS summary
       O - OSPF intra, OI - OSPF inter, OE1 - OSPF ext 1, OE2 -
OSPF ext 2
       ON1 - OSPF NSSA ext 1, ON2 - OSPF NSSA ext 2
       D - EIGRP, EX - EIGRP external
OI  2001:DB8::1/128 [110/10]
     via FE80::C001:13FF:FEC8:0, FastEthernet0/0
OI  2001:DB8::3/128 [110/20]
     via FE80::C001:13FF:FEC8:0, FastEthernet0/0
```

```
R3#show ipv6 route ospf
IPv6 Routing Table - 4 entries
Codes: C - Connected, L - Local, S - Static, R - RIP, B - BGP
       U - Per-user Static route, M - MIPv6
       I1 - ISIS L1, I2 - ISIS L2, IA - ISIS interarea, IS -
ISIS summary
       O - OSPF intra, OI - OSPF inter, OE1 - OSPF ext 1, OE2 -
OSPF ext 2
       ON1 - OSPF NSSA ext 1, ON2 - OSPF NSSA ext 2
       D - EIGRP, EX - EIGRP external
OI  2001:DB8::1/128 [110/10]
     via FE80::C001:13FF:FEC8:1, FastEthernet0/0
OI  2001:DB8::2/128 [110/20]
     via FE80::C001:13FF:FEC8:1, FastEthernet0/0
```

This is looking good, they learned about the prefixes on the loopback interfaces. Let's check out the LSDB and its LSA types:

```
R1#show ipv6 ospf database

            OSPFv3 Router with ID (1.1.1.1) (Process ID 1)

            Router Link States (Area 0)

ADV Router      Age        Seq#        Fragment ID  Link count
Bits
1.1.1.1         285        0x80000006  0            2
B
2.2.2.2         512        0x80000003  0            1
B
3.3.3.3         291        0x80000004  0            1
B

            Net Link States (Area 0)

ADV Router      Age        Seq#        Link ID     Rtr count
1.1.1.1         522        0x80000001  4           2
3.3.3.3         291        0x80000001  4           2

            Inter Area Prefix Link States (Area 0)

ADV Router      Age        Seq#        Prefix
1.1.1.1         589        0x80000001  2001:DB8::1/128
2.2.2.2         508        0x80000001  2001:DB8::2/128
3.3.3.3         451        0x80000001  2001:DB8::3/128

            Link (Type-8) Link States (Area 0)

ADV Router      Age        Seq#        Link ID     Interface
1.1.1.1         292        0x80000001  5           Fa0/1
3.3.3.3         453        0x80000001  4           Fa0/1
1.1.1.1         669        0x80000001  4           Fa0/0
```

```
2.2.2.2              525            0x80000001  4              Fa0/0

                  Router Link States  (Area 1)

ADV Router        Age            Seq#           Fragment ID  Link count
Bits
1.1.1.1           601            0x80000001  0                 0
B

               Inter Area Prefix Link States  (Area 1)

ADV Router        Age            Seq#           Prefix
1.1.1.1           509            0x80000001  2001:DB8::2/128
1.1.1.1           288            0x80000001  2001:DB8::3/128

               Intra Area Prefix Link States  (Area 1)

ADV Router        Age            Seq#           Link ID    Ref-lstype
Ref-LSID
1.1.1.1           601            0x80000001  0              0x2001      0
```

The output is similar to the OSPFv2 equivalent command. You can see that LSA type 3 (summary LSA) is now called Inter Area Prefix. You can also see the new LSA type 8 (Link LSA) and LSA type 9 (Intra Area Prefix Link). Let's redistribute something into OSPFv3 so that you can also see LSA type 4:

```
R3(config)#interface loopback 0
R3(config-if)#no ipv6 ospf 1 area 3

R3(config)#ipv6 router ospf 1
R3(config-rtr)#redistribute connected
```

Let's see if this worked:

```
R1#show ipv6 route ospf | incl E2
        O - OSPF intra, OI - OSPF inter, OE1 - OSPF ext 1, OE2 -
OSPF ext 2
OE2  2001:DB8::3/128 [110/20]
```

And here's what it looks like in the LSDB:

```
R1#show ipv6 ospf database | begin Inter Area Router
            Inter Area Router Link States  (Area 1)

ADV Router        Age            Seq#           Link ID    Dest RtrID
1.1.1.1           113            0x80000001  50529027   3.3.3.3
```

Here you can see LSA type 4 with its new name.

IOS versions 15.1(3)S and later also support another OSPFv3 configuration mode which uses **address families**. This lets you configure IPv4 and IPv6 routing under a single OSPFv3 process. Let's use the following topology to demonstrate this:

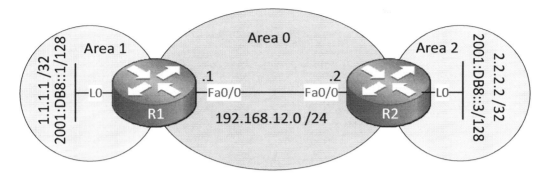

These routers have IPv4 and IPv6 addresses. We'll use a single OSPF process to advertise all these prefixes. After enabling IPv6 unicast routing and configuring the IPv4 + IPv6 addresses, this is the only thing we have to do:

```
R1(config)#interface FastEthernet 0/0
R1(config-if)#ospfv3 1 ipv6 area 0
R1(config-if)#ospfv3 1 ipv4 area 0

R1(config)#interface loopback 0
R1(config-if)#ospfv3 1 ipv6 area 0
R1(config-if)#ospfv3 1 ipv4 area 0
```

```
R2(config)#interface FastEthernet 0/0
R2(config-if)#ospfv3 1 ipv6 area 0
R2(config-if)#ospfv3 1 ipv4 area 0

R2(config)#interface loopback 0
R2(config-if)#ospfv3 1 ipv6 area 0
R2(config-if)#ospfv3 1 ipv4 area 0
```

We can use the **ospfv3** command to enable for both IPv4 and IPv6. Since I have some IPv4 addresses on the interfaces, it will automatically select one as the router ID. Let's verify if it works:

```
R1#show ospfv3 neighbor

          OSPFv3 1 address-family ipv4 (router-id 1.1.1.1)

Neighbor ID     Pri    State           Dead Time    Interface ID
Interface
2.2.2.2          1     FULL/BDR        00:00:33     7
FastEthernet0/0
```

```
        OSPFv3 1 address-family ipv6 (router-id 1.1.1.1)

Neighbor ID      Pri   State           Dead Time    Interface ID
Interface
2.2.2.2          1     FULL/BDR        00:00:30     7
FastEthernet0/0
```

The **show ospfv3 neighbor** command is new. We can see an adjacency for both IPv4 and IPv6. Let's check the routing tables:

```
R1#show ip route ospfv3

      2.0.0.0/32 is subnetted, 1 subnets
O IA     2.2.2.2 [110/1] via 192.168.12.2, 00:07:46,
FastEthernet0/0
```

```
R2#show ip route ospfv3

      1.0.0.0/32 is subnetted, 1 subnets
O IA     1.1.1.1 [110/1] via 192.168.12.1, 00:08:00,
FastEthernet0/0
```

Here are the IPv4 prefixes, and here's the IPv6 routing table:

```
R1#show ipv6 route ospf

OI   2001:DB8::2/128 [110/1]
     via FE80::20C:29FF:FEBF:A362, FastEthernet0/0
```

```
R2#show ipv6 route ospf

OI   2001:DB8::1/128 [110/1]
     via FE80::20C:29FF:FEE5:60DD, FastEthernet0/0
```

That's all there is to it.

Feel like doing a link-state exercise? See if you can configure OSPFv3 yourself:

http://gns3vault.com/IPv6/ipv6-ospfv3.html

You have now seen all the IGPS...RIPNG, EIGRP and OSPFv3. What about BGP? The "traditional" version of BGP (BGP-4) only supports IPv4 networks. Nowadays we use M-BGP (Multiprotocol BGP) which supports multiple protocols, including IPv6.

MP-BGP uses address families for different protocols, for example:

- IPv4 unicast
- IPv4 multicast
- IPv6 unicast
- IPv6 multicast

MP-BGP also has address families for some other things like MPLS VPN but this is outside the scope of the ROUTE exam.

There are a couple of new features in MP-BGP that BGP-4 doesn't have:

- **Address Family Identifier (AFI):** specifies the address family.
- **Subsequent Address Family Identifier (SAFI):** Has additional information for some address families.
- **Multiprotocol Reachable Network Layer Reachability Information (MP_UNREACH_NLRI):** This is an attribute used to transport networks that are unreachable.
- **BGP Capabilities Advertisement:** This is used by a BGP router to announce to the other BGP router what capabilities it supports. MP-BGP and BGP-4 are compatible, the BGP-4 router can ignore the messages that it doesn't understand.

With MP-BGP there are a couple of configuration options. BGP routers can become neighbors using IPv6 addresses and exchange IPv6 routing information. It's also possible to become neighbors using IPv4 and then exchange IPv6 routing information.

Let's start with the simplest example, using IPv6 everywhere:

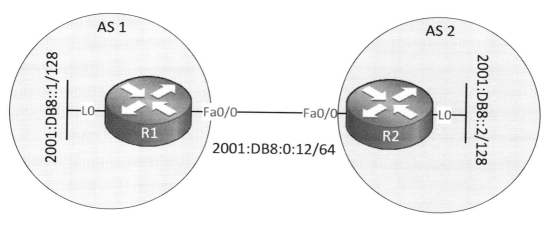

Here's the configuration of R1:

```
R1(config)#router bgp 1
R1(config-router)#neighbor 2001:db8:0:12::2 remote-as 2
R1(config-router)#address-family ipv4
R1(config-router-af)#no neighbor 2001:db8:0:12::2 activate
R1(config-router-af)#exit
R1(config-router)#address-family ipv6
R1(config-router-af)#neighbor 2001:db8:0:12::2 activate
R1(config-router-af)#network 2001:db8::1/128
```

In the configuration above we first specify the remote neighbor. **The address-family** command is used to change the IPv4 or IPv6 settings. I disable IPv4 routing and enabled IPv6 routing. Last but not least, we advertised the prefix on the loopback interface. The configuration of R2 looks similar:

```
R2(config)#router bgp 2
R2(config-router)#neighbor 2001:db8:0:12::1 remote-as 1
R2(config-router)#address-family ipv4
R2(config-router-af)#no neighbor 2001:db8:0:12::1 activate
R2(config-router-af)#exit
R2(config-router)#address-family ipv6
R2(config-router-af)#neighbor 2001:db8:0:12::1 activate
R2(config-router-af)#network 2001:db8::2/128
```

You will see the neighbor adjacency popping up the console:

```
R1#
%BGP-5-ADJCHANGE: neighbor 2001:DB8:0:123::2 Up
```

Now let's check the routing tables:

```
R1#show ipv6 route bgp
IPv6 Routing Table - default - 7 entries
Codes: C - Connected, L - Local, S - Static, U - Per-user Static
route
       B - BGP, HA - Home Agent, MR - Mobile Router, R - RIP
       I1 - ISIS L1, I2 - ISIS L2, IA - ISIS interarea, IS -
ISIS summary
       D - EIGRP, EX - EIGRP external, NM - NEMO, ND - Neighbor
Discovery
       l - LISP
       O - OSPF Intra, OI - OSPF Inter, OE1 - OSPF ext 1, OE2 -
OSPF ext 2
       ON1 - OSPF NSSA ext 1, ON2 - OSPF NSSA ext 2
B    2001:DB8::2/128 [20/0]
     via FE80::217:5AFF:FEED:7AF0, FastEthernet0/0
```

```
R2#show ipv6 route bgp
IPv6 Routing Table - default - 7 entries
Codes: C - Connected, L - Local, S - Static, U - Per-user Static
route
       B - BGP, HA - Home Agent, MR - Mobile Router, R - RIP
       I1 - ISIS L1, I2 - ISIS L2, IA - ISIS interarea, IS -
ISIS summary
       D - EIGRP, EX - EIGRP external, NM - NEMO, ND - Neighbor
Discovery
       l - LISP
       O - OSPF Intra, OI - OSPF Inter, OE1 - OSPF ext 1, OE2 -
OSPF ext 2
       ON1 - OSPF NSSA ext 1, ON2 - OSPF NSSA ext 2
B    2001:DB8::1/128 [20/0]
     via FE80::21D:A1FF:FE8B:36D0, FastEthernet0/0
```

The routers learned each others prefixes...great!

Now let's look at a more complex example, the routers will become neighbors through IPv4 but will exchange IPv6 prefixes. I'll use the same topology but with an IPv4 subnet in between:

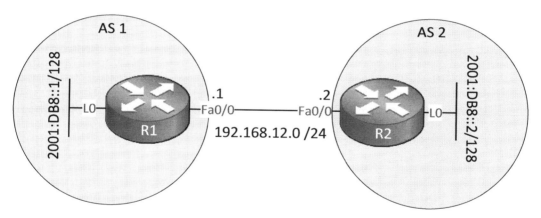

Here's the configuration:

```
R1(config)#router bgp 1
R1(config-router)#neighbor 192.168.12.2 remote-as 2
```

```
R2(config)#router bgp 2
R2(config-router)#neighbor 192.168.12.1 remote-as 1
```

Now we can configure the address-family for IPv6 unicast:

```
R1(config)#router bgp 1
R1(config-router)#address-family ipv6
R1(config-router-af)#network 2001:db8::1/128
R1(config-router-af)#neighbor 192.168.12.2 activate
```

```
R2(config)#router bgp 2
R2(config-router)#address-family ipv6
R2(config-router-af)#network 2001:db8::2/128
R2(config-router-af)#neighbor 192.168.12.1 activate
```

Once we enter the address-family IPv6 configuration there are two things we have to configure. The prefix has to be advertised and we need to specify the neighbor. The prefixes on the loopback interface should now be advertised. Let's check it out:

```
R1#show ip bgp ipv6 unicast
BGP table version is 2, local router ID is 192.168.12.1
Status codes: s suppressed, d damped, h history, * valid, >
best, i - internal,
                r RIB-failure, S Stale, m multipath, b backup-
path, x best-external, f RT-Filter
Origin codes: i - IGP, e - EGP, ? - incomplete

    Network          Next Hop          Metric LocPrf Weight
Path
*> 2001:DB8::1/128   ::                                  0        32768 i
*  2001:DB8::2/128   ::FFFF:192.168.12.2
                                                         0            0 2 i
```

```
R2#show ip bgp ipv6 unicast
BGP table version is 2, local router ID is 192.168.12.2
Status codes: s suppressed, d damped, h history, * valid, >
best, i - internal,
                r RIB-failure, S Stale, m multipath, b backup-
path, x best-external, f RT-Filter
Origin codes: i - IGP, e - EGP, ? - incomplete

    Network          Next Hop          Metric LocPrf Weight
Path
*  2001:DB8::1/128   ::FFFF:192.168.12.1
                                                         0            0 1 i
*> 2001:DB8::2/128   ::                                  0        32768 i
```

As you can see the routers have learned about each others prefix on the loopback interfaces. There's one problem though...we were able to exchange IPv6 prefixes but we only use IPv4 between R1 and R2, there is no next hop address that we can use.

To fix this, we need to use some IPv6 addresses that we can use as the next hop. We'll configure a prefix between R1 and R2 for this:

```
R1(config)#interface FastEthernet 0/0
R1(config-if)#ipv6 address 2001:db8:0:12::1/64
```

```
R2(config)#interface FastEthernet 0/0
R2(config-if)#ipv6 address 2001:db8:0:12::2/64
```

Now we have IPv6 addresses that we can use as the next hop. We are using IPv4 for the neighbor peering so the next hop doesn't change automatically. We'll have to use a route-map for this:

```
R1(config)#route-map IPV6_NEXT_HOP permit 10
R1(config-route-map)#set ipv6 next-hop 2001:db8:0:12::2

R1(config)#router bgp 1
R1(config-router)#address-family ipv6
R1(config-router-af)#neighbor 192.168.12.2 route-map
IPV6_NEXT_HOP in
```

```
R2(config)#route-map IPV6_NEXT_HOP permit 10
R2(config-route-map)#set ipv6 next-hop 2001:db8:0:12::1

R2(config)#router bgp 2
R2(config-router)#address-family ipv6
R2(config-router-af)#neighbor 192.168.12.1 route-map
IPV6_NEXT_HOP in
```

Both routers will now advertise their IPv6 address as the next hop for all prefixes that are advertised. Let's reset BGP:

```
R1#clear ip bgp *
```

Take a look now:

```
R1#show ip bgp ipv6 unicast | begin 2001
*> 2001:DB8::1/128    ::                        0        32768 i
*> 2001:DB8::2/128    2001:DB8:0:12::2
```

```
R2#show ip bgp ipv6 unicast | begin 2001
*> 2001:DB8::1/128    2001:DB8:0:12::1
```

The next hop IPv6 addresses are now reachable so they can be installed. The downside of this solution is that you have to fix the next hop yourself, the advantage is that you only have 1 BGP peering for both IPv4 + IPv6. That's all we have on MP-BGP...

Anything else you need to know about IPv4 routing protocols? Most of the commands you know for IPv4 work as well for IPv6.

```
Futura#show ipv6 protocols
IPv6 Routing Protocol is "connected"
IPv6 Routing Protocol is "static"
IPv6 Routing Protocol is "ospf 1"
  Interfaces (Area 0):
    Loopback0
    FastEthernet0/0
  Redistribution:
    None
```

Show ipv6 protocols is of course a useful example. The command is the same except now you get to see IPv6 information. My suggestion is just to get going and use all your favorite commands but substitute "ip" for "ipv6" and see what the result is.

One more thing about IPv6 routing protocols...redistribution!

All the same rules of redistribution for IPv4 apply to IPv6 but there are some exceptions:

- Of course you need to use IPv6 prefix-lists and access-lists instead of IPv4.
- The redistribute command for IPv6 will only redistribute routes that are learned from an IGP but not routes on interfaces that are enabled for that IGP. If you want to see those routes redistributed as well you need to use the **include-connected** parameter when redistributing.
- OSPFv2 needed the **subnets** parameter or it would redistribute classful. Classful/classless networks is something we don't know in IPv6 so this parameter is no longer required.
- Link-local routes are not redistributed in IPv6 (they are link-local right?).

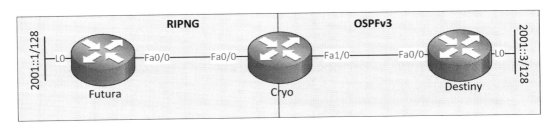

Let's look at a redistribution example. In the middle we have router Cryo that will perform the redistribution between RIPNG and OSPFv3. Router Futura and Destiny have a loopback interface that will be advertised.

```
Futura(config)#ipv6 unicast-routing
Futura(config)#interface loopback 0
Futura(config-if)#ipv6 address 2001::1/128
Futura(config-if)#exit
Futura(config)#interface fastEthernet 0/0
Futura(config-if)#ipv6 enable
```

```
Cryo(config)#ipv6 unicast-routing
Cryo(config)#interface fastEthernet 0/0
Cryo(config-if)#ipv6 enable
Cryo(config-if)#exit
Cryo(config)#interface fastEthernet 1/0
Cryo(config-if)#ipv6 enable
```

```
Destiny(config)#ipv6 unicast-routing
Destiny(config)#interface loopback 0
Destiny(config-if)#ipv6 address 2001::3/128
Destiny(config-if)#exit
Destiny(config)#interface fastEthernet 0/0
Destiny(config-if)#ipv6 enable
```

This is what we'll start with. I'm using the loopbacks to have something to advertise in RIPNG or OSPFv3. On the FastEthernet interfaces I only need a link-local IPv6 address.

```
Cryo(config)#ipv6 router rip RIPNG
Cryo(config-rtr)#exit
Cryo(config)#interface fastEthernet 0/0
Cryo(config-if)#ipv6 rip RIPNG enable
```

```
Futura(config)#ipv6 router rip RIPNG
Futura(config-rtr)#exit
Futura(config)#interface loopback 0
Futura(config-if)#ipv6 rip RIPNG enable
Futura(config-if)#exit
Futura(config)#interface fastEthernet 0/0
Futura(config-if)#ipv6 rip RIPNG enable
```

I'm configuring RIPNG on router Cryo and Futura to get things going.

```
Destiny(config)#ipv6 router ospf 1
Destiny(config-rtr)#router-id 3.3.3.3
Destiny(config-rtr)#exit
Destiny(config)#interface fastEthernet 0/0
Destiny(config-if)#ipv6 ospf 1 area 0
Destiny(config-if)#interface loopback 0
Destiny(config-if)#ipv6 ospf 1 area 0
```

```
Cryo(config)#ipv6 router ospf 1
Cryo(config-rtr)#router-id 2.2.2.2
Cryo(config-rtr)#exit
Cryo(config)#interface fastEthernet 1/0
Cryo(config-if)#ipv6 ospf 1 area 0
```

And this is what we need on router Destiny and Cryo to get OSPFv3 working.

```
Cryo(config)#ipv6 router ospf 1
Cryo(config-rtr)#redistribute rip RIPNG
Cryo(config-rtr)#exit
Cryo(config)#ipv6 router rip RIPNG
Cryo(config-rtr)#redistribute ospf 1
```

We use the **redistribute** command to exchange routing information between OSPFv3 and RIPNG. This is all you have to do to redistribute everything.

```
Futura#show ipv6 route rip
IPv6 Routing Table - 4 entries
Codes: C - Connected, L - Local, S - Static, R - RIP, B - BGP
       U - Per-user Static route
       I1 - ISIS L1, I2 - ISIS L2, IA - ISIS interarea, IS -
ISIS summary
       O - OSPF intra, OI - OSPF inter, OE1 - OSPF ext 1, OE2 -
OSPF ext 2
       ON1 - OSPF NSSA ext 1, ON2 - OSPF NSSA ext 2
R    2001::3/128 [120/2]
     via FE80::CE04:19FF:FE67:0, FastEthernet0/0
```

```
Destiny#show ipv6 route ospf
IPv6 Routing Table - 4 entries
Codes: C - Connected, L - Local, S - Static, R - RIP, B - BGP
       U - Per-user Static route
       I1 - ISIS L1, I2 - ISIS L2, IA - ISIS interarea, IS -
ISIS summary
       O - OSPF intra, OI - OSPF inter, OE1 - OSPF ext 1, OE2 -
OSPF ext 2
       ON1 - OSPF NSSA ext 1, ON2 - OSPF NSSA ext 2
OE2  2001::1/128 [110/20]
     via FE80::CE04:19FF:FE67:10, FastEthernet0/0
```

We can verify our configuration by looking at the routing tables.

If you want you can be a bit more specific with redistribution using route-maps:

```
Cryo(config)#ipv6 router rip RIPNG
Cryo(config-rtr)#redistribute ospf 1 route-map ONLYTHESE
Cryo(config-rtr)#exit

Cryo(config)#ipv6 prefix-list MYPREFIXES permit 2001::3/128

Cryo(config)#route-map ONLYTHESE permit 10
Cryo(config-route-map)#match ipv6 address prefix-list ONLYTHESE
```

Using a route-map and a prefix-list like in the example above I can select only the prefixes that I want redistributed.

Last but not least...static routes! Not a very hard subject but there are some minor details you have to be aware of. The next hop IPv6 address can be any address on your neighbor but if you use a link-local address you'll have to specify the outgoing interface as well.

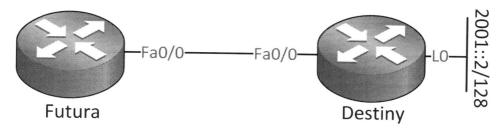

Let me show you what I mean by creating a static route on router Futura to reach the loopback interface on router Destiny.

```
Futura(config)#interface fastEthernet 0/0
Futura(config-if)#ipv6 enable
```

```
Destiny(config)#interface fastEthernet 0/0
Destiny(config-if)#ipv6 enable
Destiny(config-if)#exit
Destiny(config)#interface loopback 0
Destiny(config-if)#ipv6 address 2001::2/128
```

First I'll prepare the interfaces.

```
Futura(config)#ipv6 route 2001::2/128 fastEthernet 0/0
FE80::CE0A:22FF:FED5:0
```

This is my static route and it has the link-local IPv6 address of router Destiny as the next hop. I also specified the outgoing interface.

```
Futura#show ipv6 route static
IPv6 Routing Table - 3 entries
Codes: C - Connected, L - Local, S - Static, R - RIP, B - BGP
       U - Per-user Static route
       I1 - ISIS L1, I2 - ISIS L2, IA - ISIS interarea, IS -
ISIS summary
       O - OSPF intra, OI - OSPF inter, OE1 - OSPF ext 1, OE2 -
OSPF ext 2
       ON1 - OSPF NSSA ext 1, ON2 - OSPF NSSA ext 2
S    2001::2/128 [1/0]
       via FE80::CE0A:22FF:FED5:0, FastEthernet0/0
```

You can see the static route shows up.

```
Futura#ping 2001::2

Type escape sequence to abort.
Sending 5, 100-byte ICMP Echos to 2001::2, timeout is 2 seconds:
!!!!!
Success rate is 100 percent (5/5), round-trip min/avg/max =
0/3/4 ms
```

And a quick ping demonstrates that it's working.

Want to try some static routes yourself? Here you go:

http://gns3vault.com/IPv6/ipv6-static-route.html

That's all I have for you on IPv6 routing protocols. If you are familiar with RIP, OSPFv2 and EIGRP then I believe IPv6 routing shouldn't be too bad for you (except for the weird looking IPv6 addresses maybe).

The next chapter will be about tunneling and migration techniques!

22. IPv6 Migration & Tunneling

Since IPv4 and IPv6 are not compatible with each other we will need tools for a migration. This is going to be very interesting and I'm curious to see how it will unfold in the future. All current operating systems (Windows XP SP3, 7, Linux, OSX) are IPv6 compatible. Network hardware like routers and firewalls are also ready for IPv6. I believe one of the big problems will be the applications. It's not just your hardware and operating system that needs to support IPv6...all your current and old applications need to support it as well.

If your network has up-to-date hardware/operating systems and you only use Microsoft Office as your application things will be smooth. I've seen large companies still running very old versions of applications that are not easily replaced. Even in 2011 there are still servers running Windows NT or 2000 that nobody dares to burn their hands on ;)

This chapter will show you some techniques we can use on Cisco equipment to make our migration from IPv4 to IPv6 a bit easier. Roughly we can divide the techniques in three categories:

- Dual stack
- Tunneling
- NAT-PT / NAT64

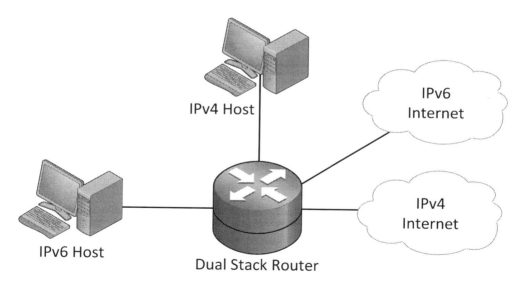

Dual Stack Router

Dual stack means that your device is running IPv4 and IPv6 simultaneously so you can serve IPv4 and IPv6 devices. It sounds interesting but it's nothing more than having an IPv4 and IPv6 address configured on your interface.

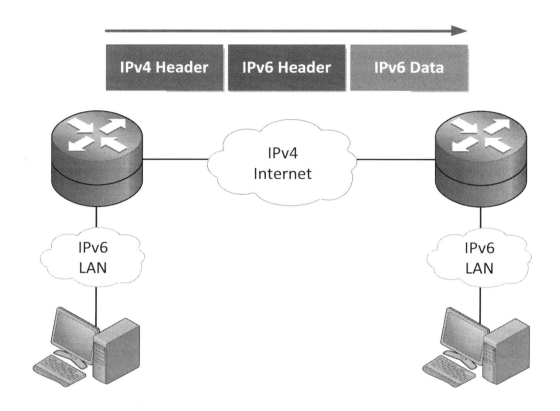

Tunneling is where we will put IPv6 packets in IPv4 packets (encapsulation) or the other way around. The internet is mostly IPv4 so this is one method to connect two IPv6-only LANs with each other over an IPv4 network like the internet.

NAT is something you have learned when you studied CCNA. **NAT-PT** or **NAT64** are used to translate between IPv4 and IPv6 or vice versa. Currently only NAT-PT is supported on Cisco IOS routers but has been deprecated as per RFC 4966. NAT64 is only supported on higher end Cisco routers at this moment.

Dual stack works very well but it means you need both IPv4 and IPv6 on all routers. When we use tunneling we need fewer hosts that require IPv6.

Let's start by looking at **static point-to-point IPv6** tunnels, there are two methods:

- **Manual tunnels**
- **GRE (Generic Routing Encapsulation) tunnels**

Both tunnel types are very similar with just minor differences. Both support IPv6 IGPs through the tunnel interface and forwarding of multicast traffic. The manual tunnels refer to RFC 4213 which defines how to encapsulate IPv6 packets in IPv4. GRE is a generic encapsulation type that rides on top of IPv4 and isn't only for IPv6. It can carry many different protocols and if you ever configured an IPSEC VPN with IGPs running through it you had to use GRE.

Let's continue by looking at some examples and how to configure the static point-to-point IPv6 tunnels.

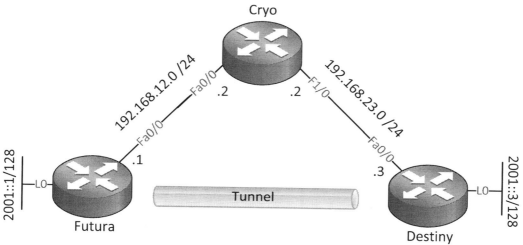

This is the topology we'll be using. Three routers are running IPv4. Router Futura and Destiny also run IPv6 and we want connectivity between them without adding IPv6 support on router Cryo.

```
Futura(config)#interface loopback 0
Futura(config-if)#ipv6 address 2001::1/128
Futura(config-if)#exit
Futura(config)#interface fastEthernet 0/0
Futura(config-if)#ip address 192.168.12.1 255.255.255.0
```

```
Cryo(config)#interface fastEthernet 0/0
Cryo(config-if)#ip address 192.168.12.2 255.255.255.0
Cryo(config-if)#exit
Cryo(config)#interface fastEthernet 1/0
Cryo(config-if)#ip address 192.168.23.2 255.255.255.0
```

```
Destiny(config)#interface fastEthernet 0/0
Destiny(config-if)#ip address 192.168.23.3 255.255.255.0
Destiny(config-if)#exit
Destiny(config)#interface loopback 0
Destiny(config-if)#ipv6 address 2001::3/128
```

First we'll fix the IPv4 and IPv6 addresses on the interfaces. Next step is to create a tunnel interface between router Futura and Destiny. They need to be able to reach each other through IPv4.

```
Futura(config)#interface loopback 1
Futura(config-if)#ip address 1.1.1.1 255.255.255.0
Futura(config-if)#exit
Futura(config)#router eigrp 123
Futura(config-router)#no auto-summary
Futura(config-router)#network 192.168.12.0
Futura(config-router)#network 1.1.1.0
```

```
Cryo(config)#router eigrp 123
Cryo(config-router)#no auto-summary
Cryo(config-router)#network 192.168.12.0
Cryo(config-router)#network 192.168.23.0
```

```
Destiny(config)#interface loopback 1
Destiny(config-if)#ip address 3.3.3.3 255.255.255.0
Destiny(config-if)#exit
Destiny(config)#router eigrp 123
Destiny(config-router)#no auto-summary
Destiny(config-router)#network 192.168.23.0
Destiny(config-router)#network 3.3.3.0
```

I'll create a new loopback interface on router Futura and Destiny. I'll use these loopback interfaces to establish a tunnel interface between the two routers. I could also use physical interfaces but they can go down. Whenever a loopback goes down our IGP (EIGRP in this example) could find another path (if there is another path).

```
Futura(config)#interface tunnel 0
Futura(config-if)#tunnel source loopback 1
Futura(config-if)#tunnel destination 3.3.3.3
Futura(config-if)#tunnel mode ipv6ip
```

```
Destiny(config)#interface tunnel 0
Destiny(config-if)#tunnel source loopback 1
Destiny(config-if)#tunnel destination 1.1.1.1
Destiny(config-if)#tunnel mode ipv6ip
```

This is how we configure a tunnel interface. By default a tunnel interface is **always GRE** so by using the **tunnel mode ipv6ip** command I changed it to a "manual" tunnel per RFC 4213. You can also configure the tunnel interface between the physical interfaces but I like to use loopback interfaces.

This will make sure that when a physical interface fails your IGP will try to find another route to the loopback interface of your neighbor.

```
Futura#show interfaces tunnel 0
Tunnel0 is up, line protocol is up
  Hardware is Tunnel
  MTU 1514 bytes, BW 9 Kbit, DLY 500000 usec,
     reliability 255/255, txload 1/255, rxload 1/255
  Encapsulation TUNNEL, loopback not set
  Keepalive not set
  Tunnel source 1.1.1.1 (Loopback1), destination 3.3.3.3
  Tunnel protocol/transport IPv6/IP
```

```
Destiny#show interfaces tunnel 0
Tunnel0 is up, line protocol is up
  Hardware is Tunnel
  MTU 1514 bytes, BW 9 Kbit, DLY 500000 usec,
     reliability 255/255, txload 1/255, rxload 1/255
  Encapsulation TUNNEL, loopback not set
  Keepalive not set
  Tunnel source 3.3.3.3 (Loopback1), destination 1.1.1.1
  Tunnel protocol/transport IPv6/IP
```

Use the **show interfaces tunnel** command to check if the tunnel is working. You can see mine is up and the encapsulation type is TUNNEL. At this moment our tunnel is working but we have some things left to do.

```
Futura(config)#ipv6 unicast-routing
Futura(config)#ipv6 router rip RIPNG
Futura(config-rtr)#exit
Futura(config)#interface loopback 0
Futura(config-if)#ipv6 rip RIPNG enable
Futura(config-if)#exit
Futura(config)#interface tunnel 0
Futura(config-if)#ipv6 enable
Futura(config-if)#ipv6 rip RIPNG enable
```

```
Destiny(config)#ipv6 unicast-routing
Destiny(config)#ipv6 router rip RIPNG
Destiny(config-rtr)#exit
Destiny(config)#interface loopback 0
Destiny(config-if)#ipv6 rip RIPNG enable
Destiny(config-if)#exit
Destiny(config)#interface tunnel 0
Destiny(config-if)#ipv6 enable
Destiny(config-if)#ipv6 rip RIPNG enable
```

I enabled RIPNG (could have chosen OSPFv3 or EIGRP as well) on the loopback0 and tunnel0 interface. You can see I also added an IPv6 address on the tunnel0 interfaces. We don't need any IPv4 addresses on our tunnel0 interfaces.

```
Futura#show ipv6 route rip
IPv6 Routing Table - 4 entries
Codes: C - Connected, L - Local, S - Static, R - RIP, B - BGP
       U - Per-user Static route
       I1 - ISIS L1, I2 - ISIS L2, IA - ISIS interarea, IS -
ISIS summary
       O - OSPF intra, OI - OSPF inter, OE1 - OSPF ext 1, OE2 -
OSPF ext 2
       ON1 - OSPF NSSA ext 1, ON2 - OSPF NSSA ext 2
R    2001::3/128 [120/2]
     via FE80::303:303, Tunnel0
```

```
Destiny#show ipv6 route rip
IPv6 Routing Table - 4 entries
Codes: C - Connected, L - Local, S - Static, R - RIP, B - BGP
       U - Per-user Static route
       I1 - ISIS L1, I2 - ISIS L2, IA - ISIS interarea, IS -
ISIS summary
       O - OSPF intra, OI - OSPF inter, OE1 - OSPF ext 1, OE2 -
OSPF ext 2
       ON1 - OSPF NSSA ext 1, ON2 - OSPF NSSA ext 2
R    2001::1/128 [120/2]
     via FE80::101:101, Tunnel0
```

You can see both routers learned about each other IPv6 networks.

```
Futura#ping 2001::3 source loopback 0

Type escape sequence to abort.
Sending 5, 100-byte ICMP Echos to 2001::2, timeout is 2 seconds:
Packet sent with a source address of 2001::1
!!!!!
Success rate is 100 percent (5/5), round-trip min/avg/max =
8/8/8 ms
```

A quick ping proves us that we have connectivity.

That's all you have to do to create a manual tunnel and encapsulate IPv6 packets in IPv4 packets. Not that bad right? How about GRE?

```
Futura(config)#interface tunnel 0
Futura(config-if)#tunnel mode gre ip
```

```
Destiny(config)#interface tunnel 0
Destiny(config-if)#tunnel mode gre ip
```

Use **tunnel mode gre ip** or type **no tunnel mode ipv6ip** so it switches back to the default (GRE).

```
Futura#show interfaces tunnel 0
Tunnel0 is up, line protocol is up
  Hardware is Tunnel
  MTU 1514 bytes, BW 9 Kbit, DLY 500000 usec,
     reliability 255/255, txload 1/255, rxload 1/255
  Encapsulation TUNNEL, loopback not set
  Keepalive not set
  Tunnel source 1.1.1.1 (Loopback1), destination 3.3.3.3
  Tunnel protocol/transport GRE/IP
```

It looks pretty much the same except it now says GRE. The only difference between GRE and the manual tunnel is that GRE has a higher MTU by default and there's something with the link-local IPv6 address of the tunnel interface:

- The link-local address for the GRE tunnel is created with EUI-64 and takes the lowest numbered interface's MAC address.
- The link-local address for the manual tunnel is FE80::/96 + 32 bits from tunnel source IPv4 address.

That's all there is to it. Do you want to see if you can configure this yourself and play around a bit with the show commands? Here is a lab you should look at:

http://gns3vault.com/IPv6/ipv6-tunneling-over-ipv4.html

Dynamic multipoint IPv6 tunnels are another migration technique we can use. It's called dynamic because we don't have to specify the end-point IPv4 address ourselves but its being automatically determined. The downside of multipoint IPv6 tunnels is that they **don't support IPv6 IGPs**. You have to use **static routes or BGP**.

There are two different flavors:

- **Automatic 6to4**
- **ISATAP**

Let's dive in the automatic 6to4 tunnel to see how it works. We don't configure the IPv4 end-point address ourselves but instead the IPv4 end-point address will be wrapped in the IPv6 destination address. Our IPv4 address is only 32-bit so it's easy to fit it in a 128-bit IPv6 address right?

The 2002::/16 range has been reserved to use for tunneling. This IPv6 address space is only for tunneling and will never be used for IPv6 global unicast addresses. If we start with the 2002::/16 prefix we create a /48 prefix for each tunnel end-point. What we have to do is take the IPv4 address of the end-point and convert it **into hexadecimal as bits 17 to 48**.

The second step is that we can create subnets from /48 up to /64 prefixes for all the subnets behind the end-point.

2002:	C0A8:1703:	Subnet::/64

Prefix   IPv4 address in HEX

Here's a graphical overview. 2002::/16 is the range we can use for the tunnels. The second part is the IPv4 end-point address converted to hexadecimal. Up to /64 we can use to create subnets. C0A8:1703 converts to IPv4 address 192.168.23.3. Do you have trouble calculating from hex to binary/decimal and vice versa?

```
Destiny(config)#ipv6 general-prefix MYPREFIX 6to4 fastEthernet
0/0

Destiny#show ipv6 general-prefix
IPv6 Prefix MYPREFIX, acquired via 6to4
  2002:C0A8:1703::/48
```

There is a neat trick on Cisco routers that can do the work for you. First you have to configure an IPv4 address on an interface and then use the **ipv6 general-prefix** command. It will convert the IPv4 address in hexadecimal and give you the correct IPv6 tunnel prefix with the **show ipv6 general-prefix** command. I'm not sure if this is available on the CCNP ROUTE exam but it's nice to know anyway!

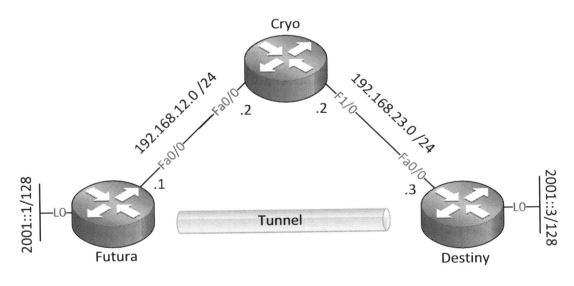

Let's look at another example and configure automatic tunneling. The idea is that I don't want to configure a tunnel destination on router Futura nor Destiny…it should be created dynamically!

```
Futura(config)#no interface tunnel 0
```

```
Destiny(config)#no interface tunnel 0
```

First I'll remove the tunnel I used previously.

```
Futura(config)#ipv6 general-prefix MYPREFIX 6to4 fastEthernet
0/0
```

```
Destiny(config)#ipv6 general-prefix MYPREFIX 6to4 fastEthernet
0/0
```

```
Futura#show ipv6 general-prefix
IPv6 Prefix MYPREFIX, acquired via 6to4
  2002:C0A8:C01::/48
```

```
Destiny#show ipv6 general-prefix
IPv6 Prefix MYPREFIX, acquired via 6to4
  2002:C0A8:1703::/48
```

This time I'm going to use the IP addresses on the FastEthernet0/0 interfaces to build the tunnel. Since the tunnel is created automatically we need to know the IPv6 equivalent of the IPv4 addresses.

```
Futura(config)#interface tunnel 0
Futura(config-if)#ipv6 address 2002:C0A8:C01::1/64
Futura(config-if)#tunnel source fastEthernet 0/0
Futura(config-if)#tunnel mode ipv6ip 6to4
```

```
Destiny(config)#interface tunnel 0
Destiny(config-if)#ipv6 address 2002:C0A8:1703::3/64
Destiny(config-if)#tunnel source fastEthernet 0/0
Destiny(config-if)#tunnel mode ipv6ip 6to4
```

Let me walk you through this configuration: The tunnel interface has an IPv6 address that starts with 2002: and then the IPv4 address in hex:

- Router Futura: 192.168.12.1 → C0A8:C01
- Router Destiny: 192.168.23.3 → C0A8:1703

The tunnel is sourced from the FastEthernet interface (I could have used a loopback as well) and there is no destination. That's why we need the **tunnel mode ipv6ip 6to4** command for. It tells the router to get the IPv4 address from the IPv6 address.

Are we done? Well almost. The tunnel configuration is OK but we still have to tell our routers how to reach the loopback0 interfaces. It's impossible to run an IGP on dynamic tunnel interfaces so we can use **static routes or BGP**. I'm going to use static routes.

```
Futura(config)#ipv6 route 2001::3/128 2002:C0A8:1703::3
Futura(config)#ipv6 route 2002::/16 tunnel 0
```

```
Destiny(config)#ipv6 route 2001::1/128 2002:C0A8:C01::1
Destiny(config)#ipv6 route 2002::/16 tunnel 0
```

The first static route we need to tell our routers how to reach the loopback0 interface of the other side. It points to the IPv6 address which has the IPv4 address in hex in it. The routers will have to do recursive routing to find an entry for 2002:: which is why we need the second static route. Since 2002::/16 is reserved for tunneling I'm creating a static that points directly to our tunnel0 interface.

```
Futura#ping 2001::3 source loopback 0

Type escape sequence to abort.
Sending 5, 100-byte ICMP Echos to 2001:3::3, timeout is 2
seconds:
Packet sent with a source address of 2001::1
!!!!!
Success rate is 100 percent (5/5), round-trip min/avg/max =
8/8/8 ms
```

A quick ping shows we can reach the loopback0 interface of the other side! Want to see this one in action? Of course I have just the lab for you!

http://gns3vault.com/IPv6/ipv6-6to4-tunneling.html

There is one more dynamic tunneling technique we have to look at:

ISATAP (Intra-site Automatic Tunneling Addressing Protocol)

What's in a name right? It is similar to automatic 6to4 tunneling with some differences:

- ISATAP embed the IPv4 address in the last two quartets.
- ISATAP doesn't use the reserved 2002::/16 range but normal global unicast addresses.
- ISATAP uses a single prefix to which all tunnel interfaces connect.
- ISATAP tunnels automatically create the tunnel's interface ID by using EUI-64.

EUI-64 works a bit different though. There is no MAC address to use so we have **modified EUI-64 rules:**

- Your router will use 0000:5EFE for quarter 5 and 6.
- Your router will use the tunnel source IPv4 address converted to hex and add it as quarter 7 and 8.

Let's walk through the ISATAP configuration together!

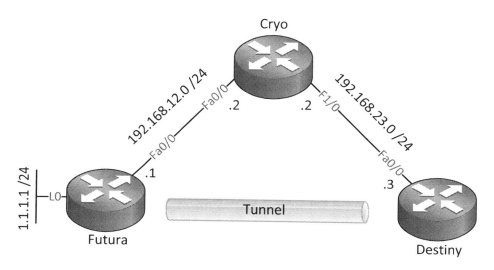

My goal is to have a ISATAP tunnel between router Futura and Destiny. Router Destiny should get its IPv6 address through the ISATAP tunnel. OSPF has been configured so we have full connectivity for IPv4.

```
Futura(config)#interface tunnel 0
Futura(config-if)#ipv6 address 2001::/64 eui-64
Futura(config-if)#no ipv6 nd suppress-ra
Futura(config-if)#tunnel source loopback 0
Futura(config-if)#tunnel mode ipv6ip isatap
```

We'll start with the tunnel configuration on router Futura. We'll have to set the tunnel mode to ISATAP with **tunnel mode ipv6ip isatap.** I'm configuring 2001::/64 as the prefix and we are using EUI-64 to create the IPv6 address. You have to use **no ipv6 nd suppress-ra** to enable router advertisements on the tunnel interface. Router Destiny can use the router advertisements to configure itself.

```
Destiny(config)#interface tunnel 0
Destiny(config-if)#ipv6 enable
Destiny(config-if)#ipv6 address autoconfig
Destiny(config-if)#tunnel source fastEthernet 0/0
Destiny(config-if)#tunnel destination 1.1.1.1
Destiny(config-if)#tunnel mode ipv6ip
```

Router Destiny has a tunnel interface and we use **ipv6 address autoconfig**
so it will use the router advertisements from router Futura to configure its own
IPv6 address. The destination of the tunnel is 1.1.1.1 (loopback0 interface of
router Futura). Router Destiny can configure its own IPv6 address this way and
we have connectivity.

```
Destiny#show ipv6 interface tunnel 0
Tunnel0 is up, line protocol is up
  IPv6 is enabled, link-local address is FE80::C0A8:1703
  Global unicast address(es):
    2001::C0A8:1703, subnet is 2001::/64 [PRE]
```

You can see that router Destiny has configured itself using the 2001::/64
prefix and EUI-64 to come up with IPv6 address 2001::C0A8:1703.

That's all I have on tunneling for you. The dynamic tunnels are fun to play with
but the downside is that you can't run any IGPs so you have to use static
routes or BGP.
Do you want to try ISATAP yourself? Check out this lab:

http://gns3vault.com/IPv6/ipv6-isatap.html

This is the end of the IPv6 chapter. What do you think? Can't wait to migrate
your network and get rid of IPv4? To be honest I'm really curious to see what
the migration will look like. On our LANs we don't have the problem with lack
of IPv4 space but we do on the Internet. Are network engineers really going to
change their own networks or will we see more NAT-like solutions? The future
will tell us!

If you want to play a bit with IPv6 on your own computer you can try a Teredo
tunnel. You can install client software on your computer and you'll get an IPv6
global unicast address to access the Internet even when you are behind an
IPv4 router. I won't go into details but you can read more on Wikipedia:

http://en.wikipedia.org/wiki/Teredo_tunneling

```
renemolenaar@RMCSWS006 ~ $ sudo apt-get install miredo
```

If you like Ubuntu like me you can install Miredo.

```
renemolenaar@RMCSWS006 ~ $ ifconfig teredo
teredo    Link encap:UNSPEC  HWaddr 00-00-00-00-00-00-00-00-00-
00-00-00-00-00-00-00
          inet6 addr: fe80::ffff:ffff:ffff/64 Scope:Link
          inet6 addr: 2001:0:53aa:64c:383d:5305:abe0:2962/32
Scope:Global
          UP POINTOPOINT RUNNING NOARP MULTICAST  MTU:1280
Metric:1
```

```
RX packets:0 errors:0 dropped:0 overruns:0 frame:0
TX packets:3 errors:0 dropped:0 overruns:0 carrier:0
collisions:0 txqueuelen:500
```

You don't have to do configure anything yourself and you will get a public IPv6 address like mine.

Take a look at this ping:

```
renemolenaar@RMCSWS006 ~ $ ping6 www.kame.net
PING www.kame.net(2001:200:dff:fff1:216:3eff:feb1:44d7) 56 data
bytes
64 bytes from 2001:200:dff:fff1:216:3eff:feb1:44d7: icmp_seq=1
ttl=57 time=747 ms
64 bytes from 2001:200:dff:fff1:216:3eff:feb1:44d7: icmp_seq=2
ttl=57 time=290 ms
64 bytes from 2001:200:dff:fff1:216:3eff:feb1:44d7: icmp_seq=3
ttl=57 time=258 ms
^C
--- www.kame.net ping statistics ---
3 packets transmitted, 3 received, 0% packet loss, time 1999ms
rtt min/avg/max/mdev = 258.687/432.220/747.425/223.263 ms
```

A little ping test proves that I'm ready for the future!

If you want to try this on Windows 7 you can read the following article:

http://www.domaincontrollertips.com/?p=88

If you want to practice a bit more with IPv6 you can see what other labs I have left for you:

http://gns3vault.com/Table/IPv6/

23. Remote Site Connectivity

In this chapter we will take a look at some different WAN options to connect remote sites to the HQ network. Back in the days, WAN connections were typically dedicated leased lines or PVCs using frame-relay and ATM. Nowadays, we have high speed internet using DSL, Cable and fibre links.

The advantage of these internet connections is that it's easy to get a connection to an ISP and they are cheap compared to dedicated connections.

Since the Internet is a public network, we'll use VPNs to create a logical connection between sites that offers us authentication and encryption. In the ROUTE exam you are only required to understand the configuration of GRE tunneling. You only need to understand the theoretical part of the other VPN technologies.

Let's start with GRE, simply said a GRE tunnel creates a point-to-point tunnel between two routers. Take a look at the image below:

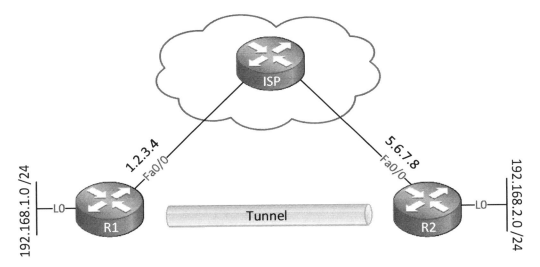

Here we have two routers, R1 and R2 that are connected to the Internet. Behind each router is a private network. By creating a tunnel between the two routers, the two private networks will be able to communicate with each other.

Tunneling basically means that we put an "IP packet into another IP packet". For example: When R1 has an IP packet from the 192.168.1.0 /24 to the 192.168.2.0 /24 network, it will **encapsulate** the original IP packet into a new IP packet that has a source IP address of 1.2.3.4 (its public IP address) and a destination of 5.6.7.8 (the public IP address of R2).

When R2 receives this encapsulated IP packet, it will **de-encapsulate** it and forwards the original IP packet to the 192.168.2.0 /24 network.

Let's take a look at an actual configuration. I'll use the topology that I just showed you, make sure that R1 and R2 are able to reach each other:

```
R1#ping 5.6.7.8

Type escape sequence to abort.
Sending 5, 100-byte ICMP Echos to 5.6.7.8, timeout is 2 seconds:
!!!!!
Success rate is 100 percent (5/5), round-trip min/avg/max =
20/33/52 ms
```

R1 and R2 are able to reach each other, let's configure the GRE tunnel:

```
R1(config)#interface tunnel 1
R1(config-if)#tunnel source FastEthernet 0/0
R1(config-if)#tunnel destination 5.6.7.8
R1(config-if)#ip address 192.168.12.1 255.255.255.0
```

```
R2(config)#interface tunnel 1
R2(config-if)#tunnel source FastEthernet 0/0
R2(config-if)#tunnel destination 1.2.3.4
R2(config-if)#ip address 192.168.12.2 255.255.255.0
```

First we create a new tunnel interface, you can pick any number you like. Secondly we need to configure the source and destination of the tunnel. In this example, the tunnel will be established between the IP address on the "outside" interfaces of the router. Last but not least, the tunnel itself has a subnet and each router has an IP address.

Here's a good way to verify this:

```
R1#show interfaces tunnel 1
Tunnel1 is up, line protocol is up
  Hardware is Tunnel
  Internet address is 192.168.12.1/24
  MTU 1514 bytes, BW 9 Kbit/sec, DLY 500000 usec,
     reliability 255/255, txload 1/255, rxload 1/255
  Encapsulation TUNNEL, loopback not set
  Keepalive not set
  Tunnel source 1.2.3.4 (FastEthernet0/0), destination 5.6.7.8
  Tunnel protocol/transport GRE/IP
```

The tunnel interface is up, we have an IP address and you can see the source and destination IP address.

A quick way to test if the tunnel is working is to ping the IP address on the other side of the tunnel:

```
R1#ping 192.168.12.2

Type escape sequence to abort.
Sending 5, 100-byte ICMP Echos to 192.168.12.2, timeout is 2
seconds:
!!!!!
Success rate is 100 percent (5/5), round-trip min/avg/max =
36/45/56 ms
```

This proves that the tunnel is working. Our goal however is to have connectivity between the 192.168.1.0 /24 and 192.168.2.0 /24 network. The tunnel works just like any other interface so we'll create two static routes so the routers know how to reach each others network:

```
R1(config)#ip route 192.168.2.0 255.255.255.0 192.168.12.2
```

```
R2(config)#ip route 192.168.1.0 255.255.255.0 192.168.12.1
```

Let's see if there is connectivity between the two networks now:

```
R1#ping 192.168.2.2 source 192.168.1.1

Type escape sequence to abort.
Sending 5, 100-byte ICMP Echos to 192.168.2.2, timeout is 2
seconds:
Packet sent with a source address of 192.168.1.1
!!!!!
Success rate is 100 percent (5/5), round-trip min/avg/max =
24/41/68 ms
```

There we go, we can ping from one side to the other. That's all there is to GRE tunneling...to help you visualize what encapsulation really looks like I have added a wireshark capture of this ping:

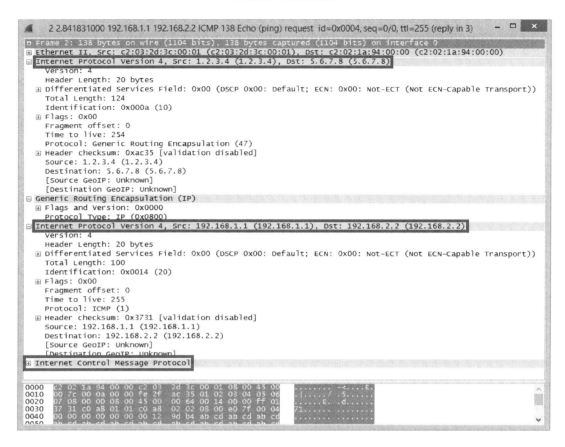

This capture is the encapsulated IP packet which carries the ICMP echo request. You can clearly see the outer and inner IP packet.

GRE does not offer any security, as you can see in the wireshark capture everything is in clear text. If you want encryption, we'll have to use IPSEC. Here is an example how to encrypt the GRE tunnel:

```
R1(config)#crypto isakmp policy 10
R1(config-isakmp)# encr aes 256
R1(config-isakmp)# authentication pre-share
R1(config-isakmp)# group 5
R1(config-isakmp)# lifetime 3600
```

```
R2(config)#crypto isakmp policy 10
R2(config-isakmp)# encr aes 256
R2(config-isakmp)# authentication pre-share
R2(config-isakmp)# group 5
R2(config-isakmp)# lifetime 3600
```

First of all we have to configure an ISAKMP policy. In the example above I specify that I want to use 256-bit AES encryption and that we want to use a pre-shared key. We use Diffie-Hellman Group 5 for the key exchange process.

The lifetime for the ISAKMP security association is 3600 seconds. Don't forget to configure the pre-shared key on both routers:

```
R1(config)#crypto isakmp key PASS address 5.6.7.8
```

```
R2(config)#crypto isakmp key PASS address 1.2.3.4
```

I will use 'PASS" as the pre-shared key on both routers. The next step is to create an IPSEC transform-set:

```
R1(config)#crypto ipsec transform-set TRANS esp-aes 256 esp-sha-hmac
R2(config)#crypto ipsec transform-set TRANS esp-aes 256 esp-sha-hmac
```

Above you can see I created a transform-set called 'TRANS' that specifies we want to use ESP AES 256-bit and HMAC-SHA authentication.

Now we can create a crypto map that tells the router what traffic to encrypt and what transform-set to use:

```
R1(config)#crypto map MYMAP 10 ipsec-isakmp
R1(config-crypto-map)# set peer 5.6.7.8
R1(config-crypto-map)# set transform-set TRANS
R1(config-crypto-map)# match address 100
```

```
R2(config)#crypto map MYMAP 10 ipsec-isakmp
R2(config-crypto-map)# set peer 1.2.3.4
R2(config-crypto-map)# set transform-set TRANS
R2(config-crypto-map)# match address 100
```

Above we have a crypto-map called 'MYMAP' that specifies the transform-set 'TRANS' and what traffic it should encrypt. I used access-list 100 for this but I still have to create it:

```
R1(config)#access-list 100 permit gre any any
```

```
R2(config)#access-list 100 permit gre any any
```

We will use a permit statement that only matches GRE traffic.

Now the final step is to activate crypto map by applying it to the FastEthernet interfaces:

```
R1(config)#interface fastEthernet 0/0
R1(config-if)#crypto map MYMAP
```

```
R2(config)#interface fastEthernet 0/0
R2(config-if)#crypto map MYMAP
```

Now let's send some traffic between the 192.168.1.0 /24 and 192.168.2.0 /24 network to see if it's encrypted or not:

```
R1#ping 192.168.2.2 source 10

Type escape sequence to abort.
Sending 5, 100-byte ICMP Echos to 192.168.2.2, timeout is 2
seconds:
Packet sent with a source address of 192.168.1.1
!!!!!
Success rate is 100 percent (5/5), round-trip min/avg/max =
8/8/12 ms
```

```
R1#show crypto ipsec sa

interface: FastEthernet0/0
    Crypto map tag: MYMAP, local addr 1.2.3.4

    protected vrf: (none)
    local  ident (addr/mask/prot/port):
(192.168.1.1/255.255.255.255/47/0)
    remote ident (addr/mask/prot/port):
(192.168.2.2/255.255.255.255/47/0)
    current_peer 5.6.7.8 port 500
      PERMIT, flags={origin_is_acl,}
     #pkts encaps: 16, #pkts encrypt: 16, #pkts digest: 16
     #pkts decaps: 16, #pkts decrypt: 16, #pkts verify: 16
```

Above you can see that 16 packets have been encrypted (encapsulated) and decrypted (decapsulated). It seems our IPSEC configuration is working.

GRE tunnels are very useful but scalability can be a problem. In the previous example we only had two routers. If we have a lot of remote sites then it is a pain to create all these tunnels. Here's an example:

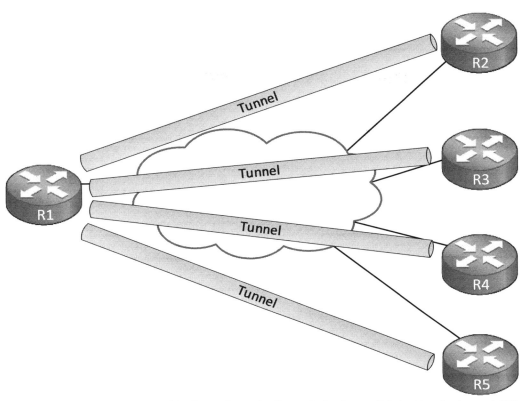

The topology above is a "hub and spoke" model where R1 is the hub and R2 – R5 are the spokes. The problem is that the spoke routers on the right side are only able to communicate with each other by going through the tunnel to R1. If you want communication between the spokes directly then you need to configure additionals tunnels between them.

To solve this issue, we can use **DMVPN (Dynamic Multipoint VPN)**. This allows us to dynamically create tunnels between routers when required. DMVPN uses **mGRE (Multipoint GRE)** for the tunnels and IPsec for security. Here's an example:

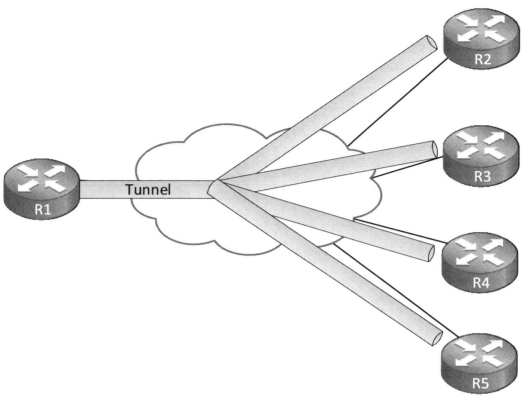

The hub router uses a single multipoint GRE interface while the spoke routers use normal GRE interfaces. Whenever a spoke has something to send to another spoke, a temporary tunnel will be created between the two spoke routers.

When a spoke wants to dynamically build a tunnel with another spoke, there is one problem...the spoke has no idea what the destination IP address of the other spoke is.

DMVPN requires **NHRP (Next Hop Resolution Protocol)**. The hub will act as a server and the spokes are clients. A spoke router will report its IP address on the outside and its IP address of the tunnel interface to the hub. The hub will add this information to the NHRP database.

When a spoke wants to dynamically create a tunnel with another spoke, it will query the hub for the outside IP address of the spoke. Once it has this IP address, it can build the tunnel to the other spoke.

The configuration of DMVPN and NHRP is outside of the scope of the ROUTE exam but it's still a good exercise to see how it works. Let's take a look at a configuration example of DMVPN. I'll use the following topology:

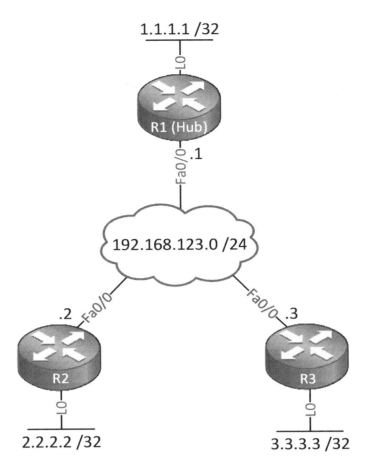

Let me explain this topology:

- R1,R2 and R3 are able to reach each other using their FastEthernet 0/0 interfaces. I used the 192.168.123.0 /24 subnet so that they can reach each other.
- R1 will be the hub router and R2/R3 will be the spoke routers.
- R2 and R3 will establish a tunnel to R1.
- When R2 and R3 want to communicate with each other they will create a spoke-to-spoke tunnel.
- We will use the 172.16.123.0 /24 subnet for the tunnel interfaces.
- Each router has a loopback interface with an IP address. The routers will reach each others loopback by going through the tunnel interface.

The configuration consists of a number of steps:
1. GRE Multipoint Tunnel configuration on all routers
2. Encryption of tunnels using IPSEC.
3. Routing configuration so the routers can reach each others loopback interfaces.

Let's start with the configuration of the hub router (R1):

```
R1(config)#interface tunnel 0
R1(config-if)#ip address 172.16.123.1 255.255.255.0
R1(config-if)#tunnel mode gre multipoint
R1(config-if)#tunnel source fastEthernet 0/0
R1(config-if)#ip nhrp map multicast dynamic
R1(config-if)#ip nhrp network-id 1
R1(config-if)#ip nhrp authentication DMVPN
```

We will configure an IP address on the tunnel 0 interface and instead of specifying a destination IP address we will configure it as **gre multipoint**. If you want to use a routing protocol like RIP, OSPF or EIGRP you require the **ip nhrp map multicast dynamic** command to automatically add routers to the multicast NHRP mappings. For each DMVPN setup you require a unique network ID that you can configure with the **ip nhrp network-id** command. Last but not least, the **ip nhrp authentication** command enables a password for NHRP queries. I've set the password to 'DMVPN'.

Now let's configure our spoke routers, R2 and R3:

```
R2(config)#interface tunnel 0
R2(config-if)#ip address 172.16.123.2 255.255.255.0
R2(config-if)#tunnel mode gre multipoint
R2(config-if)#ip nhrp authentication DMVPN
R2(config-if)#ip nhrp map 172.16.123.1 192.168.123.1
R2(config-if)#ip nhrp map multicast 192.168.123.1
R2(config-if)#ip nhrp network-id 1
R2(config-if)#ip nhrp nhs 172.16.123.1
R2(config-if)#tunnel source fastEthernet 0/0
```

Above you can see a number of commands that we didn't configure on the hub router. We use the **ip nhrp map** command to map the IP address of the **NHS (Next Hop Server)** to the outside IP address. In this case 172.16.123.1 is the IP address on the tunnel interface of R1 and 192.168.123.1 is the outside IP address of R1. We also require the **ip nhrp nhs** command to set the IP address of the NHS.

The **ip nhrp map multicast** commands configures the spoke router to send **multicast traffic only to the hub router, not to other spoke routers**.

As the source of the tunnel I specified the FastEthernet 0/0 interface with the **tunnel source** command. It's best to specify the interface as the source and not an IP address in case you are using dynamic IP address on the spoke router.

If everything went ok you should see a tunnel coming up on R2:

```
R2#
%LINEPROTO-5-UPDOWN: Line protocol on Interface Tunnel0, changed
state to up
```

Let's configure R3 which is pretty much the same as R2:

```
R3(config)#interface tunnel 0
R3(config-if)#ip address 172.16.123.3 255.255.255.0
R3(config-if)#tunnel mode gre multipoint
R3(config-if)#ip nhrp authentication DMVPN
R3(config-if)#ip nhrp map 172.16.123.1 192.168.123.1
R3(config-if)#ip nhrp map multicast 192.168.123.1
R3(config-if)#ip nhrp network-id 1
R3(config-if)#ip nhrp nhs 172.16.123.1
R3(config-if)#tunnel source fastEthernet 0/0
```

The configuration is the same with the exception of the IP address on the tunnel interface. The tunnel should come up now:

```
R3#
%LINEPROTO-5-UPDOWN: Line protocol on Interface Tunnel0, changed
state to up
```

Right now you should have a working multipoint GRE configuration so it's wise to check this before you continue configuring IPSEC.

Let's verify if the tunnels are working:

```
R1#show dmvpn
Legend: Attrb --> S - Static, D - Dynamic, I - Incompletea
       N - NATed, L - Local, X - No Socket
       # Ent --> Number of NHRP entries with same NBMA peer

Tunnel0, Type:Hub, NHRP Peers:2,
 # Ent   Peer NBMA Addr  Peer Tunnel Add  State   UpDn Tm Attrb
 -----  --------------- --------------- ----- -------- -----
     1   192.168.123.2    172.16.123.2     UP      never  D
     1   192.168.123.3    172.16.123.3     UP      never  D
```

Above you see that R1 is the hub router and that is has two peers. There's a couple of interesting items that we can find here:

- **Ent** stands for the number of entries in the NHRP database for this spoke router. Normally you will only see 1 entry here.
- **Peer NBMA Addr** is the IP address on the outside interface of the spoke router, in our example 192.168.123.2 and 192.168.123.3.
- **Peer Tunnel Add** is the IP address on the tunnel interface of the spoke router.

- **State** shows if your tunnel is up or down.
- **UpDn Tm** is the up or down time of the current state (up or down). You will see the time here once we are using the tunnels.
- **Attrb** means attributes. You can see them at top of the show command. The **D** stands for **dynamic** which you will normally see for spoke routers.

Let's use the same command on the spoke routers:

```
R2#show dmvpn
Legend: Attrb --> S - Static, D - Dynamic, I - Incompletea
       N - NATed, L - Local, X - No Socket
       # Ent --> Number of NHRP entries with same NBMA peer

Tunnel0, Type:Spoke, NHRP Peers:1,
  # Ent   Peer NBMA Addr Peer Tunnel Add State   UpDn Tm Attrb
 ----- --------------- --------------- ----- -------- -----
     1   192.168.123.1    172.16.123.1    UP 00:43:44 S
```

```
R3#show dmvpn
Legend: Attrb --> S - Static, D - Dynamic, I - Incompletea
       N - NATed, L - Local, X - No Socket
       # Ent --> Number of NHRP entries with same NBMA peer

Tunnel0, Type:Spoke, NHRP Peers:1,
  # Ent   Peer NBMA Addr Peer Tunnel Add State   UpDn Tm Attrb
 ----- --------------- --------------- ----- -------- -----
     1   192.168.123.1    172.16.123.1    UP 00:46:58 S
```

Right now the spoke routers only have a tunnel that connects to the hub router. Let's try if we can ping from one router to another...

```
R2#ping 172.16.123.1

Type escape sequence to abort.
Sending 5, 100-byte ICMP Echos to 172.16.123.1, timeout is 2
seconds:
!!!!!
Success rate is 100 percent (5/5), round-trip min/avg/max =
4/4/8 ms
```

```
R3#ping 172.16.123.1

Type escape sequence to abort.
Sending 5, 100-byte ICMP Echos to 172.16.123.1, timeout is 2
seconds:
!!!!!
Success rate is 100 percent (5/5), round-trip min/avg/max =
4/4/8 ms
```

Both spoke routers are able to reach the hub. Now let's try to ping between the two spoke routers:

```
R2#ping 172.16.123.3

Type escape sequence to abort.
Sending 5, 100-byte ICMP Echos to 172.16.123.3, timeout is 2
seconds:
!!!!!
Success rate is 100 percent (5/5), round-trip min/avg/max =
4/6/12 ms
```

The ping is working and this is the interesting part of multipoint GRE. The spoke routers will dynamically create a tunnel between each other as you can see below:

```
R2#show dmvpn
Legend: Attrb --> S - Static, D - Dynamic, I - Incompletea
       N - NATed, L - Local, X - No Socket
       # Ent --> Number of NHRP entries with same NBMA peer

Tunnel0, Type:Spoke, NHRP Peers:2,
 # Ent   Peer NBMA Addr Peer Tunnel Add State  UpDn Tm Attrb
 ----- --------------- --------------- ----- -------- -----
     1    192.168.123.1     172.16.123.1     UP 00:01:41 S
     1    192.168.123.3     172.16.123.3     UP    never D
```

```
R3#show dmvpn
Legend: Attrb --> S - Static, D - Dynamic, I - Incompletea
       N - NATed, L - Local, X - No Socket
       # Ent --> Number of NHRP entries with same NBMA peer

Tunnel0, Type:Spoke, NHRP Peers:2,
 # Ent   Peer NBMA Addr Peer Tunnel Add State  UpDn Tm Attrb
 ----- --------------- --------------- ----- -------- -----
     1    192.168.123.1     172.16.123.1     UP 00:01:42 S
     1    192.168.123.2     172.16.123.2     UP    never D
```

As you can see another tunnel has been established between R2 and R3. So far so good, multipoint GRE is working but everything is clear text at the moment.

It's time to configure IPSEC to encrypt the tunnels!

```
R1,R2 & R3:
(config)#crypto isakmp policy 1
(config-isakmp)#encryption aes
(config-isakmp)#hash md5
(config-isakmp)#authentication pre-share
(config-isakmp)#group 2
(config-isakmp)#lifetime 86400

(config)#crypto isakmp key 0 NETWORKLESSONS address 0.0.0.0
(config)#crypto ipsec transform-set MYSET esp-aes esp-md5-hmac

(config)#crypto ipsec profile MGRE
(ipsec-profile)#set security-association lifetime seconds 86400
(ipsec-profile)#set transform-set MYSET

(config)#interface tunnel 0
(config-if)#tunnel protection ipsec profile MGRE
```

When you configure the **crypto isakmp key** you should use IP address 0.0.0.0 if you are using dynamic IP addresses on spoke routers. 0.0.0.0 means it applies to **any IP address**. Let's verify if our traffic is encrypted or not...

Just to be sure, do a shut/no shut on the tunnel interfaces after the configuration of IPSEC.

```
R1,R2 & R3:
(config)#interface tunnel 0
(config-if)#shutdown
(config-if)#no shutdown
```

Next step is to check if IPSEC is active:

```
R1#show crypto session
Crypto session current status

Interface: Tunnel0
Session status: UP-ACTIVE
Peer: 192.168.123.2 port 500
  IKE SA: local 192.168.123.1/500 remote 192.168.123.2/500
Active
  IPSEC FLOW: permit 47 host 192.168.123.1 host 192.168.123.2
      Active SAs: 2, origin: crypto map

Interface: Tunnel0
Session status: UP-ACTIVE
Peer: 192.168.123.3 port 500
  IKE SA: local 192.168.123.1/500 remote 192.168.123.3/500
Active
  IPSEC FLOW: permit 47 host 192.168.123.1 host 192.168.123.3
      Active SAs: 2, origin: crypto map
```

As you can see IPSEC is active for both peers. Let's send some pings to verify if traffic is encrypted or not:

```
R2#ping 172.16.123.1

Type escape sequence to abort.
Sending 5, 100-byte ICMP Echos to 172.16.123.1, timeout is 2
seconds:
!!!!!
Success rate is 100 percent (5/5), round-trip min/avg/max =
4/4/4 ms
```

```
R3#ping 172.16.123.1

Type escape sequence to abort.
Sending 5, 100-byte ICMP Echos to 172.16.123.1, timeout is 2
seconds:
!!!!!
Success rate is 100 percent (5/5), round-trip min/avg/max =
4/4/4 ms
```

Let's see if packets are encrypted:

```
R1#show crypto ipsec sa

interface: Tunnel0
    Crypto map tag: Tunnel0-head-0, local addr 192.168.123.1

   protected vrf: (none)
   local  ident (addr/mask/prot/port):
(192.168.123.1/255.255.255.255/47/0)
   remote ident (addr/mask/prot/port):
(192.168.123.2/255.255.255.255/47/0)
   current_peer 192.168.123.2 port 500
     PERMIT, flags={origin_is_acl,}
    #pkts encaps: 26, #pkts encrypt: 26, #pkts digest: 26
    #pkts decaps: 26, #pkts decrypt: 26, #pkts verify: 26
```

As you can see packets in the tunnel are encrypted. That's all there is to DMVPN.

That's all there is for now. I have some labs that you can try to practice GRE tunneling and encrypting them with IPsec:

http://gns3vault.com/tunneling/gre-tunnel-basic/

http://gns3vault.com/tunneling/gre-over-ipsec/

24. Router Security

Routers are important devices in the network and they should be protected against a number of security risks. In CCNA R&S you learned about some basic security tasks like configuring access-lists and adding a password to privileged mode. In this chapter we'll take a look at time-based access-lists, uRPF (Unicast Reverse Path Forwarding), AAA, SNMP security and NTP authentication.

Routers are often used on the edge of our networks, connected to the Internet. The Internet isn't a very safe place so Cisco recommends that you have a documented plan detailing how you secure your routers. This document is called a **router security policy** and here are some of the things that it should contain:

- **Password Policy**: how complex should the passwords be, how often are they changed.
- **Authentication**: do we use local authentication or AAA (Authentication, Authorization, Accounting) using a RADIUS or TACACS+ server? Do we use banners that are shown to uses when they access the router?
- **Access**: What protocols do we allow for remote access? telnet? SSH? HTTP / HTTPS ?
- **Services**: What services are enabled on the router that are not required?
- **Filtering**: What access-lists do we use to block certain attacks? Do we prevent private IP addresses from accessing the Internet?
- **Routing Protocols**: What authentication do we use for routing protocols?
- **Backups**: How and how often do we backup configurations? Through TFTP?
- **Documentation**: How do we document changes to the router configuration?
- **Redundancy**: When a router fails, is there a backup router? Do we use any protocols like HSRP, VRRP or GLBP?
- **Monitoring**: What parameters do we monitor? CPU / memory utilization? Packet loss?

Let's start with access-lists. In CCNA R&S you learned about the basics of standard and extended access-lists and how you can use them to filter certain traffic to enter or exit the router. The problem with access-lists is that they are always active. What if I only want to block certain traffic during business hours?

Only permitted from 9:00 – 17:00

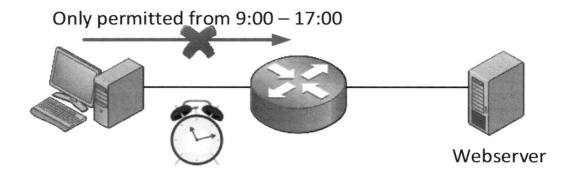

Webserver

In this example we have a computer that is trying to access a webserver. We can filter this traffic with an access-list and by adding a time-range, we can tell the router only to allow this traffic between 9:00 – 17:00.

Let's look at an actual configuration example:

R1 will simulate a host that wants to access a webserver (R3). R2 is where we configure the time-based access-list. Let's configure R2:

```
R2(config)#time-range BUSINESS
```

First I have to specify a time range, I'll call it "BUSINESS". Now we can select when this time-range is active:

```
R2(config-time-range)#periodic ?
  Friday      Friday
  Monday      Monday
  Saturday    Saturday
  Sunday      Sunday
  Thursday    Thursday
  Tuesday     Tuesday
  Wednesday   Wednesday
  daily       Every day of the week
  weekdays    Monday thru Friday
  weekend     Saturday and Sunday
```

I'll pick weekdays:

```
R2(config-time-range)#periodic weekdays 9:00 to 17:00
```

The start time will be 9:00 and the end time is 17:00, that pretty much matches business office hours. Now we can create an access-list that uses this time-range:

```
R2(config)#ip access-list extended NO_HTTP_BUSINESS
R2(config-ext-nacl)#permit tcp any host 192.168.23.3 eq 80 time-
range BUSINESS
```

The access-list is called "NO_HTTP_BUSINESS" and it has an entry that permits TCP traffic to IP address 192.168.23.3 port 80. By adding the time-range, this permit statement is only valid during the time period in the time range. Let's give it a try:

```
R2(config)#interface FastEthernet 0/1
R2(config-if)#ip access-group NO_HTTP_BUSINESS out
```

Let's check the current time:

```
R2#show clock
*00:10:49.219 UTC Fri Mar 1 2002
```

It's a Friday but it's past midnight. Let's try to reach the webserver:

```
R1#telnet 192.168.23.3 80
Trying 192.168.23.3, 80 ...
% Connection timed out; remote host not responding
```

Traffic is not allowed, we can also see that this statement is inactive by checking R2:

```
R2#show access-lists
Extended IP access list NO_HTTP_BUSINESS
    10 permit tcp any host 192.168.23.3 eq www time-range
BUSINESS (inactive)
```

Let's change the clock and try again:

```
R2#clock set 16:00:00 29 January 2015
```

```
R1#telnet 192.168.23.3 80
Trying 192.168.23.3, 80 ... Open
```

```
R2#show access-lists
Extended IP access list NO_HTTP_BUSINESS
    10 permit tcp any host 192.168.23.3 eq www time-range
BUSINESS (active) (3 matches)
```

Now it's showing up as active and we are able to reach TCP port 80 on R3. That's all there is to time based access-lists. There's one more thing I'd like to show you about access-lists. Imagine we have a router that is connected to the Internet:

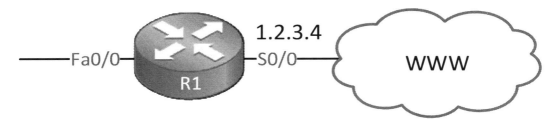

Without access-lists, this router will route any traffic from its FastEthernet 0/0 interface to the Serial0/0 interface or the other way around. If your router is connected to a public network, you really need an access-list to restrict traffic from the outside. This will really depend on your network but here's an example:

```
R1(config)#ip access-list extended OUTSIDE
R1(config-ext-nacl)#deny ip 0.0.0.0 0.255.255.255 any
R1(config-ext-nacl)#deny ip 10.0.0.0 0.255.255.255 any
R1(config-ext-nacl)#deny ip 100.64.0.0 0.63.255.255 any
R1(config-ext-nacl)#deny ip 127.0.0.0 0.255.255.255 any
R1(config-ext-nacl)#deny ip 169.254.0.0 0.0.255.255 any
R1(config-ext-nacl)#deny ip 172.16.0.0 0.15.255.255 any
R1(config-ext-nacl)#deny ip 192.0.0.0 0.0.0.255 any
R1(config-ext-nacl)#deny ip 192.0.2.0 0.0.0.255 any
R1(config-ext-nacl)#deny ip 192.168.0.0 0.0.255.255 any
R1(config-ext-nacl)#deny ip 198.18.0.0 0.1.255.255 any
R1(config-ext-nacl)#deny ip 198.51.100.0 0.0.0.255 any
R1(config-ext-nacl)#deny ip 203.0.113.0 0.0.0.255 any
R1(config-ext-nacl)#deny ip 224.0.0.0 31.255.255.255 any
```

The networks above are all private, reserved or multicast addresses and you should never see an IP packet with a source IP address in these ranges arriving on your outside interface. If you do, someone is messing around and you should drop it.

Something else you might want to drop are IP fragments, it increases the CPU load of the router:

```
R1(config-ext-nacl)#deny ip any any fragments
```

If you use any routing protocols then you should permit them, for example:

```
R1(config-ext-nacl)#permit tcp host 5.5.5.5 gt 1023 host 1.2.3.4
eq bgp
R1(config-ext-nacl)#permit tcp host 5.5.5.5 eq bgp host 1.2.3.4
gt 1023
```

This would allow BGP traffic between this router and a remote BGP peer that uses IP address 5.5.5.5. You might also want to restrict ICMP traffic:

```
R1(config-ext-nacl)#permit icmp any any echo-reply
R1(config-ext-nacl)#permit icmp any any unreachable
R1(config-ext-nacl)#permit icmp any any time-exceeded
R1(config-ext-nacl)#deny icmp any any
```

This will allow the router to responds to ICMP echo requests (ping) and it allows traceroute. All other ICMP traffic will be dropped. If you want to manage the router through SSH from the outside, make sure you create a statement that only allows certain source IP addresses:

```
R1(config-ext-nacl)#permit tcp host 5.6.7.8 host 1.2.3.4 eq 22
```

This allows a host that uses IP address 5.6.7.8 to access SSH on this router. These are just some examples but it should give you an idea of the things you should block / permit from the outside world.

Another useful technique on Cisco routers that helps to block malicious traffic from entering the network is **uRPF (Unicast Reverse Path Forwarding).**

Normally when your router receives unicast IP packets it only cares about one thing:

What is the destination IP address of this IP packet so I can forward it?

If the IP packet has to be routed it willl check the routing table for the destination IP address, select the correct interface and it will be forwarded. Your router really doesn't care about source IP addresses as it's not important for forwarding decisions.

Because the router doesn't check the source IP address it is possible for attackers to spoof the source IP address and send packets that normally might have been dropped by the firewall or an access-list.

uRPF is a security feature that prevents these spoofing attacks. Whenever your router receives an IP packet it will check if it has a matching entry in the routing table for the source IP address. If it doesn't match, the packet will be discarded. uRPF has two modes:

* **Strict mode**
* **Loose mode**

Let's take a look at the difference between both modes and how to configure them.

Strict mode means that that router will perform **two checks** for all incoming packets on a certain interface:

- Do I have a matching entry for the source in the routing table?
- Do I use the same interface to reach this source as where I received this packet on?

When the incoming IP packets passes both checks, it will be permitted. Otherwise it will be dropped. This is perfectly fine for IGP routing protocols since they use the shortest path to the source of IP packets. The interface that you use to reach the source will be the same as the interface where you will receive the packets on. Here's an illustration to demonstrate this:

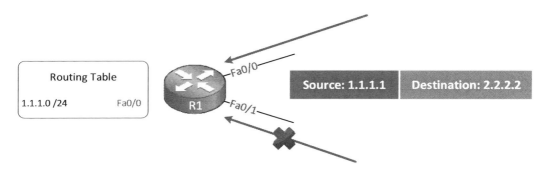

R1 has installed network 1.1.1.0 /24 in its routing table and in order to reach this network it will use the FastEthernet 0/0 interface. Suddenly this router receives an IP packet with source IP address 1.1.1.1 on both of its interfaces. The one it receives on the FastEthernet 0/0 will be accepted but the packet on the FastEthernet 0/1 interface will be dropped because this is not the interface we use to reach this source.

Let's configure the example above to see how it works. I'll use the following topology:

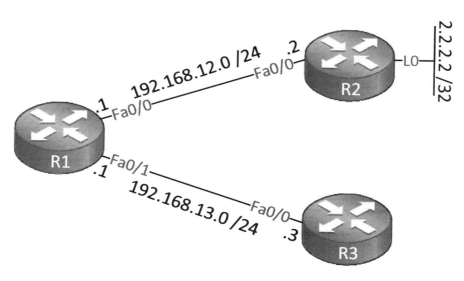

We will configure R1 with a static route so it can reach the loopback0 interface of R2:

```
R1(config)#ip route 2.2.2.2 255.255.255.255 192.168.12.2
```

This is what the routing table looks like now:

```
R1#show ip route

C    192.168.12.0/24 is directly connected, FastEthernet0/0
C    192.168.13.0/24 is directly connected, FastEthernet0/1
     2.0.0.0/32 is subnetted, 1 subnets
S       2.2.2.2 [1/0] via 192.168.12.2
```

Now we'll configure uRPF strict mode on both interfaces:

```
R1(config)#interface fastEthernet 0/0
R1(config-if)#ip verify unicast source reachable-via rx

R1(config)#interface fastEthernet 0/1
R1(config-if)#ip verify unicast source reachable-via rx
```

You can verify that it has been enabled on the interface like this:

```
R1#show ip interface fastEthernet 0/0 | include verify
   IP verify source reachable-via RX

R1#show ip interface fastEthernet 0/1 | include verify
   IP verify source reachable-via RX
```

To test uRPF we'll send some pings from R2 first, these should be accepted:

```
R2#ping 192.168.12.1 source loopback 0

Type escape sequence to abort.
Sending 5, 100-byte ICMP Echos to 192.168.12.1, timeout is 2
seconds:
Packet sent with a source address of 2.2.2.2
!!!!!
Success rate is 100 percent (5/5), round-trip min/avg/max =
4/4/8 ms
```

As expected this ping works. Now I'll create a new loopback interface on R3 with the 2.2.2.2 IP address on it so that we can spoof this IP address:

```
R3(config)#interface loopback 0
R3(config-if)#ip address 2.2.2.2 255.255.255.255
```

Now we'll send some pings from this loopback:

```
R3#ping 192.168.13.1 source loopback 0

Type escape sequence to abort.
Sending 5, 100-byte ICMP Echos to 192.168.13.1, timeout is 2
seconds:
Packet sent with a source address of 2.2.2.2
.....
Success rate is 0 percent (0/5)
```

The packets will make it to R1 but they will be dropped there, we can verify this as following:

```
R1#show ip interface fastEthernet 0/0 | include drops
  0 verification drops
  0 suppressed verification drops
```

```
R1#show ip interface fastEthernet 0/1 | include drops
  5 verification drops
  0 suppressed verification drops
```

Above you see that the spoofed packets on the FastEthernet 0/1 interface have been dropped. Now let's take a look at loose mode...

Loose mode means that the router will perform only a **single check** when it receives an IP packet on an interface:

- Do I have a matching entry for the source in the routing table?

When it passed this check, the packet is permitted. It doesn't matter if we use this interface to reach the source or not. Loose mode is useful when you are connected to more than one ISP and you use **asymmetric routing**.The only exception is the null0 interface, if you have any sources with the null0 interface as the outgoing interface then the packets will be dropped. Take a look at this illustration:

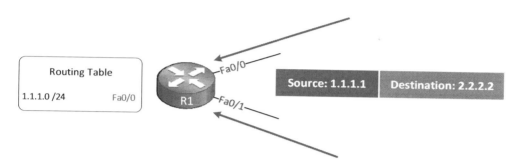

R1 has been configured for uRPF loose mode and receives an IP packet with source IP address 1.1.1.1 on both interfaces. Since it has an entry for this source in its routing table it will accept both packets. It doesn't care where it came from, as long as there is an entry in the routing table.

Let's configure uRPF loose mode on R1 using the same topology:

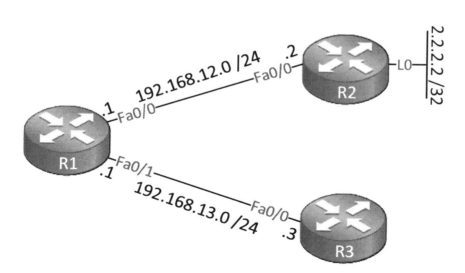

I'll install the same static route on R1 to network 2.2.2.2/32:

```
R1(config)#ip route 2.2.2.2 255.255.255.255 192.168.12.2
```

This time we'll enable uRPF loose mode on the interfaces:

```
R1(config)#interface fastEthernet 0/0
R1(config-if)#ip verify unicast source reachable-via any
```

```
R1(config)#interface fastEthernet 0/1
R1(config-if)#ip verify unicast source reachable-via any
```

Let's verify that it has been enabled on the interfaces:

```
R1#show ip interface fastEthernet 0/0 | include verify
   IP verify source reachable-via ANY
```

```
R1#show ip interface fastEthernet 0/1 | include verify
   IP verify source reachable-via ANY
```

As you can see it's enabled. To verify that it actually works I'll enable a debug on R1:

```
R1#debug ip packet
IP packet debugging is on
```

Now we will send some pings from R2 and R3 using 2.2.2.2 as the source:

```
R2#ping 192.168.12.1 source loopback 0

Type escape sequence to abort.
Sending 5, 100-byte ICMP Echos to 192.168.12.1, timeout is 2
seconds:
Packet sent with a source address of 2.2.2.2
!!!!!
Success rate is 100 percent (5/5), round-trip min/avg/max =
4/4/8 ms
```

```
R3#ping 192.168.13.1 source loopback 0 repeat 1

Type escape sequence to abort.
Sending 1, 100-byte ICMP Echos to 192.168.13.1, timeout is 2
seconds:
Packet sent with a source address of 2.2.2.2
.
Success rate is 0 percent (0/1)
```

The pings from R2 will make it as this is the valid entry. The pings from R3 won't work because we don't have a valid route but the packets will be accepted by R1...

take a look below:

```
R1#
P: tableid=0, s=2.2.2.2 (FastEthernet0/0), d=192.168.12.1
(FastEthernet0/0), routed via RIB
IP: s=2.2.2.2 (FastEthernet0/0), d=192.168.12.1
(FastEthernet0/0), len 100, rcvd 3

IP: tableid=0, s=2.2.2.2 (FastEthernet0/1), d=192.168.13.1
(FastEthernet0/1), routed via RIB
IP: s=2.2.2.2 (FastEthernet0/1), d=192.168.13.1
(FastEthernet0/1), len 100, rcvd 3
```

The router is accepting both packets, even the spoofed one by R3. You can also check the interface to see if uRPF has accepted or dropped the packets:

```
R1#show ip interface fastEthernet 0/0 | include drops
  0 verification drops
  0 suppressed verification drops
```

```
R1#show ip interface fastEthernet 0/1 | include drops
  0 verification drops
  7 suppressed verification drops
```

There are no drops on the FastEthernet 0/0 interface, the packets on the FastEthernet 0/1 interface have been suppressed. This means that the incoming interface is incorrect but that we do have a valid entry in the routing table. Let me show you what happens when R1 receives an IP packet with an unknown source:

```
R3(config)#interface loopback 1
R3(config-if)#ip address 3.3.3.3 255.255.255.255
```

```
R3#ping 192.168.13.1 source loopback 1

Type escape sequence to abort.
Sending 5, 100-byte ICMP Echos to 192.168.13.1, timeout is 2
seconds:
Packet sent with a source address of 3.3.3.3
.....
Success rate is 0 percent (0/5)
```

```
R1#show ip interface fastEthernet 0/1 | include drops
  5 verification drops
  7 suppressed verification drops
```

I'll create a new loopback interface with IP address 3.3.3.3. If I use this as the source then the packet will be dropped by R1 because it doesn't have an entry in its routing table that matches 3.3.3.3.

There are 3 more security topics we'll discuss:

- AAA
- SNMP Security
- NTP Authentication

If you have a large network with multiple routers and switches then it will become an administrative nightmare to configure local usernames and passwords on each of these devices. It's easier to have a single point of administration.

When someone tries to login a router or switch, it will check a central server to see if the credentials are correct. If so, the user will gain access. This is achieved using **AAA (Authentication, Authorization, Accounting):**

- **Authentication**: we check if the credentials are correct. This proves that the user really is who he/she is claiming to be.
- **Authorization**: we check what the user is allowed to do...one user might get full access, another user gets limited access to only certain show commands.
- **Accounting**: we can log everything that the user did on a network device.

The server that we use for AAA is typically a RADIUS or TACACS+ server. Configuring a AAA server is outside the scope of the ROUTE blueprint but you should know how to enable remote authentication on a router. Here's how to do it:

```
R1(config)#aaa new-model
```

First we need to "unlock" the AAA commands. This is done with the **aaa new-model** command. Now we can enable authentication:

```
R1(config)#aaa authentication login ADMIN group tacacs+ local
```

This command creates a list called "ADMIN" that tells the router to use TACACS+ authentication if possible. When the TACACS+ server is unreachable, it will fallback to local authentication. Make sure you have a local username / password:

```
R1(config)#username rene password something
```

If the TACACS+ server is unreachable then I can use local login using the credentials above.

We still have to configure where the TACACS+ server can be found:

```
R1(config)#tacacs host 192.168.1.2
R1(config)#tacacs key CISCO
```

This tells the router that the TACACS+ server can be found at 192.168.1.2 and that the shared key is "CISCO". Last but not least, we have to tell the router when to use AAA:

```
R1(config)#line vty 0 4
R1(config-line)#login authentication ADMIN
```

This tells the router to use the list "ADMIN" on the VTY lines.

RADIUS and TACACS+ both offer AAA, there are some differences between the two:

	TACACS+	RADIUS
Protocol	TCP	UDP
Features	Supports Authentication, Authorization and accounting	Supports Authentication and Authorization
Encryption	Entire packet is encrypted	Only password is encrypted
Standard	No (Cisco Protocol)	Yes

Next stop...SNMP.

SNMP (Simple Network Management Protocol) can be used to collect statistics from network devices including Cisco routers and switches.

SNMP consists of 2 items:

- **NMS (Network Management System)**
- **SNMP Agents**

The NMS is the external server where you want to store logging information. The SNMP agents run on the network devices that we want to monitor. The NMS can query a SNMP agent to collect information from the network device. This query is called a **SNMP GET**. Besides reading information, it's also possible to configure a network device through SNMP, this is done with a **SNMP SET**.

The "information" that we want to collect are stored in objects, these objects are stored and structured into something called the **MIB (Mangement Information Base)**.

SNMP has multiple versions:

- SNMP version 1
- SNMP version 2c
- SNMP version 3

The most popular versions are 2c and 3.

SNMP version 3 offers security through authentication and encryption which SNMP version 2c does not. SNMP version 2c however is still more common. Let me show you a simple example for SNMP version 2c:

```
Router(config)#snmp-server community ROUTE ro
```

First we'll have to configure a **community string**. Think of this as a password that the SNMP agent and NMS have to agree upon. I called mine "ROUTE". The **ro** stands for **read-only**. SNMP isn't just for retrieving information; we can also use it to instruct our routers and switches to perform an action.

```
Router(config)#snmp-server location Amsterdam GNS3Vault Lab
Router(config)#snmp-server contact info@gns3vault.com
```

These two steps are not required but it's useful to specify a **location** and **contact.** This way you'll at least know where the device is located whenever you receive information through SNMP.

```
Router(config)#snmp-server host 192.168.12.2 version 2c TSHOOT
```

The messages that the SNMP agent sends to the NMS are called **SNMP traps**. Of course we want to send these to an external server so I'll configure the IP address of the SNMP server. I also have to specify the version and the community string.

```
Router(config)#snmp-server enable traps
```

Last but not least I'll have to enable the SNMP traps.

If I use the **snmp-server enable traps** command it will enable **all SNMP traps**.

```
Router#show run | include traps
snmp-server enable traps snmp authentication linkdown linkup
coldstart warmstart
snmp-server enable traps vrrp
snmp-server enable traps ds1
snmp-server enable traps tty
snmp-server enable traps eigrp
snmp-server enable traps casa
snmp-server enable traps xgcp
snmp-server enable traps bulkstat collection transfer
snmp-server enable traps isdn call-information
snmp-server enable traps isdn layer2
```

This is only a portion of everything that you'll see in the running-configuration. This is a great way to test SNMP but on a production network it's better to take a look at the different traps and only enable the ones you feel are necessary. One of the SNMP traps in the example above is related to EIGRP. If anything happens with the EIGRP routing protocol a SNMP trap will be send towards the SNMP server.

If you never tried saving syslog information to an external server or played with SNMP I recommend trying "Solarwinds Kiwi Syslog server". You can download a 30 day trial and practice the commands above yourself:

http://www.kiwisyslog.com

Since version 3, SNMP offers strong authentication and encryption.

SNMPv1 and SNMPv2 use a community-string that is used as the password and there's no authentication or encryption.

SNMPv3 is able to use both authentication and encryption and has a new security model that works with users, groups and 3 different security levels. Users will be applied to a group and access policies will be applied to a group so that you can determine what groups have read or read-write access and which MIBs they should be able to access.

SNMP offers 3 different security levels:

- noAuthNoPriv
- AuthNoPriv
- AuthPriv

Auth stands for Authentication and Priv for Privacy (encryption).

- noAuthNoPriv = no authentication and no encryption.
- AuthNoPriv = authentication but no encryption.
- AuthPriv = authentication AND encryption.

SNMPv1 and SNMPv2 only support noAuthNoPriv since they don't offer any authentication or encryption. SNMPv3 supports any of the three security levels. When you decide to use noAuthNoPriv for SNMPv3 then the username will replace the community-string.

The community-string for SNMPv1 and SNMPv2 is send in clear-text. SNMPv3 is far more secure because it doesn't send the user passwords in clear-text but uses MD5 or SHA1 hash-based authentication, encryption is done using DES, 3DES or AES.

Let's take a look at a simple SNMPv3 configuration example on a Cisco IOS router. First we need to create a group and user:

```
R1(config)#snmp-server group MYGROUP ?
  v1    group using the v1 security model
  v2c   group using the v2c security model
  v3    group using the User Security Model (SNMPv3)
```

We'll call our group "MYGROUP" and of course we will select SNMPv3 as the security model. Next step is to select the security level:

```
R1(config)#snmp-server group MYGROUP v3 ?
  auth     group using the authNoPriv Security Level
  noauth   group using the noAuthNoPriv Security Level
  priv     group using SNMPv3 authPriv security level
```

By using the priv parameter we will select the AuthPriv security level. There are a number of options for security levels:

```
R1(config)#snmp-server group MYGROUP v3 priv ?
  access    specify an access-list associated with this group
  context   specify a context to associate these views for the
group
  match     context name match criteria
  notify    specify a notify view for the group
  read      specify a read view for the group
  write     specify a write view for the group
  <cr>
```

The first item is the access-list, you can use this to select what IP addresses or subnets should be permitted for users. Optionally you can select certain views:

If you don't specify a read view then all MIB objects are accessible. Use this if you want to limit the number of MIBs that your NMS (Network Management Software) can monitor. Without a write view then nothing is writable, you will have read-only access. The notify view is used to send notifications to members of the group. If you don't specify any then it will be disabled by default.

To keep this example simple we won't use any views for now, this means that we'll have full read access to all MIBs:

```
R1(config)#snmp-server group MYGROUP v3 priv
```

The next step is to create a user account:

```
R1(config)#snmp-server user MYUSER MYGROUP v3 auth md5 MYPASS123
priv aes 128 MYKEY123

Configuring snmpv3 USM user, persisting snmpEngineBoots. Please
Wait...
```

We'll create a new user called "MYUSER" and assign it to the "MYGROUP" group. We use SNMPv3 as the security model and use MD5 for authentication. This user will use "MYPASS123" as the password. Encryption is done using AES 128-bit and the encryption key is "MYKEY123".

This router is now SNMPv3 enabled and we can monitor it using SNMPv3 from a NMS. Let's try if we can get access...

User accounts are not stored in the configuration, take a look below:

```
R1#show running-config | incl snmp
snmp-server group MYGROUP v3 priv
```

Above you only see the group configuration, user accounts can be found with another command:

```
R1#show snmp user

User name: MYUSER
Engine ID: 800000090300C200128F0000
storage-type: nonvolatile        active
Authentication Protocol: MD5
Privacy Protocol: AES128
Group-name: MYGROUP
```

Here you can see the username, security options and to which group the user belongs.

We can also check the group configuration:

```
R1#show snmp group
groupname: ILMI                               security model:v1
readview : *ilmi                              writeview: *ilmi
notifyview: <no notifyview specified>
row status: active

groupname: ILMI                               security model:v2c
readview : *ilmi                              writeview: *ilmi
notifyview: <no notifyview specified>
row status: active

groupname: MYGROUP                            security model:v3
priv
readview : v1default                          writeview: <no
writeview specified>
notifyview: <no notifyview specified>
row status: active
```

Above you can see that we have our group called "MYGROUP" and that we use the default read view. If you are a Linux user you can use the excellent snmpwalk command-line utility that tests if your router can be accessed using SNMP. It works for SNMPv1, v2 and v3:

```
rene@linux ~ $ snmpwalk -v3 -u MYUSER -l AuthPriv -a md5 -A
MYPASS123 -x aes -X MYKEY123 192.168.82.138
iso.3.6.1.2.1.1.1.0 = STRING: "Cisco IOS Software, 2800 Software
(C2800NM-ADVIPSERVICESK9-M), Version 12.4(24)T8, RELEASE
SOFTWARE (fc1)
Technical Support: http://www.cisco.com/techsupport
Copyright (c) 1986-2012 by Cisco Systems, Inc.
Compiled Sun 09-Sep-12 04:01 by prod_rel_team"
iso.3.6.1.2.1.1.2.0 = OID: iso.3.6.1.4.1.9.1.576
iso.3.6.1.2.1.1.3.0 = Timeticks: (27513) 0:04:35.13
iso.3.6.1.2.1.1.4.0 = ""
iso.3.6.1.2.1.1.5.0 = STRING: "R1.gns3vault.local"
iso.3.6.1.2.1.1.6.0 = ""
iso.3.6.1.2.1.1.7.0 = INTEGER: 78
iso.3.6.1.2.1.1.8.0 = Timeticks: (0) 0:00:00.00
iso.3.6.1.2.1.1.9.1.2.1 = OID: iso.3.6.1.4.1.9.7.129
iso.3.6.1.2.1.1.9.1.2.2 = OID: iso.3.6.1.4.1.9.7.115
iso.3.6.1.2.1.1.9.1.2.3 = OID: iso.3.6.1.4.1.9.7.265
iso.3.6.1.2.1.1.9.1.2.4 = OID: iso.3.6.1.4.1.9.7.112
iso.3.6.1.2.1.1.9.1.2.5 = OID: iso.3.6.1.4.1.9.7.106
iso.3.6.1.2.1.1.9.1.2.6 = OID: iso.3.6.1.4.1.9.7.47
[output omitted]
```

As you can see snmpwalk is able to read information from the router through SNMP. It's now ready to be added to a NMS for monitoring.

The last topic in this chapter is about **NTP (Network Time Protocol)**. NTP is used on networks to ensure that all devices use the same time source and stay synchronized.

NTP uses something called a **stratum value** that indicates how reliable the time source is. It ranges from 0-15 where 16 indicates that the time is not synchronized. The lower the value, the more "reliable" the source is. For example, some internet based NTP server with an atomic clock could have a low stratum value like 0. When your core devices would like the time from this source then their stratum value will be 1.

When other network devices learn the time from these core devices, their stratum value will be 2 and so on.

NTP is important for logging since we require correct date and timestamps. If the date / time is incorrect then our logging information is pretty much useless. A potential hacker could try to mess with your NTP settings to mess up your logging. Other services / protocols that rely on a correct date are also in danger (like the time based access-list we saw earlier).

To prevent someone from tampering with NTP, we can enable authentication for NTP. We should enable this on our NTP servers and clients.

Here's a configuration example:

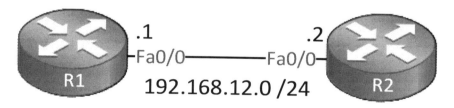

I'll use two routers for this. R1 will be our NTP server and R2 will be a NTP client:

```
R1(config)#ntp master 1
```

This configures R1 to be the NTP master with a stratum value of 1. Now we'll enable authentication:

```
R1(config)#ntp authentication-key 1 md5 MY_KEY
R1(config)#ntp authenticate
R1(config)#ntp trusted-key 1
```

The password will be "MY_KEY" and we use MD5 authentication. Authentication is enabled with the ntp authenticate command and we need to tell the router that we want to use MD5 key 1. Here's the configuration of R2:

```
R2(config)#ntp authentication-key 1 md5 MY_KEY
R2(config)#ntp authenticate
R2(config)#ntp trusted-key 1
R2(config)#ntp server 192.168.12.1 key 1
```

The configuration of R2 is similar. We configure the key, enable NTP authentication and tell the router to trust MD5 key 1. When we specify the NTP server we want to use we have to specify the key we want to use. Let's verify our work:

```
R1#show ntp status
Clock is synchronized, stratum 1, reference is .LOCL.
nominal freq is 250.0000 Hz, actual freq is 250.0000 Hz,
precision is 2**18
reference time is D874EEDF.82F76828 (17:39:43.511 UTC Thu Jan 29
2015)
clock offset is 0.0000 msec, root delay is 0.00 msec
root dispersion is 0.02 msec, peer dispersion is 0.02 msec
```

R1 is synchronized which makes sense since we configured it as a NTP master. Let's see what R2 thinks about all this:

```
R2#show ntp status
Clock is synchronized, stratum 2, reference is 192.168.12.1
nominal freq is 250.0000 Hz, actual freq is 249.9999 Hz,
precision is 2**18
reference time is D874EF3C.791C27E2 (17:41:16.473 UTC Thu Jan 29
2015)
clock offset is 10.2308 msec, root delay is 35.74 msec
root dispersion is 17.09 msec, peer dispersion is 6.84 msec
```

R2 is also synchronized and you can see its stratum value is 2. That's all there is to NTP authentication and it's also the end of this chapter.

Hopefully this have given you a basic idea how to protect your router(s). In reality, this is only real short introduction to security. There's an entire CCNA, CCNP and CCIE track for security that covers these items in much greater detail.

If you want to get some practice, I have some security related labs for you:

http://gns3vault.com/security/time-based-access-list/

http://gns3vault.com/network-management/snmpv2-server/

http://gns3vault.com/network-management/snmpv3-server/

http://gns3vault.com/network-management/ntp-network-time-protocol/

25. Final Thoughts

Here we are, you worked your way through all the different chapters that showed you how you can master the CCNP ROUTE exam. There is only one thing left for you to do and that's *labs, labs and even more labs!* The CCNP exam is very hands-on minded so you need to lab a lot to gain practical experience! If you want labs just visit http://gns3vault.com where I have about everything on CCNP ROUTE level. If you feel there is something missing drop me a message/mail/PM/twitter and I'll make sure to add a new lab.

One last word of advice: If you do a Cisco exam you always do the tutorial before you start the exam which takes 15 minutes. These 15 minutes are not taken from your exam time so this is valuable time you can spend creating your own cheat sheet for subnetting questions or anything else you would like to dump from your brain onto paper.

I hope you enjoyed reading my book and truly learned something! If you have any questions or comments how you feel I could improve the book please let me know by sending an e-mail to info@gns3vault.com or drop a message at my website: http://gns3vault.com.

I wish you good luck practicing and mastering your CCNP ROUTE exam!

Appendix A – How to create mindmaps

A mindmap is a diagram which consists of text, images or relationships between different items. Everything is ordered in a tree-like structure. In the middle of the mindmap you write down your subject. All the topics that have to do with your subject can be written down as a branch of your main subject. Each branch can have multiple branches where the pieces of information are leaves. Mindmaps are great because they show the relationship between different items where notes are just lists...

You can create mindmaps by drawing them yourself or use your computer. I prefer the second method because I can save / print them but also because I'm a faster at typing than writing.

You can download Xmind over here, it's free:

http://www.xmind.net/

Once you have installed it and started a new project you can add some items.

Here's an example I created for CCNP ROUTE with some of the items, just to give you an impression:

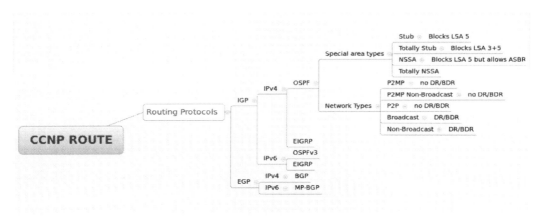

Just add all the items and build your own mind-map using your own words. Now you have a nice overview with all the stuff you need to remember but also the relationship between items. Give it a shot and see if you like it!